Introduction to Early Childhood Education

VERNA HILDEBRAND

MICHIGAN STATE UNIVERSITY

Introduction to Early Childhood Education

SECOND EDITION

Macmillan Publishing Co., Inc.

NEW YORK

Collier Macmillan Publishers

LONDON

I wish to dedicate this book to my family—to my husband, John, *without whose faith and encouragement this book would never have been written; to my children,* Carol *and* Steve, *both of whom weathered the testing of the philosophy presented; and to my parents,* Carrel *and* Florence Butcher, *who provided encouragement and an opportunity to study.*

MACMILLAN PUBLISHING CO., INC.
866 Third Avenue, New York, New York 10022

COLLIER MACMILLAN CANADA, LTD.

Library of Congress Cataloging in Publication Data

Hildebrand, Verna.
    Introduction to early childhood education.

    Includes bibliographical references and indexes.
    1. Education, Preschool. I. Title.
LB1140.2.H522   1976   372.21   75–5848
            ISBN 0–02–354210–1

Printing: 2 3 4 5 6 7 8   Year: 6 7 8 9 0 1 2

PREFACE
AND ACKNOWLEDGMENTS

INTRODUCTION TO EARLY CHILDHOOD EDUCATION is a textbook written especially for those who are concerned with teaching children ages three through six. It is an introduction to professional preparation for nursery school and kindergarten teaching. Teachers, psychologists, social workers, and administrators concerned with planning sound programs for fostering children's growth and development will find the book relevant. Parents, nurses, librarians, and Sunday school teachers will discover many useful ideas.

Introduction to Early Childhood Education was written from the experience of many years' teaching in the university classroom and in the kindergarten, nursery school, day-care center, and university laboratory school. The additional experience of being a parent of a son and daughter has provided incentive for exploring early childhood education from more than the academic vantage point.

University students and Head Start teachers provided the major stimulus for writing this book. Both wanted help with integrating knowledge about child growth and development into meaningful school programs for young children. In class and after class they questioned the curriculum and the techniques observed in the laboratory demonstration programs. A continuous search was made for improved ideas to use with young children. This book is designed to help students, teachers, and of course ultimately the children they teach.

PART ONE gives an overall view of goals, children, schools, techniques, and curriculum. It is a brief survey designed for initial orientation of the student to the field before the numerous details of a program are presented. This survey will be particularly helpful to the student beginning observation and participation in a group of children as the school term gets under way.

PART TWO examines the curriculum in detail, discussing goals and procedures and making suggestions for learning experiences. Each chapter covers a curriculum area, which makes the book an easy reference when help is desired. Guidance suggestions and interpersonal relationships are emphasized in each curriculum area. Planning is stressed throughout. Teachers and assistants are urged to sit down together and to think specifically about the why, what, and how of their teaching. For some classes, instructors may prefer to assign Chapter 16 ("Program Planning and Evaluating") at the beginning of the curriculum study rather than having it serve as a capstone chapter.

PART THREE discusses the teacher's professional relationship with parents and views the past, present, and future of early childhood education.

The school for young children is approached through the developmental tasks of early childhood. The numerous program ideas contained in this book will help with program planning and thus save time and energy for understanding and helping children as individuals. Photographs and incidents involving real children enliven and illustrate points being made.

Male readers will be quick to note the feminine pronouns. It is hoped that they will not be offended by this reference, just as women customarily overlook being referred to as "he" in books. Men in early childhood education have taken such references in good humor. I wish to encourage their participation in the exciting profession of educating young children.

Though I was aware of the excellent reception of the first edition of *Introduction to Early Childhood Education*, during the preparation of this second edition I have been especially mindful of the need to make improvements. I think nothing is ever really perfected and completed. Unless an author's knowledge and understanding fail to grow, there must be modifications and additions with the passing years. I have added a new chapter, "Structured Learning Activities," and have made numerous significant additions, updatings, and changes throughout the book.

I hope all readers, and especially instructors, student teachers, and teachers of young children, will view this book not as a straitjacket with rigid sequences, answers, and programs but as a flexible aid helping their own creativity and stimulating their minds. Improvements can be made beyond the blueprints frozen into these printed pages. Professionals are expected to modify and improve upon these efforts as experience, reason, and new knowledge guide them—especially if the well-being of our children and of all humankind is to be most effectively served. Without these corrective possibilities I, as an author, would have some trepidation concerning my impact on future generations.

To accompany the second edition, I have prepared a revised edition of *A Laboratory Workbook for Introduction to Early Childhood Education*, which is also published by the Macmillan Publishing Co., Inc. The workbook, covering suggested students' projects and laboratory observations, has been rewritten and expanded to fit the revised textbook. Where observation and participation are possible, these workbook learning activities will give realistic and practical aid to students.

In addition, I have also prepared a related textbook, *Guiding Young Children* (Macmillan Publishing Co., Inc., 1975), which focuses on interpersonal relations in young children's groups. Each textbook was structured to stand alone for a single course or to follow one another in a sequence of course work.

In this revised edition acknowledgment for specific help is due Sister Marie Hopkins, Marygrove College of Detroit; Lois Mendrygal, Madonna College of Detroit; Judy McKee, Eastern Michigan University; Rebecca Peña Hines, University of Houston; and Vern Seefeldt, John Haubenstricker, Frances Kertesz, and Lillian Phenice of Michigan State University.

In addition, I wish to renew my thanks to the following educators, who, when they were affiliated with the identified universities, read all or portions of the first edition manuscript: Josephine Stearns of California State Polytechnic; Sam Clark of Iowa State University; Helen Hostetter of Kansas State University; Beverly French of Los Angeles Valley College; Vera Borosage, Jeanne Brown, Mary Fritz, Beatrice Paolucci, and Mary Sanderson of Michigan State University; Jean Dickerscheid of Ohio State University; James Walters of Oklahoma State University; Rebecca Hines of San Jose State College; Henry Draper of Stout State University; Jessie Bateman, Wilma Brown, Bernadine Johnson, Dora Tyer, and Emma Doyle of Texas Woman's University; Catherine Landreth, University of California at Berkeley; Charlotte McCarty, University of Delaware; Phyllis Lueck, University of Guelph; and Lane Butler, University of Ohio.

Photo credits are due many photographers, teachers, students, and parents, including Rebecca Peña Hines, University of Houston; Roberta Hay and Ed Breidenbach, University of Idaho; Kathryn Madera, Iowa State University; Ivalee McCord, Kansas State University; Gladys Hildreth and Gayle Mary Clapp, Louisiana State University; Vern Seefeldt, John Haubenstricker, William Mitcham, Connie Lisiecki, Jean and James Page, Vera Borosage, Gayle and Larry Schiamberg, and Joe Kertesz, Michigan State University; Mary O'Dell, Southern University; Judith Kuipers, University of Tennessee; Billie Wolfe and Estelle Wallace, Texas Tech University; Jessie Bateman-Barns, Texas Woman's University; Johnnye Goodrich, National Institute of Education Child Study Center; Harriet Wilson, Nazarene Child Care Center; Donna Creasy, *What's New in Home Economics;* and Theda Connell, Brenda Golbus, John Naso, and Margot and Gerald Seelhoff.

Recognition is due Michigan State University for a faculty research grant that helped initiate, and Texas Woman's University for an opportunity to complete, the first edition.

Permission to use portions of some materials I had previously published in *Childhood Education* and in *The Progressive Farmer* has kindly been granted by the editors.

To my professors, fellow students, professional colleagues, and graduate and undergraduate students in several universities throughout the country, I am indebted for challenges and stimulation. To the many hundreds of nursery school and kindergarten children and their parents who have given me most of whatever understanding I have of young children, I am especially grateful.

V. H.

CONTENTS

ix

PART THREE
PROFESSIONAL CONSIDERATIONS

PART ONE

Teaching in a School for Young Children Today:
An Overview

So You Are Going to Teach
Young Children!

YOU ARE going to teach young children! Welcome to the ever-widening professional field of child development and early childhood education.

Perhaps you are among the growing number of young men and women who have planned this career from high school days. If so, you have the advantage of a planned sequence of courses utilizing current information in a rapidly growing field of knowledge. Some of you may feel long on theory and short on practical know-how. Others, who are entering early childhood education from upper elementary or secondary teaching experience, from work in other fields, or from a rest leave for motherhood may feel confident regarding practical aspects but anxious regarding recent theory. Two such different groups are often enrolled in early childhood education classes. Each has a great deal to offer the other, and moments of sharing ideas and information will add to each student's respect for the other's competencies.

Both men and women will find satisfactions in teaching young children. The field, once the province of women, willingly accepts men in preparation programs and in jobs in schools when they graduate. Women, who once were locked into career roles in helping professions, such as teaching or nursing, now can find acceptance in careers ranging from astronomy to zoology and should, therefore, remain in early childhood education only if it truly fits their needs, interests, and talents.

Teaching young children is challenging and rewarding, though at times frustrating. It is an awesome responsibility to influence the lives of children from day to day during their most formative years. This is a profession in the truest sense of the word, and anyone looking for a nine-to-five job should look elsewhere. Your teaching will

3

FIGURE 1–1. *School—a place to get a little help from a friend. (Nazarene Child Care Center, Lansing, Michigan.)*

have long-range implications for the child, the family, the school, the community, and the world. Special preparation is required in order to do well. In fact, you can never stop learning, changing, and updating your knowledge and skill. As in other professions, you must apply ethical procedures in dealing with children, parents, and fellow professionals. You will be on call when needed after hours for a conference or a meeting. Even on vacation you will be a teacher as you see new sights, read new books, or collect objects and ideas

FIGURE 1–2. *School—a place to give a little help to a friend. (National Institute of Education Child Study Center, U.S. Office of Education.)*

that will become learning experiences for your group of children. Teaching young children is one of the helping professions that needs dedicated practitioners.

The foregoing conveys the seriousness of the professional responsibility you are undertaking. Yet there is enjoyment and creativity in it too. An artist takes the elements of a masterpiece—line, color, form, and texture—and puts them together with his own perceptions to make a painting. You, as a teacher, will be creative from moment to moment and day to day as you work with a group of young children—each a creative individual in his own right. You will create for each child, for each group, for each year, in accordance with needs, goals, plans, and resources of time, money, materials, and help available. No two children will develop in quite the same way. Yes, yours is a creative profession!

Teaching young children will bring enjoyment. If you do not find joy in it, you should look for some other avenue of work, because *work* it surely will be. Young children are spontaneous, loving, curious, and creative. Working with them will keep you young at heart, on your toes, and moving ahead. Children help keep your sense of wonder alive because all things interest them. Little ones express themselves so honestly that it may relieve you to discover a social group so unpretentious.

The early childhood education profession needs happy, intelligent, energetic, and creative teachers to guide it through the years ahead. It is hoped that you will find many satisfactions in the study you have undertaken.

Types of Schools [1]

Your professional preparation will probably take you into a wide variety of children's schools for observation, training, and experience. Schools will vary as to the type of program, the ages and number of the children served, the length of the program, the purposes for the child, and the purposes of the supporting agency. The historical development of schools for young children will be given more detailed treatment in a later chapter. The present discussion will focus on the types of schools that a student is likely to observe.

The term *nursery school* typically refers to a school for children from 2½ or 3 years old up to kindergarten age. The nursery school sessions last for two to three hours a day and are held two to five days per week. The educational emphasis in the program will vary according to the professional preparation and experience of the teacher. Nursery schools usually expect to supplement rather than substitute for home care and training. The term *prekindergarten* may also designate a program for three- and four-year-olds. In some localities the use of this term may be an attempt to differentiate a program that has more "education" content than is customary in the nursery school program of that community. In Table 1–1 the term *prekindergarten* refers to schools for three- and four-year-olds. According to Table 1–1, many three- and four-year-olds are enrolled in programs called *kindergarten*.

---

[1] For further discussion on these topics see James L. Hymes, Jr., *Early Childhood Education: An Introduction to the Profession* (Washington, D.C.: National Association for Education of Young Children, 1968).

FIGURE 1–3. *School—a place to use new tools and to talk about what you learn with someone who cares. (University of Houston Parent-Child Development Center.)*

Kindergarten generally refers to schools for five-year-old children. The entry age in a kindergarten is usually determined by the legal limits for entering first grade—that is, if a state requires the child to be six before September 1 to enroll in first grade, then kindergartens in that state will enroll children who are five before September 1. The sessions are about three hours in length for four to five days per week. As with nursery school, the kindergarten teacher formulates the program. Kindergarten is part of an early childhood educational continuum that begins at birth. Because of individual differences, children's readiness for various experiences falls at different points on this continuum.

Table 1–1 shows that classroom education for young children is not yet common. In 1973 only 14.5 per cent of the three-year-olds, 34.2 per cent of the four-year-olds, and 76.0 per cent of the five-year-olds were enrolled in any school for children under six.

The lines plotted in Table 1–2 reveal the percentages of various

FIGURE 1–4. *School—a place to enjoy a game with your friends. (Michigan State University Laboratory Preschool.)*

TABLE 1–1

Preprimary Enrollment and Population of Children 3 to 5 Years Old, by Age,
Enrollment Status, Level, and Control: United States, October 1973
(Numbers in thousands)

Enrollment Status, Level, and Control	Total 3–5 years	3-year-olds	4-year-olds	5-year-olds
Total number:				
In population	10,344	3,557	3,443	3,344
Enrolled in programs	4,234	515	1,177	2,542
Percent Enrolled:				
All programs	40.9	14.5	34.2	76.0
Public	27.4	3.9	15.0	65.0
Nonpublic	13.6	10.6	19.1	11.0
Prekindergarten	12.7	13.8	21.9	2.3
Public	3.8	3.6	6.7	1.1
Nonpublic	8.9	10.2	15.1	1.2
Kindergarten	28.2	.7	12.3	73.7
Public	23.5	.3	8.3	63.9
Nonpublic	4.6	.4	4.0	9.8

SOURCE: *Nursery School and Kindergarten Enrollment: October 1973*, Series P–20, No. 268. Issued August 1974, U.S. Department of Commerce, Bureau of the Census, Washington, D.C., p. 10.

TABLE 1–2

Per Cent of 3- to 5-Year-Old Children Enrolled in Nursery School and
Kindergarten: October 1964 to October 1973

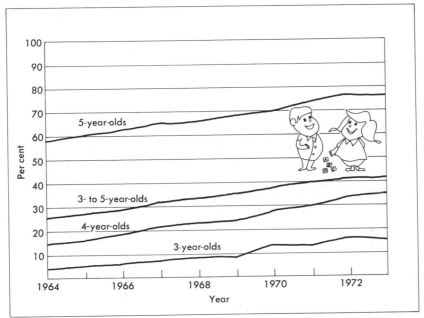

SOURCE: *Nursery School and Kindergarten Enrollment: October 1973,* Series P–20, No.
268. Issued August 1974, U.S. Department of Commerce, Bureau of the Census, Washington, D.C.

age groups enrolled in nursery schools or kindergartens during the
ten-year period from 1964 through 1973. A glance at the historical
data contained in Table 1–2 gives a quick summary of the progress
made in providing formal educational programs for a growing proportion of our young children during the decade. For example, it
is evident that approximately 26 per cent of the three- to five-year-olds were enrolled in preprimary programs in 1964; the upward trend
increased steadily to approximately 41 per cent in 1973. Yet, even at
the kindergarten level many children are still denied this important
educational opportunity—an opportunity especially critical for children from disadvantaged environments. Throughout our history
equality of opportunity has been a value widely held by Americans.
If continued progress toward equality of opportunity is to be
achieved, early childhood education must be available for *all* children.

The enrollment of children in early childhood education programs
has increased both in percentage and in total numbers in a period
when families are having fewer children. According to census data

FIGURE 1–5. *School—a place where you can make friends and climb to a secret place to talk. (University of Tennessee Gulf Range Child Care Center.)*

the absolute numbers of three- to five-year-olds dropped from 12.496 million in 1964 to 10.344 million in 1973, whereas the numbers of three- to five-year-olds enrolled in education programs increased from 3.187 million in 1964 to 4.234 million in 1973.[2] No figures are available for the numbers of infants and toddlers that are in programs outside the home.

Public Kindergartens and Nursery Schools

Public institutions are taking increased responsibility for pre-primary education. According to Table 1–1, public kindergartens and

[2] *Nursery School and Kindergarten Enrollment: October 1973*, Series P–20, No. 268 (Washington, D.C.: U.S. Department of Commerce, Bureau of the Census, August 1974), p. 1.

nursery schools enrolled 27.4 per cent of the total population of
10.344 million three- to five-year-old children in 1973, whereas nonpublic schools enrolled 13.6 per cent. Of the 3.344 million five-year-
olds, 63.9 per cent were enrolled in public kindergartens, and 9.8
per cent were enrolled in nonpublic schools.

According to Harold Howe II, former Commissioner of Education,
the trend is to lower the public school age. He suggested in a message
to elementary school principals that the word *preschool* be phased
out and that schools begin planning for a structure that includes
three- to five-year-olds. Howe predicted that by the year 2000 most
children in the United States would start school by age four.[3]

Children Today reports results from a 1972 survey by the Education Commission of the States showing that (1) 9 states (Arizona,
California, Connecticut, Florida, Maine, Maryland, Massachusetts,
Rhode Island, and West Virginia) mandate school districts to offer
kindergarten; (2) 37 additional states have enacted permissive kindergarten legislation; (3) 4 states (Idaho, Kentucky, Mississippi,
and North Dakota) have no state legislation permitting or mandating
kindergarten; (4) 42 states offer some form of state aid to kindergartens, with 26 of these states allocating funds through the state
foundation formula; (5) all 50 states have certification requirements
for kindergarten teachers, but many require only an elementary
teaching certificate; and (6) certification for kindergarten paraprofessionals and prekindergarten paraprofessionals is required by 5
states and 2 states, respectively.[4]

Head Start Nursery Schools and Kindergartens

Head Start nursery schools and kindergartens were first organized
under the joint sponsorship of the federal government and a local
agency in many American communities in 1965. The program was
begun as part of President Lyndon Johnson's War on Poverty. The
program brought children of the poor together in groups for educational, medical, and nutritional assistance in hopes of reducing the
observed handicap that such children experience when they enter
elementary school. Some Head Start programs operated only in the
summer, and others operated year round. Parent involvement has
always been an important part of Head Start programs.

Day-Care or Child-Care Centers

Day-care, or child-care, centers provide full day care for children
of working mothers. Increasingly, care is given to crib infants and

---

[3] Harold Howe II, "Phase Out Preschool," *Scholastic Teacher* (May 2,
1968), 5.

[4] *Children Today*, **3**:5 (September–October 1974), 28.

toddlers. Such centers may be privately, publicly, or philanthropically financed. Parents' fees cover costs and a profit margin in the private centers. In public and philanthropic centers flat fees are charged according to ability to pay. Some centers are opened for after-school supervision of school-aged children in a program called *extended day care.* The centers serve "latch-key" children who would otherwise be letting themselves into their own homes with a key carried on a string around their necks. Those agencies sponsoring day-care centers typically hope to provide a well-rounded educational program. Still, their first priority is to keep the child safe, nourished, and rested. It is not uncommon to find these centers understaffed and thus incapable of providing the educational programs their directors know would be desirable. With the ever-increasing number of women in the labor force, additional and improved day-care facilities are in great demand.

FIGURE 1–6.   *School—a place where they let you try new things like playing a guitar. (Michigan State University Spartan Cooperative Nursery School.)*

FIGURE 1–7.   *School—a place to enjoy a joke with your friends. (Nazarene Child Care Center, Lansing, Michigan.)*

Parent-Cooperative Nursery Schools and Kindergartens

Parent-cooperative nursery schools and kindergartens are operated by parents who organize to provide schooling for their own children. They pool their time, energy, and money and hire a qualified teacher. In addition, they take turns serving as the teacher's assistant. Parents meet to build equipment, paint the facility, or plan outings for the children. Tuition is lower than at the area's private schools. Programs will vary from simple playground groups to highly organized programs—depending on the training and experience of the teacher and the interests of the parents.

Some parent cooperatives include well-organized classes for parent education in addition to the child's participation in the school. Since the parents (usually the mother) must participate, cooperatives are ordinarily not feasible for working mothers.

Church-Sponsored Schools

Church-sponsored schools, such as nursery schools, kindergartens, parent-cooperative nursery schools and kindergartens, and day-care centers are common in various localities. Tuition may be nominal if the sponsoring church provides the facility and furnishings without cost to the group. Programs may have denominational emphasis or be entirely secular. Nevertheless children of church members usually receive preferred status if there is a waiting list. And, of course, churches often provide other programs for young children—choirs, one-hour-a-week Sunday schools, and week-long Bible schools.

Private Nursery Schools, Kindergartens, and Day-Care Centers

Private nursery schools, kindergartens, and day-care centers are fee-supported commercial ventures. Many are well known and have built a reputation on sound educational philosophy. However, others are more susceptible to pressure and follow current fads "guaranteed to bring outstanding results." A popular service of private schools is the bus service that they frequently provide.

Schools for the Handicapped

Schools for the handicapped are organized for children who are mentally retarded, emotionally disturbed, and physically handicapped. These schools for exceptional children focus on early detection and training, and they usually encourage parental participation in the child's education. The recent increases in public funds for educating young children with handicaps have enlarged the demand for professionals with a knowledge both of young children and of the handicap.

Hospital Schools

Hospital schools are becoming increasingly popular. Hospitalized children are brought to the classroom on the children's floor for as much school as their illness will permit. Not only is the child's education fostered, but there is therapy in getting together with other children. The teacher may also provide activities for children unable to be moved to the classroom.

Laboratory Schools

Laboratory schools have been established on college and university campuses since the 1920s to provide students a laboratory for observing and working with children of nursery school and kindergarten age. Research and teacher-preparation programs are usually car-

FIGURE 1–8. *School—a place where your creativity finds many avenues of expression. (Michigan State University Laboratory Preschool.)*

ried on in these groups. Increased interest in the young child is taxing the laboratory schools. Many groups have become overobserved, overtaught, and overresearched. To alleviate the situation, moving some research and practice teaching out into the community is becoming the new trend. High schools occasionally provide groups of children for laboratory experiences. Some of these groups are organized on a temporary basis.

FIGURE 1–9. *School—a place to be responsible for your own things.* (*Michigan State University Laboratory Preschool.*)

High School Preschools

Preschools connected with secondary education are becoming increasingly common. With the trend toward vocational education increasing, many high schools have moved into preparing their students to work as child-care aides. In order to give these students practical experience, some schools have built their own child-care facilities, whereas others have used those already existing in the community.

In some high schools infant and toddler programs have been developed to care for children while parents finish their high school work. The parents also receive guidance in the care and feeding of their children.

FIGURE 1–10. *School—a place where young children enjoy being taught to cook fluffy rice in a science project carried out by high school child development students. (Ferndale High School, Ferndale, Michigan.)*

Some high school nursery schools are organized on a temporary basis while students are studying a particular parenting or child-care unit. They may recruit students' siblings and local faculty children.

Experimental Groups

Experimental groups of young children provide research subjects. For example, the researchers may test teaching techniques, curricula, and theories. Often these studies are related to the educational problems of the disadvantaged child.

Family Day-Care Homes

Family day-care homes are operated by neighborhood mothers who care for children in addition to their own. Of course this type of care has been informally organized for many years. Some states regulate day-care homes to some extent, and other states largely disregard them in the monitoring system. These homes are popular with many families because they keep the child in his neighborhood and because they offer care for latch-key children, who might otherwise be left alone for several hours after school.

Recently some public effort has been made to help those who run family day-care homes with the nutritional, educational, and social problems of the children and families they serve, for example, in workshops run by professional teachers and groups.

Home Start Programs

Home Start programs have four major objectives: to involve parents directly in the educational development of their children; to help strengthen parents' capacity for stimulating their children's development; and to demonstrate and evaluate methods of delivering services to the parents and children for whom a center-based program is not feasible. The program is federally funded. A trained visitor helps the parents develop an educational program for their children and helps them learn how to carry the program out.

Informal Groups

Informal groups differ from schools in that they are not continuous programs and children may attend on an irregular basis. These groups may be organized by a group of mothers, a dancing teacher, or such institutions as the YWCA, a recreation department, or a library. All bring children together for particular purposes. Informal groups do offer an opportunity to observe children in a group situation.

Observing in the Nursery School or Kindergarten

Students in early childhood education usually have regular observations scheduled from the beginning of the term. Thus they can see children in action and relate their observations to the theoretical material they are studying in the classroom. Sometimes students may be asked to seek out children to observe. Children may be observed in laboratory schools, in schools not associated with the university, in informal groups, or in a family. In your preparation to become a teacher of young children, it is most helpful to observe situations similar to those in which you may later teach.

The purposes of observation are to help you to relate theory to practice, to understand what it means to be three, four, or five years old, to become acquainted with methods and materials used in the school, and to sense the complications and satisfactions of being a teacher of young children.

To accomplish these purposes you will want to see a typical group of children behaving in typical ways. The following suggestions will help a new observer learn and be welcome.

1. Determine what you expect to see. Your instructor will indicate the points to look for during each observation. You may be given specific questions to answer as you observe.

2. Study the observation assignments for the entire course, if they are available. This will help you in observing, in understanding, and in collecting meaningful examples for your assignments.

3. Be sure to read your text, listen to your instructor, and ask questions so that each assignment will be clear. Children are fascinating, and you may enjoy just watching. However, observation should be done with a purpose if you are to benefit most from it.

4. Take with you an outline of questions you have to answer.

5. Secure or copy a list of names and ages of the children. For easy reference, arrange the list according to chronological age. For some assignments, it is helpful to list the number of months or terms in school and the number and ages of siblings of each child.

6. Generally, it will be necessary to take notes, then write the report of the observation later. A hardbacked notebook is convenient for note taking.

7. An observation booth facilitates observing and makes it easier to watch behavior without affecting it. Safely behind a one-way-vision screen, you can be more objective and will not have to wonder whether you should interact with the child.

8. Be quiet in the booth in order to avoid attracting the children's attention and to avoid disturbing other observers. Sound equipment will, of course, make hearing easier.

9. When it is necessary to observe in the room with children, it is important to be as quiet and unobtrusive as possible. You should sit on a low chair, usually along a wall. Children who are accustomed to observers won't pay much attention to you unless you dress in a startling fashion or talk to them.

10. If a child talks to you, answer him briefly and return to your writing. If he continues to seek your company, you can move to a new location and quietly tell the teacher that this child seems to need someone to talk to. Children have been observed going from observer to observer for short chats. Even though each conversation was short, the total effect was that the child made many contacts with adults but few with children. This situation does not help students to ob-

serve child-child interaction. Often no contribution is made to the goals the teacher has for the child.

11. Unless your presence will interfere, you should move to areas where you can clearly see what the children are doing.

12. Avoid congregating with other adults. This tends to interfere with children's activity and with students' responsibility.

13. Stand near groups of children, or sit on the benches provided, but not on the children's equipment.

14. Identify each set of observation notes by date, time, group, teacher, activity, names, and a description of the setting so that you can recall it later with ease.

15. Include the child's age in your reports because behavior is much more understandable when related to a specific age. For example, use 3–5 to indicate three years five months.

16. If the assignment calls for an *anecdotal record,* the observer records incidents as the child interacts.

17. If the assignment calls for a *diary record,* the observer writes down a running account of the behavior of a particular child. Because writing is tiring, diary records may be taken for several minutes followed by a period of rest, then repeated.

18. In both anecdotal and diary records use quotation marks and quote the exact words of the children and adults. Exact words are often significant, as we shall discuss in a later chapter.

19. In reporting either type of observation, carefully separate facts from interpretations. Interpretations include what you think the behavior means and what questions arise in your mind about it. Evaluative words, e.g., *good, bad, pretty, ugly, happy, angry,* are part of your interpretation.

20. You may be called on to observe as you work with children. In this case your observation notes will of necessity be briefer. A small notebook and pencil should be carried in your pocket. A short word or phrase can suffice to help you remember a situation to write about in your reports or to discuss with the teacher. Such notes should be expanded immediately after the children leave, or the notes will soon be of little help.

21. Do not ask about or make statements about children in front of children or parents.

22. Discuss your observations with the teacher after the children leave. A teacher is usually too busy to give students' questions sufficient thought while attending the children.

23. No one, on the basis of a short observation, is justified in making sweeping statements about what children "always" or "never" do. Remember, even the child's total week in school is only a small part of his total experience.

24. Ethical treatment of observation data requires that discussions regarding the material be kept within the classroom. Here observations can be discussed in the light of other observer's experience and the knowledge and experience of the course instructor.

Participating in the Nursery School or Kindergarten

For most students, participating directly with children is a long-awaited and valuable part of preparation to become a teacher. Through participating, you will begin feeling, thinking, and reacting as a teacher. You will be seeing children live and learn together. Not only will you watch teachers, but you will try your own skill and eventually develop a teaching style of your own.

Because students are often scheduled to participate with children at the beginning of a term, before learning the whys and wherefores of nursery school or kindergarten procedures, the following list of participation hints will help during the first confusing weeks. As the course develops, you will gain an understanding of the reasoning contained in these hints.

Hints for New Student Participators

1. Wear clean, comfortable, colorful, washable clothing during your participation. When you are dressed comfortably in washable clothing you need not worry about your clothing and are free to concentrate on the children around you. A wraparound apron is handy to wear around the finger paints.

2. Wear a badge with your name clearly printed on it. Write "student helper" under your name so visitors or parents will know you.

3. Arrive on time at the designated school and check with the teacher for your particular assignments. Note any posted schedules or directions.

4. Attend any conference the teacher holds prior to the arrival of the children or at the end of the day.

5. Ask for advice in handling teaching material with which you are unfamiliar.

6. Avoid making patterns or models in any media for the children.

7. Write the children's names on pictures, starting in the upper left-hand corner and using manuscript writing in upper- and lower-case letters as shown on the next line and in Figure 1–11 overleaf.

John Mary George

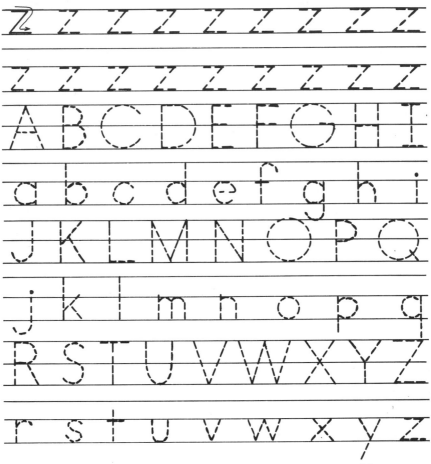

a b c d e f g h i j k l m
n o p q r s t u v w x y z

8. Sit down to work with the children whenever possible.

9. Talk quietly, using distinct words and short sentences.

10. Sit with the children during group times, for example, story, rest, music, and snack.

11. The children will help with cleanup if you make a game of it. Try singing your directions. Try suggesting, "You bring them to me

and I'll help you put them on the shelves." Smile and say, "Thank you, John," after each bit of assistance. You'll marvel at how quickly the room or yard gets straightened up.

12. Be an alert observer and you will know when assistance is needed. Move in to help, that's how you learn.

13. Avoid unnecessary conversation with other adults in the room or yard.

14. When you have serious doubts about a procedure, say to the children, "Let's ask the teacher."

15. Always keep the children's safety in mind.

In the Locker Room

1. Sit on a low chair in a central location so that you'll be at the children's level and can see what help they need. Sitting saves the teacher's back, too!

2. Snowpants usually must be put on before boots. Lay the snowpants out in the correct position in front of the child as he sits on the floor. You can arrange several children around your chair like spokes on a wheel. The same circular arrangement works well for helping with boots too. A plastic bag over a shoe helps stubborn boots slip on.

3. Give praise generously as you encourage self-help.

4. Give both verbal directions and demonstrations as you help.

5. Jackets can be laid in open position on a low table. The child turns his back to the table and reaches backward, first with one arm and then with the other, to put his arms in the sleeves. Or the jacket can be placed in front of the child with the opening upward and the collar closest to the child. The child slips his hands into the sleeves, raises his arms, and the coat flips over his head into the correct position. Children enjoy this trick. Zippers and buttons require a number of demonstrations. You may have to start them partially to avoid overfrustrating a child trying to help himself. Watch closely and help only when the child needs you.

6. For snowy boot removal, sweep snow off the children's boots and snowpants with a small broom while they are still outdoors. Arrange a number of small chairs around an absorbent rug in the entryway. Preferably, let only a few children enter at a time to avoid congestion. The children sit on the chairs and remove their boots before proceeding to the locker area to remove their other wraps. The rug absorbs moisture and keeps it out of the locker area. An adult can sit in the circle and tug at stubborn boots. Boots may have to be drained and dried before being stored in the lockers. A clothespin with the child's name on it is helpful for clipping pairs of boots together. Boots can be marked with a felt pen.

7. Learn where extra clothes are stored. Three- and four-year-olds need a complete set of extra clothing stored in their lockers for emergency use. Each school needs its own collection of clean "extras" for unusual emergencies. A supply of paper bags should be stored nearby to use for soiled clothes.

8. Kindergarteners usually learn to tie their shoes, but younger children as a rule have difficulty with this skill. If you teach kindergarteners to call the loops "bunny ears" as you demonstrate tying, they will often become interested in learning.

At Storytime or Singing Time

1. You may be asked to read to a small group. You should read the book to yourself before reading to the children.

2. Be sure that the children can see the pictures. When the children sit with their backs to the windows, the light is usually best on a book held up for them to see.

3. Give them opportunities to respond to the story and pictures.

4. If someone else is reading or singing with the group, you should sit with the children. If a child becomes disruptive, quietly remind him about appropriate behavior by tapping his knee or shoulder. Avoid saying "Shhh" and causing more distraction than the child.

5. Sing along with the children softly so that your voice does not overshadow their voices.

6. If a child leaves the group, keep an eye on him so that the teacher can attend to the total group. If the child does not want to return to the story or singing time, help him find a quiet activity that does not disturb the other children who are enjoying the group activity. Such a child might enjoy a story alone, so you could try reading to him, perhaps encouraging him to sit on your lap.

7. Should a visitor enter when the teacher is conducting story or singing time, see if you can assist the visitor until the teacher is free. Should the teacher be called out, you should assume responsibility for the group so as to minimize the disruption.

In the Bathroom

1. Certain points in the schedule are usually designated for the toilet routine. However, at other times keep alert for a child who is holding his genitals—usually an indication he needs to urinate.

2. Don't offer a child a choice when you are virtually certain he needs to urinate. Tell him, "Let's go to the bathroom." Take his hand and guide him quickly to the bathroom.

3. When helping in the bathroom, sit on a low chair in order to

be comfortable while assisting children with straps, buttons, zippers, and belts. By sitting nearby you avoid pressuring the child.

4. Boys need to learn to raise the seat, aim accurately as they stand to urinate, then lower the seat. These steps usually require many gentle reminders.

5. Children may worry about the noise of the toilet flushing. If the child hesitates when you suggest that he trip the lever, then you flush it until the child gains confidence.

6. Since girls and boys use the same bathroom at the same time, be matter-of-fact and factual when answering questions regarding differences in their bodies. Don't be embarrassed when they look at each other. They are learning.

7. Toilet accidents are not unusual in groups of three-year-olds. They are less common in older children but still may happen. Wet pants are more common than a bowel movement. If a child has an accident, suggest that he try to use the toilet—sometimes he isn't finished and may only wet again as soon as you get him changed. Get the child's dry clothing from his locker and dress him. Put the soiled clothing in a sack and label it with his name. Be matter-of-fact when other children ask about what has happened. The teacher will report the accident quietly to the parents so that the child doesn't feel betrayed and the parent doesn't feel inclined to punish the child. The teacher might say, "We'll be able to work out this problem. We'll just remember to encourage Jimmy to go to the bathroom right after snack."

8. Children usually enjoy washing their hands. Watch the temperature of the water. Usually, long sessions at the lavatory indicate that the children would enjoy some water play. Help the children dry their hands well to avoid chapping.

9. Late four-year-olds and fives can usually manage the bathroom routine without much adult help. Sometimes they play. If they spill water, let them mop it up.

10. Avoid having children wait in the bathroom. Keep the number entering in accordance with the number of toilets and lavatories available.

At Snack Time or Mealtime

1. If you are required to serve the meal, ask for advice on procedures.

2. Sit with the children at the small table.

3. Have a quiet conversation with the children. Avoid intertable conversations.

4. Give quiet directions to aid the children in learning the routine.

5. Tipped-over glasses of beverage are probably the most common mealtime accident. Therefore, encourage the child to keep his glass moved toward the center of the table.

6. Use a sponge to wipe the table as you leave. A child might be encouraged to help you.

During Outdoor Activities

1. Dress for the weather from head to toe. Boots, gloves, scarves, and plenty of warm clothing are a must in winter. Comfortable loose clothing is important when it is hot.

2. Go where the children are. Adults should be spaced throughout the yard.

3. Keep off the children's equipment. Children won't use it if adults are sitting on it.

4. Go to a child and get his attention before giving directions.

5. Encourage and assist the children in putting things in the storage areas at the end of the period.

At Rest Time

1. Sit by a child who is having difficulty being quiet.

2. A child may quiet down more quickly if he lies on his stomach. Some like to have their backs massaged.

3. Sing lullabies or say quiet poems to the children.

4. If a child needs to go to the toilet, help him leave the group quietly. Assist him in the bathroom.

5. Rest time should be a pleasurable experience free of punishing admonitions.

Conclusion

An organized program for visiting, observing, and participating in groups of children under the leadership of experienced teachers will benefit the student expecting to teach young children. Suggestions on observing and participating have been made at the outset to help students beginning those experiences. On-the-spot experience with children's groups reveals many of the pleasures and challenges of working with young children.

ADDITIONAL READINGS

HECHINGER, FRED M. (ed.). *Pre-School Education Today.* Garden City, N.Y.: Doubleday & Company, Inc., 1966.

HURD, HELEN B. *Teaching in the Kindergarten.* Minneapolis, Minn.: Burgess Publishing Company, 1955.

LEEPER, SARAH H., RUTH DALES, DORA SKIPPER, and RALPH L. WITHERSPOON. *Good Schools for Young Children*. New York: Macmillan Publishing Co., Inc., 1974.

Montessori in Perspective. Washington, D.C.: National Association for Education of Young Children, 1966.

RUDOLPH, MARGUERITA, and DOROTHY H. COHEN. *Kindergarten—A Year of Learning*. New York: Appleton-Crofts, 1964.

TODD, VIVIAN E., and HELEN HEFFERNAN. *The Years Before School: Guiding Preschool Children*. New York: Macmillan Publishing Co., Inc., 1970.

NOTE: The following journals will be important resources for further exploration of every topic in this book. Students are urged to become familiar with each journal. The index issue will guide you to particular topics. Many of the associations publishing the journals offer special memberships to students, making it easy to join and become influential in the early childhood education field.

Childhood Education. Published by the Association for Childhood Education International, 3615 Wisconsin Avenue, N.W., Washington, D.C. 20016.

Children Today. Published by the Children's Bureau, Department of Health, Education, and Welfare, Washington, D.C. 20013.

Educating Children. Published by the Department of Elementary, Kindergarten, and Nursery Educators of the National Education Association, 1201 Sixteenth St., N.W., Washington, D.C. 20036.

International Journal of Early Childhood. Published by the Organisation Mondiale pour l'Education Préscolaire (O.M.E.P.), The United States Committee, 81 Irving Place, New York, N.Y. 10003.

Journal of Home Economics. Published by The American Home Economics Association, 2010 Massachusetts Ave. N.W., Washington, D.C. 20036.

Offspring. Published by Michigan Council of Cooperative Nurseries, Box 1734, East Lansing, Michigan, 48823.

Young Children. Published by the National Association for Education of Young Children, 1834 Connecticut Ave., N.W., Washington, D.C. 20001.

Voice for Children. Published by The Day Care and Child Development Council of America, 1012 Fourteenth St., N.W., Washington, D.C. 20005.

Philosophy

"WHY DO the children do this?" "How do they know what to do next?" "What is your reason for planning this activity?" "Is play all they do?" These are questions that as a beginning student you may ask the teacher of a nursery school or kindergarten. Students in early childhood education classes are often asked to observe and participate in organized schools as part of their training. Through observation and participation in ongoing groups you can sense many aspects of a program that might escape your notice if they were discussed only in a purely classroom situation. You will also have an opportunity to confirm the correctness of your professional choice as you try out personal reactions to real live children.

After you have observed several different groups taught by different teachers you may be more confused than enlightened until you attempt to isolate various factors from each observation. How are the groups similar and different? How are the teachers alike and different? Do teachers' attitudes differ toward children, parents, other teachers, curriculum, or goals?

What Does the Nursery School or Kindergarten Teach?

The modern, technical, fast-moving age we live in is putting more and more pressure on teachers and parents of young children to be sure that meaningful learning experiences are available in homes and schools. Young children can learn, want to learn, and must learn. The evidence is convincing that the early years of a child's life set the stage for the later years.[1] The problem for the teacher centers on what to teach and how to go about teaching it.

In some sense, if we are honest, we really don't know exactly what

[1] See Elizabeth Hurlock, *Child Development* (New York: McGraw-Hill, 1972), pp. 40–49, for numerous references to document the importance of the early years.

these children we teach will need to know in order to function effectively in their adulthood. If we take a three-year-old, should we project him into his college years—17 years hence—or into his middle age—37 years hence? Can the reader evaluate his own education? What did the teachers of your early years teach you that prepared you for the world today? What changes would you have made? Even for the youthful college student today, the world has changed with tremendous rapidity since he entered nursery school or kindergarten some 17 to 20 years ago. The middle-aged person today, caught up in the rapidly changing technology, finds himself involved in a job, social relations, and world interrelationships for which no one really prepared him. If a crystal ball had been able to tell him what today would be like, he wouldn't have believed it. He may be critical of his education and want schools to be better for his children.

Robert Maynard Hutchins, a distinguished educator, wrote, "About all we can say today is that the one certain calling is citizenship and the one certain destiny, manhood." He concluded his article with this statement: "The aim of American education in an age of rapid change should be to do what it can to help everybody gain complete possession of all his powers." [2]

When we say we don't know what kind of world these children will find, it doesn't excuse us from trying to make some predictions. Modern society calls for basic tools in language, mathematics, the social and physical sciences, and the arts. The future demands self-confidence and an ability and desire to continue to learn in order to cope with inevitable changes. Creativity will be required to take existing media and ideas, combine them with new media and ideas, and come up with better products or better ways of doing things. Progress requires that children find answers to questions that teachers can't answer or haven't even asked. In addition, emotional health and successful family and personal relationships will surely be important to individuals. Education for citizenship will be vital. At all ages, the ability to cope with leisure time may be significant to the individual's feeling of satisfaction. Throughout life, learning how to learn and developing a zest for learning may be the most important outcomes of the educational experience.

What does this discussion about an individual's future needs tell us about planning to help young children reach their full potential today? There is no question but that we should hope to foster their mental development and prepare them well in the basic subjects—reading and language arts, physical and social sciences, mathematics,

---

[2] Robert M. Hutchins, "Permanence and Change," *The Center Magazine*, 1:6 (September 1968), 6–8.

and the arts. Every effort should be made also to help build strong bodies and teach children to care for these bodies. Longevity figures warn us that these children's bodies will be with them a long time. Sports should play a significant role in physical development and in the use of leisure time. Teachers should help children build a personal self-confidence that prepares them to cope with life. We should be concerned with the total aspects of mental health. We hope that children will learn to get along with others in order to live peacefully on this planet. Closely related is the individual's creativity—his ability to see new relationships, push boundaries beyond present knowledge, and organize ideas aesthetically.

From the foregoing we can now sift out several areas to emphasize in our planning for young children: (1) mental development, (2) physical development, (3) emotional development, (4) social development, and (5) creativity. These areas are not independent for either adults or children. They are interrelated, and a deficiency in one can create inadequacies in the others. The conclusion follows, then, that in planning for the child to reach his fullest potential, we must plan for the totality of experience for the whole child.

Goals for Early Childhood Education

Establishing goals must come before attempting to make plans. What do we want to accomplish? Let us agree our goals are that each child live a happy childhood, reach his potential, and become a happy, fully functioning adult.

To define goals in terms more helpful to teachers, the concept of developmental tasks as outlined in the work of Carolyn Tryon and J. W. Lilienthal is useful.[3] Developmental tasks are those common tasks each individual of a given age must master within a given society in order to be happy and to master the tasks of the next age. The developmental tasks are like rungs on a ladder; they are too far apart for the person to scale the wall of maturity without stepping on each rung. Sufficient experience and skill in each task must be achieved before the next task can be reached successfully. When

---

[3] Carolyn Tryon and J. W. Lilienthal, "Guideposts in Child Growth and Development," *National Education Association Journal* (1950), 188–189. For a somewhat different and more comprehensive approach to developmental tasks, see Robert J. Havighurst, *Developmental Tasks and Education* (New York: McKay, 1952).

FIGURE 2–1.   *Early childhood—a time to discover something, to touch it to see what you can learn that way, and to tell someone who'll listen what you've discovered.*

FIGURE 2–2. *Early childhood—a time to learn new motor skills like riding a tricycle.*

conditions are right, and if the teacher is prepared, she can help a child master his tasks.

Goals will be stated in terms of the nursery school and kindergarten child. A developmental continuum exists, and each child may reach a particular task at a somewhat different calendar age.

1. The child needs to grow in independence. He begins to think of himself as an independent, capable individual. This goal is always in the teacher's mind as she plans the program, equipment, materials, and guidance for children. A teacher remembers this goal as she decides whether or not and how much to help a given child with his boots or zipper. The objective is to help the child learn to make decisions and choices. She is responsible for helping each child reach a level of independence appropriate for him.

2. The child needs to learn to give and share as well as receive affection. From a typical pattern of self-centered affection, the child will grow in his ability to give and share affection with others his age and with adults other than his family. The teacher helps him to feel secure and loved in his new environment. For a child whose home background has not fostered feelings of love and security, the teacher makes special plans for working with the child and the parents in hopes of changing some of the negative aspects of the home setting.

3. The child needs to learn to get along with others. As the child moves out of the social unit of the family into the social unit of the school, the teacher wants his experiences to be happy. She protects him until he is ready for social relationships. She helps him learn techniques of interaction that will bring him positive responses from others.

4. The child needs to develop self-control. The teacher thinks of discipline as a skill to be developed over time and one for which there are few absolutes. She works toward the child's becoming self-disciplined, self-guided, or self-directed. She wants him to learn certain behavior responses and the reasons for them. She explains how appropriate responses provide protection for him as well as for the safety and well-being of others. As a child gains understanding he develops a sound basis for appropriate behavior. Fear of an authoritarian figure does not provide an adequate basis for developing self-control. Experience in making judgments and decisions is provided in order that the child will become confident that he can make decisions when the teacher isn't nearby.

5. The child needs to learn human, nonsexist roles. Though biological sex roles differ, sex stereotyping is to be avoided. Teachers must be constantly alert to set expectations and use guidance that encourages children, regardless of sex, to develop all aspects of their personalities and talents. Equal treatment and equal career opportunities for either sex are now generally required by state and national laws.

6. The child needs to begin understanding his body. The teacher fosters understandings about feeding, caring for, and appreciating the body.

7. The child needs to learn many large and small motor skills. A program is designed by the teacher to challenge the child's small and large muscles. Motor skill development is assisted through careful support and guidance.

8. The child needs to begin to understand and control his physical world. The teacher develops the child's intelligence by encouraging curiosity, thinking, reasoning, and the gathering and using of

information. Every effort is made to help children fit together some of the pieces of their world puzzle through careful planning and selecting of materials, equipment, and experiences. She hopes to provide a background of experiences and attitudes that will make living and learning more meaningful.

9. The child needs to learn new words and how to use words in his social and intellectual activity. Every opportunity is used by the teacher to foster the child's use of language and his understanding of his surroundings. Encouragement is provided for all aspects of learning.

10. The child needs to begin to develop a notion about his relationship to the world. The teacher's role is to help the child develop a positive self-concept—a good feeling about himself and his expanding world. As the child makes his initial adjustment to new people,

FIGURE 2–3.   *Early childhood—a time to learn to work together. (Michigan State University Laboratory Preschool.)*

FIGURE 2–4. *Early childhood—a time to talk new things over with a friend.*

places, and expectations, the teacher provides protection and encouragement. Because these group experiences are the child's first experiences away from home, it is very important for these to be positive, happy experiences. School should be so personally exciting and meaningful that fuel is added to the child's drive to learn. In this way the mechanics of learning—reading and writing—will seem worth the effort in the next phase of schooling. Unavoidably, the child forms an opinion of school from his early educational experiences. We should strive to help the child become self-confident in the school situation. We want him to be positively attracted to school, teachers, friends, experiences, books, and learning. If we send him on to elementary school with these positive feelings, we will have accomplished a great deal that will serve him for a long time.

Using the foregoing ten developmental tasks for guides, teachers can plan nursery school or kindergarten programs that foster all

FIGURE 2–5. *Early childhood—a time to try out the roles you see around you. (Michigan State University Laboratory Preschool.)*

areas of a child's development—physical, mental, emotional, social, and creative. Each of the ten tasks is important for a balanced program.

There are other frameworks that might help the teacher establish goals. One framework, by Foote and Cottrell, defines six areas of interpersonal competence: health, intelligence, empathy, autonomy, judgment, and creativity.[4] Whatever the framework chosen the teacher must guard against choosing one that does not develop the whole child. She must avoid getting carried away by schemes that would emphasize one aspect of development and neglect others.

[4] Nelson Foote and Leonard S. Cottrell, Jr., *Identity and Interpersonal Competence* (Chicago: University of Chicago Press, 1955), p. 61.

How Are Goals Achieved?

The first time you visit a nursery school or kindergarten you may wonder how the teacher survives the day or how the children ever learn anything. There is usually a free-flowing informality that is far different from the organization any adult is likely to remember in his own schooling.

PLANNING. Despite the apparent informality and lack of regimentation, a great deal of planning and organizing takes place before, after, and even during the school day. The teacher and her assistants meet regularly when the children are not at school to map out the days, weeks, and months ahead. Plans are flexible, but a good program for children does not develop haphazardly. The teacher keeps goals for the children firmly in mind. She thinks of goals in terms of individual children. She does not lump all children together and say, "All children must learn to. . . ." There will be a range of skills, behaviors, and competencies in any class. The teacher should expect differences and plan for them.

LEARNING CENTERS. The school will generally be arranged in learning centers, or zones. That is, in various parts of the room there will be a place for children to work in art, in science, or in music. They will find zones with blocks, books, and materials for dramatic play. Other zones will display perceptual and number games. In colder climates there may be an indoor zone for vigorous climbing, which substitutes for outdoor activities during bad weather. Though outdoor zones may not be as numerous as those for indoors, the observer will find zones for both quiet and vigorous activity outdoors.

SELF-SELECTED ACTIVITY AND THE TEACHER'S ROLE. Finding children talking, laughing, and moving about may be one of the biggest surprises to a new observer. Yet, further observation will reveal that the children are actively learning as they choose their own activities. During the *self-selected activity period* they work individually and in small groups throughout the room or yard. The largest part of the child's day is self-selected.

The informal teaching style may also be a surprise. The teacher's role is to organize the learning centers and see that there is appropriate and sufficient equipment in each for carrying on activities from which the child can choose. Then the teacher relates to each child as he learns. The role is far more than supervisory. The teaching involves moving about, putting in a word here, redirecting there, listening to children's comments and questions.

The assistants and the teacher work as a team. For example, one day the assistant may provide a science experiment in one zone

FIGURE 2–6. *Early childhood—a time to enjoy swinging with friends.* (*National Institute of Education Child Study Center, U.S. Office of Education.*)

that requires her close attention. Another day the assistant may keep an eye on all the zones while the teacher concentrates on teaching language arts at the literature table. Through many one-to-one contacts the teachers contribute to the total growth of each child.

TEACHER-INSTIGATED ACTIVITIES. Routine activities such as clean-up, storytime, and snack time are also part of the child's day. These are teacher instigated, requiring some compliance with the teacher's plan. However, they are loosely organized to leave room for individual differences in response. Group activities contribute to the child's learning and develop an *esprit de corps* in the group.

As a student participator you may be asked to select a zone in which you can begin to develop a relationship with children individually and in small groups. For example, you may sit near the table games or puzzles, observing and helping where needed. The teacher may brief you on procedures, schedules, and the like, or may offer advice when it seems warranted. For the most part, though, you will be left to handle your assignment as well as you can—applying your knowledge from readings and other sources. After you are acquainted with the children, you may move into situations in which you work with larger numbers of children. After the children have

FIGURE 2–7. *Early childhood—a time to try out new games. (Louisiana State University Nursery School.)*

gone, you will have an opportunity to question the teacher and seek recommendations for handling special problems.

How Does Organization Facilitate Goals?

Do children really learn anything worthwhile in such a free setting? This may be the student's first reaction and question. Doubt is usually common among teachers who are already experienced in teaching upper elementary and secondary grades.

Almost inevitably problems arise in groups of small children when an adult tries to get all the children doing the same thing at the same time. A young child is not accustomed to sitting still, and his attention span is short. But the attention span of many children is longer when they are involved in a self-chosen activity, not an adult-initiated one.

Children have a natural inclination to explore and manipulate. This inclination is to be exploited when the educational environment for the young child is being planned. Put a puzzle on the table so that the child can see it. He can't resist taking the puzzle apart. And when he is successful at working it, the child has developed both physically and mentally. The effective nursery school and kindergarten provide for numerous learning experiences with a variety of enticing equipment that openly invites the child's use.

The teacher plans learning experiences that permit the child to educate himself. As he makes discoveries through his senses—sight, touch, taste, smell, and hearing—he will communicate with other children and teachers, developing language vital to all learning. Also he will concentrate because he is doing something that interests him. He will investigate, manipulate, and create, thereby contributing to his intelligence and storehouse of knowledge.

Through individual, small group, and whole group activities, the teacher structures a flexible, individualized, and academically sound program. To observe or participate in a nursery school or kindergarten where children are dynamically involved in their own learning is to become convinced that "worthwhile" learning is taking place.

To the casual observer, children who are exercising their free choice during the self-selected activity periods are "just playing." Writers such as Bereiter and Engelmann advocate reducing the

FIGURE 2–8.   *Early childhood—a time to see what happens if you beat soap in the water. (Iowa State University Nursery School.)*

FIGURE 2–9. *Early childhood—a time to develop climbing muscles. (University of Tennessee Gulf Range Child Care Center.)*

amount of self-directed play activity by "focusing upon academic objectives and relegating all nonacademic objectives to a secondary position." [5] However, Lawrence K. Frank, a distinguished scholar of child growth and development, would not consider the self-directed activity previously described as "nonacademic." He wrote, "Hence through play the child continually rehearses, practices, and endlessly explores and manipulates whatever he can manage to transform imaginatively into equivalents of the adult world. He experiments with and tries to establish the meaning and use of a variety of symbols, especially language, as he tries to cope with this often perplexing grown-up world." [6]

Indeed, play is very valuable. Frank and Theresa Caplan, writing in *The Power of Play*, discuss the following sixteen values of play.[7]

[5] Carl Bereiter and Siegfried Engelmann, *Teaching Disadvantaged Children in the Preschool* (Englewood Cliffs, N.J.: Prentice-Hall, 1966), p. 10.

[6] Lawrence K. Frank, "Play and Child Development," *Play—Children's Business, Guide to Selection of Toys and Games: Infants to Twelve-Year-Olds* (Washington, D.C.: Association for Childhood Education International, 1963), pp. 4–5.

[7] Frank and Theresa Caplan, *The Power of Play* (Garden City, N.Y.: Anchor Press, Doubleday, 1973), pp. xii–xvii.

FIGURE 2–10. *Early childhood—a time to get acquainted with books.* (*Michigan State University Laboratory Preschool.*)

1. Play aids growth.
2. Play is a voluntary activity.
3. Play offers a child freedom of action.
4. Play provides an imaginary world a child can master.
5. Play has elements of adventure in it.
6. Play provides a base for language building.
7. Play has unique power for building interpersonal relations.
8. Play offers opportunities for mastery of the physical self.
9. Play furthers interest and concentration.
10. Play is the way children investigate the material world.
11. Play is a way of learning adult roles.
12. Play is always a dynamic way of learning.
13. Play refines a child's judgments.
14. Play can be academically structured.

15. Play is vitalizing.
16. Play is essential to the survival of humans.

The advocates of more academic activities are really suggesting more teacher-instigated or structured activities. Bereiter and Engelmann recommend that drill on teacher-chosen topics consume most of the child's school day.[8] There is no doubt that there are significant problems for teachers who teach disadvantaged youngsters—the youngsters Bereiter and Engelmann had in mind when they proposed their much discussed methods. However, it is doubtful that long-range goals for stimulating the child's love for learning, teachers, and books are accomplished through methods such as they propose.

Conclusion

A developmental philosophy of early childhood education has been described. Teachers establish goals before planning programs. Suggested goals for the young child have been stated in terms of the developmental tasks of early childhood. Goals are achieved through careful planning and through arranging centers in which the child can learn as he uses the materials and equipment he himself selects. Routine activities are organized in a way that leaves room for individual differences.

As you read, observe, participate, and plan for a career in teaching, you must judge the merits of various teaching approaches. In what sort of school atmosphere does a child best learn academically significant concepts? What teaching methods are most appropriate to the philosophy, ideals, and needs of a democratic society?

The teacher is of utmost significance. Perhaps you can sense through your observation and participation what Moustakas calls "the bond" between teacher and child from which "opportunities and resources emerge which enable both child and teacher to realize hidden potentials, to release creative capacities, and to stretch to new horizons of experience, together and alone, where learning has an impact on total being and where life has a passionate, enduring character." [9]

ADDITIONAL READINGS

ANKER, DOROTHY, et al. "Teaching Children as They Play." *Young Children*, Vol. 29, No. 4, May 1974, pp. 203–213.

[8] Carl Bereiter and Siegfried Engelmann, op. cit., p. 10.
[9] Clark Moustakas, *The Authentic Teacher* (Cambridge, Mass.: Howard A. Doyle Publishing Co., 1967), p. 58.

BEREITER, CARL, and SIEGFRIED ENGELMANN. *Teaching Disadvantaged Children in the Preschool.* Englewood Cliffs, N.J.: Prentice-Hall, Inc., 1966.

CALDWELL, BETTYE M. *Project Head Start Program II: A Manual for Teachers.* Washington, D.C.: Office of Economic Opportunity, 1968.

Feelings and Learning. Washington, D.C.: Association for Childhood Education International, 1963.

HAVIGHURST, ROBERT J. *Developmental Tasks and Education.* New York: David McKay Company, Inc., 1952.

HYMES, JAMES L., JR. *Teaching the Child Under Six.* Columbus, Ohio: Charles E. Merrill Publishing Co., 1974.

LAW, NORMA, et al. *Basic Propositions for Early Childhood Education.* Washington, D.C.: Association for Childhood Education International, 1965.

LEEPER, SARAH H., et al. *Good Schools for Young Children.* New York: Macmillan Publishing Co., Inc., 1974.

Montessori in Perspective. Washington, D.C.: National Association for Education of Young Children, 1966.

Murphy, Lois B., and Ethel M. Leeper. *Conditions for Learning.* Washington, D.C.: U.S. Government Printing Office, 1973.

NIMNICHT, GLENN, ORALIE McAFEE, and JOHN MEIER. *The New Nursery School.* New York: General Learning Corporation, 1969.

READ, KATHERINE. *The Nursery School: A Human Relationships Laboratory.* Philadelphia: W. B. Saunders Company, 1971.

TODD, VIVIAN E., and HELEN HEFFERNAN. *The Years Before School: Guiding Preschool Children.* New York: Macmillan Publishing Co., Inc., 1970.

WEBER, EVELYN. *The Kindergarten.* New York: Columbia University, Teacher's College Press, 1969.

WEBER, EVELYN. *The English Infant School and Informal Education.* Englewood Cliffs, N.J.: Prentice-Hall, Inc., 1971.

WILLS, CLARICE, and LUCILLE LINDBERG. *Kindergarten for Today's Children.* Chicago: Follett Publishing Company, 1967.

Getting to Know Children

"WE GET to help more with the three-year-olds than we did with the fives." "I feel useless. These fives don't need any help." "Whew! There is never a dull moment in here with the four-year-olds."

Such comments are common when early childhood education students talk about their observing and participating assignments in the nursery school and kindergarten groups. When given an opportunity to see different age groups, students discover common characteristics of an age. They also note wide differences between children who are the same age.

Teachers and parents can make use of normative-descriptive data derived from research by investigators such as Arnold Gesell (1880–1961).[1] Gesell and others carefully observed large numbers of children and described typical behavior and other characteristics of each age. Although a child may never completely fit the "typical" pattern, it helps to compare his growth with such norms. Normative data help adults plan new experiences and guidance measures for the child. Comparing the behavior of a child with these data helps adults recognize severe deficiencies and initiate appropriate measures to correct deficiencies.

Teachers combine normative-descriptive data and goals in order to plan appropriate programs for children. The following are general characteristics of nursery school and kindergarten children as they might be observed in the school situation.

Characteristics of Children

Late Two-Year-Olds and Young Threes

If you observe a group of late twos and young three-year-olds, you may find there is very little conversation. Most children's vocabularies

[1] Arnold Gesell and Frances L. Ilg, *Child Development* (New York: Harper & Row, 1949).

FIGURE 3–1. *Children's first drawings are scribbles made with a crayon held in a fist.*

are limited at this age. They get what they want by physical rather than verbal means. Children may be playing quite far apart, yet never seem to feel left out. Even if they are playing close together, each will be playing his own game. This is called *parallel play.* You will see little interaction between the children.

Physical skills interest twos and threes. They may seek compliments on how high they are on the slide or jungle gym. They may need encouragement, help, and reassurance the first few times they use a piece of equipment. Twos may prefer to push a kiddie car, but the tricycle usually attracts the threes. Twos look clumsy and precarious to many visitors, who worry that they will fall. However, they generally won't fall if they climb from their own motivation. If they are encouraged by another child or an adult to go beyond what they

FIGURE 3–2.   *Students who have had baby-sitting experience feel at ease with children.*

personally feel is a safe height, then the teacher should be nearby to avoid accidents.

For most twos and young threes, the school is the first group experience away from home. This age group should have a sufficient number of adults ready to provide individualized attention. The ability to play the mother role when necessary is a characteristic of a good teacher for this age group. Introduction to group living may be painful for some of the children. It may be difficult for the child's mother, too! Children enter nursery school with differing amounts of experience outside the home. One child may readily accept a teacher because he has had pleasant experiences with baby-sitters, relatives, or Sunday school teachers. If his previous experience has been unpleasant, however, the teacher may be in for a difficult time. Many young children will have had virtually no experience away from home. When they arrive at nursery school among strange adults and children, they are overcome with fear.

Teachers of twos and young threes must be on the alert for signs indicating a child's need to use the toilet. The child may fidget restlessly, or become unusually quiet, or hold his hand pressing his genitals. As soon as the signs are noticed, the teacher heads straight for the bathroom with the child in hand. Young children can't wait! The teacher talks in a quiet voice as she leads the child to the bathroom. Although schools generally prefer to enroll children who are toilet trained, every teacher of two- and three-year-olds knows that bladder control is frequently not well established. She alerts herself to prevent accidents. Her guidance will vary from child to child as she understands each one. Some may need a helping hand, others may need only a reminder. A mature child will go to the toilet when he needs to without attention. Some may fear the noise of the flushing water. If this is true, do not require the child to flush the toilet until he matures and overcomes this fear.

FIGURE 3–3.   *Techniques for working with children develop during baby-sitting experiences.*

FIGURE 3–4. *Sharing books with children helps new students feel comfortable in their role. (Michigan State University Laboratory Preschool.)*

Lunch or snack with twos and young threes is a serious business. They eat well and talk little. Often they spill food and milk. Fingers are the popular eating tool.

Resting time should provide a closeness to the teacher or other adults. In groups that meet only a few hours, children may not be required to lie down to rest. However, in day-care centers, where children stay a full day, nap time is essential. These youngsters may get exhausted because of the amount of stimulation they receive in the group and because most arrive at school quite early. Bedtime has many associations for the child. He may be weepy because his mother is not there. Many hands and much patience are required to get a happy, restful nap time under way.

Comparing the teaching in a group of young children with the teaching in an older group, you will note that the younger child gets more help, more demonstration, more reassurance, and more assistance as he tries a new skill. The teacher uses words, gestures, and actions because the young child's verbal understandings are being developed. Action cues help the child to understand.

Late Threes and Fours

Three-and-a-half- and four-year-olds have many characteristics in common. During their first days in nursery school they may have anxiety periods, just as do the two-year-olds and young threes. Generally, anxiety periods will be of short duration because the child has had more occasions to leave his mother and enter into groups. He knows his mother always returns. Because he is more experienced, he will be more curious about what the other children are doing and will move in the direction of the action. If the mother remains at school, she will probably find she is not needed.

FIGURE 3–5.   *Directed observation of children draws students' attention to characteristics of children's growth and behavior. (University of Idaho Nursery School.)*

FIGURE 3–6. *The youngest children usually play alone but will enjoy a "peek-a-boo" game with a teacher.*

Children of this age ask many questions. They ask some questions because they really want to know. They ask some simply because they want attention. Others they ask because they wish someone would ask them that question—they know the answer and enjoy a chance to show off. Verbally they have developed by leaps and bounds from the younger age discussed previously. They understand more vocabulary than they are able to use.

At this period there is a rapid increase in reasoning and concept building. They want to know about everything and to experiment with any material provided for them. Interest is maintained over a longer period of time than in younger children.

These children are more active. They run faster, climb more easily, and swing higher. Many can now pump the swing. They ride their tricycles fast, bumping into things and people, and even upsetting the tricycles deliberately.

Socially, late three- and four-year-olds play closer together, sometimes sharing toys. The more mature will make suggestions for the

FIGURE 3–7. *Children need to rest from time to time. While they are resting, their eyes may be alert to the actions of others nearby.*

others. This is parallel play, showing the beginning of cooperative play. Increased verbal and motor ability seem to be facilitating factors.

During the fourth year boys often choose activities traditionally thought of as masculine. For example, they select big blocks and cars. Girls often like the housekeeping area or other more "feminine" activities. However, there is still a great deal of interaction between the sexes as they play in the learning areas. Imaginative themes develop in the group.

Teachers can help avoid sexist orientations by encouraging all children to participate in all activities. For example, with our newer understanding of the impact of socialization and sex role stereotyping, the teacher may not only permit but encourage girls to be more rambunctious, physical, and loud in their play and boys to be more loving, helping, and aesthetic. Societal gains from removing sex role, racial, and ethnic stereotypes can be substantial.

The four-year-old vacillates between wanting to be big and enjoying

FIGURE 3–8.   *Five-year-olds use verbal skills to plan and carry out co-operative ventures.* (*Michigan State University Laboratory Preschool.*)

FIGURE 3–9. *Students preparing to teach gain much from observing a dynamic teacher working with children. (Michigan State University Laboratory Preschool.)*

being little. One day he can do a thing for himself, the next day he would like you to do it for him—or at least give a little help.

The late threes and four-year-olds may be picky eaters. They may indicate their likes and dislikes strongly, thus asserting themselves. Their growth rate has slowed down and they require less food. Therefore, avoid pressuring children to eat.

Toileting is generally quite routine in these groups. A wise teacher is quick to note indications of a child's need and will remind him to go. Most four-year-olds prefer to take care of toileting without help.

At this age the child usually thinks he's too old to rest. Rest time is therefore better received if it is called quiet time. However, a three- or four-year-old still needs to slow down or he may become exhausted, hyperactive, or grouchy. In day-care centers adjustments may have to be made for older children who aren't sleepy. Sometimes they can be given resting and reading privileges in a room away from the sleepers.

Three-year-olds are known for their negativism. Wording questions and requests to avoid that "No" seems to be the key to living harmoniously with threes. Fours, instead of saying "No," typically find

FIGURE 3–10. *"Best friends" are made, especially among girls, during the late four- and five-year-old period. (Michigan State University Laboratory Preschool.)*

other ways (dawdling or talking) to resist what adults want them to do. Almost all have difficulty waiting for their turn.

Fives and Young Sixes

The fives and young six-year-olds found in kindergartens are different from the groups we have been discussing. They are much easier to organize into a group because of their increased use and understanding of words. They seem more patient and can wait for their turn—though not indefinitely. They seem to have a genuine interest in pleasing their teachers, their mothers, and anyone else who shows interest in them.

In addition to their increased verbal skills, they are highly curious about everything they see or hear. They want to know. They like to experiment. They often wonder how something works and will take it apart in an effort to find out. They are highly creative if their previous experience has stimulated their imagination. They will be creative in every aspect of their learning if the atmosphere is conducive to experimentation.

Socially these children enjoy each other. Cooperation on intricate projects may last several days. Each group usually has a number of strong leaders with creative ideas for projects or dramatic play. Boys and girls often play together. However, girls tend to choose a "best friend"—often resulting in easily hurt feelings if the friend finds someone else. Boys are less inclined toward a single friend and usually enjoy activities that incorporate a large group of boys at a time. All activity is not cooperative, however. Because of a longer attention span, a child may work on a project alone while everyone else does something else. This type of independent activity frequently occurs with the more socially secure children.

A charming characteristic of children of this age is their growing sense of humor. At the younger ages children are too literal to appreciate a joke. Now they enjoy jokes, riddles, and nonsense songs and poems. They like to rhyme words and may taunt their friends verbally.

Motor coordination is well developed. Kindergarteners enjoy learning new skills. Chinning, skating, and riding a two-wheel bike are challenges they appreciate. Small motor coordination is also developing, so that a crayon marks where the child wants it to mark. More complicated puzzles and building toys are enjoyed.

With so much growth in all areas of development, the teacher's role is to provide a wide varity of activities. Activities must be constantly new, different, and appealing. When a teacher knows that children have not learned something thoroughly, she must present the concept in a fresh way; otherwise her group will let her know that they are bored. Because of the wider variety of interests, she must plan to have many activities going on in her group at once. When kindergarteners have had previous nursery school experience or are from advantaged homes, an even wider variety of challenging activities is crucial. There is so much in this world to learn that it is a severe indictment of the teacher if a group of kindergarteners becomes bored.

FIGURE 3–11. *Independence is a goal to be fostered in school activities.* (*Michigan State University Laboratory Preschool.*)

Some typical behaviors and other characteristics of children found in nursery schools and kindergartens have been described. Each child differs regarding these characteristics. When it is said that three-year-olds are typically negative, it means that most, but not necessarily all, three-year-olds are negative. The same is true of the other behaviors described. Normative data only indicate typical characteristics and therefore are not really an evaluation of behavior.

Any plan for learning must take into consideration the ages and stages of the children in the group. To master advanced skills, the child must first succeed in the more elementary ones. This fact is important in all areas of learning and must be taken into account as teachers provide experiences and set expectations for individual children. A three-year-old may advance along the developmental continuum and master some skills that are typical of five-year-olds. A five-year-old may have a slower rate of development and be like three-year-olds in some skills.

It is important for teachers to become knowledgeable about child growth and development, to learn to assess accurately a child's level of development, and to incorporate this knowledge into planning for children at school.

Age for Entering School

Ideally a child should enter a nursery school or kindergarten when his level of development indicates that he is ready for the expanded

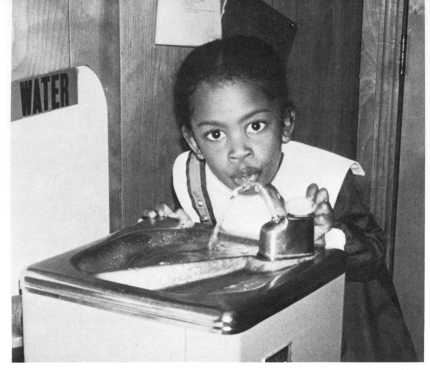

FIGURE 3–12. *Children need plenty of water. If a fountain is not available, then pitchers of water and cups should be available in playroom and play yard. (Louisiana State University Nursery School.)*

environment. However, in practice the teacher may be required to cope with children who are not really ready for school. For example, day-care centers receive children who are not ready for school, because their mothers must work and they have no other place to send them. Head Start schools enroll children at a young age to begin the compensatory efforts that are needed. Even in the more exclusive schools, children may be sent to school before they are ready because their name is next on a waiting list and the parents know they may have a long wait if they relinquish the place. Public kindergartens set arbitrary chronological age limits without regard for a child's level of development. When situations of this sort occur, the teacher's skill in blending mothering with teaching may be challenged.

Research points out the immature child's lack of success in school.[2] Immature boys especially have difficulty competing against girls and older boys.[3] When a child will be among the youngest in his class, school officials may urge parents to seek an evaluation of his readiness. His ability to cope with a class of older children and to partici-

[2] Katrina De Hirsch, "Potential Educational Risks," *Childhood Education,* **41**:4 (December 1964), 178–183.

[3] Ibid., p. 183.

pate in regular school activities must be considered. Boys appear to be less academically oriented than girls and may have more difficulty than girls with small muscle coordination of the sort required for handwriting.[4] Parents who want their boy's first school experiences to be successful may be encouraged to enroll him in nursery school or kindergarten a year longer. These children simply need time to mature and one year may make the difference between school success and difficulty. School counselors support this move. They find their biggest caseload among immature, hyperactive boys who are not ready for the sitting still that many first grades require.[5] When this type of counseling is taking place in a community, the nursery schools and kindergartens may enroll a number of children somewhat older than the typical ages described.

Catherine Landreth summarizes research findings as follows: "In clinics for children with speech and reading problems, there are many more boys than girls. Why? This sex difference could be due to differences in the frequencies with which boys and girls inherit characteristics that lead to speech and reading problems. It could also be due to differences in their rate of development. It may well be that many boys are not ready for the kinds of learning tasks that most girls are ready for at ages 5 and 6." [6]

Grouping Children

Schools vary in their policy of grouping children. A single group may range from ages three to six. In other schools separate homogeneous age groups of threes, fours, and fives exist. Flexible grouping is followed in some programs. For example, if there is a physically skillful late three-year-old, he may be allowed some time with the four-year-old group. The teacher may even transfer him if all areas of his development justify it.

A case can be made for nearly any age combination. Some teachers like to have older children with the younger. They reason that older children learn to help out the younger ones. In a classroom with a wide age range an immature older child can find a playmate with similar skills. In a single-age classroom he may feel inferior.

Some teachers object to a wide-age-range classroom because the wide differences make it difficult to plan activities with sufficient

[4] See Elizabeth Hurlock, *Child Development* (New York: McGraw-Hill, 1972), p. 141, for a discussion regarding development of handwriting skills.
[5] Katrina De Hirsch, "Potential Educational Risks," *Childhood Education*, **41**:4 (December 1964), 180.
[6] Catherine Landreth, *Preschool Learning and Teaching* (New York: Harper & Row, 1972), p. 3.

challenge for the most mature children. Frequently a teacher has little to say about the ages of the children in her group. She may simply be handed a list of children who are enrolled. In a public school she may have to enroll any child who registers. Sometimes church officials or welfare officers recruit children with little regard for age. But even if the children were all the same age, teachers would find wide variations in development. With a mixture of ages the range of differences is still greater. Teachers must plan a variety of activities for self-selection—some to challenge the most skillful child and others to encourage the least skillful.

Size of Group

Fewer than twenty children per group is best from the viewpoint of both the children and the teachers. A small group permits the teachers to know the children and the parents better. Children, too, get better acquainted with their teachers and each other if the group is small. Also, it is easier to avoid overstimulation and fatigue. Every group should have a minimum of two adults in order to cope with emergencies. A ratio of one adult per five children is suggested, especially in groups of disadvantaged children, where individualized teaching is of special importance. Research indicates that the larger the group the more authoritarian the leadership becomes in order to maintain control.

Knowing Children as Individuals

Classroom Observation

Teachers begin accumulating information about the children from the first moment they know which children will be in their group. Because each child is unique, understanding each one is a difficult task. The teacher makes a systematic effort to learn about each child. She may carry a notebook in which she records information. She may periodically check a progress report for each child. She may ask an observer to take diary records of each child's activity and manner of response. Combining observations and information from various sources, the teacher plans a program to fulfill each child's needs. Students will benefit from the teacher's careful study as she provides them with background information for understanding more about the children.

Home Visits

Besides working with the children at school, most teachers make periodic visits to the home in order to get better acquainted with the child and the family. A student may be invited to accompany the teacher on a home visit. Students, and even some teachers, are often hesitant about making home visits. However, once they have made a few visits they realize their value in developing understanding, appreciation, and rapport.

The home visits made prior to the opening of school can be one of the teacher's most important activities of the entire year. Arranging introductions on the family's home premises gives the family a chance to feel more at ease. The focus is on the family and their concerns. If the introduction occurs at school, the focus becomes almost entirely school-centered. The goal for the first visit is to learn from the parents about their child and his home environment.

The teacher makes an efficient visiting schedule by grouping children according to their neighborhoods and making telephone calls to arrange a convenient time for a short visit. If the visits are scheduled every half hour, there is a little time to allow for getting mixed up on directions or waiting while the baby's diaper is changed. The home visit can be presented as a routine event and as an opportunity for the child to get to know the teacher before he enters school. Cooperation is usually excellent.

For an icebreaker a teacher can show the child a packet of snapshots of former classes of children busily at work at school. Pictures always interest children and help them get over some of their shyness. A toy or a book can substitute for pictures. As the child looks at the pictures or plays with the toy, the parents and the teacher can talk over a few details.

The teacher can provide the parents a school policy statement for later reading, a list of children's names and addresses, a field trip permission blank, health forms, a brief informational questionnaire, and forms for any research data needed. She explains when the forms are to be returned and why they are needed and assures parents that personal documents are confidential.

The teacher discusses with parents their role on the first day of school and seeks their estimate of how much support they feel the child will need. Because the first days are so crucial to the child's attitude toward school, it seems worthwhile to ask the parents to stay with the child if necessary. It is rarely necessary for a five-year-old, especially if the home visit has been thoughtfully done. With younger children it may or may not be necessary for the parent to stay. Sometimes the teacher's role is one of helping the parent permit the child to become independent. Sometimes the parent may be more concerned than the child about the new experience.

One of the values of a short visit early in the year is that, as yet, there are no problems to discuss. The parent or child can't worry that a teacher comes with bad tidings—as she may later on. The parent may welcome the chance to forewarn the teacher of a possible problem area and will be grateful for the opportunity to discuss it. Parents, teacher, and child can visit without feeling that others are waiting for their turn or that others are listening—as they might be at the school or at a parents' meeting. The young child is reassured when he later says to his teacher, "You know where I live." He feels real security in this knowledge and believes that in any emergency the teacher could find his house—and she sometimes may have to!

Home visits often give information about family activities, interests, or hobbies. This information may also provide ideas for involving a family in class activities. For example, if Johnny brings out his daddy's banjo, the teacher can remember to ask Mr. Smith to play his banjo at school when the class is studying vibrations or stringed instruments. Questions such as "What did you do this summer?" can help a teacher include the child in future class discussions. For example, a teacher learned that shy Ronnie had flown by jet to visit his grandmother. Ronnie then became the class's jet expert when flying was mentioned.

A classroom storybook featuring the children themselves can begin to take shape during home visits. The teacher carries her camera and uses this opportunity to photograph each child. Looking for siblings, pets, or toys to include in the photo brings about informal visiting that adds further to the rapport among all present. See the chapter on literature for more discussion about this storybook. Pictures may also be placed on lockers to help the child identify his personal space.

On parting from the home visit the teacher can tell the parents, "Please call me at school or at home any time a question comes up that concerns the school and your child. We want to work together to make a good year for Johnny." Usually they quickly respond with the counterpart of that statement, "You call us too if anything comes up or if we can help." If they do not so respond, the teacher can add, "And I'll want to feel free to call you if I have any questions." In addition, parents are extended an open invitation to visit during the school year at any time, for a minute or all day.

Parents may have some anxiety concerning their lack of nice furnishings, but a wise teacher does not concentrate on these things or appear to notice. She is building a relationship with people with whom she expects to work at least a year. The human element interests her more than the quality of sofas. After this informative get-acquainted visit, they'll know each other the next time they meet.

Throughout the year the teacher can realize tremendous value from this brief home visit. In the first place, the child's name and face can more easily be remembered after she has had some time to talk to him individually. Calling the child by name, perhaps asking about a pet or a baby sister, can make him feel more at home those first days at school. Following this procedure, teachers find fewer children who cry on opening day. In addition, during the visit she gains some feeling about the psychological climate of the child's environment. For example, she may sense quite accurately the competition between siblings or the laissez-faire attitudes of parents. Home visits are as unique as families. Teachers should relax, enjoy these new friends, and not feel any compulsion to teach but only to learn.

When home visits are not feasible before school begins, they should be planned as quickly as possible after the opening of school. On visits later in the year, parents will expect the teacher to tell them about their child. Visits or conferences that are held when there are problems that must be discussed are far more difficult than the initial meeting. They, too, require thoughtful preparation. However, when initial meetings have built a feeling of confidence and respect between teacher and parent then the relationship can withstand a discussion about a child's problem.

Teachers should write notes on all visits and conferences. These can be written after the session and filed for future reference. Further discussion of the school's partnership with parents in extending the classroom goals to the home follows in the chapter on teacher-parent relations.

Family Visits to the School

During the home visit a time can be agreed upon for the family to see the school facilities. These family visits to the school afford university students assigned to that laboratory an excellent opportunity to get acquainted with children.

As a result of the home visit, the teacher and family now greet each other as old friends. Student helpers can be available to help quietly as the child looks around. The child usually explores quickly, finding his locker with his name on it, the bathroom, the various learning centers, and the playground. Sometimes he meets new classmates because several families (including siblings) may drop in for their visits at the same time. If a child had any worries, they are usually allayed by now. He is ready for school to begin.

Teacher's Files

Teachers will keep files for each child containing various types of information. Since dealing with families is a highly personal relationship, professional standards and adherence to ethical procedure require that personal information revealed by parents be kept strictly confidential. For this reason, teachers are not at liberty to open all files to the students or to tell them all they know about a child's family. Some teachers keep two separate files: one containing objective data, to which the students have access; the other containing more subjective notes and evaluations that are not open to the students.

Students also may have occasion to obtain very personal information about a family. They too must treat the information as confidential. It is sound policy for a school to ask students to discuss a child only with the child's teacher or in the theory class that accompanies the course. Using anecdotal material for dormitory conversation is a sure way to embarrass the student, the teacher, and the parents. In a social situation, information becomes gossip. Parents can quickly lose confidence in the school if they feel their personal lives are not being protected. Imagine the nursery school teacher's chagrin when a mother reported that her husband had learned from one of his students that their son was "the holy terror of the nursery school." Even if the story were true, the teacher should be the one to bring the child's conduct to the parents' attention and to discuss the problem in the light of possible remedies.

Health forms, questionnaires, and tests are objective data that may be open to students. When teachers provide parents with health forms they are asking for information, examinations, and immunizations that meet the local and state health codes. For the school to secure all the needed information and examinations, parents may need some help on what is required, where it can be obtained, and what it costs. The teacher may give the parents exact information on days and hours that clinics are open, or names and addresses of physicians who give the examinations. Occasionally arrangements are made for a physician to administer examinations at the school.

Questionnaires should be short and ask only for necessary information. They should be tried out on a few parents before they are used for everyone: a trial run will indicate unclear questions and unnecessary duplications. If research questionnaires are to be used, it is best to include these in the original package to avoid the constant request for information. If questionnaires become a nuisance to parents, they will fill them out haphazardly. Further, a single request facilitates the teacher's checking and filing of questionnaires. Parents should be reassured that personal data will be kept strictly confidential.

Conclusion

Getting to know children is a continuing process. Real understanding requires a depth of perception that comes with training and experience and, of course, may never really be completely achieved. Information regarding children can be obtained from research, from parents, and from previous experience with children. Each child has characteristics that are similar to those of other children of his age. He also has unique characteristics. The similarities enable the teacher to work with children in a group. A range of interests and abilities will exist in every age group. The teacher and the student of early childhood education are challenged to learn to gauge the level of a child's development and to plan a program that meets the needs of individual children.

ADDITIONAL READINGS

BRECKENRIDGE, MARIAN E., and MARGARET N. MURPHY. *Growth and Development in the Young Child.* Philadelphia: W. B. Saunders Company, 1969.

COHEN, DOROTHY, and VIRGINIA STERN. *Observing and Recording the Behavior of Young Children.* New York: Teachers College Press, Columbia University, 1965.

DUVALL, EVELYN. *Family Development.* Philadelphia: W. B. Saunders Company, 1971.

GARDNER, D. BRUCE. *Development in Early Childhood.* New York: Harper & Row, 1973.

GESELL, ARNOLD, and FRANCES L. ILG. *Child Development.* New York: Harper & Row, 1949.

HAVIGHURST, ROBERT J. *Developmental Tasks and Education.* New York: David McKay Co., Inc., 1952.

HURLOCK, ELIZABETH. *Child Development.* New York: McGraw-Hill Book Company, 1972.

HYMES, JAMES, L., JR. *The Child Under Six.* Englewood Cliffs, N.J.: Prentice-Hall, Inc., 1963.

JANIS, MARJORIE G. *A Two-Year-Old Goes to Nursery School.* Washington, D.C.: National Association for Education of Young Children, 1965.

LANDRETH, CATHERINE. *Early Childhood: Behavior and Learning.* New York: Alfred A. Knopf, Inc., 1967.

LANDRETH, CATHERINE. *Preschool Learning and Teaching.* New York: Harper & Row, 1972.

LEFEBVRE, SUE. "Valuing a Curious Child," *Childhood Education,* Vol. 51, No. 5., March 1975, pp. 257–260.

MAIER, HENRY W. *Three Theories of Child Development.* New York: Harper & Row, 1965.

SMART, RUSSELL, and MOLLIE SMART. *Children: Development and Relationships.* New York: Macmillan Publishing Co., Inc., 1972.

Setting the Stage

"How did you get your group started?" "Was it hard to work with all new children at the beginning of school?" Such questions are often asked by students who watch a smoothly functioning nursery school or kindergarten group during the latter part of a school year. These students are experienced enough to realize that the smooth operation does not happen by accident.

Some early childhood education students have the opportunity to help the teacher make the necessary preparations for the beginning of school. They see exactly what is required for starting a new group.

Planning for the Opening of School

Planning is similar for both nursery schools and kindergartens. The kindergarten teacher, however, organizes a program containing a wider variety of learning experiences than a nursery school teacher needs to provide. Also, kindergarteners, as opposed to nursery children, are of more assistance to the teacher and can take better care of their personal needs.

Basis for Planning

When making class plans the teacher considers the following:

1. The goals for the young child (Chapter 2).
2. The rationale for self-selected activity (Chapter 2).
3. The characteristics of the particular age (Chapter 3).
4. The information about individual children (Chapter 3).

The week before the children arrive, the teacher should (1) arrange the facility where school is held, (2) plan the daily schedule, and (3) choose the learning experiences for the children. Arranging the facility and organizing a workable schedule are covered in this chapter. Learning experiences are referred to only briefly in this chapter but are discussed in detail in Part Two.

Planning the Arrangement of the Facility [1]

Equipping and arranging the schoolroom and yard are similar to furnishing and arranging a house or an apartment. The teacher takes inventory of the functions that must be performed and plans for the most efficient use of the space available. Everyone knows that it is exciting to plan new space before it is built. Using old space may be a greater challenge. More creativity is often required on the part of those planning to operate in old space designed for other purposes.

Careful planning of room arrangement, storage spaces, and equipment can facilitate the teacher's handling of the children. There are many functions the children can perform for themselves. They can help with others if the facilities are carefully arranged. Children learn favorable attitudes toward helping, care of equipment, and cooperation when they are expected to help and are taught to help. For example, children can wash the easel and the paintbrushes if the cleanup sink is at their height and sponges are provided. When children put away their own toys, the teacher's time and energy can be used for other educational purposes.

A large rectangular playroom containing about 50 square feet per child is usually satisfactory. More space is desirable in colder climates, where longer periods of the day are spent indoors. Where weather permits extensive use of outdoor space, less indoor space might suffice. Space should be allowed for the number of adults in the program. One large room is superior to several small ones in terms of supervising and teaching.

The room is divided into learning centers or zones. There are centers for (1) art activities, (2) science activities, (3) literature-language activities, (4) music activities, (5) dramatic play, (6) blockbuilding activities, (7) manipulative toys and games, and (8) carpentry or sand activities when space permits. Also, provision must be made for eating, toileting, resting, and storing a child's belongings. Shelves and other storage facilities can serve as dividers between learning centers at the same time that they hold the equip-

[1] For a comprehensive analysis of play spaces, floor plans, and recommendations, see Sybil Kritchevsky, Elizabeth Prescott, and Lee Walling, *Planning Environments for Young Children: Physical Space* (Washington, D.C.: National Association for Education of Young Children, 1969). Also, for detailed drawings of several children's centers throughout the country, see Fred Lynn Osmon, *Patterns for Designing Children's Centers*, 1971, and Paul Abramson, *Schools for Early Childhood*, 1970, both available from Educational Facilities Laboratories, 477 Madison Avenue, New York, N.Y. 10022.

ment and materials needed in those centers. Care should be taken to keep the storage facilities low so that the teacher can observe the action in each center. Also, low shelves encourage children to get out and put away materials and thus develop independence. In some climates it is necessary to have a large muscle activity center indoors.

The rooms should have a light, airy, warm look and be friendly and inviting. An artistic use of color—such as subdued walls, with color supplied by equipment and children's art products—is aesthetically pleasing and gives a feeling of happiness without being over-stimulating. Soft light and enough electrical outlets with safety features are important. There are many new materials with washable, durable finishes that are useful for decorating and equipping rooms housing young children.

Every effort should be made to reduce the noise level in the rooms by the use of draperies, carpeting, acoustical tile, and other sound-proofing. Carpeting is particularly desirable in block, dress-up, and story areas. Flooring that can be readily mopped should be provided for painting, eating, and water-play areas until carpeting proves itself and janitorial services are equipped to cope with carpet cleaning. One corner can be used for quiet activities, and the opposite corner for active and noisy events.

TRAFFIC PATTERNS.   The teacher visualizes how she expects the children to move through the room. Where do they enter and leave the school? Where will they store their wraps? Where do they go to get to the bathroom? Which entrance will they use going to and coming from the outdoors? Where will the snack be served? Where will the children rest? The best arrangement will require a minimum amount of reminding children what to do next. The teacher will study traffic patterns and organize the room to minimize the children's getting in each other's way.

LOCKER SPACES.   Locker spaces should be close to the door where parents will enter and call for the child. If lockers are in out-of-the-way places, reminders will be required to get coats into the lockers. This little space, sometimes just a modest hook, becomes a child's place to call his own. Parents, teachers, and child will know where to look for his belongings. It is convenient if a cubicle or locker is included where the child's treasures can be placed. Names clearly printed by hand in capital and small letters should be placed above the locker. A symbol or picture is used by some teachers to help a child identify his locker. However, most will quickly learn to locate the locker by its position in the room—or by the name above it.

BATHROOM.   The toilet often requires rapid entry and should be readily accessible. Toilets and sinks should be at the children's

FIGURE 4–1. *Individual lockers help a child know where her belongings will be found. The child's picture in the locker is an aid for identifying her locker.* (*Michigan State University Laboratory Preschool.*)

height. A minimum of two toilets and two lavatories for each group of children is recommended. Both sexes use toilets in the same room. Doors are not needed on toilets for children up to five years old. The absence of doors facilitates supervision. Five-year-olds usually are beginning to appreciate privacy, so shutter-type doors that spring closed can be installed. Even for five-year-olds there is no need for separate bathrooms for boys and girls.

LOW SINKS.   Bathroom lavatories should be about 22 inches high. Faucets that work by the pressing of a lever with the knee or by a foot lever will eliminate running water in an empty bathroom. A low sink in the creative arts center is convenient; here paints can be mixed, paper and sponges moistened, and children and supplies washed without the art cleanup interfering with the bathroom routine. A low drinking fountain both indoors and out permits children to help themselves to a drink—a frequently neglected need.

RESTING SPACE.   A quiet time of songs and stories will rest children; hence a space should be designated for quiet-time activity. Ideally this space should be located away from distracting toys. Short rest periods can take place without formal stretching out. If the room is carpeted, the children may stretch out without being told. Where there is no carpeting, a few throw rugs will cushion the lying down or sitting. It should be noted that severe efforts to get everyone lying down often yield negative results and negative attitudes toward sleep.

In day-care groups, where napping is essential, cots with sheets and blankets will be required. Sufficient storage space and space to place the cots will be necessary. When you are putting a number of children together for sleeping, it is urgent that the utmost care be taken that fire exits are accessible.

EATING SPACE.   Snack or lunch is more conveniently served near the kitchen area. Serving carts or trays can be used if food must be carried some distance. Lists of required utensils should be attached to the cart to prevent the forgetting of needed items. Sanitary and aesthetic aspects must be kept in mind. Small tables and chairs are required for serving lunch. Some teachers prefer that all children sit down at the same time for midmorning and midafternoon snack. Others serve snacks in a come-and-go fashion, as the children sit on the floor or the grass, and fewer chairs and tables are needed.

SPACE FOR LEARNING CENTERS AND STORAGE.   Each learning center should have open storage space available for the materials and equipment that the children will use in the center. Closed storage space is best for materials and equipment that are seasonal or that are brought into the room only occasionally. Thought should be given to where the children will use a toy. Toys should be stored close to where they will be used. For example, puzzles are best used on tables, so the storage should be near the tables. Blocks require open building space and should be stored and used in an out-of-the-way area so that other children who are merely passing by will not interfere with block building. Toys, such as cars, that are used with blocks should be on open shelves near the blocks.

The housekeeping corner and dress-up clothes suggesting dramatic play should have sufficient storage space so that the children can constructively select materials for their dramatic games. If possible, the teacher should keep all materials available so that the children can readily get them. When space is limited, the children should know what materials are available and feel free to ask for them to supplement any idea they may have. If props are stored close by, the teacher too will be able to add them quickly to support dramatic play that she sees developing.

A literature–language arts area should be located in a quiet nook with a low table and with books on an open shelf so that children can use them freely as they are interested. The teacher will also use this learning center for planned language experiences for small groups of children. A collection of science books should be kept as a permanent resource so that the children, assistants, and teacher can develop the habit of looking things up whenever an occasion arises.

A music area can consist of a simple record player for children to operate and a few suitable records in a rack. If it is located adjacent to open space, the children may respond with a dance or organize a band from instruments stored nearby.

The creative arts center needs natural lighting, a close water supply, and materials for artistic endeavors. The following should be easily accessible to the children: drawing paper, crayons, glue, scissors, stapler, string, masking tape, and paper punch. These supplies will be incorporated into many kinds of play if available on a low, open shelf. Art materials that the teachers feel need closer supervision can be stored near the art area sink.

A science center is best located near a window because sunlight is helpful in many experiments. A small table or shelf will encourage children to display their specimens for others to see and handle. Room should be available to seat several children so that planned discussions can take place in this area.

Arranging learning centers and areas for quiet activity is as important outdoors as indoors. Water available for drinking, for wetting sand, and for mixing and cleaning up paints increases the ease with which the yard functions for the total program. Proper storage is essential for outdoor equipment. Children can be taught proper care of the equipment if storage is designed so that they can easily remove and return equipment.

Planning the Daily Schedule or Sequence of Events

Choosing a schedule is another requirement before the first day of school begins. A schedule becomes the structure within which the teacher and the children work. To an outsider it may appear as if there is no structure at all—the children seem to be doing just what they want to do. Yet it *is* in fact a framework or structure, with flexibility and room for individuality. When you have a planned sequence of events, the children will soon learn to guide themselves. If you

FIGURE 4–2. *In a city playground crossties are arranged to give children experience in heights. (National Institute of Education Child Study Center. U.S. Office of Education.)*

implement the plan in a flexible manner, interpreting the needs of individuals in your group, the activity will move with ease. There will be a maximum of learning, a minimum of teacher direction, and a minimum of child tension. The following is an example of a child whose behavior was entirely self-directed because he was well aware of the planned sequence of events: Mike noticed the children entering the kindergarten room as he slid down the slide. Finishing his ride, he ran to the door, which was being held open by his teacher. He smiled at her, entered, and ran up the stairs. After putting his hat and coat in his locker, Mike went directly to the bathroom. Here he urinated, flushed the toilet, and washed his hands. He went to the snack table and found the place marked with his place card and sat down. He visited with his friends as they too found their places and sat down for a snack.

This short episode occurred without the teacher's telling Mike any of the steps he was to take. The routine was the same every day, and Mike was happy knowing and doing what was expected of him. The routine seemed to fit his needs because there was no looking back at the slide or detouring to other areas as he progressed through the routine.

The teacher had planned carefully in the beginning to develop the sequence that fitted the children's needs. She reminded the children of that squence for a few days. Most learned quickly. Some children reminded those who forgot, until eventually all the children mastered the routine without reminders.

If the routine had not fitted her group, the teacher might have observed resistance, such as children taking one more slide or otherwise not being ready to go indoors. If lockers had been in an out-of-the-way place, Mike might have dropped his coat on a chair and needed a reminder to put it in the locker.

The teacher plans the schedule or the sequence of events by designating big blocks of time that will constitute the framework for fitting in the learning opportunities, which will be discussed in detail in Part Two. The half-day program typically has three large blocks of time; the day-care center, six. See Figures 4–5 and 4–6.

FIGURE 4–3. *When an activity is very popular, an additional setup is often needed to prevent problems that insufficient space or toys may provoke. (Michigan State University Spartan Cooperative Nursery School.)*

FIGURE 4–4. *A place for everything and everything in its place helps make cleanup time easier. Note the designs drawn on the back of the shelves to show which blocks go where. (National Institute of Education Child Study Center, U.S. Office of Education.)*

The major considerations for scheduling activities are (1) goals for the group, (2) special needs of the group, (3) time of day the children arrive, (4) how long the children stay at school, (5) what happens at home before the child goes to school, and (6) season of the year.

Time Block I

A block of about 60 minutes for self-selected activity—either indoors or outdoors—is a good way to start the day. As children arrive, they find an activity that interests them. If they are slow starters, nobody rushes them to socialize; they are free to choose a puzzle and be alone. If they want to socialize, they can approach a friend in the housekeeping corner or one using the slide. Latecomers need not feel unduly uncomfortable, as they may when a group assembly occurs first. Beginning with a self-directed activity period enables teachers to talk to parents and also to give each child a little attention as he

DAILY SCHEDULE

A.M.	P.M.	
9:00–10:00	1:00–2:00	Self-selected activity indoors.
10:00	2:00	Cleanup time (can vary a few minutes either way). As the child finishes helping with cleanup, he goes to the toilet, if necessary, and washes his hands.
10:15–10:25	2:15–2:25	Snack. With older children, sharing time* goes on at the same time as snack.
10:25–10:45	2:25–2:45	The children move to a story group or groups. They sit on the floor. They select a book for "reading" as they pass the shelf. They look at the book or just talk quietly. The teacher finishes the period with some songs, a special story, planning, or discussion.
10:45–11:30	2:45–3:30	Outdoor self-selected activity.
11:30–11:40	3:30–3:40	Cleanup time. Preparation to go home.
11:45	3:45	Dismissal.

* Sharing time—A period when children are called on to share some article or news they have brought from home. Discussed in detail in the chapter on language arts.

FIGURE 4–5 *Sample of a daily schedule.*

enters the school. Children should never feel as one little girl put it to her mother after school, "I don't know if my teacher even knew I was there. She never called my name once."

The first large block of time might vary from 30 to 90 minutes, depending on all the factors mentioned above and the number of special learning experiences the teacher may have planned for the day. There should always be provision within each time block for both quiet and vigorous activity to take care of the differing needs and interests of the children.

TIME BLOCK PLAN *

Time Block I	Self-selected Activity (Indoors)

Art   Music
Science   Dramatic play
Table games   Small, wheeled objects
Blocks   Language arts
Books

Time Block II   Teacher-Instigated Activity

Cleanup
Toileting, washing hands
Snack
Quiet time:
    looking at books
    music
    storytime and discussions

Time Block III   Self-selected Activity (Outdoors)

Climbing   Riding tricycles
Swinging   Sand play
Running   Science

Time Block IV   Lunch Period

Washing hands, toileting
Resting prior to lunch
Eating
Washing hands
Going home or preparing for nap

Time Block V   Nap Time

Dressing for bed   Toileting
Sleeping   Dressing

Time Block VI   Self-selected Activity

New activities
Snack
Outdoor play

* Blocks I, II, and III are typical of half-day programs in nursery schools and kindergartens where lunch is not served. The six blocks are more typical of day-care centers. Blocks I and II may be interchanged for variation and for meeting the needs of the children as discussed elsewhere.

FIGURE 4–6   *Sample of a Time Block Plan.*

FIGURE 4–7. *A sharing table attractively arranged encourages children to explore and discover concepts on their own. (National Institute of Education Child Study Center, U.S. Office of Education.)*

Time Block II

The second block of time is more teacher-instigated or -directed. It includes a period of cleaning up, washing hands, toileting, serving snack, singing, and listening to a story. It is a slowing down and relaxing time of day. This period could last from 30 to 45 minutes. There is some movement between the various activities. The story and singing groups, especially for younger children, contain, at most, four or five children rather than the entire group.

This quiet group time provides for rest without being called that, since the words *sleep* or *rest* may create strongly negative feelings in children. As the teacher considers the needs of the children, a decision can be made about how much rest the children require. What time do they go to bed? What time do they get up? It is unrealistic to assume that a healthy child who has had 12 hours of sleep and barely gets up in time to reach nursery school or kindergarten by 9 A.M. will need to rest on a cot at 10 or 10:30 A.M. As one child said, "I thought we came here to learn stuff. I already know how to sleep!" However, rest routines can provide positive learning experiences.

Time Block III

The third block of time will be another self-selected activity period. If the first one was indoors, then the second one will be outdoors, and vice versa. Again there will be a variety of activities so that a child can choose or be guided into quiet or active play as seems to fit his need. Every school should provide outdoor activities daily.

Time Block IV

If the program calls for lunch, another block of time will be used in preparing for and in eating lunch. Many people feel that a quiet time just prior to lunch rests the children and helps them eat better. Considerable time is required to move the children from their learning activities to toileting, washing, resting, and finally to eating.

The schedule after lunch is also important, and a definite plan for this next step is crucial. Is it time for the children to go home? Or take a nap? Or go outdoors to play? Or begin their nursery school day? Some afternoon groups may begin with lunch as some morning groups may begin with breakfast. Having next steps clearly in mind helps the teacher guide children in the routine. Some children will need to wash again after lunch and frequently will need to use the toilet. In order that all adults are not distracted from attending the children left at the lunch tables, it is usually best to have one adult assigned to supervise the children after they leave the lunch table.

Time Block V

Where naps are given, they usually follow the lunch hour immediately. The sleeping area should be prepared while the children are in the lunchroom. After a busy morning that starts early for many, the subdued light, soft music, and comfortable bed should be welcome. Efforts to keep the voices low, the pace slow, and a positive attitude toward the nap period will pay dividends. Because excessively long naps may interfere with the home bedtime schedules, it is well to confer with parents regarding a reasonable length of the nap period for their children.

There may be a few children who won't sleep. Some children get adequate rest at night. Provision can be made to keep nonsleepers from interfering with the sleeping children. Usually the older children do not need sleep. They can rest in an adjacent room while "reading" a book. Some children who seem to need sleep but are alert to all movement can be encouraged to sleep face down. Sometimes if the teacher gently massages the shoulders, the child will relax and go to sleep. Children have varying feelings about bedtime and may become lonesome for their parents. At no time should bedtime become a period for harsh discipline or punishment.

Time Block VI

Following nap time, toileting, and dressing, self-selected activity can again take place. In day-care centers there may be a new shift of personnel because the morning staff comes to work early. For in-

FIGURE 4–8. *On warm days virtually the whole program can take place outdoors. (Texas Woman's University.)*

secure children the new shift may present problems that teachers should be prepared to handle. The new teachers with their different ways will add variety for the children. New materials should be offered that were not available in the morning. Outdoor play is usually enjoyed by children after a nap. Working mothers coming home to family responsibilities may not have time to supervise their children outdoors and are happy that the school provides outdoor play. However, every effort should be made to avoid exhausting these children physically. Tired children will be cranky. Cranky children are not pleasant for mothers who are tired themselves after a full day's work. For this reason a quiet group for listening to stories and singing songs is popular in late afternoon.

FIGURE 4–9. *Cartons make useful additions to the classroom or play yard, inviting dramatic play to take place. (University of Houston Parent-Child Development Center.)*

Departure Time

Before it is going-home time, children's belongings, art products, and so forth should be checked to see that all are ready to be sent home. Having everything ready avoids the strain of looking for things that cannot be found and paves the way for a smooth and happy departure of the children with their parents.

Transition Times

Transition points between activities and big blocks of time should be planned carefully. The teacher should plan just what she expects the children to do and then state the directions clearly. If planning is adequate, the children will move with ease through the routines, will not be running into each other, will know what comes next, and will not have to wait. Waiting, to young children, is tedious and probably just as uninteresting as it is for adults, and therefore it should be avoided. It may help to have one teacher start an activity while another teacher brings up the stragglers or forms a new group.

Examples of helpful and interesting techniques for grouping and moving children during transitions follow. These techniques help children make a game of listening and waiting until their turn comes and also avoid the stampeding effect of everyone moving at once.

Name tags may be color coded and the children can be told, "All children wearing red name tags may go to snack." Another day the teacher may say, "The children with *black* shoes may tiptoe to snack." The teacher might suggest that all boys (or all girls) go first. In a mixed age group the teacher might ask the three-year-olds to go first. Adapting a song to include the names of different children in each verse can signal them when it is their turn to move. For example, to the tune of "The More We Get Together" the teacher and the children can sing:

> The more we get together,
> Together, together,
> The more we get together
> The happier we'll be.
> We're ready for Becky, and Jimmy,
> And Susie, and Milton.
> The more we get together
> The happier we'll be.

Providing for Flexibility

The sample schedule, Figure 4–5, is a flexible guide. Each period of time can be adjusted shorter or longer as needs warrant. If children are just beginning to use something they have spent all hour building, then an additional 10 or 15 minutes will give them a feeling of greater satisfaction. Advising the children a few minutes ahead that there will be a change in activities enables the children to terminate projects to their satisfaction. If presented in a positive manner, cleanup time can be fun for the children—especially if the teacher is assisting. It can also be a learning experience for children and a big help to the teachers.

Providing for Weather Changes

Any plan must be judged against how well it adapts to days of inclement weather. Ideally, the teacher hopes to disturb the routine as little as possible on bad days because she knows that changes tend to confuse young children. On a rainy day the first self-selected activity period can be extended about 30 minutes and other routines can occur in sequence until after the story period. Then if, instead of the outdoor activity, the teacher plans some singing games, tumbling activities, or the like, the children will probably move through a rainy

FIGURE 4–10. *Unusual places to climb can be designed by teachers, inviting children to explore various levels. (National Institute of Education Child Study Center, U.S. Office of Education.)*

day without realizing a difference in schedule until the teacher announces the time to go home. They may then ask, "Well, aren't we going to play outside?" If a rainy-day room or a protected porch or patio is provided, only minor schedule adjustments need to be made on a rainy day. A walk in the rain with boots and umbrellas can provide learning opportunities and can also provide the energy release ordinarily gained in outdoor activities.

The teacher makes the schedule to fit the needs of the particular group of children. A plan is required that takes care of all needs. The plan must be one in which the teacher has confidence and with which she feels comfortable working. Morning groups in early fall or late spring or summer may be anxious to have outdoor activities when they arrive. In that case, the teacher may choose a self-selected outdoor activity period as the first large time block.

In cold seasons or wet climates the early morning may be too cold or wet for outdoor activities. The outdoor period would then be postponed until late morning, when the dew is off the grass and the sun has warmed up the atmosphere. In snowsuit climates the schedule may be adjusted to minimize dressing and undressing. For example, in an afternoon group, mothers were asked to send the children to school already dressed in snowsuits for outdoor activity. Outdoor self-selected activities were scheduled for the first part of the afternoon at school. This schedule had additional merit because these children were staying indoors during their mornings at home. Their exuberance during the outdoor period, even in very cold weather, indicated that a need was being met.

Children who were not interested in outdoor activity were allowed to enter the indoor play area when they chose. This suggests another alternative a teacher may use. Indoor and outdoor activity may take place at the same time when the spaces are adjacent or when there are enough adults to supervise activities going on in both places.

During warm weather it is possible to provide almost the entire program outside if the teacher moves some activities out that are normally done indoors. Teachers note that when the weather turns warm the children will begin playing outside in their neighborhoods during the morning. If the children are playing vigorously in the morning, the afternoon program should be restful to avoid excessive fatigue.

Additional Tips for the First Days of School

Introducing a Few Children Each Day

When a teacher is starting a new group of children, she can assure time to give attention to each child's needs by dividing the group and introducing only a few new children each day. Perhaps by the fifth or sixth day all the children can be attending. If such a plan is not feasible, a number of assistants should be available to handle routines while the teacher is kept free to work with children who are uneasy about being at school. First days make a lasting impression on the child. Every effort should be made to ensure that every child has a happy time.

Beginning with Easily Supervised Activities

The activities offered the first day or two should be ones that are very easily supervised. For example, crayons are likely to be familiar to the children and thus require no special help or encouragement for the children to use. Getting involved in finger painting will be fine later on. These first days, when the teacher may be needed other

FIGURE 4–11. *A plank across the corner of a sandbox invites children to mix their cakes where the sand can fall back into the box. (Michigan State University Spartan Cooperative Nursery School.)*

places on short notice, she would not want to be delayed because her hands were in the finger paints.

Name Tags

The first day of school the teacher should prepare name tags for everyone. Convention badges work fine for adults. For children excellent name tags can be made from two layers of art sponge or felt glued with a piece of muslin between and trimmed with scalloping shears. Sponge and felt come in pretty colors and might be coordinated into a color scheme or a teaching plan. Tags can be about two inches wide and cut to fit each name. Names are lettered in manuscript printing with a marking pen. The tag is pinned to the front of the child's shirt with a large safety pin. Pinning the name tag on the child's back discourages children from trying to pin their own, and consequently tags last longer. However, if the tags are pinned in front, the children will feel great satisfaction when they are able to open and close that pin!

Health Measures

Health inspection has been omitted so far. This does not mean that the child's health is not an important concern. Far from it. Parents should be urged to send only healthy children to school. They should be advised to look at their child and say, "If he were someone else's child, would I want my child exposed to him?" Parents should know that if a child becomes ill, they will be called. Mothers who are working are urged to leave telephone numbers of neighbors or relatives that would care for their sick child. Actually, all children's records should carry a second telephone number because mothers often run errands during a child's hours in school and might not be available immediately.

Parents' cooperation on health matters is probably more effective than having an inspection. Persons without training will see very little in the throats of young children. Even registered nurses will miss significant symptoms. Children who attend morning schools may not seem ill at nine o'clock but may be quite ill by eleven. Teachers must always be alert for signs of illness. They should isolate the sick child under proper supervision and call the parents.

In afternoon groups parents are advised that if a child has symptoms in the morning, he will be much better off taking a rest at home in the afternoon than going to school, where he might get overtired and might also expose his friends to a communicable disease. Attention to vaccinations should be given in admission procedures. With good vaccination programs some communicable diseases can be nearly eliminated.

If a child gets a communicable disease, the parents of children who, according to school records, have not had the disease are notified. Parents may then be on the lookout for symptoms and avoid sending their children to school on days they might expose the entire group to a disease.

When inspections are necessary, the nurse should wear regular street clothes to avoid arousing the anxiety that a uniform often creates.

Staff Assignments

Staff assignments are important every day, but especially on opening days. Students or other assistants who have accompanied the teacher on the home visits or have helped when the family visited the

FIGURE 4–12. *Older children who do not feel the need for sleeping can be allowed to "read" quietly while others sleep. (Nazarene Child Care Center, Lansing, Michigan.)*

school will know the children. The staff should get together and pool their guesses regarding individual children's needs. Staff cooperation is important. Team teaching has always been common in nursery schools and is increasingly common in kindergartens. No one will be able to predict with much accuracy how these first days will go. Brief daily discussion of goals, children, routines, and procedures will give teachers confidence in each other as unpredictable situations arise.

A democratic plan of operation enables all teachers, student teachers, mother assistants, or volunteers to be on an equal plane. The head teacher, who in the final analysis is responsible, must assume the lead. However, more creative teaching will develop within the staff if each adult feels that her contribution is significant and that she can follow her own creative teaching ideas without unnecessary interference. Teachers may vary in their teaching styles. Differences need not confuse the children if all adults are working toward common goals.

A head teacher needs at least one assistant, no matter how small the nursery school or kindergarten. If each person is to gain personal satisfaction when working with young children, all responsibilities— the good and bad, the hard and easy, the clean and dirty, and the pleasant and unpleasant—should be shared fairly. The children are the winners when adults work together, the losers when they don't.

Just as each child is unique, so is each adult. Each person has strengths and weaknesses. The individual's strength should be capitalized upon and the weak areas overcome. As one assistant said during a planning session, "I'm not as good as Betty Kay in music, but I'd love to try leading the singing." Another said, "Could I be responsible for the finger painting? I've never supervised that before." The assistants were volunteering to learn. Learning means growing and becoming a better teacher. The stage must be set so that each adult can make a satisfying contribution. Planning and posting of responsibilities help achieve the goals of the center.

Conclusion

Setting the stage for the opening of school includes arranging the facility, planning the daily schedule, and choosing the learning experiences for the children. The teacher takes an inventory of the functions that must be performed and plans the most efficient use of the space available. Learning centers are arranged along with storage for the needed equipment and supplies. Traffic patterns are a consideration. The schedule or sequence of events is the structure within which the teacher and children work. All planning is of a tentative nature until the teacher becomes acquainted with a particular group of children. Definite planning is required as the teacher sets the stage for the children's behavior and learning.

ADDITIONAL READINGS

BERSON, MINNIE PERRIN. *Kindergarten Your Child's Big Step.* New York: E. P. Dutton and Co., Inc. 1959.

BEYER, EVELYN. *Teaching Young Children.* New York: Western Publishing Company, Inc., 1968.

HILDEBRAND, VERNA. *Guiding Young Children.* New York: Macmillan Publishing Co., Inc., 1975.

KRITCHEVSKY, SYBIL, ELIZABETH PRESCOTT, and LEE WALLING. *Planning Environments for Young Children: Physical Space.* Washington, D.C.: National Association for Education of Young Children, 1969.

LEEPER, SARAH H., RUTH DALES, DORA SKIPPER, and RALPH WITHER-SPOON. *Good Schools for Young Children.* New York: Macmillan Publishing Co., Inc., 1974.

LUECK, PHYLLIS. "Planning an Outdoor Learning Environment." *Theory into Practice,* Vol. 12, No. 2, April 1973, 121–127.

MOORE, SHIRLEY, and SALLY KILMER. *Contemporary Preschool Education: A Program for Young Children.* New York: John Wiley & Sons, Inc., 1973.

NIMNICHT, GLENN, ORALIE MCAFEE, and JOHN MEIER. *The New Nursery School.* New York: General Learning Corporation, 1968.

READ, KATHERINE. *The Nursery School: A Human Relationships Laboratory.* Philadelphia: W. B. Saunders Company, 1971.

ROBISON, HELEN F., and BERNARD SPODEK. *New Directions in the Kindergarten.* New York: Teachers College Press, Columbia University, 1965.

RUDOLPH, MARGUERITA, and DOROTHY H. COHEN. *Kindergarten—A Year of Learning.* New York: Appleton-Century-Crofts, 1964.

SALOT, LORRAINE, and JEROME E. LEAVITT. *The Beginning Kindergarten Teacher.* Minneapolis: Burgess Publishing Co., 1965.

SPODEK, BERNARD. *Teaching in the Early Years.* Englewood Cliffs, N.J.: Prentice-Hall, Inc., 1972.

TODD, VIVIAN E., and HELEN HEFFERNAN. *The Years Before School: Guiding Preschool Children.* New York: Macmillan Publishing Co., Inc., 1970.

WILLS, CLARICE, and LUCILLE LINDBERG. *Kindergarten for Today's Children.* Chicago: Follett Publishing Company, 1967.

The Teacher and the Techniques She Uses

E ACH teacher is unique, just as each child is unique. Good teachers develop a teaching style all their own. Each teacher's style will be different from all other teaching styles she has known either in training or on the job.

Developing a Unique Teaching Style

A teaching style is the teacher's manner and method of teaching. The individual's personality is an important factor in determining a teaching style. As each teacher develops a program and builds a relationship with children, she consciously and unconsciously integrates all she knows with all she feels—thus developing a personal teaching style. The teacher's knowledge of herself, the children, and their families will affect her teaching style. Her philosophy of education and her political and moral value systems will influence her teaching style.

Teaching styles may be placed on continuums ranging between democratic and authoritarian, organized and haphazard, passive and active, formal and informal, child-oriented and subject-matter-oriented. Students in training are often frustrated by the differing teaching styles they observe among demonstration teachers. Universities deliberately assign students to a variety of nursery school and kindergarten groups to give them opportunities to see different teachers in action. This practice should assure students that no one teaching style is the "correct way." For those who still insist on a "right way," this practice may bring confusion. Yet if demonstration teachers can use differing teaching styles while achieving similar goals for young children, a student should reason that she too will be free to develop her own style of teaching.

A demonstration teacher worthy of her position is creative, innovative, and inquisitive. She experiments and evaluates continuously. She handles both children and university students differently from class to class. She looks upon teaching as a creative profession and never expects the factors to be enough alike for everything to remain the same. Neither would she expect her student teachers to duplicate her style of teaching.

The student should be encouraged to go forth and develop her own teaching style in the light of her own personality, her own experience, the age she teaches, and all other pertinent information. It is of crucial importance that the professionals in early childhood education keep a questioning attitude and endeavor to make improvements. Each teacher who works with young children should feel this challenge.

Using Methods Appropriate for Young Children

Methods of teaching include lecturing, recitation, discussion, laboratory experiments, demonstrations, field trips, and audiovisual aids. Every teacher uses each of these methods within her own teaching style. However, because of the way the young child learns, certain methods are more appropriate than others. For example, the teacher rarely lectures to young children. She quickly discovers that lecturing is ineffective. Methods that allow one-to-one contacts with the child are far more in keeping with the needs and interests of young children.

Identification is a process of silent teaching discussed by Hymes. The child feels with the teacher, likes her, and wants to be like her. The teacher is the heroine. Through this intimate relationship teachers have a potent educative force. Identification works only when relationships are close, warm, and friendly.[1]

The student is challenged to observe experienced teachers using various teaching methods with young children. She should question the use of each method and continue to question as she establishes her own groups and incorporates teaching methods into a unique teaching style.

Qualities of a Good Teacher of Young Children

A significant contribution to society is made by a good teacher. The contribution cannot be measured, but it will affect the present generation and, indirectly, the generations to come. The good teacher

[1] James Hymes, Jr., *Teaching the Child Under Six* (Columbus, Ohio: Merrill, 1974), pp. 107–109.

FIGURE 5–1. *A teacher offers a helping hand to a child having a problem with his clothing. (Michigan State University Laboratory Preschool.)*

likes children and is dedicated to instilling in children a desire to learn and to become independent learners. She permits children to express themselves. She arouses their curiosity, gives them understanding and affection, and supports them when needed; yet she lets them grow up.

The good teacher believes in herself and in her ability to cope with her responsibility. She believes that her job is important and that her teaching will make a significant contribution to the lives of the children. She believes that she is accepted and liked by children, parents, and colleagues. A good teacher is a happy individual on and off the job. Though serious at times, she enjoys life and can laugh and be gay. She encourages others' sense of humor and gaiety. She finds some fulfillment outside her work with children and thus avoids the crippling effect that results when teachers gratify all needs through work.

The teacher has confidence in people. She believes that both children and parents are basically good. She recognizes that behavior has meaning and seeks to discover the meaning. She believes that children *can* learn and that through the efforts of all they *will* learn. She is deeply committed to seeking a new and deeper understanding of individuals and families in every walk of life. She can empathize or feel with the parents and children with whom she works.

An effective teacher can adapt information to the young child's level. The university curriculum can become the curriculum of the nursery school and kindergarten. For example, a university freshman wrote to her little brother, "I am taking botany. We put a plant in dye to watch the vascular tissue carrying it up through the leaves. You did that in kindergarten with celery, remember?"

The teacher's scholarship should go beyond what she expects to teach. Her obvious enthusiasm for understanding the political, social, scientific, and aesthetic world she lives in will infect her young learner. Beauty has priority in her classroom—in arrangements and relationships. She understands the implications of educating the child in a democracy as opposed to education in an authoritarian society. She understands applications of scientific method in social as well as physical science.

The teacher is well informed about human growth and development. Therefore she knows what to expect and how to plan for the growth and maturation she observes in the children.

The teacher of young children works constantly to improve her ability to guide children's learning. She helps parents learn to contribute effectively to their child's education. She makes a serious effort to discover effective methods of working with children and parents individually and in groups.

A good teacher strives to mold all her skill and knowledge into a teaching style that is comfortable and unique. With each new experience the student who is preparing to teach moves a step forward in developing her own teaching style.

Guidance and How the Teacher Can Use It

Many students can accept the philosophy of a democratic, child-centered program for nursery schools and kindergartens. They can also accept the rationale for an individualized, self-selected learning environment for the young child. Students are often baffled, however, when confronted with the problem of operating a classroom and relating to children within such a framework.

FIGURE 5–2. *A teacher takes time to comfort a child when the need arises. (Michigan State University Laboratory Preschool.)*

Most students remember their elementary and secondary classrooms. They may even recall their first grade, when they had 15 minutes of morning news followed by reading circles or seatwork, then 15 minutes of recess followed by science. Teachers who try to organize young children in such a rigid fashion court disaster. Trying to get everyone to do the same thing at one time is virtually impossible. A contest results between the teacher and the children. When silence is highly valued, as it is in some classes, the only way silence can be maintained is through coercion, punishment, and threats.

Order can be maintained within the framework of an individualized, self-directed learning environment. The teacher should feel sure that she can stop the activities of individuals and groups of children when necessary and that the children will listen and respond. Limits that protect each child, the property, and the learning environment should be set. The teacher should exercise the obligation to set limits (make rules) so that the group can learn together harmoniously. There is no place in either nursery school or kindergarten education for a total free-for-all.

Democratic living can begin with very young children. They will learn and respond to rules that keep the group functioning on an even keel. They will not learn all the rules overnight. Transgressions are often due to forgetting or misunderstanding and normally occur with only a few children at a time.

What Is Guidance?

The term *guidance* is used here to mean anything the adult does to influence the behavior of the child. The teacher manages her group of young children through carefully conceived teaching techniques and the special personal relationship she develops with her class. A self-guided or self-disciplined child is the teacher's goal. The teacher wants the child to assume as much responsibility for conducting himself as he is ready to assume. The teacher helps the child to grow in ability until he can assume the responsibility for conducting himself when teachers, parents, police, or other authority figures are not present to enforce correct behavior. She does not want the child to be like Janet, who wanted to jump over a bonfire and kept saying "My mother didn't tell me *not* to!" The teacher knows parents will not always be present to say "No." Each child must learn to make decisions that affect his safety—perhaps his life. One of the goals for the young child is to develop self-control.

Guidance can be either *indirect* or *direct*. Indirect guidance includes all the teacher's behind-the-scenes work that sets the stage for the behavior the teacher expects. Through direct guidance the teacher deals directly with the child.

Indirect Guidance

The teacher guides the child indirectly through the arrangement of learning centers in the room and the yard, through daily schedule, and through work with parents. The type of equipment selected and the richness of the curriculum or learning experiences provided indirectly affect the ease with which children do what is expected. James Hymes, Jr., says in his book *Behavior and Misbehavior:* "Bored children will be bad." [2] Keeping that in mind, the teacher will provide plenty of learning experiences that are neither too hard nor too easy. She will keep her youngsters so actively involved in learning that

---

[2] James Hymes, Jr., *Behavior and Misbehavior* (Englewood Cliffs, N.J.: Prentice-Hall, 1955), p. 57.

FIGURE 5–3.   *A teacher stops by to show interest in a child's drawing and to write his name on his picture. (Southern University Nursery School.)*

they will have little time for misbehavior. Detailed procedures for enriching the curriculum follow in Part Two.

As an example of indirect guidance, the teacher alters the physical environment and thereby influences the behavior of the child. To illustrate: The teacher sees a large group of children having a lively game on top of a large packing box. The teacher is foresighted. She knows from experience that this type of setting often creates difficulty. Falling or pushing may occur. The teacher quietly moves another packing box near and, using a walking plank, makes a bridge between the boxes. The children move to include the second box. The game takes on new dimensions with the additional space. Through quietly changing the physical environment, the teacher averts a possible conflict or danger.

As another example, the teacher may note that a number of children are waiting for a turn to swing. Knowing how hard it is for them to wait, the teacher thinks of an activity that might attract the swingers, or at least give the waiters an interesting activity while they wait. She lines up a few tricycles and gets out the traffic signs. In a moment she has a line of traffic and a policeman directing it. As anticipated, the swingers leave their swings, and no longer is there a line at the swing set. The teacher has not only extended the play of the children but has averted what might have become a difficult problem of sharing the swings.

The teacher can use indirect guidance by taking care of the children's needs for stretching, shifting position, or getting attention as she works with a group. For example, during quiet time the teacher notes that the children are being distracted by a child who is kicking his neighbor's foot. Rather than call further attention to the fidgeting child, she chooses to teach a new singing game that requires everyone to stand up. The teacher regains the attention of all the children and the quiet time proceeds smoothly.

Indirect guidance is a very effective tool for the teacher to use in managing her group of children. If she uses it well, many observers will remark that "the children seem to be doing just what they want to do." She can smile, knowing that she has set the stage for the behavior being observed. Success is greater than if she spends hours lecturing the children on how to behave.

Direct Guidance

Direct guidance includes all of the *physical* and *verbal* means the teacher uses to influence the child's behavior. It includes speaking, teaching, demonstrating, helping, leading, loving, approving, disapproving, compelling, restraining, punishing, and even ignoring. The good teacher uses the positive methods in this list far more than the negative. She feels that the positive methods contribute more to the goal of the child's becoming self-directed. Frequent use of compelling, restraining, or punishing should serve as a warning that the teacher's guidance leaves something to be desired. There is virtually no place in teaching for physical or mental punishment. Punishment produces feelings that may not be conducive to learning, creates negative attitudes toward school and teachers, and does little to help the child develop self-direction.

Verbal guidance is a form of direct guidance. In guiding a child, the teacher gets the child's attention and speaks to him in words he will understand. The teacher stoops or sits at the child's level in order to allow him to see her face. If he doesn't fully understand her words, he can interpret what she means from facial expressions and ges-

FIGURE 5–4. *A teacher relaxes a moment while a child explains his digging project to her. (Michigan State University Spartan Cooperative Nursery School.)*

tures. She speaks quietly to individual children, seldom to the whole group. Verbal statements may be accompanied by action such as leading, helping, or demonstrating—whichever seems to be required for fuller understanding. She learns from experience that shouting across the room or yard seldom brings forth the desired behavior. Directions given on a to-whom-it-may-concern basis are seldom heeded.

The teacher remembers to be clear in giving directions. Reasons are given for her requests. Direct positive statements are best. They tell the child what *to* do instead of only what *not* to do. A "don't" command leaves him uncertain as to how to proceed. The first part of the statement should contain the action clause. Reasons are then added. For example, "Walk around the blocks, Peter. John isn't ready to have his building knocked down yet." "Mary, hold your glass up straight. The milk will spill." In each example, the child knows immediately what to do and why.

The teacher generally speaks in a slow, calm, quiet manner with her eyes on the listener. On rare occasions she might speak with obvious alarm if the situation warrants it and calls for quick compliance; for example, if a serious danger arises. She will use the latter technique sparingly so that the children will not get accustomed to the technique and fail to respond when there is real reason for quick action.

The teacher's tone of voice as well as what she says will guide the children's response. They will know by the firmness in her voice and their previous experience with her guidance that she expects them to comply. For example, children generally respond willingly to the teacher's call, "Time to go inside." She stands at the door waiting for them to come. They learn the first day that if they linger, the teacher reinforces her statement by taking their hands and leading them indoors. Through reinforcing her direction, she teaches them to do as she asks. Contrast this technique with a parent who makes a similar announcement to the child—that it is time to leave at once—then lingers, visiting with friends and neighbors. Is it understandable why his child doesn't come when called?

The teacher gives a minimum number of directions. However, when she gives directions, she will reinforce them if necessary and see to it that they are carried out. Reinforcing or following through simply means that the teacher leads the child to do what she asks. The number of direct commands is limited and appropriate for the children. However, split-second responses are not expected. The child is given some leeway in the time allowed to carry out a direction. For instance, in giving direction to children whom she wants to go indoors, she'll first remind them that they will be going in soon. This practice helps children bring to an end any activity they have started. When given time to terminate their activity, children are less likely to feel the teacher's decision is unfair.

The teacher should avoid giving too many directions at a time. Often teachers are guilty of giving a long series of unrelated directions to young children. If they are given one at a time, the child is more likely to remember the requests until the task is accomplished.

The teacher guides children by helping them make choices. She wants them to have experience in making up their own minds, in deciding things for themselves. The teacher may offer a child a choice between playing indoors or out, between listening to a story now or later, between painting or not painting. When giving a choice, she should leave the choice up to the child. It is easy to use the phrase, "Would you like . . . ," when one really intends the child to do something specific. A teacher avoids this phrase unless she will accept the choice the child makes. The teacher can narrow down choices in order to give the child experience in decision making. Instead of asking a new child, "What would you like to play?" she might say, "You could paint or play with blocks. Which would you like?"

Detouring or redirecting children from unsafe or unsociable behavior requires imagination. When children are doing something unacceptable, the teacher's task is to think of an activity that requires behavior of about the same type that is acceptable. For example, if the children holding their fire hoses are climbing on a storage shed that is too steep for safety, the suggestion to move to the packing boxes for their house-on-fire will be acceptable to them.

There are many examples of detouring or redirecting children's behavior. One day three children were piling up locust beans that had fallen from the trees. Two children began pelting the third with the beans. The teacher knew this type of play would not be fun for the third child for long. "Let's see if we can throw the beans over this packing box," she said. They responded to her suggestion, and a probable crisis was averted. Distraction works well with toddlers but is less effective as the child matures. The teacher simply redirects the child's attention to a new object or situation.

Motivating the child is a common use of verbal guidance. Self-motivation is by far the most desirable type of motivator. The child should develop plenty of self-confidence. He needs to feel competent and important. If the learning environment is set up so that the child's natural curiosity is aroused, then little has to be said to motivate him. As he sees others involved in an activity, he usually wants to observe and to try it. Care should be taken to keep competition at a minimum. Avoid motivating by asking who is best, fastest, or tallest. A better method is to motivate according to the child's own record. For example, "You are swinging higher than you did yesterday." It should be remembered that children who are highly competitive are seldom friends. Failing in competition contributes to a lack of self-confidence.

Embarrassing the child is also a poor motivating technique. Calling him a "baby" or "naughty" or drawing attention to a difficulty such as wet pants in no way contributes to the happy self-confidence for which teachers strive.

Physical guidance is the second form of direct guidance. When the teacher uses such techniques as helping, demonstrating, leading, restraining, removing, ignoring, and punishing, she is using physical guidance.

Demonstrating is effective with young learners because their language development may be too inadequate for them to learn only through words. Nearly anyone learning a new skill is helped by watching a demonstration. It is even more helpful if the person demonstrating goes slowly enough so that the learner can concurrently copy the motions. An example follows: The four-year-olds were having difficulty opening the door to the nursery school. Tell-

ing them to hold down the thumb lever, then push, was ineffective. However, when the teacher took time to show each child how and supervised his practice for a few minutes, many were able to accomplish the task.

The teachers of younger children frequently have to give a supporting hand to encourage them and help them feel safe while trying a new activity. For example, some children were climbing the newly cut log left in their yard. The most skillful children climbed up quickly, walked along the trunk, and jumped off the end. Though more cautious and hesitant, the less agile children still wanted to try. The teacher offered a steadying hand until each had practiced enough to increase his confidence.

The teacher faces many decisions about whether to help a child. She, of course, wants him to grow in independence. Persistence or sticking to a task is also valued. Children vary as to how much frustration they can tolerate. Some children react to frustration by giving up or getting angry. The teacher must decide when and how much to help. Sometimes she helps the child get beyond an obstacle so that he can complete the task. For example, Jamie had unzipped his boots. He was struggling to get them off. The teacher watched his effort. Then she reached over and showed him how to slip the boot an inch or two beyond the heel. Jamie was elated as the boot yielded to his final tug. Soon he could do the task alone.

Teachers may have to restrain children to prevent their hurting others or damaging property. The teacher must protect the entire group. It is much better to stop a child than to allow him to harm others. Efforts should then be made to help the aggressive child reduce his angry feelings. Often such activities as hammering nails, pounding clay, or punching the punching bag will help. When restraint is needed frequently with the same child, the teacher must ask, "What does this behavior mean to the child? What are the circumstances that prompt it?" With closer study of the child the teacher may develop more appropriate guidance.

FIGURE 5–5. *Teaching the young child to become independent in swinging.*

(A) An inclined plank placed under a swing sets the stage. Holding the swing chains tightly, he walks backward up the plank. He sits down and magically swings forward.

(B) "Touch my fingers," challenges the adult, using verbal guidance to encourage the child to raise his feet and point his toes, both motions essential to swinging alone.

(C) "You did it!" praises the adult while bending low in front of the child so smiles and eyes can help communication.

(Michigan State University Laboratory Preschool.)

Removing a child from the group is another way of guiding a child who is having difficulty in a group. Difficulties that arise when a child loses control are often due to overfatigue. When a child cannot cope with a situation, the teacher may choose to remove him completely. She may lead him to a quiet nook and then talk, read, or sing to him for a while. She may ask him to help her find the play dough or some favorite toy. By involving the child in a way that will relax him, she averts problems. If a firm, loving, nonpunishing attitude is maintained, the child will welcome the respite. He may even seek help another time when he feels his control slipping.

Ignoring some behavior is appropriate, depending on the individual and his age. James Hymes, Jr., advises teachers not to make an issue over every little fall from grace and says it is often helpful to be half deaf and nearsighted.³ Surely the teacher cannot make a supreme court case out of every transgression. And transgressions may actually be progress for certain children. For example, Mary never did anything "wrong" and never said "No" to anyone. She was painfully shy and always proper. The teacher's rule was that children stay out of certain pieces of the housekeeping equipment. However, one day Mary was seen in the dollhouse kitchen climbing up through the opening left for the dishpan "sink," the teacher turned her back and allowed Mary to go ahead without the customary disapproval.

Approval and disapproval of certain behavior are direct guidance techniques. Verbally labeling behavior helps the child learn. In the following example, John knows the teacher will approve if he repeats the behavior. "John, I like the way you shared the cars with Mark," said the teacher. "When you let Mark use your car, you are sharing." Sharing is one of those vague attributes that most adults wish for in children and one that is very difficult to explain to the child. Sharing should be labeled so that children can begin to recognize it and know what the teacher means when she says, "We are learning to share our toys."

The use of praise should be sincere and given for merit—even if small. When a child makes a number of paintings, the teacher need not praise them all. She can say, "You have been working hard. Which painting do you think is the prettiest?" Insincere praise will be suspect even to children. Children should not need praise for all good behavior. That is, in the long run, they should find satisfaction in their behavior and not just the praise received for doing the appropriate act.

Praise and approval should come to children for jobs well done. Likewise, disapproval should focus on the child's act, not the child.

³ Ibid., p. 29.

"We don't like spitting, Brad. When we need to spit, we spit in the toilet." In this example no accusation is made that Brad is "bad" when he spits.

A silent smile across the room or a pat on the head conveys approval. Privately bestowed verbal praise avoids confusing the other children and discourages competition. For example, Peter heard the teacher exclaiming over David's art project. Peter looked at the praised art product and immediately rearranged his own project to fit the praised model. Peter's self-confidence and creativity were unwittingly undermined by the praise for David's picture. No amount of persuasion would convince Peter that the teacher also liked the way he had first made his picture.

The teacher's interaction with a young child should help keep communication open and help the child feel better about himself. Teachers should be aware that because children are immature and inexperienced they do not see a situation in the same way that teachers do. Before we judge a situation or react strongly or drastically we should try to get the child's view. Thomas Gordon, in his book *T.E.T.: Teacher Effectiveness Training,*[4] gives teachers a framework for practicing interactional skills with their students that are positive and growth producing. He calls it a "No-Lose Method." Based on humanistic psychology, Thomas' method allows both children and adults to feel good about the methods used.

Conclusion

The distinct manner and method of teaching make up the teacher's teaching style. The good teacher develops a unique teaching style. She uses guidance to influence the behavior of the children. Guidance can be thought of as either indirect or direct. Children are guided indirectly as the teacher arranges the learning centers, plans the daily schedule, and works with parents. Verbal and physical guidance make up direct guidance techniques.

The teacher relaxes and enjoys the children. Yet she is ready to use any of the guidance techniques described above as she supervises her group. At times she may appear to have eyes in the back of her head, as she gives attention to a single child and yet is able to respond readily to a difficulty in the far corner of the room or yard. In some ways the teacher is like the cowboys of the Old West who rode with the herd. According to the historian J. Frank Dobie, they "knew how to linger; they had 'ample time'; but their repose was the repose of

---

[4] Thomas Gordon, *T.E.T.: Teacher Effectiveness Training* (New York: Peter H. Wyden Publisher, 1974).

strength, capable of steel-spring action and not that of constitutional lethargy." [5]

After teaching nursery school or kindergarten, you may feel certain that Frank Dobie was describing you. Nursery school and kindergarten teaching requires almost instantaneous response to situations. The response that contributes to goals for educating each child so that he can reach his highest potential demands insight, knowledge, and empathy from teachers.

ADDITIONAL READINGS

BEYER, EVELYN. *Teaching Young Children.* New York: Western Publishing Company, Inc., 1968.

COMBS, ARTHUR. *Professional Education of Teachers: A Perceptual View of Teacher Preparation.* Boston: Allyn & Bacon, Inc., 1965.

DREIKURS, R., and V. SOLTZ. *Children: The Challenge.* New York: Duell, Sloan & Pearce, Inc., 1964.

HARTRUP, WILLARD W., and NANCY L. SMOTHERGILL (eds.). *The Young Child.* Washington, D.C.: National Association for Education of the Young Child, 1967.

HILDEBRAND, VERNA. *Guiding Young Children.* New York. Macmillan Publishing Co., Inc., 1975.

HYMES, JAMES L., JR. *Behavior and Misbehavior.* Englewood Cliffs, N.J.: Prentice-Hall, Inc., 1955.

LANDRETH, CATHERINE. *Preschool Learning and Teaching.* New York: Harper & Row, 1972.

MOUSTAKAS, CLARK. *The Authentic Teacher.* Cambridge, Mass.: Howard A. Doyle Publishing Co., 1966.

MOYER, JOAN E. and JEAN T. KUNZ, "Trust Is Everything," *Young Children,* Vol. 30, No. 2, January 1975, pp. 107–112.

READ, KATHERINE. *The Nursery School: A Human Relationships Laboratory.* Philadelphia: W. B. Saunders Company, 1971.

ROSENTHAL, ROBERT, and LENORE JACKSON. *Pygmalion in the Classroom.* New York: Holt, Rinehart and Winston, Inc., 1968.

SMITH, JAMES A. *Setting Conditions for Creative Teaching in the Elementary School.* Boston: Allyn & Bacon, Inc., 1966.

TODD, VIVIAN E., and HELEN HEFFERNAN. *The Years Before School: Guiding Preschool Children.* New York: Macmillan Publishing Co., Inc., 1970.

WILLS, CLARICE, and LUCILLE LINDBERG. *Kindergarten for Today's Children.* Chicago: Follett Publishing Company, 1967.

[5] J. Frank Dobie, *The Longhorns* (New York: Bramhall House, 1961), p. xix.

PART
TWO

The Curriculum of the Nursery School and Kindergarten

Learning Activities in the Outdoors

BABY'S eyes light up when mother reaches for outdoor clothing and says, "Let's go bye-bye." Nursery school and kindergarten children run for their coats when their teacher says, "Time to go outside." Older children's eyes sparkle and books get shoved into desks when the recess bells ring. Even some elders are happy when friends invite them to go jogging.

Each day nursery school and kindergarten teachers plan outdoor activities for children. Students are called upon to observe and to help. The first chapter of this section on curriculum is devoted to children's learning activities that take place out of doors. Students who appreciate these activities will be able to make meaningful contributions when they are outdoors with children during the term.

Motor Skill Development [1]

Motor skills are required to control the body. When skills for moving the body such as running, jumping, or climbing are discussed they are called *large motor* or *gross muscular skills*. When skills such as writing, tying, or using scissors are discussed they are called *small motor* or *fine muscular skills*. According to developmental studies the pattern of motor development is predictable in its broader aspects with individual differences occurring in the timetable.[2]

Motor skill development is usually the first value of outdoor play activity that comes to mind. Large motor skills are critical to the individual's development and to his enjoyment of life. The long lives that our children can be expected to live make it even more critical that their physical bodies and motor skills be developed adequately.

[1] The author is indebted to Drs. Vern Seefeldt and John Haubenstricker of Michigan State University for permission to use research results, descriptions of sequential stages of motor skill development, and photographs, and for consultations on the content of this section of this chapter.

[2] Elizabeth B. Hurlock, *Child Development* (New York: McGraw-Hill Book Company, 1972), pp. 133–150.

FIGURE 6–1. *A three-year-old child catching a ball with a Stage 3 pattern. Catching a ball at the third developmental level (Stage 3) involves placing the arms in front of the body in preparation to receive the ball. The arms begin moving toward the body while the ball is still airborne. The first point of contact occurs when the ball strikes the chest. At that instant the arms and hands encircle the ball and secure it by pressing it next to the body.*

In the typical indoor classroom, vigorous activity is not encouraged and children may not be allowed to run, jump, climb, or catch. Although such restrictions might be expected indoors, often these large motor skills are also being curtailed outdoors. Teachers may excuse this lack of large motor skill practice by indicating that they are afraid for the children's safety, that there is little or no equipment, or that they place priority on mental tasks. However, children need

FIGURE 6–2. *Punting a ball, using a Stage 3 pattern. Punting is the act of striking a ball with the foot before the ball, projected by the punter, has a chance to descend to the surface. The Stage 3 punt shows the performer in a stationary position prior to releasing the ball in a forward, downward motion. The striking foot moves forward as the ball moves toward the surface. Ideally the ball should be contacted by the foot at a level between the ankle and the knee of the supporting leg. Note that as the right foot moves forward the left arm moves ahead and the right arm moves backward, in an attempt to maintain an upright posture and yet achieve maximum rotation of the force-producing body parts.*

teachers who will plan opportunities for them to practice needed large motor skills.

At Michigan State University Drs. Vern Seefeldt and John Haubenstricker have been engaged in a longitudinal research program designed to examine small children's physical growth, motor maturity, and motor development. The research team observes the same children every month over a period of years, and they are finding

FIGURE 6–3.   *Kicking a ball with a Stage 2 pattern. Kicking involves striking a stationary ball with the foot. Kicking is learned with less difficulty than punting because the former eliminates the need to relate to an approaching object during the performance. The body remains stationary during the contact phase, but the performer generally steps backward after the kick to regain the balance that was lost momentarily during the contact phase. Note that there is cross-body opposition of movement in the arms and feet after the ball is contacted.*

that "rudimentary stages of the fundamental motor skills which include walking, running, hopping, jumping, skipping, leaping, throwing, catching, etc. must be established very early in life if a child is to advance to more mature stages." [3]

In addition to this research, Seefeldt and his co-workers have organized remedial groups for children referred to them for the assessment of physical motor skills. Seefeldt says, "The children who come to us at age five with poorly established preliminary stages in fundamental motor skills are unlikely to become highly skilled, even though we provide additional sessions with a one-to-one teacher-pupil ratio." [4] As a result of their work these researchers have grown increasingly convinced that parents and nursery school and kindergarten teachers must engage children in practicing these skills.

[3] Vern Seefeldt, "The Role of Motor Skills in the Lives of Children with Learning Disabilities," paper presented to the Conference of the Association for Children with Learning Disabilities, Detroit, Michigan, March 1973.
[4] Ibid.

The Seefeldt team has been able to analyze the sequential stages children go through in learning many of the fundamental motor skills. They have grouped the skills as follows:

Locomotor skills—moving from place to place.

walk	jump	hop	stop	fall
run	gallop	skip	start	dodge
leap	slide	roll		

Nonlocomotor skills—moving body parts, with child stationary.

swing	stretch	turn	lift
sway	curl	bend	pull
rock	twist	push	

Projection and reception skills—propelling and catching objects.

catch	punt	dribble	trap
throw	strike	kick	bounce

If you have compared the way a baby and an older sibling throw a ball, you know there are differences in the manner of handling the ball and of managing the body during the throw. Through the use of movies Seefeldt's team has been able to describe in detail the developmental sequence of some of these skills. Seefeldt believes that knowing these stages of development will assist parents and teachers in providing appropriate experiences for individual children. The child should be helped to the next stage in the hierarchy rather than encouraged or pressed to skip a stage or two, as, for example, when a child whose father wants him to become a baseball great is encouraged to throw and catch in advanced stages before his body has mastered the fundamental stages.

Skills are not specifically related to chronological age but are a result of a combination of maturation and experience. Teachers and parents must remember that grouping children by chronological age, body size, or sex will still leave a wide variation in the sequential stages of motor skill development. Alert adults can make a contribution to the experiences children are offered for large motor skill practice. Adults can sequence tasks for each child that will help assure success and minimize the possibility of failure.

Seefeldt and Haubenstricker have identified, described, and made available the following developmental sequences for catching, kicking, throwing, and the standing long jump.

FIGURE 6–4.   *Throwing a ball with a Stage 4 pattern. The throw at a Stage 4 developmental level involves opposition of movement between the arms and the feet; as the throwing arm (right) moves backward in the preparatory phase, the left foot moves forward to receive the weight as the arm moves forward to release the ball. The force of the throw is shifted to the left foot as the body "follows through" its motion after the throw.*

FIGURE 6–5.   *Striking a ball from a tee, using a Stage 4 pattern. Striking at the Stage 4 developmental level involves a shift of the body weight to the rear or right foot of a right-handed batter. As the bat moves forward the weight is transferred to the forward or left foot. At the point of contact the body weight has rotated so that it is over the left foot, with the right foot in position to provide stability during the follow-through phase.*

DEVELOPMENTAL SEQUENCE OF CATCHING

Stage 1   The arms of the performer are directly in front of the body, with the elbows extended and the palms facing upward or inward. As the ball contacts the hands or arms the elbows flex and the arms and hands attempt to secure the ball by holding it against the chest.

Stage 2   The child prepares to receive the object with the arms in front of the body, the elbows extended or slightly flexed. Upon presentation of the ball the arms begin an encircling motion that ends when the ball is secured against the chest. The arm action in Stage 2 begins before the ball contacts the body.

Stage 3   The child prepares to receive the ball with arms that are slightly flexed and extended forward at the shoulder.

Substage 1   The child uses the chest as the first point of contact with the ball and attempts to secure the ball by holding it to the chest with the hands and arms.

Substage 2   The child attempts to catch the ball with the hands. Failure to hold it securely results in an attempt to guide the ball to the chest, where it is controlled by the hands and arms.

Stage 4   The child prepares to receive the ball by flexing the elbows and presenting the arms toward the approaching ball. Skillful performers may keep the elbows at the sides and flex the arms simultaneously as they bring them forward to meet the ball. The ball is caught with the hands and does not contact any other body part.

Stage 5   The upper body movement is identical to that of Stage 4. In addition, the child is required to change the stationary base in order to receive the ball. Stage 5 is apparently difficult for many children when they are required to move in relation to an approaching ball.

DEVELOPMENTAL SEQUENCE OF KICKING

Stage 1   The body is stationary as the striking foot is flexed in preparation for the kick. Knee flexion is limited, resulting in a pushing rather than a striking motion. There is little follow-through of the contact foot, and frequently it is withdrawn from the ball after contact.

Stage 2   The body is stationary just prior to the kicking motion, although some performers may run or walk to the ball prior to assuming the preparatory kicking position. Opposition of the upper and lower extremities is present during the kicking motion; that is, as the right (kicking) foot moves forward, the left arm also moves forward. The body pivots on the supporting leg, but the force of the kick usually is not sufficient to move the body forward after the ball is struck.

Stage 3   In the preparatory phase the performer approaches the ball by walking or running toward it. The striking foot remains near the surface in its approach, indicating a reduction in knee flexion in contrast to Stage 2. The force of the striking foot is less than maximum, reflected by the upright posture of the trunk and a poststriking position in which the body remains near the point at which the ball was contacted.

Stage 4 The performer approaches the ball by walking rapidly toward it. Just prior to striking the ball he brings the support foot into position near the ball by a leap. The trunk leans backward as the kicking foot moves forward. The performer reduces the force of the kicking foot, after it contacts the ball, by stepping in the direction of the kick or hopping on the supporting foot.

DEVELOPMENTAL SEQUENCE OF THROWING

Stage 1 The motion is essentially in a back-to-front or posterior-anterior direction. The feet remain fixed with little or no trunk rotation. The force of movement comes from hip flexion, moving the shoulder forward, and extending the elbow.

Stage 2 The feet generally remain stationary with a wide base of support, but a step with the right or the left foot in the direction of the throw may be taken. The force is directed more toward a direction parallel to the floor, with the hips and trunk moving as one unit.

Stage 3 The primary change from Stage 2 is that the movement of the foot on the same side as the throwing arm strides in the direction of the throw. The trunk rotation may be decreased in relation to Stage 2, but the hip flexion is increased.

Stage 4 The movement of Stage 4 shows opposition of movement in that the foot opposite the throwing arm strides forward in the "wind-up" phase, thus allowing a greater range of motion. The time over which the forces can act and the number of body parts involved in producing force are increased, so that the throwing motion of Stage 4 involves greater velocity and distance than in any of the other stages.

DEVELOPMENTAL SEQUENCE OF THE STANDING LONG JUMP

Stage 1 The child bends the knees and moves the arms backward in preparation for jumping. Just before the body is lifted from the floor, the knees straighten and the arms move forward to a position in front of the body. However, at the point of takeoff the arms again move backward in an attempt to keep the body upright and in a safe landing position. The angle of the jump is more vertical than horizontal.

Stage 2   The movement of the arms and legs in preparation for the jump is similar to Stage 1 behavior. However, after the takeoff the arms move to the side of the body with the elbows bent and the hands at shoulder height. The angle of the jump is slightly lower than in Stage 1.

Stage 3   The arms swing backward and then move forward vigorously during the preparatory phase. Upon takeoff the arms extend and move forward to approximately the height of the head. The arms remain in this position during the first half of the jump and then move down and backward in preparation for landing. The knee extension at the takeoff is nearly complete, but the angle of the jump still exceeds 45 degrees.

Stage 4   The arms extend vigorously forward and upward upon takeoff, reaching full extension above the head at "lift-off." The hips and knees are extended fully, with the takeoff angle at 45 degrees or less. In preparation for landing the arms are brought downward and the legs are thrust forward until the thighs are parallel to the surface. The center of gravity is far behind the base of support upon landing, but at the moment of contact the knees are flexed and the arms are thrust forward in order to keep the body from falling backward.

Other Values of Outdoor Activity

Mental, Social, and Emotional Development

Outdoor activity makes outstanding contributions to young children's lives. The goals for motor skill development are interrelated with goals for mental, social, and emotional development.

FIGURE 6–6.   *Jumping at Stage 1. The preparatory phases of jumping are essentially the same for all developmental levels of jumping. However, the force-production phase—especially those actions that occur immediately before, during, and after the point at which the feet leave the surface— distinguish the various levels of performance. The performer moves his arms backward immediately upon takeoff in an attempt to restrict the forward movement of the trunk. In Stage 1 jumping behavior the arms act as "brakes" to forward momentum.*

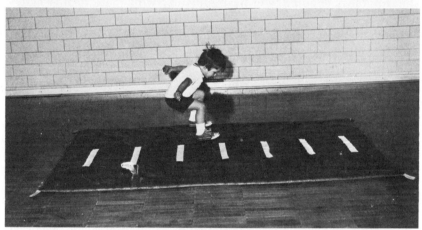

The reason outdoor activity is so popular with every age is that it honestly meets the needs of the individuals. Why do elementary children answer, "Recess," when asked, "What do you like best at school?" Recess is popular because it is freer of adult interferences— interferences that must at times be frustrating and stifling to children. A time for outdoor activity provides a release from tensions that build up from prolonged sitting, thinking, creating, being quiet, and trying to be "good."

The outdoor period provides the child additional stimuli to meet his friends and talk over mutual interests. Children talk, shout, laugh, and sing outdoors with less restraint than may occur in classrooms. Language flows naturally. Children use their outdoor period to make plans and do things together. Sharing and other social skills develop. Outdoor activity may provide social acceptance and leadership for those children who have difficulty with more formal activities.

Individual motor skills, such as pulling, pushing, lifting, balancing, running, climbing, pedaling, steering, riding, jumping, throwing, and swinging, are practiced. These skills contribute to a child's self-assurance, making him more confident when facing new experiences. Interaction with people of all ages is facilitated through motor skills. Skill in swimming dramatizes this fact. Once a young child swims with confidence he can swim with adults and teenagers as well as with children his own age. Until he develops swimming skills he is relegated to the shallow pool and his fellow nonswimmers. Or a five-year-old who has graduated to a two-wheel bicycle not only is king in his own crowd but he also is admitted to the school age set and is ready for family rides.

Negative and hostile feelings can be drained off through the activities the out-of-doors provides. Throwing balls and beanbags, punching the punching bag, or pounding nails are examples of acceptable outlets for "bad" feelings. Vigorous running and riding also provide release for pent-up feelings.

Of course, the mind continues to develop out of doors. In fact, the new environment will stimulate curiosity and exploration in the child. He can make many observations on his own. He can test out his ideas and come to many conclusions. The child may seem to be only exercising his legs or vocal chords, but his mind is also developing. Physical and mental development are closely related. For example, such concepts as fast and slow, high and low, long and short, and hard and easy are readily experienced. The child expresses much of his intellectual understanding through motor skills. Adults make inferences about intellectual growth through observing a child and his activities.

FIGURE 6–7. *A push-pull swing allows the child to be independent sooner.* (*Michigan State University Laboratory Preschool.*)

Developing large muscle coordination during vigorous play leads to improved small muscle coordination. Small muscle coordination is required in order to write, draw, cut, tie, or manipulate such things as puzzles and equipment.

The imaginative games and dramatic play observed during children's outdoor activity challenge the child's creativity, concepts, percepts, and memory. All are part of the child's mental development.

Vigorous physical activity stimulates all vital processes, such as circulation, respiration, and elimination. Eating habits improve, and rest is more welcome.

Dr. Jean Mayer, professor of nutrition at the Harvard School of Public Health, states that physical activity is the most important environmental variable affecting obesity in children. Obese children exercise less than lean children, yet often eat the same amounts. In diet therapy a long-term regime of increased exercise is needed.[5]

[5] Myron Winick, "Childhood Obesity," *Nutrition Today,* **9**:3 (May/June 1974), 9.

FIGURE 6–8. *A rope ladder is an additional challenge to climbing skills.* (*University of Houston Parent-Child Development Center.*)

Prime values of the outdoor self-selected activity period are the opportunities it affords children to feel free and to enjoy fresh air and sunshine. Children's happiness in outdoor activities is clearly expressed in laughter, squeals, and shouts.

Requirements of a Good Outdoor Program

A good nursery school and kindergarten program includes plans for a daily outdoor self-selected activity period. It is possible in some climates to hold virtually the entire school day outdoors. If the outdoor period is to make the maximum contribution to the development of the child, the following are required: (1) careful planning, (2) adequate space, (3) appropriate equipment, (4) sufficient time, and (5) appropriate guidance.

FIGURE 6–9. *When dressed warmly, children are delighted to be out in the snow.*

Careful Planning

Teachers should plan outdoor and large motor activities as thoughtfully as they do indoor activities. Too many teachers simply turn children loose in the outdoor play yard with little or no thought about variety, sequencing, or challenging activities. Children should have an opportunity for outdoor activities every day. During severe weather, gymnasium activities may be substituted. Typically, children desire lively action and need little urging to participate.

Referring to the list of fundamental motor skills, the teacher will plan to involve each child in these activities regularly. She must observe each child to see where he is in his skill mastery, then plan activities to encourage the child to practice the skills at his present stage, and, when he is ready, encourage him to move to the next stage in the sequence.

Locomotor skills can be practiced through such games as follow-the-leader, with a few children at a time following an adult through several skills on the list. For example, the leader could move from running, to jumping, to galloping, to leaping, as the group of children is led around the play yard. Another day several of the other skills can be practiced. Such games are helpful on cold days to get children moving, warmed up, and having a good time. The activities serve similar ends for teachers and help them release the energy and tension that inevitably build up.

An obstacle course may be set up with various pieces of equipment, and the children may be required to climb up on a packing

FIGURE 6–10.   *A tire swing gives children another experience in moving through space. (University of Houston Parent-Child Development Center.)*

box, jump across a plank held up by saw horses, climb through the rungs on the jungle gym, and run down an inclined plane attached to the jungle gym. Such a game gives children the opportunity to practice several fundamental skills.

The teacher can encourage jumping by placing one end of a bamboo fishing pole on the ground and the other end on a sawhorse or jungle gym for the children to jump over. The fishing pole should be loosely held, so that if the child hits the pole while jumping, the pole will fall easily and the child will not be hurt. The angle of the pole allows the child to jump where he is ready—high or low. This exercise requires the propelling of the body up and over. The teacher can encourage the long jump by marking a V shape on the grass or tumbling mat and encouraging the children to jump where they can make it across. Children typically fall after a jump, making the softer surface important. Avoidance of failure is important, and competition between children should also be avoided. Games of hopscotch give good hopping and jumping practice. Boys and girls should be equally encouraged to practice all skills.

FIGURE 6–11. *Another type of rope ladder requiring new skills. (Michigan State University Laboratory Preschool.)*

Nonlocomotor skills can be combined with locomotor skills through music and rhythm activities. A tom-tom, a tambourine, maracas, or recorded music may accompany the activity. The teacher should draw the children's attention to or get them to suggest different ways of using the body. Carrying ribbons or scarves or wearing full skirts encourages using the body to sway, twist, and bend. The hula hoop also encourages body movement.

Keeping an inflated beach ball, sponge ball, or balloon in the air encourages children to stand on tiptoe and to stretch and leap. Balls and beanbags encourage the practice of projection and reception skills. Children may like to throw the balls against a wall or into a large receptacle, such as a packing box. The smaller the child the larger the ball required.

A whiffle ball—a lightweight, hollow, molded polyethelene ball—may be tied to an elastic rope and suspended from a tree limb at the right height to allow children to practice batting with a plastic bat. Because the ball is attached, the child can practice alone without

FIGURE 6–12. *A felled tree can contribute to imaginative games and add experience with a rough texture. (Michigan State University Laboratory Preschool.)*

having to chase the ball each time he hits it. A ball may also be placed on a rubber cone (the type used to mark a street) or on a tee to enable the young batter to practice striking a ball that is stationary. Because young children are not skilled in throwing, they make less than satisfactory partners for friends who want to catch or bat; therefore adults usually must help children individually with batting and catching. A sponge ball, called a Nerf ball, is harmless to the people or furnishings it might hit while the young child practices throwing, catching, punting, and batting.

Teachers should plan outdoor activities as thoughtfully as they do indoor activities. Movable equipment should be regrouped from time to time to stimulate new use of it. Close observation of the children's interests will guide the teacher in planning activities and arranging equipment. She can enlist the children's advice and assistance. For example, when cowboy play is popular, the packing boxes are called "barns," and a corral is needed for the cowboy's tricycle "horses."

The teacher assists the cowboys in getting the barn in the correct position.

The teacher's attitude toward the outdoors is quickly indicated by what she plans and what she permits children to do outdoors. Teachers who don't particularly enjoy the outdoors should make an effort to learn to enjoy it. They should dress appropriately for the weather. With proper attire from head to toe, the teacher will begin to appreciate the exhilarating freshness of a winter day or the peaceful sunshine of a spring afternoon just as much as the children enjoy the out-of-doors.

The teacher should make plans to stimulate children's mental development while they are out of doors. Many indoor experiments, such as those using inclines or balances, can be repeated outdoors. Spontaneous learning about weather, plants, insects, and animals are all natural for the yard. Specimens can be observed, discussed, classified, labeled, imitated, and taken indoors. It is helpful to have science books, specimen jars, butterfly nets, and magnifying glasses available to use in extending the learning. The teacher's close involvement in children's learning will guide her to ask questions that help children see relationships and make comparisons between their discoveries and the adult world. Planned experiences should be initiated for children who don't seem to have questions.

Quiet activities have a definite place outdoors. Children should always be able to choose between active and less active outdoor activity. Music, perhaps with guitar or autoharp, is delightful. Stories told or read to small groups are pleasant. Children enjoy a period of looking at books alone, so books should be available. Even resting takes on positive dimensions when a blanket is spread under a tree.

Adequate Space [6]

Children probably often feel cooped up. They need the outdoor space that a good school affords. At home their living space may be shared with a number of siblings. Their playground may be the city streets and sidewalks. Even where parks and playgrounds are available, the parent may curtail the child's use of them. When playgrounds are overcrowded, the young child may feel insecure among the many strangers.

Children who live in mansions with plenty of room both indoors and out may also need the outdoor activities offered at school. These children may have few friends their age with whom to enjoy their

[6] For a comprehensive analysis and recommendations regarding amounts and use of space, see Sybil Kritchevsky, Elizabeth Prescott, and Lee Walling, *Planning Environments for Young Children: Physical Space* (Washington, D.C.: National Association for Education of Young Children, 1969).

elaborate home setting. They may stay indoors to have the companionship of their mother or the maid.

In the microscopic yards of some hillside slums and suburbs the child is unable to use a ball or bike. Even a good run is impossible because the terrain is too steep, and gravity is against him.

Space, then, becomes a cherished item in the modern world. Nursery school and kindergarten teachers should endeavor to provide 75 to 200 square feet of outdoor space for each child. Careful planning is required to see that all space is used judiciously.

The outdoor space should be safe from traffic so that the children can use it without fear and without constant reminders to protect themselves. The fence should permit children to see the outside world, yet be high enough and designed to discourage climbing. Gates with secure latches are needed. One practical aspect to consider when planning the fence is to provide some way for trucks with sand and equipment to make deliveries.

The space should be large enough for the number of children who may use it at any given time. When space must be shared with other groups, it is well to agree on a time schedule to avoid conflict from overcrowding. In schools housing older children it is wise to take nursery children and kindergarteners outdoors when older children are at work in the building. Thus the fear and confusion younger children feel when older children play at the same time may be avoided.

The best outdoor space is adjacent to and on the same level as the indoor room. The toilet must be near the entrance. Time and energy for both teachers and children are used more effectively when indoor and outdoor space are adjacent. Materials can be easily moved in and out. Supervision is simpler. Children's needs can best be met if the whole group is not required to be outside or inside at a given time.

Good playground space provides a variety of levels and challenges to the children. There should be knolls and flat surfaces, grassy expanses and hard-surfaced areas. Open space is necessary for exuberant play. A quiet nook for resting and reflecting is just as important. There should be protected areas so that the benefits of the outdoors can be enjoyed when the rains come. Shade is pleasantly cooling when the sunshine is very hot. Protection from prevailing winds makes space usable on wintry days. The space should be located where children can be allowed to be noisy.

Phyllis Lueck designed a creative outdoor learning environment at the University of Guelph in Ontario, Canada. The tricycle paths had various textures and finishes—pebbly, smooth, gravel, asphalt, and cement ridged like a washboard. A bridge across a little gully required careful driving, for it had narrow tracks that just fit the tricycle tires. In addition, various types of wind chimes gave the children an opportunity to hear variations in sounds when they rang the chimes.[7]

Adequate drainage is important. A sloping yard of slightly sandy soil dries off quickly after a shower. Wood chips, gravel, and other materials can be used to weatherize the surface and keep the children out of the mud. When planning a riding lane for wheel toys one should remember that a ribbon of hard surface encircling the play area simplifies driving rules. Ramps, inclines, or knolls add interest and challenge young riders.

The play yard should be designed to facilitate teaching. Out-of-the-way corners, equipment, and foliage that block the teacher's view prevent good teaching and supervision.

The space should be attractive. A variety of plantings can provide interesting natural science experiences as well as beauty. Special attention to finishes and colors will make the yard more inviting to all.

In some schools there is space to house several animal pets, which provide learning experiences for the children. In other schools the yard might be used for a day to house someone's pet rabbit or a lamb borrowed from a farmer friend. From watching a wriggling worm or a soaring bird the children can be stimulated to observe and learn about living creatures.

Children may not get enough vigorous outdoor exercise in climates that are extremely hot or cold. In such situations protected space for large motor activities—climbing, sliding, running, and riding—should be located elsewhere. For example, a protected patio, a rainy-day room, or a gymnasium can serve this purpose if it is carefully planned and equipped.

Appropriate Equipment

Equipping the school yard is a major endeavor. A knowledge of children's needs, interests, and abilities is required for choosing appropriate equipment. Money, planning, and imagination are also required.

There should be equipment for climbing, swinging, balancing, pulling, lifting, chinning, sliding, riding, building, and pounding. Some large boxes or structures are needed that lend themselves to imaginative games for children to develop. Sand, mud, and water are essentials.

There must be enough equipment so that all children using the

[7] Phyllis Lueck, "Planning an Outdoor Learning Environment," *Theory into Practice,* **12:2** (April 1973), 121–127.

FIGURE 6–13. *A playhouse shell contributes to dramatic play outdoors.* (*Michigan State University Laboratory Preschool.*)

yard at one time may find a suitable activity. If there is a shortage of equipment, then children direct their energy against each other and toward climbing on gates and fences. Ample equipment is essential if the outdoor program is to make its rightful contribution to the child's overall development.

Large packing boxes of varying sizes and colors can become the center for dramatic play. To imaginative children a large box can be a "barn" for tricycle "horses" or the "living room" of the little "house." Several boxes built from sturdy pine lumber ranging down from 54″ × 54″ × 54″ and painted with high-quality outdoor paint will be invaluable in the outdoor program.

Other accessory pieces such as barrels, ladders, sawhorses, and planks have many uses. Planks can become bridges between packing boxes. A jumping board can be made from low blocks or sawhorses placed under each end of a plank. A sliding board can be made from a plank with one end resting on the jungle gym.

A collection of large hollow blocks painted or varnished for use out of doors adds to the quality of the play. Corrals, roads, bridges, and houses are designed by young "engineers" when they are provided with an adequate supply of blocks. Out-of-the-weather storage is required for most blocks. Block storage and movement will be facilitated if blocks are stored on a wheeled dollie that is easily rolled in and out.

A sufficient number of sturdy wheel toys should be available so that children can perfect their cycling skills. Wheeled equipment is also useful in dramatic play. In a group of twenty children about ten wheel toys—tricycles of various sizes, wagons, tractors, and the like —should be available.

Rocking-boat-type equipment, either to stand or to sit on, provides pleasant opportunities for developing arm and leg muscle coordination.

Judgment and coordination in throwing, kicking, and chasing can be fostered if many balls are available. Beanbags, made from heavy cloth and partly filled with dried beans, are better than balls for young children learning to catch. A box or basket encourages the children to play "basketball."

The equipment should contain a few pieces that the children will find somewhat difficult to master at the beginning of the school year. For example, only one five-year-old was able to use the trapeze in September. However, during the final weeks of school almost every child went hand over hand on that trapeze.

A good choice of swing is the glider type requiring two children to face each other and cooperate in a push-pull motion. With this type of swing, goals for self-help, cooperation, and socialization are fostered in ways not achieved with traditional swings.

For younger children traditional swings should have strap seats. This seat, which resembles a horse saddle cinch, does not harm the child as a hard seat may if the child gets hit with it. The seat curves to fit the child's body so that he's less likely to fall out. Because children cannot stand up easily in strap seats, they will be less popular with older children. For older children the swing should have a rigid seat made of lightweight plastic material.

The tire swing is the favorite swing in many yards. It is a tire hung from a tree limb with a chain. The tire may be suspended in only one place or anchored with three chains that hold the tire parallel to the ground, making room for three children.

The jungle gym offers a challenge to children's climbing muscles and their imagination. It should be sturdy. Though the steel gym is cold to the touch, it does not become as dangerously deteriorated as a wooden one. A jungle gym is best located on a grassy surface or over tanbark so that falls will be cushioned.

A slide should be low enough for the teacher to reach the child at the top. This is important for a young group. Also, the slide should be flat enough at the bottom so children will not shoot out into the dirt from a fast ride. Popular slides in some schools are those built into tree houses or other structures. Children can then incorporate the slide into imaginary play more readily than when it is a single, isolated piece of equipment.

Live trees in the yard can provide challenging climbing experiences, refreshing shade, and outstanding opportunities to watch nature's sequences. A fallen tree trimmed down to two or three major forks provides children a gnarled surface for climbing, sitting, and jumping. As the bark loosens the children will enjoy helping to remove it. With years of use the surface will become shiny. The tree trunk will contribute to imaginative play, serving as a spaceship, an airplane, or a train, depending on the idea of the moment.

Old cars, trucks, boats, and even airplanes have been used in school yards to stimulate imaginary games. Usually these are mere skeletons with doors, windows, and all loose gadgets removed. They should be colorfully painted to avoid giving the area a junkyard appearance.

A sand pile provides a quiet, restful area and an inexpensive medium for children. A good-quality sand can be purchased. A wood frame box with a 10-inch ledge provides a seat for the children when the sand is wet. Children will use the ledge as a "table" as they turn out their "cakes." A lid for the sandbox is essential in neighborhoods where cats might contaminate the sand. The lid can be hinged along the edges in such a way that it becomes a seat when opened.

Sand should be kept moist. Dry sand gets in hair and eyes more readily than damp sand. Moist sand is more easily molded into cakes or tunnels. Numerous containers should be provided. Kitchen castoffs are excellent: juice cans, old pots and pans, plastic milk cartons, and funnels made from the tops of plastic bottles are all suitable sand toys. The teacher should examine the collection from time to time and replace broken items. A large number of metal shovels makes sharing less difficult. The sandbox with numerous containers of various sizes gives children opportunities to measure, count, and label the products they are making so carefully. The sandbox affords a place to rest, yet keep busy and in touch with friends.

When an area in the yard is set aside for the spring garden or the fall bulb planting, sturdy short-handled garden tools are useful. Quality tools should be purchased to encourage a young gardener. A corner can be reserved for "just digging."

Water play is delightful outdoors when the weather is warm. Plastic aprons are essential to keep clothes dry. A specially made portable water table with a galvanized lining that makes a 10-inch deep sink

FIGURE 6–14. *A sand-covered yard eliminates problems with mud, and children can shovel the sand wherever it suits their fancy. (University of Tennessee Gulf Range Child Care Center.)*

is convenient for both indoor and outdoor water play. Children, however, will enjoy even a dishpan or a bucket of water. When children are furnished soap, they will happily wash the doll clothes or tricycles. A wading pool is popular in summer. Of course, for safety, utmost care must be taken to have the water play supervised at all times.

When given a can of water and a small paintbrush, the young child likes to "paint" the side of the storage shed or the jungle gym: he will paint as carefully as any painter. A paper cup of water with detergent suds and a drinking straw make bubble blowing easy. Both activities are fun on warm sunny days.

Wintertime, with its snow and ice, gives children water in another form. When dressed properly, children enjoy the snow. Children often lie in the snow making snow angels, like Peter in Ezra Jack Keats's *A Snowy Day*, and gaining information about their body shapes and sizes. Sleds are standard equipment in nursery schools in snowy climates. Only a small knoll is necessary to bring joy to young sledders. Pans of snow can be taken indoors for measurement or experimentation.

Young carpenters will enjoy pounding and sawing in the play yard. Carpenter's benches, old work tables, or packing boxes can provide space on which to work. Real tools should be purchased and kept in good working condition. Separate clamps or vises attached to the tables are handy for helping the child hold the wood. Water paints can be made available so that little carpenters can finish up their projects in style. Nuts and bolts make interesting manipulative and sorting experiences and may be used in wood projects. Wrenches may be needed for some projects.

Cabinetmakers will usually give teachers the scraps of wood from their scrap bin. Sometimes the teacher is able to interest the craftsmen in her children's projects, and they will save unusual shapes as they cut them out. Under saws, planes, and drills the teacher will find sawdust and shavings of various sizes that are useful in numerous art projects.

A playhouse structure—which can double as a storage room—stimulates children's dramatic play. When it is designed with a variety of stairs and ladders, the child's climbing skills are developed. A fireman's pole, a rope ladder, or a metal slide can be built into the structure for the child's quick "escape." Doll carriages and dress-up clothes contribute to imaginative outdoor play.

Children get thirsty when they are very active. Drinking water should be available, from either a drinking fountain or a pitcher of water brought outside. It is very convenient to have weatherproofed tables so that an outdoor snack or lunch can be served.

Various table toys from inside can be used outside also. Finger painting and clay take on new possibilities when used outdoors. Easels can be set up outside for painting.

Storage for all outdoor equipment should be designed to encourage the children to help put things away. Proper storage of toys teaches children desirable habits. At the same time children can be very helpful to the teacher. Most equipment deteriorates in wet weather; therefore proper storage is essential.

An adequate budget is needed to keep equipment properly maintained. Equipment with pieces that are loose or missing is often frustrating and unsafe for children's use. Equipment represents a substantial investment in time and money.

Sufficient Time

The time block set aside for outdoor, self-selected activity should be at least 30 minutes long. Thirty minutes or more are needed to encourage the children to go beyond the level of just letting off steam. With a large block of time children will engage in constructive, thoughtful activity. Teachers may observe that the first few minutes outdoors children often seem compulsive in activity. They may grab at the first toy they see, or monopolize the tricycle, or hold a swing with an "I got here first" attitude. After 10 to 15 minutes, when they realize they will have time left over, they begin to plan activities. When children accustom themselves to long outdoor periods, many satisfying learning experiences take place.

In warm climates virtually the entire school day, and most of the school's learning centers, can be carried on out of doors. Care should be taken to avoid overtiring those children who use the large muscle equipment extensively in an effort to keep up with a special friend. Routine quiet times should be incorporated in the planning.

Sufficient time outdoors should be considered a must for large motor activities, fresh air, and sunshine. With modern clothing even snowy and rainy days can be enjoyed by children and teachers. Teachers in day-care programs must realize that when children are kept indoors in the center for eight to ten hours, there will be little or no daylight hours left for outdoor activity when the child gets home—even assuming he has a productive learning environment in which to play at home. The school's outdoor activities become critical in these cases.

Appropriate Guidance

Teachers will enjoy guiding children's learning out of doors if they understand the stages of physical and motor development. This understanding will help adults overcome excessive concern that children will hurt themselves, provide clues to when children's safety requires the teacher to stop an activity, and preclude unnecessary labeling of activities as "dangerous."

Many adults are fearful when children climb. A general rule followed by most experienced teachers is that a child will climb only as high as he feels safe. If he is overencouraged by adults or other children to go beyond the point where he feels safe, or if he appears to be showing off, then the teacher should stay close by to prevent accidents.

Teachers must be willing to set limits that protect the safety of the children, protect the learning environment, and protect property. The teacher will define and give reasons for the limitations set— "Your sand is for digging. Sand hurts Jane's eyes." She may remove a child from the sandbox or other equipment if he does not abide by the rules.

When a teacher sees only a single child or two on a piece of high equipment, she may not need to worry. However, if several children are climbing on a slide, a jungle gym, or a packing box, she knows it is a situation to watch. Crowding invites pushing. The teacher can first move closer to the group. If all is peaceful, she need not say anything. She is close enough to know when guidance is needed to ensure safety.

In practice the mere movement of the teacher close to a play group is a reminder to the children to play according to the established rules. Therefore, without saying anything, the teacher will influence the behavior of the children. In addition, if the group is too large for the equipment, she can directly or indirectly extend the play to a larger area. She may set up an enticing new climbing arrangement nearby that will attract some children and thus reduce the size of the first group to a safe number.

Using traditional swings, a child consciously or unconsciously may isolate himself from the group. Guidance may help a child who swings alone all the time to feel confident enough to try other activities.

Some children monopolize a teacher by having her push them in the swing. If the school has a traditional swing, the teacher will want the children to learn to pump themselves. The following is one way to help children learn to pump. The teacher places a plank straight behind the swing, extending from the spot where the child's feet rest. The far end is elevated with a large hollow block or sawhorse, making an inclined plane. Holding the swing chains tight with the seat under him, the child then walks backward up the plank. As he sits down on the seat his feet go up in the air and he "takes off." The child will be thrilled at his new-found independence in being able to make himself go in the swing. He will practice the feat over and over again. In some schools the incline is built as a ramp under the swings used by the younger nursery school children.

Another useful method to encourage pumping is to pull the child forward in the swing, grasping his feet instead of pushing from behind. The teacher warns the child, then gives both his feet a slight tug. She encourages the child, as he swings forward, to reach with his feet for her hands, which are held up higher and higher. This reaching gets his feet up, and eventually he feels secure enough to relax and let his shoulders and torso move with the swing. Verbal encouragement and the accompanying words, "bending and stretching," will label the action of his legs and help him get the rhythm. Children enjoy the socializing with the teacher that this technique encourages.

Sharing is one of those elusive qualities that adults would have all children develop. The teacher's guidance is often required in problems of sharing. In addition to social learning, sharing affords children concrete experience with quantity, number, and division—all mathematical concepts. Sharing toys is easier when there is a sufficient quantity, because a child does not like to wait indefinitely for a desired toy. A new toy may have to be rationed so that each child can have a turn. Rationing and sharing are different. With rationing one hopes to ensure equal use of a given supply. With sharing one finds joy and satisfaction in mutual or partial use of a thing.

There is a feeling that goes with sharing that comes from having "enough." Adults may tell the child that he has had the toy long enough, but only he really knows. How would you react if someone told you that you had had "enough to eat"? You'd probably think, "How does she know I've had enough?"

People share voluntarily, willingly, happily, and frequently when they feel that they can decide. Children who feel loved and self-confident are more willing to share. Significant sharing can be observed when two children are having a happy time together. There will be a mutual give-and-take that is the real essence of sharing. Statements like "We share in this school" or "You've got to learn to share" do not really help the child learn. He interprets these statements to mean you expect him to divide up the goods and will force him to do so if he refuses.

It is helpful to identify activity verbally as "sharing" so that the child will grasp what is meant by the expression. For example, Jack arrived in the kindergarten and observed the children petting some new guinea pigs. He walked up and immediately said, "You've got to share." His behavior indicated that he expected everyone to step aside and give him a guinea pig. When at last he got his turn, he quickly forgot his admonition to the other children. "Sharing" was in Jack's vocabulary but was not in his repertoire of behaviors and feelings. The next time the teacher saw Jack share, she should have told him, "There, Jack, you shared with Bill." To promote sharing the teacher provides a sufficient number of toys, then works to establish a climate of mutual love and respect that brings sharing about voluntarily.

A new toy in a school may have to be rationed, but the sooner it can become "yours while you are using it," the better. This "yours while you are using it" policy allows a child to use equipment until he feels he has had enough. Then he will be able to share. The policy also avoids having the teacher become a timekeeper.

Teachers often have difficulty with some children monopolizing certain equipment. Monopolizing may occur because children are unable to think of anything else to do. For example, the boys in one group monopolized the tricycles. The teacher decided to give the girls a chance at the tricycles by dismissing them to the yard first for a few days. Another day she chose everyone wearing red to go to the yard first. Such procedures gave others a chance to use the tricycles. Guidance in helping the boys find suitable alternatives to tricycle riding was called for. Teachers should be observant and prevent the practice of one child or clique tyrannizing the others in order to get certain equipment.

Toys brought from home handicap the teacher in her "yours while you are using it" policy. Personal toys are usually unsuited for use by a group. Some are so fragile that they may get broken if they are shared. It is well to discourage children from bringing personal toys to school. There are cases in which children need their own toys for personal security. This, of course, will be an exception. In these cases a frank explanation to the other children that "Jill feels better today with her own doll; perhaps tomorrow she will enjoy our dolls" is sufficient.

The teacher's guidance is often required to keep children from getting overheated outdoors or in. Many wraps that are appropriate when the child is moving slowly in the early morning are unnecessary when he's going full speed in the sunshine later on. A good rule, of course, is to encourage the children to decide for themselves when they need to shed their wraps. The teacher should err on the side of letting the children take off coats if they wish. It is hard for adults to realize how hot children get from their vigorous activity.

In some climates boots are kept in the locker all the time because of the prevailing wet grass in the yard. Extra boots, mittens, and hats stored in the school closet can supply the child who does not have his own. Parents often need suggestions as to appropriate clothing to send, and even to purchase.

Emergencies

If a child falls while playing, it is better for the teacher to comfort him on the ground for a few minutes while she tries to determine how serious the injury is. For the teacher to jerk the child up on his feet or into her arms will certainly frighten him and may do serious damage to a limb if one is broken. In time of emergency a teacher's calmness can relax the hurt child, reassure the other children, and guide the assistants' efforts to be helpful. A coherent report is required by the parents or the doctor if either must be called.

In case of a serious accident a full account should be typed immediately to ensure recall of all details. Reports should be filed with appropriate authorities. If the school is covered by insurance, this report will be helpful, perhaps required.

Conclusion

The teacher should realize the value of offering a rich outdoor program to young children. Adequate plans ensure that goals are achieved for each child. The teachers should make wise use of space and be creative in selection and arrangement of equipment. In addition, appropriate guidance and teaching techniques assure meaningful outdoor learning experiences for all the children.

ADDITIONAL READINGS

BAKER, KATHERINE READ. *Let's Play Outdoors*. Washington, D.C.: National Association for Education of Young Children, 1966.

BEYER, EVELYN. *Teaching Young Children*. New York: Western Publishing Company, Inc., 1968.

D'EUGENIO, TERRY. *Building with Tires*. Cambridge, Mass.: Educational Arts Association, 1971.

ENGSTROM, GEORGIANNA (ed.). *Play: The Child Strives Toward Self Realization*. Washington, D.C.: The National Association for the Education of Young Children, 1971.

ENGSTROM, GEORGIANNA (ed.). *The Significance of the Young Child's Motor Development*. Washington, D.C.: The National Association for the Education of Young Children, 1971.

GERHARDT, LYDIA A. *Moving and Knowing: The Young Child Orients Himself in Space*. Englewood Cliffs, N.J.: Prentice-Hall, Inc., 1973.

HYMES, JAMES L., JR. *Teaching the Child Under Six*. Columbus, Ohio: Charles E. Merrill Publishing Co., 1974.

KRITCHEVSKY, SYBIL, ELIZABETH PRESCOTT, and LEE WALLING. *Planning Environments for Young Children: Physical Space*. Washington, D.C.: National Association for Education of Young Children, 1969.

LANDRETH, CATHERINE. *Early Childhood: Behavior and Learning*. New York: Alfred A. Knopf, Inc., 1967.

LEEPER, SARAH H., RUTH J. DALES, DORA SKIPPER, and RALPH L. WITHERSPOON. *Good Schools for Young Children*. New York: Macmillan Publishing Co., Inc., 1974.

LUECK, PHYLLIS, "Planning an Outdoor Learning Environment," *Theory into Practice*, Vol. 12, No. 2, April 1973, 121–127.

READ, KATHERINE. *The Nursery School: A Human Relationships Laboratory*. Philadelphia: W. B. Saunders Company, 1971.

RUDOLPH, MARGUERITA, and DOROTHY H. COHEN. *Kindergarten—A Year of Learning*. New York: Appleton-Century-Crofts, 1964.

STONE, JEANNETTE GALAMBOS, and NANCY RUDOLPH. *Play and Playgrounds*. Washington, D.C.: The National Association for the Education of Young Children, 1970.

TODD, VIVIAN E., and HELEN HEFFERNAN. *The Years Before School: Guiding Preschool Children*. New York: Macmillan Publishing Co., Inc., 1970.

WILLS, CLARICE, and LUCILLE LINDBERG. *Kindergarten for Today's Children*. Chicago: Follett Publishing Company, 1967.

Creative Art Activities

"I'M GONNA paint," said four-year-old Greg, lifting the long-handled brush out of the red paint and stroking it on the easel paper. "You know," he continued, turning to his companion at the adjacent easel, "when we're in kindergarten, we won't ever get to paint. My brother goes to kindergarten and he never gets to do anything that's fun."

Greg's comments regarding kindergarten attracted several listeners. His predictions brought thoughtful, worried expressions to the faces of his young friends. They couldn't imagine a school where they couldn't paint or have fun.

Children enjoy the many and varied art experiences offered in good schools for young children. Through these activities children integrate all areas of their growth—creative, physical, mental, social, and emotional. Greg's forecast of the grim life ahead in kindergarten need not be the reality. Teachers at all levels are accepting the importance of encouraging the inventive, original, self-initiated, and self-motivated behavior that is the creative potential in each child.

Creativity

What Is Creativity?

Creativity, according to Eisner, is a capacity possessed in some degree by all human beings.[1] Creativity is part of human intellect, which Hofstadter differentiates from intelligence. "Intellect," Hofstadter writes, "is the critical, creative, and contemplative side of the mind. Intelligence is an excellence of mind that is employed in a fairly narrow, immediate, and predictable range."[2] Creativity is the

[1] Eliot W. Eisner, "Research in Creativity," *Childhood Education*, **39**:8 (1963), 371.

[2] Erhard Hofstadter, *Anti-intellectualism in American Life* (New York: Knopf, 1966), pp. 24–25.

FIGURE 7–1. *Easel painting is a favorite activity of young children. They readily make their own spaces and fill them in. (Michigan State University Laboratory Preschool.)*

ability to see new relationships between previously unrelated objects or ideas, to push boundaries beyond present knowledge, and to organize ideas aesthetically. Originality in action or thought is creativity.

Adults are often confused about creativity. Rigid, stifling, or unsupported early experience may have made them doubt their own creativity. They may think that only artists are creative. It sometimes helps to think of creativity as a personal resource that is part of everyday decision making. Each person has some unique ways in which he applies what he knows to the tasks of everyday living. That's creativity in operation.

Creative potential gives people the motivation to change, to shift gears in a rapidly changing society. From a very practical point of view, it is extremely important that a person's creativity be fostered

FIGURE 7–2. *Controlling the glue flowing from the plastic bottle is an intriguing outcome of collage making. (Michigan State University Laboratory Preschool.)*

to its fullest extent. The village blacksmith of grandfather's day may have lamented that there were no more horses to be shod, but he turned to repairing the wheels of the tractors that replaced the horse. He used many of the same materials and skills. He saw the possibilities and learned new ways of using his resources. He didn't let the need to change throw him into psychological or economic despair.

A walk down any street on any day reveals how someone's creativity has made life easier: the window washer uses a rubber blade on a long stick; the painter uses a roller instead of a brush; the street sweeper now rides a big machine instead of carrying a broom and a pail; the businessman has his computer buttons; office forces have automatic machines; the bus driver serves customers faster because buses have two doors to speed the process of moving people on and off. All are the result of someone's creativity. Industry encourages creative suggestions from employees through incentive payments.

A look in the household section of a historical museum shows how pioneers used their creative ingenuity to lighten household tasks. The pioneer housewife must have said, "I wish there was a better way to peel these apples besides sitting here with this knife." Having made the complaint, she not only set her own creative thoughts in operation but perhaps those of her husband or sons, who came up with a gadget for peeling and coring apples.

Modern society needs people who will ask important questions and seek solutions. When people are encouraged to question and are encouraged to engage in creative thought and experimentation, problem solving and progress will come more rapidly. The questioning attitude will contribute to creative thinking whether the question deals with a household task or problems of world peace. Progress can take place only if individuals ask the question, "Couldn't we do this a better way?"

The aesthetic aspects of creativity are available to all. Individuals live more fully when they appreciate beauty, whether in nature, in work, or in human relationships.

Teachers must believe that all children have creative potential, just as they believe that children have the physical potential to grow to adulthood. That teachers' expectations of pupil performance become self-fulfilling prophecies are documented in *Pygmalion in the Classroom* by Rosenthal and Jacobson.[3] To restate an old saying— look for creativity; you will find it if you do.

The teacher's creativity is challenged in both her personal and her professional life. Every day she takes the raw material of life and through creative leadership creates her own life canvas. Each school day the teacher contributes significantly to the life canvases of the children in her class. Creative teaching requires sensitivity to people and things, to ideas and issues, to feelings and moods, to colors and textures. Community resources of time and money are coordinated with energy, ability, experience, and training. Independently and collectively, a group of children has all human potentials. Perhaps no other profession takes as many variables or as many unknowns and attempts to make a creative picture each day. Through careful planning, weighing of goals and values, combining of technique and human understanding, a teacher shapes tomorrow's citizens. Teaching is a creative task—an awesome responsibility.

[3] Robert Rosenthal and Lenore Jacobson, *Pygmalion in the Classroom* (New York: Holt, Rinehart and Winston, 1968).

Fostering Creativity Through the Arts

"The goal for art education is to use the creative process to make people more creative regardless of where their creativeness will be applied," wrote Viktor Lowenfeld in *Creative and Mental Growth*.[4] Lowenfeld and Brittain, in a later edition of that book, wrote, "Art education, as an essential part of the educative process, may well mean the difference between a flexible, creative human being and one who will not be able to apply his learning, who will lack inner resources, and who will have difficulty relating to his environment. In a well-balanced educational system, in which the development of the total being is stressed, each individual's thinking, feeling, and perceiving must be equally developed in order that his potential creative abilities can unfold." [5]

In the high-quality nursery school and kindergarten opportunities abound for children's creativity or divergent thinking to find expression. In every segment of the curriculum there is room for children to "put it together" in new ways. The teacher values the unique, spontaneous, fresh, and imaginative manner with which the child faces the challenge of learning. The child's use of art materials is a regularly offered part of the program.

The end products of the creative process, such as paintings, collages, or other works of art, may have little value in the market, yet the creative process involved is of great value to the developing child. Patterns are not used to get products that look "just so." Coloring-book-type line drawings for the child to fill in are not provided. The teacher has faith in the child. She often tells him so. She refrains from helping the child outright. She demonstrates her confidence in him time and again. She bolsters his self-confidence, encourages his experimentation, and commends the unique way in which he solves a problem.

If the teacher loses faith in the child's creative ability or falls victim to pressures to produce products, she will hurt the child and his future creativity. Henceforth, the child will wait for her idea, her "correct" way, before beginning. The child won't enjoy his products or the process.

Max is an example of a child whose creativity suffered when products were emphasized. He was a child who had creative teachers during his nursery school and kindergarten years. He used new materials with great confidence. In the first grade Max was told that

4 Viktor Lowenfeld, *Creative and Mental Growth* (New York: Macmillan, 1957), p. 5.
5 Viktor Lowenfeld and W. Lambert Brittain, *Creative and Mental Growth* (New York: Macmillan, 1970), p. 6.

FIGURE 7–3. *Finger painting gives children an opportunity to mix colors, to practice small motor skills, and to use a messy medium. (Texas Tech University Kindergarten.)*

Christmas drawings would be selected for a display in an uptown department store. Max became anxious and practiced diligently so that his drawing might be chosen. It was selected.

Upon seeing the picture, his kindergarten teacher felt something was amiss. She later commented to Max, "Max, I saw your picture in the exhibit uptown." Max responded, "Did you see those angels? My teacher did those and she ruined it." Max had enjoyed neither the process nor the product. He did not enjoy winning with help. The first-grade teacher surely got little satisfaction from displaying her work as child's art.

Fostering Perceptual-Motor Skills Through the Arts

Creativity should be reason enough for offering children a wide array of art media and for helping them find one that especially allows expression of their feelings, moods, and ideas. However, other important reasons are apparent. The skills developed through the art materials are both prewriting and prereading skills. Clearly, the

FIGURE 7–4. *Play dough gives children a medium for molding or for cutting cookies "just like mother." (Nazarene Child Care Center, Lansing, Michigan.)*

small motor skills are being developed. One has only to watch in a three-year-old class as children draw and cut, then move on to a four- or five-year-old class to see how much skill the threes can be expected to develop in the next year or two.

Eye-hand coordination is continually practiced as the hand draws a head in the "right" place or puts a wheel on a "car" in the customary spot. Picking up and placing the collage materials requires eye-hand coordination, as does squeezing the glue bottle to drop the glue in the right spot. Using scissors to cut on a line is a complicated coordination task to learn.

The art table is usually the site of the child's first attempts to write his name, which must be from left to right in our language. The teacher teaches the child to use manuscript printing (see

Chapter 1) and to start in the left-hand corner of the page in order to avoid scrambling and crowding letters, as he will if he starts too far over to the right and doesn't have enough room for all the letters. Forming those letters is clearly an early reading experience as well as a writing experience.

Through art activities children learn to concentrate their attention on the figures or designs they place on the page or background, helping them develop figure and ground concepts. Later, in writing, a child must concentrate on the black squiggles, not on the white space surrounding them. Through art media children also gain experience putting pieces together to make a whole, learning whole-part relationships. For example, when children add eyes, ears, nose, and mouth to a circle to make a face, they are learning with some precision the parts of the body. One five-year-old looked at a picture he had drawn of himself a few months earlier. The picture had six fingers on the hands. "Hum," he laughed, "I put six fingers on my hand." In only a few brief months he had become more discriminating. Now he would add the correct number of parts to his figure.

Experience with colors, their various shades and hues, is provided in most of the activities. Children easily learn the names and dis-

FIGURE 7–6. *Drawing requires concentration and thought and is a pre-writing experience in eye-hand coordination. (Southern University Nursery School.)*

cover the combinations of primary colors that make secondary colors and so on. Watch them at the finger painting table, for example, as they combine blue and yellow. "Look! Teacher! Teacher! I made green!" shouts Cindy.

Concepts of shape are also required in reading and are common among the art materials. Shapes are cut out, drawn, compared, and named. Likenesses and differences in shapes are frequently discussed. "I want some shiny squares like yours," said Jack. "Here," said Todd handing him a piece. "No, I want gold shiny squares, not silver shiny squares." said Jack.

Stages

Self-expression, as with other areas of development, has its typical ages and stages. When the teacher and parent understand the various levels, they can help, not hinder, the child's creative growth. In *Creative and Mental Growth* Lowenfeld and Brittain describe several stages of particular importance to teachers of young children.[6] Knowing these developmental stages will help teachers (1) plan art activities at an appropriate level; (2) set an appropriate level of expectations for children; (3) appreciate children's drawings and art projects; and (4) have an appropriate basis for discussing children's art with parents.

SCRIBBLE STAGE. The scribble stage is the first stage described by Lowenfeld and Brittain. The child's first scribbles are random and disordered. He progresses to controlled scribbling, then finally mixes horizontal, vertical, and circular motions and enters the named scribble stage. At this stage the child can think of an object to represent but as yet is unable to draw it. The several scribble stages cover the second to the fourth year. However, if an older child has had no opportunity to use art materials, he passes through this sequence before going on to the next.

It is natural for anyone faced with a new art material to experiment in a scribbling or "disordered" fashion. This impulse should be understood and permitted when children work with new materials.

PRESCHEMATIC STAGE. The preschematic stage occurs from the fourth to the seventh year. In this stage the child achieves his first representation, usually a head. He becomes excited and is highly satisfied with his success. He begins consciously to create forms. Circles and rectangles are the first forms he makes. The child will fill the spaces very carefully. He gains the same practice that advocates of coloring books say the child gets from filling in ready-made spaces. However, when he encloses a space himself, that space has personal meaning for him. He creates out of his own experience. He expresses an idea that *he* wants to express.

SCHEMATIC STAGE. The schematic stage, described by Lowenfeld and Brittain for the seven- to nine-year-old, may sometimes be seen in classes of five- and six-year-olds who have had many opportunities to observe and create. In this stage the child focuses his attention on drawing a human figure—usually himself or his family. With experience, the parts of the human figure take on more realistic proportions, and the child begins to place his figures on a baseline— grass, ground, or sidewalk. The child in this stage is not ready to produce depth in his drawings. According to Harris, the more details the child puts into his picture the more intellectual and perceptual growth one can assume is taking place.[7] The amount of repetition or

[6] Ibid., pp. 91–187.
[7] D. B. Harris, *Children's Drawings as Measures of Intellectual Maturity* (A Revision and Extension of Goodenough Draw-a-Man Test) (New York: Harcourt, Brace & World, 1963).

FIGURE 7–7.   *Drawings provide information about each child's level of representation. The above array, done in private sessions, is typical of a four-year-old group near the end of the school year. The numbers refer to the child's age in years and months. Drawings range from the scribble stage to the schematic stage including a base line. The teacher asked, "Draw a man, the best man you know how."*

exaggeration of a theme can guide the teacher in understanding the child's emotional growth. Social growth is indicated by the themes the child's work takes and how much the themes are related to his actual experience.

The child's creative growth can be inferred from the number of independent themes he produces and whether or not he seems to be imitating other children. Physical growth may be indicated by his skill with tools and by his exaggeration of some body part and the vigorousness of his participation.

Children may occasionally regress to previous levels of artistic behavior just as they may regress emotionally. When attempting to understand or to explain a child's art products, one should be careful not to draw conclusions from an inadequate sample of a child's work or from scanty knowledge about the child's experience.

Arlie, for example, worried many observers because he painted a solid sheet of black. However, the teacher was not alarmed, because she often heard Arlie talk about the fire that burned the garage next door to his home. The teacher knew that the fire had been an alarming event in the neighborhood. She allowed Arlie to paint. Finally, one day Arlie painted his paper yellow. He reported that the painters had used yellow paint to paint the neighbor's garage. Arlie's opportunity to paint as he chose for all those days undoubtedly relieved him of tensions associated with the fire.

Pete's mother worried because her five-year-old was drawing armless human figures. In a discussion with the teacher the mother realized that she had seen only a couple of pictures in which he had tried to draw human figures. The teacher also explained to Pete's mother that it was not unusual for Pete to be enticed away from the drawing table by another child or by another activity before his drawing was finished. The teacher might discuss the armless drawings with Pete, asking, "What is the man doing?" "What does your man need to throw a ball?" Such questions would help him think of the relationship between activities and body parts.

General Classroom Procedures

Atmosphere

An atmosphere of freedom is important if the child is to develop his creative potential. Children who feel free to try new ways of using materials will be more creative than children who are taught there is only one right way to do everything. From the very first day the teacher must allow her children to be experimental. She believes and says, "I know you have ideas. Let's see how many different pictures we can make." If her faith falters or she gives children patterns, then the children will wait for the teacher's intervention every day.

To say there is freedom does not mean the teacher does not have rules. She logically limits the location of the messy activity to where it can be cleaned up. She sets rules about splashing paints, dropping clay, and washing hands.

An uncritical atmosphere will help the child feel safe, secure, and unthreatened by the teacher, his peers, or his family. Expectations should be kept at a reasonable level so that the child can hope to succeed. Children will set their own pace. In any class there will be a wide range of abilities; therefore materials must be suited to this wide range. For example, in a three- or four-year-old group the stages will range from scribbling to preschematic. Caution should be taken to protect the child's right to "just paint."

When commenting to a child, it is best to say, "Would you like to tell me about your picture?" rather than to guess what the child is painting. Too many questions may invite casual naming that may not have much relationship to the original ideas. For example, Doug alarmed his father because he always reported having painted a "monster." The father asked the teacher about the paintings, and she recalled quite a different theme during Doug's time at the easel. Apparently Doug was pleased with the increased attention this picture title drew from his father.

The teacher protects the child from the criticism of his peers. She verbally sets the stage for acceptance of all children's creations. "We each can paint what we are thinking" and "Each of us sees an object a little differently" are examples of comments she can make to set the stage for individuality. The teacher displays something from everyone. As some children do like to take art products home, it is well for the teacher to ask permission to keep a painting for display. She refrains from choosing only the "best" for exhibit. She avoids arousing competition between children. She keeps her hands off children's products no matter how much she might think she could improve them.

Parental criticism of a child's art can be devastating. Therefore the teacher makes efforts to communicate to parents the expected standards and the level of their child's creative development. For example, reassuring parents that scribbling is typical of their Johnny's age group and that other children in the group are scribbling, too, helps the parents become more accepting of Johnny's products. Parents may have to be alerted so that they can curb older siblings' criticisms or efforts to improve a young child's products.

Not infrequently a young child competes with a school-age sibling.

The young child may carelessly splash paint on many pages to have as many products to show his parents as his school-age sibling brings home. When this happens, parents may then be counseled to lay out the array of paintings and let the child choose his favorite. This technique can help steer the child away from mass production and back onto a track of self-expression. However, the problem of sibling rivalry is also one the parent may need help with. Some young children react to home competition by refusing to create any product the teacher might encourage them to take home. Parents may pressure the child to bring something home. When he spends his day playing with blocks or cooperating in the doll house, he has nothing to take home. Parents need this information so that they do not over-value art products.

The teacher should feel obligated to provide painting aprons that help protect children's clothing. The parents' complaints at home about messy clothing will adversely affect the child's creative expression. The wise teacher will guide parents in choosing appropriate clothing for the child to wear to school in order that he can participate fully in all activities.

In case of an unusual amount of spilling, the teacher can advise parents about helpful laundry procedures. When sending home children's painted or glued products, the teacher should take care that smearing of clothes and cars en route home is avoided. Some products can be sent in paper bags and others rolled together and held by a rubberband. Such measures may sound overprotective of parents; however, some empathy on the teacher's part results in better co-operation from parents.

Children who feel skillful and self-confident will make the most effort to be creative. Therefore a teacher should give children opportunities to practice skills. Teachers should create an environment in which the child feels safe to practice a new skill. The child should receive instruction when he asks or seems mature enough to benefit from it. Such skills as holding a crayon, cutting with scissors, using the stapler, tying a bow, or squeezing the glue bottle may profitably be demonstrated to a child who is ready to learn them. Most small motor skills contribute eventually to writing skill. Self-confidence is fostered through the mastery of skills.

Organizing the Art Centers

Most art materials are presented in nursery school and kindergarten during the indoor self-selected activity period. In mild climates art materials should be moved outdoors. Having a smorgasbord of art materials available along with other activities enables a child to create when he wants to and enables the teacher to work with small groups of children. With a wide variety of materials no one activity attracts all the children at one time. They naturally move to learning centers that attract their attention. After satisfying their need, they move to another center. They may be stimulated by the attractiveness of the center per se or to a valued friend who happens to be interested in that activity. The wise teacher will make the art centers as much self-service from the children's standpoint as she can. Children enjoy independence. When not tied too closely to one center, the teacher is freer to assist in other centers as needed.

The activities of the art center often require using water and washing hands. The logical location of the art center is near the water supply. An ideal situation is to have a low sink in the art center in order to keep the children from running to the bathroom with paint-covered hands and aprons. A dishpan or a bucket of water can substitute for some of the needed water if a sink is not available. Remember to bring along the paper towels.

An area for drying products is required—preferably one that the children can use themselves. Newspapers under drying racks or shelves can eliminate difficult cleanup problems later on.

If supplies are carefully stored and labeled, the teacher can get needed items in a hurry. The stage can be set so that the children can help with cleaning up the art center. They wash easels, brushes, and tables with as much enthusiasm as they paint—sometimes with more enthusiasm.

Children will use art materials spontaneously and incorporate them into other play if they are stored on an open shelf where they can reach them without asking for assistance. Newsprint, colored mimeograph paper, crayons, scissors, bottles of glue, stapler, paper punch, felt pens, masking tape, and string are items children use frequently. Two examples support this idea. The five-year-olds had just returned from a trip to a farm. They were getting their drinks and discussing all they had seen. Sherry quietly walked to the art center, found materials, and created a pig in a basket. Both were made from paper in three dimensions. Sherry used the scissors and stapler. Her spontaneous creation showed clearly what Sherry had liked best about the trip.

Four-year-olds were playing store. A child expressed a need for money in the cash register. One enterprising young man hastened to the art center, cut green mimeograph paper into squares, and returned to set himself up as a banker, giving money to the housewives who were shopping at the store.

Places to display children's art products should be available throughout the room. Art gives the room a personal, colorful appearance. The objects should be changed frequently to keep the interest high. Children lose interest in their own products quickly and may not even want to claim them a day or so after working on them. When a child seems to have a special need to take products home, the teacher can ask the child if he would like to make something special to put up in the display. If he indicates he would not, then of course it isn't important to him.

Planning so that the art center is efficiently arranged encourages the children's use of the center and facilitates the teacher's supervision. Following are suggestions of materials and procedures that can be used in presenting the art smorgasbord to groups of young children.

Painting

EASEL PAINTING.   Easel painting is an enjoyable activity for young children and most teachers feel it should be available every day. Such painting helps the child develop his motor skills. He is able to express his concepts and his feelings. He learns to judge space size and to fill the space. He learns about colors and lines.

Tempera paints in either liquid or powdered form are available from art shops and school supply houses. A cup of liquid starch mixed in a quart of water used to mix dry tempera will prevent the watery consistency caused by the settling out of the paint. Watery paint is unpopular with children. About a quart of each color should be mixed and stored to be ready when needed. For very young children one primary color at the easel at a time is sufficient. As they gain skill and show interest in more color, then all of the primary colors are added. Older children will enjoy variety in the paint, including brown and black. Pastels delight children and are made by the addition of color to white. White paint is popular when colored paper is available. Jars or disposable plastic or styrofoam cups may be used for paints. Disposables save a tedious washing chore.

Brushes to use at the easel should be a long-handled (12-inch) variety that allows a full shoulder stroke. A stiff bristle is best. A variety of brush sizes is appreciated by older children.

Mixing or stirring paint with brushes breaks off the bristles. To avoid damaging brushes, care should be exercised in the washing and drying of brushes. A useful aid in washing and drying brushes can be made from the bottom half of a plastic milk bottle. Puncture the bottom with holes so that water will run through, then place the brushes in the container and set it under running water for a few minutes. The paint on the brushes will soak loose. Place the brushes to dry, handles down, in a storage container. Washing the easel brushes is a popular activity with children. Perhaps it runs a close second to clapping the erasers!

Several styles of easels are available commercially. Also, excellent ones can be homemade. A board can be hung along a wall to be used for an easel. A 4-inch wedge at the bottom will hold the board out from the wall and give the board an appropriate angle. Or two masonite boards can be hinged and held folded as a triangle with a metal strap. This easel can be used at the table. You can also make easels from large cardboard boxes by cutting through them diagonally. Paper is held with large tack pins. Painting paper can be placed on the wall, the table, the floor, or the sidewalk. The easels used should be the correct height for young children. Easel legs can be sawed off to an appropriate height.

Painting on large sheets of newsprint with the large brushes is suggested for young children. Large materials encourage the use of their large muscles and accommodate their large designs. A minimum of 20″ × 27″ is suggested. Paper cut to size is available from school supply houses. Some newspaper shops will cut newsprint for the school. Other publishers may donate roll ends to the school. If donations are common at the school, a paper cutter such as is used for cutting wrapping paper in stores might be a good investment. A cutter speeds the preparation of the paper.

Manila paper 12″ × 18″ is appropriate for some painting. Colored paper is available and is especially delightful with white paints on a snowy day. For variety, textured paper such as the back of embossed wallpaper is interesting. Outdated wallpaper sample books can be secured from wallpaper companies. Printed newspapers can be used occasionally. Large shapes like pumpkins or hearts can be cut out and used for painting to add further variety.

Attention must be given to attaching the easel paper to the easel. The common manner of using clamps or clothespins is not satisfactory because young children can't operate the clamps without dropping the paper. Some easels have two smooth-headed nails placed about 24 inches apart at the top of the easel. The newsprint is then punched with a paper punch so that the holes match the nails. A day's supply of paper can be hung on the easel. Each child can then easily remove his paper when he is finished and hang the painting to dry. He is more self-sufficient, having taken care of the job himself. The busy teacher is helped at the same time. Paper supplies should be stored close by the painting area.

Easel painting is very popular and is commonly planned on a daily basis. A stampede of painters results when easel painting is offered infrequently. Regular usage helps avoid complicated problems of sharing. Children who desire to produce a detailed painting or several paintings need not be rushed to finish. Closure or completion is an important aspect to encourage in creative people. Thus allowing a child to finish a product to his satisfaction is important if we are to foster a habit of becoming finishers as well as starters. The child who wants to paint and is required to wait can be reassured that paints will be available the next school day.

There is good reason to place easels side by side so that children can socialize as they paint. They may share both paints and ideas. If easels are available daily, two easels are usually sufficient for a group of twenty children. More places to paint will be necessary if painting is planned only occasionally.

Guidance may be required to encourage children to squeeze their brushes against the side of the jar—especially if the teacher notes that the child is disturbed by the drips. Teachers can encourage the use of the same brush for each color by saying, "Keep the red brush in the red paint." Children's names are printed at the top of the painting in manuscript letters to help identify paintings, to stress the importance of the child's name, and to teach him eventually to recognize his name.

Custodians will appreciate the use of a speckled throw rug under the easels to catch the occasional drips. Throw rugs are easily washed and are more aesthetic than newspapers.

Suitable paint aprons can be made from cottonbacked plastic. (See Figure 7–8.) The edges need no finishing. The neck strap of elastic and ties of cotton tape are quickly attached by sewing machine. Some schools use men's shirts for painting smocks. Big brother's shirts are a better size for children under six than are men's sizes.

It is well to pour only a small amount of paint in the paint jars for a class of young painters. With close observation for a few days teachers can judge the approximate amount of paint needed for a session. Children normally overlay one color on the others when making their paintings. Overlaying is not to be discouraged, because children learn about the mixing of colors this way. They frequently forget, or as yet don't understand, about matching up the brush in hand with the color from which it came, so that further mixing results. Mixing and matching are, of course, two of the important learnings from the painting experience. Even though the teacher knows paints will get mixed up, she should feel obligated to start with clear colors each day. If she starts with a small amount of paint and replenishes it as needed, the wasting of paint is avoided and clear colors are more likely.

If children are painting a mural on the floor, the wall, or a table, or if makeshift easels do not have the usual tray for holding paint jars, then some arrangement should be made to prevent paint jars from tipping over. Muffin tins can be used to hold jars containing paint. A cardboard serving tray from the drive-in hamburger stand is just

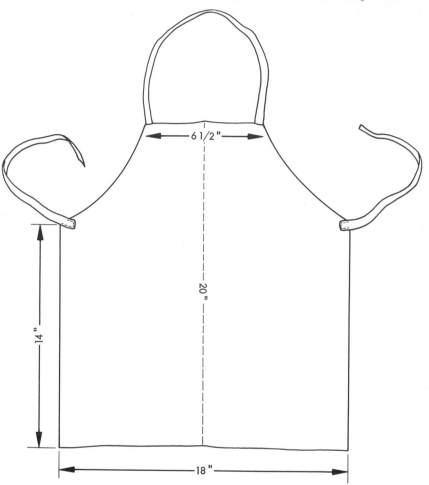

FIGURE 7–8. *An easy-to-make painting apron made of cotton-backed plastic with an elastic neck strap and cotton tape ties.*

right to hold paint jars. Simply place the paint jars where soft-drink bottles are usually set. A similar holder can be cut from a cardboard box.

STRING PAINTING.   The same mixture of tempera paint as discussed above is used for string painting. The child holds one end of a 15-inch string, such as twine, yarn, or thread, and drops the string into the paint. Slowly he pulls out the string and lets the paint drip off. The wet string is moved around on the paper to make various patterns. Several colors can be available, with different strings in each color.

For variation the child may pull the string through folded paper.

For example, he arranges the paint-covered strings on one half. He folds over the paper. Holding the folded paper together, he pulls the dry end of the string with his free hand. Interesting variations in designs result. The child observes the shading and blending of colors.

BLOCK PRINTING. The same mixture of tempera paint is used for block printing. A shallow pan is used to arrange stamp pads of various colors. Pads are cut of several layers of paper towel, cheesecloth, or thin sponge and saturated with color. There should be only enough paint to leave color on the object without dripping. Prints can be made from a variety of objects, such as clothespins, a potato masher, a sponge, vegetables, toys, pieces of wood, and spools. Children enjoy making prints from designs cut in potato halves.

You may make rollers by dipping heavy strings in glue and wrapping them around tubes from paper towels. When the glue is dry, roll the roller on a paint pad, then roll it across paper. Fingers too make interesting designs. In fact, children may see any painting activity as an opportunity for finger painting—a response that teachers should be prepared to accept.

SQUEEZE-BOTTLE PAINTING. Squeeze bottles with small openings are available with everything, from soap to mustard. Teachers save such bottles to fill with tempera paint. Using the bottle tip as a painting tool makes an acceptable substitute for dribbling the white glue that children seem inclined to do. Practice in using the squeeze bottle helps the child control the amount of paint he uses. Tempera is used with manila or construction paper. The children use the bottle tip to draw their design. They may like to place drips of color on the paper, then fold the paper. Unusual designs are discovered as they unfold the paper. Shoe polish bottles and roll-on deodorant bottles can be used in a similar fashion.

SPLATTER PAINTING. Splatter painting is done by the brushing of a paint-filled toothbrush across a wire screen. A kitchen strainer works fine for a screen. You can also make a screen by attaching a square of window screen to a wooden frame of about 6 inches to 8 inches square. The child places his paper on the table. Then he places an object such as a leaf or a key on the paper. Over this goes the screen. The child brushes the paint-filled toothbrush back and forth, getting the splatter effect around the outline of the object. A similar finished product is accomplished when a small sponge dipped in paint is used to stipple around the object.

BLOT PAINTING. Blot painting is the result when paper is folded in half and the child then brushes, squeezes, or strings paint on one side of the fold. The paper is then folded back over the painted side, and the palm of the hand is rubbed across the paper. Children enjoy the surprise of the blending and duplicating effect.

SAND OR SAWDUST PAINTING. Sand or sawdust is mixed with moist tempera. A shaker with large holes is used to shake the mixture onto paper covered with paste. Sand painting is best done out of doors to avoid difficult cleaning problems.

OBJECT PAINTING. Using the tempera to paint wood and box collages and carpentry projects is a worthwhile conclusion to three-dimensional projects. Children enjoy painting props for their dramatic play, such as a cardboard train or a valentine mailbox.

COLOR ABSORPTION. A thin solution of tempera or vegetable coloring is placed in a small dish. Several colors are provided. The child folds paper towels or squares of old sheeting and dips corners into the various colors. Children will be fascinated by the blending and shading of colors. A surface well padded with newspaper is necessary for drying these drippy products.

FINGER PAINTING. Finger painting provides both an outlet for children's creativity and a medium for messing. This latter objective is important because modern children are often under a great deal of parental pressure to stay clean. Designs with finger paint can be made, erased, and made again. Personal problem areas can be expressed, then obliterated with one stroke—a behavior that gives evidence that finger painting has therapeutic value. The medium is highly relaxing for children. Children learn concepts through their experimentation with the mixing and blending of colors. Pictures are rarely a pure color because children can't resist trying to find out what happens if they add a little blue here or a little yellow there. Teachers and parents should not be disturbed that paintings turn out a uniform muddy color. The only way to obtain pictures of pure color is to limit the choice to one color. If the child knows there are several colors available, he will certainly feel deprived if he is not allowed to choose from all of them and mix them together.

The majority of children will enjoy finger painting. The teacher may encourage the children to participate by sitting with them and actually manipulating the paint as she talks to them. Seeing the teacher get her hands in the paint will reassure the doubters that she really means that it is all right to get messy. The teacher may involve a hesitant child by permitting him to help mix the paint with a beater or a spoon. However, some children prefer to watch for a long time and may never feel comfortable with finger paints. They should, of course, not be forced to finger-paint.

If finger paints are provided frequently, there is less necessity for the teacher to permit large numbers of children to finger-paint on a given day—which would make supervision difficult. From the practical side it is much easier to have five children painting on four different days than to try to manage finger painting for twenty on one day. It is well to limit the number of painters to a number the teacher can supervise and still keep an eye on the other activities in the room. Actually some teachers store the finger paints where children can help themselves whenever they desire to paint. The less pressure there is to give many people turns, the more satisfying the experience will be for the individual child.

Of course, the only tool needed for finger painting is the child's hands. The child gets full shoulder and arm movement from his standing position. He can use hands, knuckles, fingernails, and even the whole lower arm to produce various effects. Questions like "How does it look if you use the side of your hand?" will encourage the child to experiment.

Music with soothing rhythms is especially appropriate while the children are finger painting. If the teacher plays staccato music, she shouldn't be surprised that the children splash the paint all around.

There are five necessities for finger painting—finger paints, a place to paint, aprons, a place to wash up, and a place to dry paintings.

Finger paints can be obtained commercially or mixed in the nursery school or kindergarten. Two types are available commercially: one is the consistency of a thick paste; the other is a powder that the child shakes onto the wet paper from a shaker-type container. The young child likes lots of paint per picture and enjoys making many pictures. Commercial finger paints are quite expensive when provided in the amount that is necessary in the average class. Therefore a less expensive material is usually essential. Homemade products fulfill all the objectives of the medium. However, the exception is the quality of the finished picture. If a finger painting is desired for a placemat or a book cover, the teacher can use the commercial paint on that occasion.

RECIPES FOR HOMEMADE FINGER PAINT

INSTANTIZED-FLOUR UNCOOKED METHOD (TIME: Three Minutes)

Mix in a large bowl:
1 pint water
1½ cups instantized flour (a food product for thickening gravy)

Put the water in the bowl and stir the flour into the water. Add color.

WHEAT-PASTE OR WALLPAPER-PASTE UNCOOKED METHOD (TIME: Three Minutes)

Mix in a large bowl:
1 pint water
1¼ cups dry wallpaper paste

Put the water in the bowl. Using a quick stirring motion with one hand, pour in dry wallpaper paste with the other. Keep stirring and adding paste until the proper thickness is achieved. Pour into jars and stir in tempera paint for color. A drop or two of wintergreen (purchased in a drugstore) will disguise the odor of the mixture if it seems unpleasant. *Caution:* Some wallpaper pastes have a chemical that has a mouse deterrent, so teachers should be sure the materials do not contain chemicals harmful to children.

COOKED-STARCH METHOD (TIME: Ten Minutes Plus Cooling Time)

Mix in a large bowl:
1 cup laundry starch or cornstarch dissolved in a small amount of cold water
5 cups boiling water added slowly to dissolved starch

Cook the mixture until it is thick and glossy. Add 1 cup mild soap flakes. Add color in separate containers. Cool before using.

LIQUID-STARCH METHOD (TIME: None)

Give the children a tablespoon of liquid starch. Let them shake tempera on with a salt shaker. (If you feel this is wasteful of the paint supply, then mix the color in the starch before presenting it to the children.)

SOAP-FLAKE METHOD (TIME: Ten Minutes)

Mix in a small bowl:
Soap flakes
A small amount of water

Beat until stiff with an eggbeater. Use white soap on dark paper, or add color to the soap and use it on light-colored paper. Gives a slight three-dimensional effect.

Finger painting may be done on paper, on trays, or directly on the table. Suitable paper is of a glossy variety available in 20″ × 24″ sizes from school supply companies. Shelf paper and pages from glossy magazines can be substituted. Painting directly on wet trays, heavy plastic, oilcloth, or a wet table is practical because young children gain much of their satisfaction from the finger-painting process and little from the resulting picture. Some parents have reported allowing their child to use a soap-base finger paint on the tile wall around the bathtub. The tub and the child are quickly cleaned when the shower is turned on. These latter suggestions do save the cost of the paper and the problems of wetting the paper and drying the paintings. A suggested variation is to let the child paint on the table or tray and then make a print of his final design by covering the painted surface with a sheet of paper and smoothing the paper with the palm of the hand. As the paper is peeled back, the transferred design is revealed. Printed newspaper gives an interesting effect when used for these prints.

Aprons are essential if the children are to participate freely and not receive criticism at home for soiled clothing. Aprons are discussed in detail in the section on easel painting in this chapter. Teachers can instruct the children to push up their sleeves. When the children wear their paint-splattered aprons as they go to wash their hands, paint will rub off on the edge of the sink as they reach forward to turn on the water. The teacher can remind the children to use the sponge to wash off the front of the sink so that the next child using it won't get his clothing covered with paint. Children frequently enjoy the cleanup as much as or more than the painting activity.

Drying space for finger paintings is a problem in nearly every school. A folding wooden rack (a clotheshorse) such as a homemaker uses for drying clothes and household linen may be satisfactory, or a clothesline, a shelf, a table, or the floor can be used. The children will use a great deal of paint if the amount is not limited by the teacher. The paintings will be excessively wet and may have to be laid flat to dry. Drying areas should be protected by a layer of newspaper, because the starch material used to make finger paints sticks like glue and is therefore difficult to clean up. When the teacher plans ahead, cleaning up after finger painting is not difficult.

If the children paint on trays or on the table, a container to hold the used paint may be necessary. A rubber spatula or a wooden tongue blade from the nurse's station is useful for scraping up paint. Trays and plastic table coverings are readily washed under the faucet.

When the teacher establishes a routine and has everything ready before the children arrive, the finger-paint project will go smoothly. Materials can be organized in an assembly-line fashion. For example, a table should contain a stack of glossy paper stacked upside down so that names can be written on the back, a dark crayon for writing names, a dishpan with enough water for wetting the paper, and sponges and a bucket of water for cleaning up. With guidance from the teacher the children can learn to handle the preparation and drying of their finger-painting paper themselves.

Teachers commonly complain that finger paints are "too messy" or that children or furnishings get paint all over them. Careful organization eliminates some of these complaints. To minimize messy problems, it helps to cover the table with several layers of newspaper; then when one child uses a large amount of paint that oozes over the side of his paper, you can easily prepare his place for the next child by peeling off a layer of newspaper. Also, less mess results if the children stand up to paint. Without thinking, children will handle chairs with paint-covered hands, so chairs should be removed. The teacher may choose to wear a long apron to eliminate concern that children will touch her skirt or that her skirt will accidentally brush against the paint table.

FOOT PAINTING.   Foot painting is a variation of finger painting that you might like to try on a warm spring or summer day when the children are wearing light shoes and shorts and you can work outside without shoes. The children will have the unusual experience of seeing their footprints and perhaps creating designs on a paper or on the sidewalk. This project might create real havoc inside a classroom unless many adults are present to help with shoes and other problems that do not occur outdoors on warm days. Outdoors the garden hose can be of great help in cleaning up the painters' feet and the painting area.

Drawing

Drawing offers the child a prewriting experience. Using a tool, he gains experience making lines and filling in the spaces. He develops small muscle coordination in order to control the tool. The stages discussed earlier also apply to this technique. Drawing is likely to be more familiar than other techniques when children enter school.

CRAYONS.   Crayons are probably the art medium most familiar to children. If a child has any art material at home, he surely will have crayons. Crayons give the child a medium that expresses his creativity and permits him to see clearly the results of the movement of his tool. In comparison with other media crayons make it harder for a small child to obtain depth of color without prolonged effort and are therefore somewhat unsatisfactory. By unwrapping the paper from the crayon, the child can use the side as well as the tip of the crayon. Some of the new types of crayons are softer and make it easier for the child to obtain depth of color. Children enjoy the type of crayon that is dipped in water as it is used.

FIGURE 7–9. *Tracing within stencils gives children practice in small motor skills. (University of Idaho Nursery School.)*

Because crayons are likely to be familiar, the teacher often plans the use of this medium during the first days of school. The teacher wants the child to feel at home and begin participating freely. He is more likely to do so if he sees materials he knows.

Children should be allowed to create their own designs on newsprint, manila paper, or colored mimeograph paper. Coloring-book-type material stifles the child's creativity and is not recommended. A teacher should have confidence in the child's ability to create his own designs—and to fill in the color within his own borders. She can encourage him to explore with various types of lines and shapes. Crayon prints can be made if a flat object—a leaf, a penny, or a piece of lace—is placed under the paper, which the child covers with color, using the side of the crayon.

CRAYON RESIST.   Crayon resist is a technique of making a drawing in crayon, then painting over the design with a thin wash of water color. Especially effective is a white wash on black or blue paper or a black wash over Halloween pumpkins. This technique works best with fives and sixes, who will be willing to overlay their drawings with several layers of crayon. Without the thick layer of wax the resist effect doesn't work. The wash is a thinned tempera paint. The teacher should experiment with the materials before she presents them to the children.

FELT PENS.   Felt pens come in many colors and some have washable ink, making them appropriate for use with young children. Though these are a more expensive medium, they may well encourage learning activity by some children who are not happy with other media. The colors are intense and come off easily. Teaching children to cap their pens tightly after use will help make the ink last longer.

CHALK.   Using chalk on the chalkboard gives the child another drawing medium. It too is a worthwhile prewriting experience. A chalkboard can be made from a wall or a piece of plywood or heavy cardboard painted with blackboard paint. (It need not be black.) Chalks in many colors are available. Children will enjoy the large pastel chalks because the color comes off readily. Pastels come in bright colors and are about 4 inches long and an inch thick.

Wet chalk is a creative medium that the child uses on paper. The pastel chalks (mentioned above) are used on manila construction paper. Wrapping-paper murals are interesting when done with this chalk. The paper is dipped in water; then the child draws with his chalk. Buttermilk is sometimes used to moisten the paper and gives a shiny effect when dry. Because of the size of the chalk the child is able to make large motions and large objects in his drawings. Children like this medium because they get deep color quickly.

Pastels also work well for making murals using large paper tacked to the wall or spread on the floor or a table.

Children need aprons. They occasionally see wet chalk as another finger paint. The table is more easily cleaned up if it is covered with newspaper. A drying area is required. Care should be taken when you are sending chalk drawings home, because chalk will rub off on clothing and car upholstery, making parents unhappy. It is sometimes convenient to roll the drawings and secure them with a rubberband. A fixitive can be sprayed on the drawings to keep the chalk from rubbing off.

Gluing, Cutting, and Tearing

A collage is an artistic composition of fragments of paper and other material. The word comes from a French word meaning "gluing." The opportunity to be creative with odds and ends of "junk" is very popular with young children. They develop skills while using the scissors, glue bottles, and paste brushes. They develop eye-hand co-ordination; a sense of balance, size, color, and proportion; and a sense of the third dimension (depth).

The collage invites creativity even by adults because they have a habit of seeing a creative use for many things one might throw away. What can one do with those colorful bags that department stores put your purchases in? Those perfume and makeup boxes? Or the towel and toilet paper rolls? Your roommate or spouse will probably be dismayed as you hoard such "junk" for creative art activities, so plan early to organize the materials and minimize the fire hazard and the clutter. In a time of high costs and pollution, recycling is of in-creasing importance—and you get fine materials for children's art activities without cost. In one day-care center the children who were pasting pieces of cold breakfast cereal on collages might have been better off if the cereal had been served to them with milk. Art uses made of clean, edible foods can be costly and wasteful.

TEARING AND CUTTING. Tearing and cutting are two methods of preparing material for the collage. Young children simply enjoy an opportunity to tear and cut. Well before the child can manipulate the scissors, he is able to tear paper into bits. Every mother remem-bers a time when her child tore up the unread newspaper or ripped a favorite magazine. Children can be encouraged to tear paper for their art work. Even after they can use the scissors, they may like to use the tearing method to obtain certain effects. Cutting with scissors requires finer eye-hand coordination and more mature motor skills than does tearing. Older children who have not had experience with scissors will pass through a stage of awkwardness in using them. Older children benefit from suggestions as to how to use scissors more than do younger children. Both groups seem to need ample time to experiment with scissors until they discover a satisfactory way to hold and use them.

Blunt-end scissors should be provided. They should be kept free of paste and glue and in good operating condition. Nothing is so frustrating as scissors that don't cut. The teacher should try scissors out occasionally to be sure they are usable.

Left-handed scissors should be purchased for the left-handed chil-dren. This fact seems to surprise some people, but a right-handed teacher need only try to use right-handed scissors with her left hand to see why left-handed children have difficulty cutting with them. They can't see the line that they are trying to cut unless they hold their work far to the right so they can see over the blade of the scissors. Some left-handed scissors come with colored handles to aid children in distinguishing them from right-handed ones. If they are not clearly marked, the teacher may tie colored yarn to the handles of the left-handed scissors.

If a child has difficulty learning to cut with a scissors a teacher may want to try double ring training scissors. This scissors has an extra set of rings allowing the teacher's hand to fit over the child's hand helping him develop the cutting technique.

It is interesting for children to experiment with cutting different lines—jagged, wavy, straight, fringed, or some combination of these. Kindergarteners will enjoy cutting strips of lightweight paper and curling them with the edge of the scissors' blade. These curls may be used to decorate various objects. Old magazines provide a stimulus to the young cutter. He can choose one type of object to look for— i.e., cars, food for Thanksgiving dinner, toys, animals, or babies. However, adults should not be surprised when he gets sidetracked and cuts out other interesting objects.

The light weight of colored mimeograph paper makes it especially useful for free cutting by young children. Mimeograph paper is easier to fold and cut than construction paper. Also, five sheets of mimeograph paper cost the same as one sheet of construction paper. Scraps of leftover paper can be prepared for collage work. When the teacher plans to let the children practice cutting—say, hearts—squares of paper can be prepared ahead of time to enable the children to get several objects per page. When it is left up to the child, he will cut his object out of the center of the large sheet, leaving the remainder for scrap.

GLUING OR PASTING.   Gluing or pasting is a skill children learn to help them complete their collages. Children may at first manipulate the paste or glue much as they do finger paint. They use excessive amounts when judged by adult standards. Using the white glue in squeeze bottles is very interesting to children. They often use this glue as a white paint, making designs on their paper. To curb this use of glue the teacher can give the children white tempera paint in plastic squeeze bottles to be used for making designs. Occasionally the teacher can demonstrate the amount of glue required by saying, "The white glue is very strong. See, it takes only a tiny spot to hold this big piece of paper." Sometimes such a demonstration helps reduce the amount of glue children use. Because white glue holds more securely than paste, it is better to give children white glue for structures that have considerable weight or strain. When cherished objects fall apart, it is very frustrating to children. White glue can be purchased in gallon bottles, then transferred to a smaller squeeze bottle with a large opening, such as those used for mustard. For some projects white glue can be diluted with water and brushed with paste brushes. Some white glues wash out of clothing.

Paste can be made with flour and water. It can also be bought in quantity. Since paste dries quickly, it should be kept covered as much as possible. Children may like brushes or sticks to use with paste.

The variety of materials for collage is limited only by the imagination of the teacher and the children. The home, the yard, the workshop, the park, or construction sites are places to look for castoff materials suitable for three-dimensional art projects. The teacher's role is to see that there is an interesting assortment of materials, and the children's creativity will do the rest. Most of the materials can be castoffs—helping ease the strain on the center's budget. Labeled shoe boxes or coffee cans containing collage materials help keep cupboards tidy and materials easily obtainable.

Suggested materials are

1. Acorns.
2. Beans, peas, and seeds—shelled or in the pod.
3. Bird gravel.
4. Boxes, tubes, and egg cartons from the kitchen.
5. Cellophane and tissue paper.
6. Confetti.
7. Corn—start with corn on the cob. Let the children shell it.
8. Cotton, cloth, wool, yarn, and fur.
9. Cupcake papers and candy cups from boxed candy.
10. Doilies (paper).
11. Eggshells—colored or white, to cover collages or to be glued to bottles for vases.
12. Excelsior or other packing material.
13. Feathers.
14. Glitter.
15. Grass, twigs, leaves, flowers.
16. Gummed paper, stamps, and holiday stickers.
17. Macaroni—shells, curls, and rings. Large rings may be strung for beads.
18. Magazines and catalogs.
19. Match sticks, toothpicks, popsicle sticks, or tongue blades.
20. Paper cups—the cone-shaped cups are especially interesting.
21. Paper scraps, construction paper, wrapping paper, holiday cards, foils, wallpaper, corrugated paper.
22. Nutshells.
23. Precut shapes—hearts, diamonds, squares, triangles, and circles.
24. Sawdust and wood shavings.
25. Salt or sand colored with tempera.

26. Spools and wood pieces.
27. Straws (drinking).
28. Strips of newspaper or magazines.
29. Styrofoam curls and pieces.
30. Wire and pipe cleaners.

THREE-DIMENSIONAL ART.   Sculptures made with three-dimensional materials form another type of collage. Box art is one form; the children create their structures from an assortment of disposable containers, such as boxes and tubes. Scraps of wood offer another texture and can be glued together to form designs of the children's choosing. Wood scraps can be obtained from carpentry and cabinet shops. White glue is essential for these structures. After drying, these art objects can be painted.

Modeling

Plastic modeling materials give children another medium for creative self-expression. The form changes as the child uses the material. Material such as ceramic clay, play dough, plasticene, salt ceramic, sawdust with wheat paste, and sand are common materials for modeling. Children enjoy the opportunity to be messy with these materials. Children can change the material and can add or subtract from the amount. They can experiment with shapes—forming the same piece first into a long worm, then into a flat pancake. There is opportunity to pound and squeeze, which may help a child work out hostile or aggressive feelings. Children imitate and socialize during the activity.

The products will be quite primitive. The same stages apply in modeling as in drawing. The teacher and the parents will have to be content with simple products. Most teachers of young children make no attempt to save the products.

CERAMIC CLAY.   Ceramic clay—sometimes called mud clay—will attract children, especially if the teacher works at the table with them. A visit to an art center to see a potter at work offers an opportunity to observe the relationship of the potter's work to vases, pitchers, and plates. Such a visit will encourage many nonparticipators to use this "messy" medium.

The teacher's role is to provide modeling materials in good condition. She should manipulate the clay herself to be sure that it is soft enough for the children to use. She may sit with the children and use the clay in the manner that they are using it. She will not make models for them, for this invites them to become spectators and does not fulfill goals for individual development.

Ceramic clay may be purchased ready to use or in a powdered

FIGURE 7–10.   *Children can help mix the paint or play dough before they use it and thus learn the ingredients it contains. (Michigan State University Laboratory Preschool.)*

form that must be mixed with water. The clay can be used and reused. If it becomes dry, the clay is reclaimed by the adding of water. If the clay dries in large lumps, it may be placed in a cloth bag and pounded to a powdery consistency, then moistened again. Children can be taught to leave the clay molded in large balls with a big thumb hole in the side; then water can be added to the thumb hole to help keep the clay a proper consistency. The storage container should be covered tightly. Boards for use on the table where the children will use the clay may be made of masonite and should be about 15 inches square. Covering the table with newspapers makes cleaning up easier. The children need no tools. A tongue blade from the nurse's station is useful for scraping clay up from the board. Aprons for the children are important.

PLAY DOUGH.   Play dough provides many of the same experiences as clay. However, most children do not think of dough as being dirty, as they do clay. Therefore they do not have the inhibitions they may have in working with clay. They are inclined to imitate their mothers, saying, "I'm making cookies, like my mommy." If cookies or pancakes have been recent group projects, this experience may be played out with the play dough.

The play dough can be made with little difficulty. The homemade varieties are usually superior to commercial doughs and are, of course, cheaper. Teachers should test the consistency of the doughs they give the children. Play dough should be soft and moist enough so that the child can readily manipulate it. The salt content should be low, so that the dough does not dry out the child's hands. Additional flour may be required if the dough is sticky. Cutters, rolling pins, and plates may add to the child's enjoyment. Mothers appreciate play dough recipes because play dough is a good home activity. Play dough is easily cleaned up and makes a good gift.

RECIPES FOR PLAY DOUGH

UNCOOKED PLAY DOUGH

Mix in a large bowl:
2 cups flour
1 cup salt
6 teaspoons alum (from drugstore)
2 tablespoons salad oil
1 cup water plus desired color (vegetable color or tempera paint)

This recipe is simple enough so that a group of children can help the teacher make it. Of course, let them use the dough immediately. If stored in a plastic bag, it will keep several weeks.

COOKED PLAY DOUGH

1. Mix in a large bowl:
   1 cup flour
   ½ cup cornstarch
   1 cup water
2. Boil in a pan:
   4 cups water
   1 cup salt
3. Slowly pour the boiling water into the bowl mixture until they are mixed thoroughly. The mixture will have a white-sauce appearance. Then put this mixture back in the pan, cook it over low heat, stirring, until it is thickened and stands stiff. Cooking time: 10–15 minutes.

4. Cool.
5. Stir in 4 to 5 cups of flour until a dough consistency is obtained. More flour may have to be added to make the dough workable.
6. Then knead in as much flour as is required to obtain a good, pliable, soft, but not sticky, consistency.
7. Store the dough in a plastic bag. Refrigerate it for best keeping. Allow it to warm before using it. If it becomes sticky, add flour. Children enjoy working in flour. Makes 15–20 medium-sized balls.

SALT CERAMIC

1. Heat in a saucepan until boiling:
   2 cups salt
   ⅔ cup water
2. Add while stirring quickly:
   1 cup cornstarch dissolved in ½ cup cold water
3. Mix with the hands. The mixture may need a few more drops of water to make pliable dough. Use it to make a child's handprint, tree decorations, or beads. Hardens at room temperature in two days. Can be painted.

SAWDUST DOUGH

Mix in a large bowl:
Wallpaper paste with water
Add sawdust until dough consistency is produced.
Let figures dry thoroughly for several days. Paint or shellac.

PLASTICENE. Plasticene is a commercial plastic medium. It is less useful for young children than the materials discussed above. However, it introduces some variety for the children if offered occasionally. The plasticene must be warm to be malleable for small hands. The teacher may set it near a radiator or work it in her own hands before offering it to the children. Variety and art stores sell plasticene.

SAND. Sand can be provided indoors in a sand table or outdoors in the yard. It lends itself to quiet, individual creative play or to creative group interaction. Older children develop themes and carry them out cooperatively. Sand should be of beach quality and clean. It should be kept moist so the children can pack it tightly into molds or tunnels and it won't fly into hair and eyes. Plenty of shovels should be available. Sifters and containers to fill are popular. Kitchen castoffs, such as pans and cans, encourage the playing of homemaker roles. Small cars or trucks or chunks of wood to substitute for cars

FIGURE 7–11. *Moist sand packs best for "cakes and pies" children enjoy turning out. (Michigan State University Laboratory Preschool.)*

will stimulate road building. When used indoors, sand may damage floor coverings and finishes. The sand table can be located on a cement floor if available. Firm rules (limits) regarding proper conduct around the sand should be established from the beginning. Avoid overcrowding.

Building

Blocks are mentioned here because of the creative opportunities they offer children. They will be discussed in other chapters because of their contribution to outdoor play, to concept building, and to

FIGURE 7–12. *Scraps of wood, good tools, and ideas make a creative carpentry project for children. (Texas Tech University Kindergarten.)*

dramatic play—all interrelated. The "whole child" learns when he plays with blocks. Gross motor skills and minute small-motor co-ordinations will be challenged by blocks. Some children who are not attracted to other creative media are happy using blocks. Parents may have to be reassured that the child who uses blocks is indeed creative. Because the child's creativity is expressed with school blocks, he is unable to take products home for parental approval.

CARPENTRY. Carpentry is a creative medium that offers emotional release and opportunities to develop large and small muscle skills. A table with vises and clamps to hold the wood for sawing or hammering is a big help to young children. Real tools that work well should be purchased. Scrap lumber can usually be obtained from cabinet shops or lumberyards. Bottle caps and spools make wheels for objects.

The safe use of tools is a major item to learn. Rules for using tools must be carefully set by the teacher. Supervising and limiting the number of children at work around the carpentry table are important safety precautions.

The use of glue in place of hammering can satisfy children who like to use wood but don't like to hammer. Paints can be available to paint the products. Of course, outdoors is the best place for this noisy activity. A separate indoor space with acoustical tile can, however, be prepared for young carpenters, and other quiet activities can still be enjoyed in the playroom.

Conclusion

Creativity is a human potential that integrates physical, mental, social, and emotional growth. Creativity is fostered in good schools for young children by a free, flexible, accepting, and open environment and by teachers who are openly discovering, inventing, and creating. Many activities have been suggested to help start the teacher toward creative teaching. For neither the children nor the teacher are patterns presented—only raw materials have been suggested and the reassurance that "you can do it."

In addition to the opportunity for creative self-expression, the child is practicing many small motor skills, eye-hand coordination, left-to-right progression, and whole-part relationships, all of which are foundations for later reading and writing. The first opportunity of self-expression should be enough to sell an art program, but the additional benefits further strengthen the reasons for providing art activities.

ADDITIONAL READINGS

BARRY, JAMES C., and CHARLES F. TREADWAY. *Kindergarten Resource Book.* Nashville, Tenn.: Broadman Press, 1965.

BURNS, SYLVIA F. "Children's Art: A Vehicle for Learning" *Young Children,* Vol. 30, No. 3, March 1975, pp. 193–204.

CHERRY, CLARE. *Creative Art for the Developing Child.* Belmont, Calif.: Lear Siegler, Inc., Fearon Publishers, 1972.

COHEN, ELAINE PEAR. "Does Art Matter in the Education of the Black Ghetto Child?" *Young Children,* Vol. 29, No. 3, March 1974, 170–181.

ELLIS, MARY J. *The Kindergarten Log.* Minneapolis: T. S. Denison & Co., Inc., Vol. I, 1955, Vol. II, 1960.

GETZELS, J. W., and P. W. JACKSON. *Creativity and Intelligence.* New York: John Wiley & Sons, Inc., 1962.

HARRIS, D. B. *Children's Drawings as Measures of Intellectual Maturity.* New York: Harcourt, Brace & World, Inc., 1963.

HOFFMAN, JAMES, and JOAN HOFFMAN. *Prekindergarten Discoveries.* Minneapolis: T. S. Denison and Co., Inc., 1966.

HURD, HELEN B. *Teaching in the Kindergarten,* 3rd ed. Minneapolis: Burgess Publishing Co., 1965.

KELLOG, RHODA. *Analyzing Children's Art.* Palo Alto, Calif.: National Press, 1969.

LEEPER, SARAH H., RUTH J. DALES, DORA SKIPPER, and RALPH L. WITHERSPOON. *Good Schools for Young Children.* New York: Macmillan Publishing Co., Inc., 1974.

LOWENFELD, VIKTOR. *Your Child and His Art.* New York: Macmillan Publishing Co., Inc., 1957.

LOWENFELD, VIKTOR, and W. LAMBERT BRITTAIN. *Creative and Mental Growth.* New York: Macmillan Publishing Co., Inc., 1975.

PITCHER, EVELYN G., et al. *Helping Young Children Learn.* Columbus, Ohio: Charles E. Merrill Publishing Company, 1974.

READ, KATHERINE. *The Nursery School: A Human Relationships Laboratory.* Philadelphia: W. B. Saunders Company, 1971.

SAUNDERS, EVERETT E. *Print Art.* Racine, Wis.: Whitman Publishing Co., 1966.

SMITH, JAMES A. *Setting Conditions for Creative Teaching in the Elementary School.* Boston: Allyn & Bacon, Inc., 1966.

SPARLING, JOSEPH, and MARILYN SPARLING. "How to Talk to a Scribbler." *Young Children,* Vol. 28, No. 6, August 1973, 333–341.

TAYLOR, BARBARA J. *A Child Goes Forth.* Provo, Utah: Brigham Young University Press, 1975.

TORRANCE, E. PAUL. *Guiding Creative Talent.* Englewood Cliffs, N.J.: Prentice-Hall, Inc., 1962.

TORRANCE, E. PAUL. *Encouraging Creativity in the Classroom.* Dubuque, Iowa: Wm. C. Brown Company, 1970.

Fostering Mental Growth
Through the Sciences

THE YOUNG child greets each day ready to learn. He is constantly exploring. He relates, remembers, and organizes the information he is receiving. Typical questions of children under six are "What is it?" "Where did it come from?" "What is it for?" Though parents often lament that their child never runs out of questions, most are pleased that he is inquisitive. Questioning behavior is evidence to parents that the child is alert and intelligent.

Children have natural inclinations to learn. They want to learn. They can learn. The role of adults in children's lives is to provide an environment with stimulating materials and experiences, and an empathetic leadership that keeps their curiosity alive.

Parents and teachers must have an optimistic belief in children's desire and ability to learn if each child is to reach his potential.[1] Some adults give up hope, faith, and optimism when confronted with a "slow" or "handicapped" child. It is important for such adults to become knowledgeable about the particular handicap in order to help individual children.

Goals for Children's Mental Growth

Fostering the child's mental growth before he is six is an important goal. Developing and utilizing children's curiosity is a prime objective. The ability to think, reason, infer, and generalize is to be de-

---

[1] See Robert Rosenthal and Lenore Jacobson, *Pygmalion in the Classroom* (New York: Holt, Rinehart and Winston, 1968) for documentation regarding the self-fulfilling prophecy related to the teacher's expectation and pupils' intellectual performance.

FIGURE 8–1. *Planting her own miniature garden is a satisfying science experience for this child.* (*Louisiana State University Nursery School.*)

veloped. Children need to be aware of and to interact with the world around them.

Landreth's Types of Intellectual Operations

According to Landreth, a child may be capable of five different types of intellectual operations:

1. He may perceive or recognize a problem: *cognition.*
2. He may be able to retain what is recognized and recall it: *memory.*
3. He may use the information he has perceived and retained to find the one right answer: *convergent thinking.*
4. He may take off from information already possessed, seeking a novel, a different kind of answer: *divergent thinking.*

5. He may evaluate critically the solution he has hit upon or sense a deficiency in his problem solving and try to correct it: *evaluative thinking.*[2]

The teacher will plan learning experiences to foster each of these five operations.

If teachers and parents hope to stimulate learning meaningfully they must determine their children's concerns by observing and listening. Adults willingly help the child organize his knowledge in meaningful ways. Children are accepted and not ridiculed for their lack of knowledge. They are supported in their need to learn from firsthand experience. Selecting and planning experiences to satisfy children's mental needs are important in both the home and the school.

Piaget's Stages of Mental Growth

In recent years the work of Jean Piaget, the Swiss child psychologist, has received considerable attention from early childhood educators and psychologists. Many of Piaget's observations began as he watched the development of his own three youngsters. His observations and research have been carried on for many years. Piaget has described four stages of cognitive or intellectual development.[3] Two of these stages are of major interest to those who are caring for and teaching young children in homes, day-care centers, nursery schools, and kindergartens.

Table 8–1 is a conceptualization of Piaget's stages. It indicates a few important characteristics of each stage and helps you think of each stage as an undergirding support for the next and ensuing stages, an important concept in human development. For progression from infancy upward, read the table from bottom to top.

SENSORIMOTOR.   Piaget called the earliest stage *sensorimotor.* This label and stage link movement with stimuli perceived through the senses. The stage includes the months from birth to age two. This period is one in which the child learns to control his body in space. It is a period of reflexes and a period when intelligence exists without language or symbols. During these first two years the infant or toddler learns by exploring space bodily and by handling objects and exploring them through touching, tasting, seeing, hearing, and smelling.

[2] Catherine Landreth, *Early Childhood: Behavior and Learning* (New York: Knopf, 1967), pp. 258–259.
[3] See Jean Piaget, *The Psychology of Intelligence* (London: Routledge and Kegan Paul, 1950) for additional details of Piaget's theory.

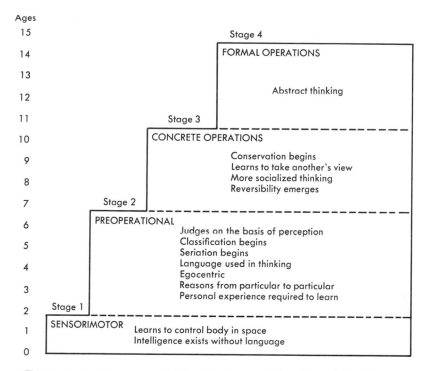

Ages

15	Stage 4
14	FORMAL OPERATIONS
13	
12	Abstract thinking
11	Stage 3
10	CONCRETE OPERATIONS
9	Conservation begins
	Learns to take another's view
8	More socialized thinking
	Reversibility emerges
7	Stage 2
6	PREOPERATIONAL
	Judges on the basis of perception
5	Classification begins
	Seriation begins
4	Language used in thinking
	Egocentric
3	Reasons from particular to particular
	Personal experience required to learn
2	Stage 1
1	SENSORIMOTOR
	Learns to control body in space
	Intelligence exists without language
0	

TABLE 8–1. *Summary of Piaget's Stages of Intellectual Development*

PREOPERATIONAL. The preoperational stage, Piaget's second stage, follows the sensorimotor stage. As the label implies, it is the period prior to logical thinking or operations. It lasts approximately from ages two years to seven years.

The preoperational is a self-centered or ego-centered stage, the child viewing his surroundings only in terms of himself. His learning requires experiences with real objects and things as opposed to being told about things. The child now begins to think of things that are not present. You can observe examples of this as you watch children play family, pet, or worker roles in dramatic play.

Piaget says a child receives stimuli from the environment and acts on the stimuli with whatever prior experience he has in a process called *assimilation.* For example, the toddler flails his spindle toy the same way he learned to shake his rattle. This, of course, creates a problem because it is heavier and more harmful to himself and others. Therefore, he must learn some new behavior; for example, putting the discs over the spindle instead of shaking the toy vigorously. He thus *accommodates* to the new toy by learning new behaviors.

The preoperational child reasons from the particular to the particular. That is, he might think, "Mother is getting her coat, so she is going to leave," and be correct. Or the child can be incorrect, like the four-year-old whose mother told her that the new baby would arrive "when cantaloupe are ready to eat." This was the mother's effort to relate the time of the birth in the future to something she knew the child liked about summer. However, she found her daughter expecting the baby immediately when the first imported cantaloupe appeared in the grocery in the spring. The child was reasoning that cantaloupe would cause the baby's arrival.

The preoperational child uses his perception of how things look to him rather than complex reasoning to provide his knowledge. Cross mothers, teachers, or neighbors are believed by him to dislike him—that's the way their behavior appears to him and no amount of reasoning will change his mind.

In this stage the young child begins to classify objects according to some criterion. When the child has sorted objects according to one criterion, he cannot shift and classify according to another. For example, after he sorts beads according to color, he will not be able to cancel that perception and re-sort the beads according to shape. Following this finding, we would only confuse children by presenting them multifaceted problems when they are in this stage of development.

CONCRETE OPERATIONS. The third stage in Piaget's scheme is called *concrete operations*. Now the child can reason logically about things and ideas. This stage occurs from the seventh to the eleventh year and is generally beyond the preschool child's capabilities. In this stage the school-age child learns to take another's view. He learns that substance, weight, length, area, and numbers remain the same regardless of changes in position. Piaget called this process *conservation*. The classic experiment that is simple for anyone to try is to show the child liquid in a tall glass, then pour it into a squat one and ask the child which glass has the most liquid. During the preschool years the child says the tall one has the most, while during the period of seven to eleven years he is said to "conserve" when he reasons that changing the size of the container doesn't change the amount of liquid.

Piaget discusses the aspect of *reversibility* in flexible and controlled thought, which, he says, emerges when the child is from seven to eleven years old. Now the child can think of an act and think it undone. For example, he can stand in the kitchen door in his muddy boots and think of the muddy tracks he'll make if he enters and walks across the floor. He can mentally think of his deed undone (tracks removed). During the early years (0–6) he cannot do this much reasoning. If you ask him after he walks across the floor, "Did you make those tracks on the floor?" he may deny it honestly, being unable to reverse his thoughts or think about the floor when it was clean. By placing reversibility in this older age bracket Piaget helps us understand that our young children are generally unable to do the mental scheming that sometimes is attributed to them. For example, when three-year-old Billy's mother says, "He's flattering me so I'll let him play with his battery car," it is highly improbable that Billy is sophisticated enough to scheme in that way.

FORMAL OPERATIONS.   Piaget's fourth stage is called *formal operations*. This stage begins around the eleventh year and continues through maturity. Now the adolescent can think about his own thinking. He can think about what could be as well as what is, something he could not do earlier. He can now think about and deal with concepts in the abstract. At a personal level, for example, he can understand his bank account and the amount of money he has available. He does not have to have his bank book in his pocket to know when he has funds for a certain need. A young child whose favorite toy or security blanket is left at his grandmother's can't reason that it is safe. He must have it in hand to be sure.

Clearly stages three and four are far out of the range of early childhood education, but they are presented here because our understanding and designing of programs for the development and education of young children will be aided. The sensorimotor and preoperational stages are of concern to us in our planning. Being familiar with the more advanced stages helps us know what is too complicated for our young children. Piaget's work is helpful to teachers because it guides us in setting expectations for children. We understand that the child is the center of his reasoning universe. We realize that we should not be critical of the child for being self-centered; it is simply part of being a young child. Knowing future stages we can provide experiences that will help the child move comfortably into advanced stages when he is ready.

Piaget, like most researchers, sets age brackets cautiously knowing that many deviations from what appears "normal" in research are still normal for a particular child. Because no child is 100 per cent consistent in a behavior, it is unwise to say, "Johnny always does . . ." It is even more unwise to say, "All children do" so and so.

Piaget himself has suggested that it is foolish to set out deliberately to "teach" these stages. He thinks they evolve from a child's step-by-step development as he uses things and socializes in his environment. When he was asked whether teachers should present the

FIGURE 8–2. *Collecting insects is an adventure in science for these budding entomologists. They carefully transfer their catch to a collecting jar. (Texas Tech University Kindergarten.)*

same types of tasks to children that he did in his research, Piaget said, "if the aim is to accelerate the development of these operations, it is idiotic."[4]

Kamii, after many experiments and attempts to build a Piaget-type curriculum for nursery school, has said, "I found in Piaget's theory many reasons why dramatic play, painting, block building, paper folding, Jell-O making, etc., were so relevant to education. The more I studied Piaget's theory, the more I came to respect the intuitive wisdom of the traditional nursery school."[5]

[4] Eleanore Duckworth, "Piaget Takes a Teacher's Look," *Learning*, **2**:2 (October 1973), 22.

[5] Constance Kamii, "An Application of Piaget's Theory to the Conceptualization of a Preschool Curriculum," *The Preschool in Action*, ed. Ronald K. Parker (Boston: Allyn and Bacon, Inc. 1972), p. 119.

What Is Science for Young Children?

Science can be defined as systematized knowledge. In the adult world, knowledge is grouped into the physical, natural, biological, and social sciences, literature, music, mathematics, and the arts. These are man-made systems. All have important concepts for young children.

It has been said that the university curriculum can become the curriculum for the nursery school or the kindergarten. The teacher needs a liberal education to teach the concepts and to appreciate the meaning of those concepts for the child and the society. No matter how extensive a teacher's education, children will confront her with questions to which she will answer, "Let's find out," or "Let's go and look that up." There will be surprises. Today's children have amazing bits and pieces of information they are trying to fit into meaningful packages. Brad, for example, thought Juarez, Mexico, had something to do with war because of the way it was pronounced in Spanish.

Teachers are faced with words, concepts, and feelings that they have never imagined. Educated parents, television, and travel are all factors contributing to the breadth of a child's knowledge. One boy's "I'm going to be an ichthyologist," sent the teacher scurrying to her dictionary. Many teachers have drawn on concepts from biology class to respond to "Was I in my mommy's stomach before I got borned?" "Today is Hanukkah" need not embarrass a teacher who has studied the world's great religions in humanities classes.

What Does the Teacher Consider When Planning Science Education?

Children's Needs and Interests

The teacher begins with the children. She assesses continuously what they know and what they want and need to know. At first she makes plans based on her general knowledge of young children. As she gets to know her group personally, she individualizes her plans. She uses a building-block approach. This is an approach that lays a firm foundation, then continues building, one block at a time. No chimneys are built before the basement is dug here. The child becomes personally and actively involved in his own education. He is helped to find concrete ways of relating new knowledge to what he already knows. Learning takes time and lots of repetition. This is a trying-it-out experimental laboratory approach. Children are more likely to understand and remember information that they discover themselves.

FIGURE 8–3. *Hooking up the dry cell batteries to make a bell ring or a light flash requires discovering the principle that makes it work. (Michigan State University Laboratory Preschool.)*

Without a teacher's continuous thought and evaluation there is real danger that only limited mental stimulation will take place in schools for young children. It is true, as some teachers argue, that spontaneous and incidental events should be valued highly for their learning potential. However, to rely entirely on spontaneous events for an entire program results in missing much of importance. Planned projects may be temporarily postponed when children are learning from an incidental event. For example, the children find a caterpillar. While other plans wait, this furry creature becomes the focus of learning for several days. The children observe how the caterpillar moves, how it eats, and finally how it spins a cocoon. The teacher tells about the stages of metamorphosis. Good teaching results when a teacher is able to capitalize on a spontaneous interest such as this one. It is also true, however, that children who do not happen to discover a caterpillar may benefit from being introduced to one by the teacher. The motivation may not be as high as when they discover something themselves, but if they are allowed to watch and hold the caterpillar the teacher brings to them, their knowledge will be enhanced. Later, when they find a caterpillar, they may recognize it and learn new facts. Knowledge is seldom a once-over-all-is-learned event. Each time a person confronts a concept his previous experience helps add to its meaning, a fact that should be taken into consideration in planning. Concepts worth learning should be introduced numerous times and in a variety of ways. Each time the child will add new information to his storehouse of knowledge.

Cumulative Plan

A cumulative plan is the name given to this building-block approach just described. This plan is continuous, starting with a simple concept at the beginning of the year and adding experiences throughout the year. As each new experience is added, the children are helped to reflect back to the related experiences they have had. Six broad themes are suggested to run concurrently as cumulative plans. The themes are

1. The child—his name, sex, health, safety, and relationship to his family, the school, the community, and the world.
2. The community—its people, workers, institutions, and traditional festivals.
3. The world of plants—especially those the child sees every day and those that provide his food.
4. The world of animals—especially those the child sees every day and those that provide his food.
5. The world of machines—including vehicles and other large and small machines.
6. The physical forces in the world.

Following is a brief example of a cumulative plan as it develops in relation to plants in the child's world (item 3 above). In September and October the children pick fall crops—corn, apples, and pumpkins. They collect leaves and make a book of them. They plant crocuses and tulip bulbs in the yard and pot geraniums for their classroom. In November and December they make pumpkin custard and pumpkin bread and talk about the leaves in their book as they observe the bare branches of the trees. New plants are brought into the classroom to brighten it up, and they are compared to the geraniums. Apple sauce is made in February, and the children discover crocuses peeking out of the snow and recall having planted them in the fall. They plant seeds in the window box in March and plan to transplant the seedlings to the play yard or to their homes in the spring. Trees and shrubs are observed as they bloom and get their new leaves. The geraniums are reset in the garden. The children plant lettuce, anticipating a salad later on. They watch a farmer planting corn and recall the corn they picked in the fall. From these activities the children begin to understand the interrelatedness of their learning.

Each of the six themes suggested, and perhaps others, can be developed as a cumulative plan. Teachers in different localities would develop the sequence differently.

Environment

The school environment is the second major consideration when the teacher is planning science education. The total learning environment can stimulate the young child to want to learn. An intriguing array of challenging activities, many displays to look at, and materials available for experimenting will stimulate curiosity. Readily available reference books will promote questions and provide answers. A science table or corner can be arranged where new science projects begin and ongoing projects continue. A special table or shelf can hold treasures children bring from home or yard. They can share and discuss discoveries with friends.

A want-to-know attitude permeates the atmosphere. No shame follows a mistake, as it is safe for a child to admit he doesn't know. Experimenting is encouraged. If some idea fails to work, there is always something else to try. The teacher encourages exchanging ideas and helping others answer questions. Alert teachers note questions children ask and plan experiences to answer those questions. The self-selection-type organization in the classroom facilitates an individual or small group lesson. Such learning is more meaningful than large group lectures at this age.

Teachers work with parents and encourage their participation in their child's learning. Open communication invites teachers and parents to share the learning experiences that are available to the children. This information better enables both teacher and parent to understand the child and helps parents supplement the school activities. Teachers may need to discuss levels of expectation with parents. The teacher may help one family enrich the child's experience; she may encourage another family to let up on the pressure.

Questioning the Children

Questions have an important place in the nursery school and kindergarten. The children's questions, as well as the teacher's, must be held in high regard. A child's curious questioning must be encouraged. These questions may often be answered by his peers, or after the child explores the environment, they may be answered by the child himself. Often a child's questions require the teacher to encourage his further exploration rather than to answer immediately. Normally a child is more enthusiastic about seeking answers to questions that he himself is asking. Therefore we should encourage children to ask their own questions and seek answers.

Questioning children skillfully is an essential technique for teachers. It is important for the teacher to establish communication with each child and to indicate her recognition of each child. Teachers use questioning to stimulate the child's awareness of new information. Questioning signals the child that it is his turn to speak and to display his knowledge, thoughts, and feelings verbally.

In planning learning activities for children, the teacher must give attention to questioning. Many un-thought-out questions lead only to a "yes" or "no" answer and not at all to the goal the teacher had in mind.

Types of teachers' questions were the subject of a research project by Zimmerman and Bergan.[6] These researchers identified the following seven categories of questions based on the intellectual operations required by the questions. Note the similarity of these categories with the types of intellectual operations identified by Landreth.

1. Perceptual—questions concerning the characteristics of objects; e.g., "What (shape, color, size) is your name tag?"

2. Cognitive—questions about comprehension or knowledge; e.g., "What's wrong with this (picture, wagon, shoe string)?"

3. Memory—questions asking for the recall of information that was received earlier; e.g., "What did the man say he fed the (cows, horses, ducks, pigs)?"

4. Divergent—questions asking for several student ideas regarding the presented stimulus; e.g., "What other ways can you put these (materials, colors, shapes) together?"

5. Convergent—questions asking for a single correct response from the child from a field of alternatives; e.g., "How many (mittens, children, shoes, fingers) do we have?"

6. Evaluative—questions asking for student responses concerning the extent to which information matches criteria; e.g., "Which car went (faster, slower, farther)?"

---

[6] Barry J. Zimmerman and John R. Bergan, "Intellectual Operations in Teacher Question-Asking Behavior," *Merrill-Palmer Quarterly*, **17:1** (January 1971), 19–26.

7. Other—questions that do not fit the above categories; e.g., "Would you like to bring the (book, puzzle, chair)?"

The researchers found that first-grade teachers placed an unusual amount of emphasis on factual knowledge, thereby largely omitting other critical intellectual operations. Teachers who had experience and training in question asking gave more emphasis to teaching those intellectual skills stimulated by divergent and evaluative questions. The researchers said that questions guiding children to perceive and process relevant stimuli would help them become aware of the subtle sensory discriminations they can make in the environment. Increased motivation is an expected result.

Teachers should become aware of the type of intellectual operation they have in mind as a learning goal and develop questioning for children accordingly. Caution is suggested to teachers to avoid over-zealous concern for emphasizing every aspect of a learning activity in a single learning episode. Learning is never a one-session experience. We must realize that there will be other days to add new information and learning.

Eric Berne, in the book *Games People Play*, wrote the following about awareness, giving food for thought to questioners, whether parents or teachers. "Awareness means the capacity to see a coffee-pot and hear the birds sing in one's own way, and not the way one was taught. It may be assumed on good grounds that seeing and hearing have a different quality for infants than for grownups, and that they are more esthetic and less intellectual in the first years of life. A little boy sees and hears birds with delight. Then the 'good father' comes along and feels he should 'share' the experience and help his son 'develop.' He says: 'That's a jay, and this is a sparrow.' The moment the little boy is concerned with which is a jay and which is a sparrow, he can no longer see the birds or hear them sing. He has to see and hear them the way his father wants him to. Father has good reasons on his side, since few people can afford to go through life listening to the birds sing, and the sooner the little boy starts his 'education' the better. Maybe he will be an ornithologist when he grows up. A few people, however, can still see and hear in the old way. But most of the members of the human race have lost the capacity to be painters, poets, or musicians, and are not left the option of seeing and hearing directly even if they can afford to; they must get it second hand. The recovery of this ability is called here 'awareness.'"[7]

---

[7] Eric Berne, *Games People Play* (London: Andre Deutch Ltd., 1966), p. 178.

Suggested Science Experiences

Understanding Oneself and Others

Developing understanding of oneself and others involves intellectual, social, physical, and emotional learning that must receive prime time in schools. Feelings of self-worth are invariably linked to the individual's success in school and throughout life. The school should seek to build the child's feeling of self-importance, his feelings of autonomy, his skill in dealing with the expectations of home and school, and his ability to express himself through words and deeds. Teachers should think of the child's self-concept as a subject for study throughout the school years.

The total environment of the school should be designed to offer children a maximum of success and a minimum of frustration. Equipment is child-sized and it works. Little is off limits or has to be protected. The teacher-pupil ratio assures each child a teacher who has time for him as an individual. The expectations of the school are individually based and developmentally sound.

THE PSYCHOLOGICAL SELF. "That means me!" exclaimed a five-year-old as he found his name on a list. The answer to the child's question of "Who am I?" only begins when he knows his name. The school helps the child learn his personal symbol by using names in conversation, by making the child a name tag, and by writing his name on his products and on his locker.

The child's self-image is formed largely from how he thinks others feel toward him. In the free-flowing small groups that are typical in schools for young children the teacher can help the child learn that he is a creative, intelligent, important member of the group. "Mary is smiling, she is glad you gave her some clay." The teacher helps the child learn that he can make changes in situations—that he can act as well as be acted upon. "Just tell Jack you aren't through" helps a shy child defend his rights and moves him a step toward self-confidence in dealing with his peers.

Teachers can become effective listeners, and through their responses to children's conversation they can help children understand their own feelings. The teacher frequently hears a child's opinion about how other significant people (parents, siblings, children, teachers) feel toward him. If a child says, "My daddy hates me," the typical adult wants to say quickly, "Oh, all daddies love their little boys," and change the subject to something more pleasant. The child notes at once that the teacher doesn't want to hear about his feelings. He guesses that she is really on his daddy's side. He bottles up his feelings. However, the teacher could respond to "My daddy hates me" with "Tell me about it." If she could use the tone of voice that she would use if he had said "My daddy has red hair," then the child might feel free to discuss his thoughts and feelings. Through a discussion he would become more able to cope with his situation. When the teacher serves as a sounding board without taking sides or making judgments, she may discover that she needs to work more closely with families or make referrals.

THE PHYSICAL SELF.   "How do I look?" is a question regarding the physical self that can best be answered by a look in the mirror. Each classroom should have a high-quality, full-length mirror placed in a strategic spot. Many homes do not have a low mirror and some have no mirrors at all. Children may literally not have seen themselves. With a good mirror the child can admire the way he looks, see the smudge on his face, straighten the fireman's hat he's wearing, or adjust a flowing dress before beginning a dance. Mirrors over lavatories are useful but show only the face.

Photographs, too, make a significant contribution to the child's understanding of his physical appearance. A child's picture can be used over his locker to identify his own space. Group photos hung at the children's eye level can be used to decorate the room. *Our Very Own Story Book* can be made using individual photos on 10″ × 12″ tagboard pages put together with notebook rings. Exclamations such as "That's you!" and "That's me!" will continue throughout the year and show the continued satisfaction the children receive from having pictures of themselves continuously available to them.

Attendance charts can become more graphically symbolic and meaningful for the children. Figure 8–4 is an example of a chart that shows the names of the children present. The children learn the concepts of present and absent. They often learn to read the names and count the number of children.

Children talk freely about their ages. They are proud to become four, or five, or six. However, they may worry about their size. One petite five-year-old girl began quizzing her mother at length about midgets. The mother learned through their discussion that her daughter believed she might never grow up because she was the smallest in her class. Another observant five-year-old was heard to say as he stood beside his three-year-old playmate, "Well, you're taller but I'm older." Occasionally being the tallest or the smallest in a group is cause for deep concern to a child. Teachers should sense whether it bothers a tall child to be chosen frequently to reach something "because you are tallest." Teachers can likewise observe a child's reaction to being chosen to ride in the baby carriage "because you're the smallest." The child's size may be a fact the child would like to

FIGURE 8–4. *A chart placed on a low bulletin board will encourage children to count, to read names, to differentiate between symbols, and to understand the concept of being absent or present. The dolls are made of a double thickness of colored paper. A thumb tack inserted between the layers before the two layers are glued together makes the dolls easy to move on the board. A piece of masking tape under the tack makes the dolls more durable.*

discuss, but he might not enjoy having group attention focused on his size. Any comparisons that unnecessarily cause one child to feel inferior to another should be avoided. To help a child build a positive self-image, teachers should avoid comparing children on the basis of tallest-shortest, biggest-smallest, oldest-youngest, fastest-slowest, best-worst, or prettiest-ugliest.

Many opportunities arise to teach about growing. Children get new shoes because their old ones are too small. New teeth replace baby teeth. Hair and fingernails require cutting. Because children seem to want to grow, teachers should use any cue to enlighten or reassure children about growing.

The child's actual motor skills are an important part of the self-concept. Also the way a child compares his motor capabilities to those of his peers is important. Development of large and small motor skills is fostered in good schools for children under six. For example, Jeff was the oldest and tallest child in a four-year-old group. He was one of several children trying a new rope swing that required standing on the packing box, holding on to the rope, swinging away from the box, and dropping to the ground. Jeff hesitated, obviously afraid but wanting to try it. By explaining the sequential steps to him and protecting him while he practiced, the teacher helped him constructively solve his dilemma. He grew in his self-confidence as he practiced his new skill.

SEX ROLE IDENTIFICATION.   Another important aspect of the child's self-concept is sex role identification. Most children are happy with their own sex, and the teacher should help a child to play and understand the roles of maleness and femaleness. Feelings regarding sexuality are laid in the early years. Occasionally teachers need to work with parents who seem to be unaccepting of the child's sex so that parents' negative attitudes will not harm the child's self-concept.

Unisex is common in preschools, with all activities and equipment being used equally by boys and girls. Teachers should evaluate books and activities critically to see whether they arbitrarily assign sex roles. Often teachers themselves must broaden their ideas of male and female roles, both in society and in the family. Modern thinking has merged the roles into more of a single, humanistic one.

Boys and girls under six typically share the same bathroom at school. Such an arrangement provides a healthy environment for learning valuable sex information. Children will look at each other's bodies during the toileting. They will ask questions that can be answered factually. Their concerns over being made differently can be recognized and discussed. Correct terms are used in discussions. Children may seek clarification of information they are receiving at home or elsewhere. It is therefore necessary for the teachers and the parents to compare notes in order that the child is not left more confused than enlightened.

The handling of the genitals, or masturbation, is generally a harmless activity and is often observed among young children. Masturbation may have various meanings, so a child must be observed individually so that the purpose of masturbation for a given child can be discovered. Of course, masturbation can mean that the child is insecure and unhappy. However, it can also mean that the child is bored and needs more active play, that his clothing is too tight, that he has a rash on his penis, or that he needs to urinate. Teachers must have an enlightened attitude and avoid shaming the child—a technique that would harm the child's positive self-image. Teachers may also need to assist parents in their understanding and handling of this behavior.

When one child's mother has had a new baby, the interest in the event can be used to help the children verbalize questions and seek answers regarding human reproduction, which they may not have had occasion to discuss before. All children enjoy hearing about when they were babies. Teachers can involve children in discussions that will bring out both information and feelings about babyhood. A recognition and an open discussion of the feelings children have toward their younger siblings or how they, as younger siblings, are treated by their older brothers or sisters can help children work through their jealous or ambivalent feelings.

THE FAMILY—A PART OF THE SELF. The family constellation can be the subject of a great deal of learning. Each teacher of young children hears examples of children's confusion about kinship. "Is that your daddy?" is the usual question when children see the teacher with any man. Youthful aunts or uncles were called "my grandma's kids" by one five-year-old.

Children's literature typically shows a family with one boy and one girl, both about the same age. A discussion can help children talk about their families and begin to understand the variations existing among families. Foster children and grandparents may be part of the family. The teacher may have most uncertainties with those children who have no parents or only one parent. If a recent divorce or death has occurred, the child may need someone who will listen to him talk about the event without prying for more information than he is ready to give. Teachers should know their children's families well in order to avoid creating unnecessary heartaches for already troubled children. For example, the kindergarten teacher who directed her class to mold ashtrays from ceramic clay for "your father's Christmas present" should have remembered that one child's father had died only days before school started in the fall. Thus, the project was one he could not do with pleasure and likewise such a specific assignment probably would not be suitable for a child from a non-smoking family.

Fascinating studies about race, language, and culture can be developed from a child's experience in a family. A teacher must first seek to understand and appreciate children and families, including those who differ from herself. She should strive for mutual understanding and greater appreciation for all racial and ethnic groups.

THE COMMUNITY—A PART OF THE SELF. A study of the community is relevant to children. Learning about the houses people live in helps to orient children to the world outside their families. Walks can be taken from neighborhood schools to see houses, yards, and pets belonging to members of the class. Occasionally children feel different because they live in a mobile home or an apartment, while others live in single-family dwellings. A suitable study can help each gain some appreciation of his own home and more understanding of those of his friends.

The whole subject of the world of work can be approached from where "my mother or daddy works." The study takes on added meaning when John's dad is the highway patrolman who shows the class his patrol car. Or they'll look at buses with increased interest after Bettie's dad arranges for the bus to take the class on a tour of the city when he has a day off from his job at the bus station. The police station loses its fearsome aspects when the policeman is Cathy's daddy, whom the children have met at school in his sports shirt. They listen attentively as the policeman tells them how to be safe on city streets. They'll like to look at his badge.

The first and most obvious place to look for learning resources is among the parents of the children in the group. Parents can be encouraged to suggest the names of members of their family and friends who may also be called on to help. There is no particular list of people young children must know, so the enthusiastic cooperation of their families is a worthwhile place to start. Any community helper —fireman, grocer, filling station operator, or mechanic—could be studied.

The search for people with special talents, hobbies, exhibits, and the like that can be shared with the group of children is well worth the teacher's effort. It may be a father who comes to school to twang his banjo, a retired railroader who displays his electric train hobby, or a mother who has the lead in the civic theater. When it's the child's parent, he, of course, gets special recognition through the experience, and other children gain understanding of the diversity among people. The people themselves learn something of the value of educating children under six.

Kindergarten children can begin learning concepts of democracy, government, and voting. Decisions can be arrived at by voting. Leaders can be elected for a day or a special event. Important state or national events can be discussed at school. One inauguration day the teacher said, "Here is a picture of our new President. Tonight when your parents listen to the news watch to see if you can see our new President." A week later one of the shyest children in the group led her to the picture on the bulletin board and reported that he'd seen "him" (the President) on TV.

THE WORLD—A PART OF THE SELF.   Older children are often fascinated by people and customs from faraway countries. This is true especially if they have occasion to know someone from faraway, or if the teacher or a child has had some foreign experience. Parents or grandparents of children may make valuable contributions.

In one group a student from India observed the kindergarten children once each week. They were curious and asked her many questions. She talked with them about school, food, and children in India and showed them pictures and souvenirs. She danced and sang songs from her country. The children were entranced as she demonstrated how her sari was wrapped. The warmth and understanding that developed between the Indian girl and the kindergarten children was heartening to see.

In another instance, some Vietnamese students let kindergarten children try on their rice-straw hats when they came to dance. They invited the children to dance and sing. The next time the Vietnamese girls were to visit, the children suggested that they would like to make hats so that they could dance "better." Before the day of the return visit the children each made a paper Vietnamese hat. Acquaintance with these Vietnamese students occurred during a period when the TV news brought the Vietnamese war raging into nearly every living room. These lovely students showed the children a striking contrast to the one-sided picture they had of Vietnam.

A father's business trip or the teacher's vacation can stimulate interest in travel, maps, and faraway places. Discussion and role playing of travel experiences by the children can follow. A teacher may initiate such study by sending children post cards when she is away.

Outer space intrigues young children just as it does their elders, perhaps more. Children can imagine making a trip in a rocket. Having eaten their baby food during the blast-off of moon explorations, children today want to talk about and play out the roles of space explorers. Teachers will search for ways to answer their questions.

CARING FOR THE SELF.   Caring for the self is an important part of the learning of a child under six. The routines related to eating, eliminating, resting, and bathing will require many reminders before they become comfortable routines. Each routine invites many questions before the child fully understands. School and home supplement each other. Efforts should be made to keep the expectations in line with the child's developmental level and to help the child understand the reasons for learning these routines. Children feel grown-up when taking care of their own needs. It is during routines that a child may first show that he has a concept of "self" as a separate entity. He may refuse to eat, to sleep, or to eliminate as prescribed.

The teacher uses the lunch or snack period to help children think about foods and learn how foods make them grow. Cooking projects may serve to interest children in their nutrition. The teacher may also develop an experiment with two white rats to demonstrate the striking results of a balanced diet for one versus a diet of soft drinks and candy for the other. After three weeks the children will be commenting about the differences between the two rats. If desired, the

DUTIES

 Wake up Smiling

 Wash Face Wash Hands

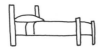 Brush My Teeth

Make My Bed

 Dress Myself

 Put Away Toys

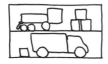 Take My Bath

 Clean Finger Nails

 Go to Bed Early

Parents: Please post this reminder note. Your 4-year-old should be learning
to do these things for himself daily. Ask him, "Have you checked
your list?"

FIGURE 8–5. *A reminder chart to help children become independent.*

smaller (soft drink and candy) rat may then be shifted to a balanced diet and the weight gains recorded.

Caring for teeth, nails, and hair can be brought to children's attention. Teachers demonstrate their interest in good grooming by helping a child comb his hair after his nap or by helping him find a fresh outfit when one gets soiled or damaged. In some day-care centers a special holder is made for each child's comb and toothbrush.

The parents' cooperation can be solicited so that they too will encourage and teach the child to help himself. Figure 8–5 is a visual aid that can be duplicated and sent home with the child to encourage and remind him to become more independent. In a note to parents the teacher suggests that the chart be attached to his wall with plastic tape. She suggests that parents say to the child, "Have you checked your chart?" and avoid nagging about specifics. This is an effort to get the child to take responsibility for his routines. The chart helps some parents realize how capable their child can be.

Safety is an obvious area of study. No one is as vulnerable to accidental death as the child under six. For the first two to three years adults assume total responsibility for a child's safety. After that the child must be relied upon to take more and more responsibility for his safety. The teacher's role is to develop an understanding of safety in the home, school, play yard, street, and family car. Developing an understanding of the rules for personal self-preservation is important. The child's conscience must be encouraged to function. Developing inner control with an understanding of rules, not blind adherence to them, can be a major accomplishment of the young child's life.

The young child is at first basically egocentric. He develops into a social being who wants to know about and to relate to others in his environment. He will eventually want to know about people far away in time and place. A great number of meaningful learning experiences can stem from a continuing emphasis on helping the child to understand himself and others. Learning experiences, both planned and incidental, must be related personally to the children. The learnings will "take" only if the children are personally involved.

Understanding the Physical World

Understanding the physical world is a lifelong pursuit that begins in early childhood. The child picks up a piece of ice covering a puddle in the play yard; he plucks a dandelion; he buttons his coat against the chilly winds; each time he is responding to the physical world. Each response contains learning experience and motivation that will serve the teacher as she uses the incidents to help the child understand what is taking place in his world.

WEATHER AND SEASONAL CHANGES. Weather and seasonal

changes are worthy subjects for the child's science lessons. Weather limits what the child can do and determines his dress; he hears it discussed frequently among adults. There will be numerous opportunities for the teacher to include concepts about the weather, the seasons, and atmospheric changes in the planned experiences for the young child.

A school for young children should use opportunities to observe and discuss all weather conditions—sun, rain, clouds, wind, snow, even hurricanes and tornadoes if the children are interested. Personal experiences reinforce weather concepts. For example, children who take a walk in the rain wearing boots and carrying umbrellas have a chance to see, hear, smell, and feel the effects of the rain. Through questions the teacher can help alert the children to the logic for wearing appropriate clothing. The children eventually learn to choose clothing that is appropriate for the weather. The teacher can ask: "You wore your raincoat today. Can you tell me why?" "If you go outdoors today, what will you need on your hands?" "Why?" "How does it happen we aren't wearing our coats today?"

When studying the seasons, teachers should remember that the child's frame of reference is not well developed. If the child is three years old in the spring of the year, for example, the teacher should remember that a year earlier in the spring he was only a two-year-old. It is unlikely that anyone spent much time with him then discussing the seasonal changes that were taking place or that he would remember, if someone did. Parents, commenting on a child's increased knowledge, often say, "This year the holiday means something to him."

The secrets of nature are awe-inspiring. Yes, nature may be overlooked in our busy, technically oriented world, unless thoughtful teachers keep youngsters tuned in on it. Having a sense of wonder that is alive is surely a prime requisite for teachers of young children. Children will enjoy the tiniest dandelion that "nobody cares if you pick." They will be joyous when they find the crocus they planted in the fall. A spring walk to see, hear, feel, and smell the evidences of spring is surely a delight to all, especially if the children are permitted to bring back a few sprigs of blossoms to decorate the room. A fall walk has equal beauty, with its glorious colors. In fall there are leaves to push into a pile and jump into, and perhaps apples or cotton to pick.

Beauty too is morning after a snow. Adults so often ruin such days by complaining about the traffic snarls and the problems with shoveling. Snow is no problem to children. They'll shovel if someone will just let them have a snow shovel. They'll roll in the snow, taste it, and jump into any "mountain" of snow they see.

Some teachers really have to force themselves to enjoy nature. It may take effort to awaken the senses so that one can appreciate how fresh and exciting all nature is for small children. Once awakened, teachers won't be able to pass a fallen hedge apple, a dandelion seed, or a budding shrub without thinking, "Oh, I must let the children see this." Reading Henry David Thoreau's *Walden*, Rachel Carson's *The Sense of Wonder*, or Anne Morrow Lindberg's *Gift from the Sea* may help a teacher appreciate nature when she has faced the city's gray walls and streets too long.

GROWING PLANTS. Growing plants is interesting to children all year long. Classroom projects can involve children in planting, watering, and observing. Plants also add a cheery note to the room. An indoor window box containing a variety of plants with room for adding new ones from time to time is worthwhile. Geraniums, petunias, ivy, philodendrons, tomatoes, and beans are all grown with relative ease. Sometimes the teacher may like each child to have his own plant to care for. Beans, pumpkins, and tomatoes can be planted in milk cartons or styrofoam cups; then when the danger of frost is past, the child can transplant his plant outside, either at home or at school. He can then continue to watch the plant develop. One child's pumpkin vined into the cherry tree. The child thought it was a big joke to tell people that her cherry tree had pumpkins in it—and it did!

When seeds are planted in clear plastic cups, the children can see the root systems develop. Learning is also facilitated if some seeds are kept damp on a wet sponge wrapped in a damp cloth. Each day the children can unroll the cloth to see if the seeds are sprouting. They can use the magnifying glass to examine the sprouts. This observation can be related to the seed they have planted under the soil.

The plant's need for sunlight, soil, and moisture can be studied. One experimental cup can be kept without light and another can be kept without water, so that the children can learn what happens if the plant does not have these necessities.

An outdoor garden is popular in many schools where space permits. Some children planted Kentucky Wonder beans along their kindergarten fence. The vines grew to cover their fence. Imagine the fun they had picking and tasting their own beans! An attractive indoor plant can be grown from a sweet potato placed in water. Because growers dry sweet potatoes artificially to keep them from sprouting, a teacher may have difficulty finding one with a few purple eyes that will sprout. Sweet potatoes may require several weeks to sprout. It helps to use warm water and to keep the container in a warm place. Tops from carrots, beets, turnips, and pineapples can be planted in water or wet sand. The top should include about one inch of the vegetable or fruit. The children will watch the new shoots grow.

Onions or garlic can be suspended with toothpicks about half immersed in water. The children will watch new green shoots and roots grow. Mothers can snip the young onion and garlic blades for salads when this project is carried on at home.

Watching the plant "drink" is a favorite experiment. If celery, a white carnation, or an iris is placed in colored water, the leaves and petals will become tinged with color overnight. The children can observe that the vascular tissue carries the water to the leaves.

Tulips, hyacinths, and daffodils can be planted in pots in the fall, stored outdoors during the winter, then brought indoors to force early spring blooms. Pussy willows and forsythia will bloom if cut in the bud stage and brought indoors. Early spring bouquets are especially welcome after long cold winters. In some localities fall is the time to plant bulbs outdoors so that children can discover their blooms in the spring.

Study of the seeds of various plants and observation of their travel by wind and water are interesting to children. One group of children who had been alerted to notice tree seeds in the spring called the maple seed the "helicopter blade" and delighted in tossing them up to watch them twirl to the ground. Such labeling is an example of the child's attempt to relate new concepts to those he already knows.

Tree leaves, buds, cones, fruit, and bark can be collected by the children during various seasons to help increase their awareness of trees. Trees' value for lumber and papermaking should not be overlooked. Leaf collections can be pressed between layers of clear plastic adhesive and kept in a book.

In the fall, Indian corn, pumpkins, and bouquets of dry seeds and beans can add color to the room. A mobile of colored leaves is very effective. Coat leaves with wax by pressing between layers of wax paper with a hot iron before arranging them. The wax helps keep leaves from curling up as they dry.

A study of local crops that contribute both to the nation's food and fiber and to the livelihood of families in a community can offer numerous learning experiences for young children. Several field trips a year may be possible to follow a crop from planting to harvesting. Even in a farming community where a crop is the mainstay of the economy the teacher will have some children who have no contact with its production. All children will profit from observing and discussing the growing and harvesting process in relation to finished products. The farm children who already know about the crop can be the teacher's outstanding information source. The farm child's own farm and his parents may contribute to the learning.

A Texas child invited his class to his cotton farm during harvest time. The children ran among the rows of cotton plucking white bolls for a "bouquet." They watched the cotton-picking machine called the cotton stripper pick the bolls and fill huge wagons with them. En route back to school the group stopped at a cotton gin and saw farmers bringing in the wagons piled high with cotton. On the other side of the gin they watched huge trucks being loaded with five-hundred-pound bales of cotton. A few weeks later the children excitedly reported that cotton bales had been placed along the street in the downtown area. (It was cotton promotion week.) They knew where those bales had come from. They felt very knowledgeable. Further discussion and recall of their trip followed. The total experience increased their understanding of cotton as a plant. The study was related to the children personally through the clothing they were wearing and alerted them to the community in which they lived. They appreciated more fully the jobs of their families and friends.

Projects such as picking fruits for eating or making jelly, picking pumpkins for the classroom jack-o'-lantern, or cutting the Christmas tree at the Christmas tree farm add to children's information regarding plants.

A teacher is encouraged to find resources of her community that can provide highly relevant learning experiences for children studying the world of growing things. An action program of planting, watering, harvesting, and using plants should be included.

A supply of reference books to supplement discussion and experiments is essential. The more the teacher knows about the subject the more she can help the children learn. The children will learn to refer to books for information, a good habit to cultivate.

THE ANIMAL WORLD.   The animal world offers valuable material to the teacher of young children. Studying the familiar animals first is best in a class of young children. Parents who take their children to a zoo consistently report that the favorite exhibits are ducks and other farm animals. These are the animals most frequently seen and most often pictured in children's books. Exotic animals from far away and prehistoric animals are for the older under-six children.

Rabbits, gerbils, guinea pigs, white rats or mice, turtles, and fish are common animals that may be kept for a time in the classroom. Advice concerning the health, safety, temperature, feeding, watering, and exercising of the animals may be needed from a specialist. The animals must be treated kindly and not overhandled or used as toys. Children can be taught how to care for the animal properly. If adequate care or housing is not available for an animal in the classroom, the teacher should consider keeping the animal for only a few hours so that the children can have some experience with it.

Children learn from sharing their new pups or kittens with their classmates. Pets can be brought to school while they are still young enough to remain in a box or a basket. The teacher can arrange a tour to children's homes to see their mature pets. She may take pictures of pets and their owners on a home visit. Children who have pets can tell the non-pet-owners practical pointers on pet care. A visit to a local pet shop can be arranged to increase the children's knowl-

FIGURE 8–6a. *Feeding and caring for animals offer endless opportunities for children to learn as they are involved personally with the animals. (Texas Tech University Kindergarten.)*

FIGURE 8–6b. *An aquarium provides a fascinating science experience as children watch the fish swim and feed. (Michigan State University Laboratory Preschool.)*

edge of the animals used for pets. Here the children will find some of the more unusual pets too.

Animals as a source of food and fiber will provide valuable learning experiences for children. The sources of familiar foods will interest the children. Teachers should be alert to the specialized nature of modern agriculture. The storybook farmer who owns every kind of animal is a rarity today. To avoid the teaching of misconceptions, up-to-date ideas of farming and farm equipment should be understood by teachers. Watch especially the accuracy of some of the storybooks you choose to use with farm studies.

A visit to a dairy to see a cow being milked is very worthwhile because milk is a familiar food. Visits to farms where pigs, sheep, beef cattle, turkeys, or chickens are raised help children learn about the sources of common foods. The sight, sound, smell, and touch experiences can be related to taste experiences they have at home and school. Farm visits during the spring months show children the mother animals and their young—a subject of high interest to young children.

An egg-hatching experience can help children learn answers to some of their questions regarding reproduction. However, incubating the fertile eggs and waiting the twenty-one days required for a chicken to hatch may be too tedious for young children. It may be more feasible to obtain eggs from a hatchery that have been incubated for nineteen or twenty days. A warm box can be arranged with an electric light for heat. If the teacher secures about a dozen eggs, it is probable that a few will hatch during the day. The box should be large enough so that the hatched chicks can move away from the light if they are too warm. Chicks will move closer to the light if they are chilled. Chicks might be kept in the classroom for several days. The teacher should seek advice from a hatchery regarding the proper care and feeding of the chicks. Some hatcheries and museums have exhibits in which the hatching process and day-old chicks can be observed.

Ducks, geese, and swans may be available for the children to visit and feed in a public pond. Dry bread crumbs offered by the children will encourage the ducks to come close to the child. Children seem to be especially attracted to ducks. Robert McCloskey's book *Make Way for Ducklings* is both a delightful story and a help to the teacher who is teaching the ways of the duck world. The children will learn from having a duck visit their classroom and swim in their water table. The teacher should be prepared for the fluttering of wet wings, puddles on the floor or grass, and excited children. This close-up view will help the children see the use the duck makes of his webbed feet.

Bird life will interest the children. A small bird such as a parakeet or a canary can be enjoyed in the classroom. The children can learn a great deal from the care and feeding of the bird. Some teachers may prefer having the bird visit school for only a few days or weeks.

Birds in their natural habitat can be observed with interest. Children can learn the names of birds and their housing and eating habits. Children can be encouraged to listen to the birds' songs and may learn to recognize some songs. Children will like to discuss information about reproduction. Bird houses and feeders can be made from plastic milk bottles or cartons. Ready-cut wooden bird houses are available in variety stores. Bird feeders can be made to attract birds to the school yard. Advice regarding the appropriate food to attract local species of birds is available from the wildlife service in each state. Drinking water may be provided for birds in cold climates where water sources freeze up. A birdbath will attract birds. A collection of strings, yarn, and bits of cotton or hair for birds to use in building nests will also attract them and give children an incentive to watch birds closely and quietly.

The world of insects offers children opportunities to discover, to observe, to question, to classify, and to relate. A butterfly net and a collecting jar may be enough to encourage an interest in entomology.

Ant farms are easily made. Clean and dry a large glass jar and make a lid of a double layer of nylon net held with a rubberband across the top. Scoop up an anthill—sand, dirt, and ants—filling the jar and covering it with the nylon net. A queen ant (winged) should be included. Wrap a dark paper around the jar for a number of days. The ants will restore order to their empire. The darkness will encourage the ants to redig their tunnels close to the glass. Once the ants feel at home they will go about their business. The children can provide bits of various foods to see what foods the ants like best and what they do with it. A tablespoon of honey or overripe fruit will be popular. A flashlight and a magnifying glass will help the child follow the ants in the trails. There is a great deal for teachers and children to learn about ants. The children can be taught some safety precautions regarding them. Ant farms are also available through school supply houses.

Butterflies, moths, beetles, and even spiders will be interesting to children. Discovering a spider's web and using a magnifying glass to watch the spider work can be very educational. A class collection of insects can be started. Collections can sometimes be borrowed from libraries or science departments.

Schools located within travel distance of the sea, lakes, or rivers will give children a special opportunity to learn about animals that make their homes in water. When the families of the children vacation near the water or make their living through fishing or a related industry, marine life is a significant subject for children to study. Some marine animals can be brought into the classroom. Visits can be made to public displays.

Watching tadpoles develop into frogs intrigues nearly everyone. Tadpoles can be secured from ponds. They can be kept in an aquarium until the legs form. The children can use the magnifying glass to observe the leg buds appearing.

The care and feeding of fish is another worthwhile classroom project. A teacher can choose a single bowl with one gold fish or a complicated balanced aquarium with collections of tropical fish. If she has the knowledge to build an aquarium or is willing to learn, young children will be eager helpers.

Earthworms are favorites of children, but may be far down the list for teachers. Nonetheless, children learn many things from observing and handling earthworms, and teachers should lay aside their prejudices and learn to tolerate worms. Worms can be collected in dirt and kept in a container for some time. If children have a spot for digging in their yard, they may collect enough worms for a "fishing trip."

Horny toads are harmless pets. They are common in arid regions, where children frequently bring them to school. They may also be purchased from pet stores.

The concept of death frequently comes up during incidental or planned studies of animals. The presence of a pet may encourage children to talk about the death of their own pets. In one five-year-old group the children began telling stories about how their pets had died. The children listened politely to each other and vied for a chance to tell their story. When a lull came in the discussion, the teacher thought it might be time for a pet story with a happy ending, so she told one. Again they listened attentively. However, the second she was through another child had a story of his pet's death. The teacher concluded that the talk of death was meeting a need for these children and took her cue from them as to when to terminate the discussion.

The world of animals offers almost unlimited opportunities for enriching children's experience. The teacher must search for worthwhile experiences for her group. She seeks accurate information. She uses correct terms. While an encyclopedia is helpful, she may have to call specialists for localized information. Sufficient time is given the children to observe and to verbalize their findings. She carefully indicates points for observation and tells about relationships that may not have been discovered by the children. She is prepared to answer such questions as the following:

What is it called?
How and what does it eat?
How does it move?
How does it reproduce?
Where does it live?
What sounds does it make?
How does it see, smell, and hear?
How does the animal protect itself?
How do humans use the animal?

Physical Forces and Their Interaction

The following suggestions will give teachers a few ideas for helping children learn how physical forces interact in their world.

AIR.   Provide opportunities to show that air is all around. Make or buy pinwheels to watch in the breeze. Build and fly a kite. Fill balloons with air. Have the child hold his nose and mouth to see how long he can go without breathing. Place a glass over a lighted candle to demonstrate that fire needs air to burn. Have the children learn words like *air, wind, breeze, oxygen,* and *movement.*

ELECTRICITY.   Electricity is used to produce light, heat, and energy. Dry cell batteries can be used to ring bells and to light bulbs. Children can learn to complete the circuit to make it work. Show the children the electric element on the hot plate or the electric frying pan used for cooking projects. They can learn such words as *battery, circuit, outlets, plugs, bulbs,* and *switches.* Static electricity is produced as a child walks across the carpet or rubs balloons on his slacks. Children enjoy the game of shocking their friends.

MAGNETISM.   Children learn that only certain objects are attracted to magnets. Avoid overgeneralizing that all metals are attracted to a magnet because some metals are not, for example, copper and brass. Make a fishing game using a stick with a magnet on the string and a paper clip on paper fish, numbers, colors, or letters. The children can be encouraged to talk about their catch.

TEMPERATURE.   Temperature can be related to the children, the room, water, or the outdoors. Temperatures can be compared by the use of two thermometers. A cardboard thermometer can be made so that the child can duplicate the reading of the real thermometer. He can observe whether the real thermometer goes up or down. Teachers can provide experiences with steam, with freezing foods, with drying clothes. The children can set water outside to freeze on a very cold day or bring ice or snow indoors to melt. Gelatin dessert cooled outdoors helps children conclude that the air outside is as "cold as the refrigerator." Thus children learn about materials that are solid at one temperature and liquid at another.

VOLUME.   Volume can be studied at the water table as the child pours from one container to another. A number of containers of various sizes should be provided. Funnels, cups, sieves, and a toy water wheel all make interesting experiments. Volume is experienced at the snack table as he pours his beverage, or during cooking projects as he measures ingredients.

LENGTH AND DISTANCE.   Length and distance can be learned by comparisons of the lengths of pencils, nails, pegs, or blocks. The teacher uses "shortest" or "longest" to designate the plank or table she's seeking. Concepts of length and distance can be experienced in the room or the yard or around the block.

SIZE, SHAPE, AND WEIGHT.   As the child uses blocks and packing boxes of various sizes, he learns about size, shape, and weight. Concepts such as big-little, large-small, high-low, wide-narrow, and long-short are learned through the motor activities involved in building. Learning names for geometric shapes and relating the concept of shape to toys and materials in the environment are important. Children may use functional labels such as *window* for a square. At that point they are ready to learn to label it a *square.*

BALANCE.   Balancing is needed on teeter-totters, walking planks, and rocking boats and to walk a railing or wall. During block play this concept can be demonstrated if the children fail to grasp it themselves.

SPEED.   Opportunities to learn concepts of fast and slow are developed through the use of wheel toys and swings or through rolling objects of different sizes and weights down an inclined plane.

GRAVITY.   Children experience the effects of gravity when rolling down a hill, sliding down the slide, flying paper airplanes, and throwing handkerchief parachutes. The teacher can teach this concept when cautioning children about taking heavy objects into high places.

FIGURE 8–7.   *Pouring, filling, measuring, and straining are all experienced at the water table. (Michigan State University Spartan Cooperative Nursery School.)*

FIGURE 8–8. *"What happens if you blow into this mixture?" asks the teacher, giving the children a bowl of detergent and water and a drinking straw. (Texas Woman's University Nursery School.)*

MACHINES AND TOOLS. Americans are gadget minded, and the typical child today has had more experience with large and small machines than many adults of other generations. Machines and tools make work easier. The children help the teacher hammer nails in a favorite packing box. The children use carpenter's tools. She asks them how they would hammer or saw if there were no tools. They help the teacher use pliers to correct a screw on a tricycle handlebar. Could they do this with their fingers? When a wheel comes off a toy, there may be an opportunity to examine the axle and perhaps the ball bearing. An inclined plane can help the group move a heavy object up on a packing box. A pulley can be fashioned with a rope and a box to show that through the use of the pulley the child can lift an object he is unable to lift outright. It is an interesting game. A collection of bolts and nuts of varying sizes provides a sorting experience related to the world of machines. Small motor skills are practiced as the children screw the nuts on the bolts. Tools and other construction toys give children opportunities to become inventors— discovering new combinations each time.

The opportunity to watch large machines working should not be passed up. Children learn about the world of work, machines, the construction of buildings or roads, sounds, and the roles of various workers as they watch a bulldozer, cement mixer, crane, train, or

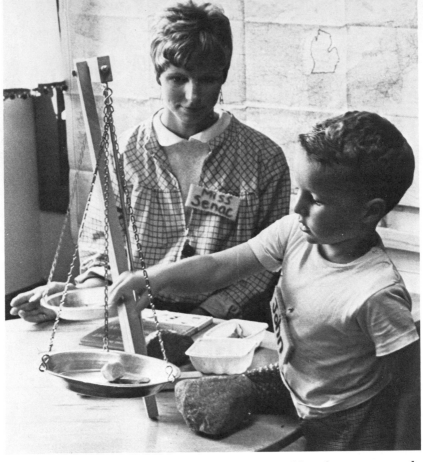

FIGURE 8–9. *Making the scales balance helps children become more observant and knowledgable about weights and densities. (Michigan State University Laboratory Preschool.)*

the like. A study of transportation combines concepts of machines, of travel, and of the world of work.

SOUNDS. Sounds are of interest to children. Most young children learn such parlor tricks as "What does a dog say?" Teachers know that children run to the window or become fearful when a siren is heard near the school. Because children are usually alert to fine differences in sounds, they are good imitators. Their attention may have to be directed so that they learn to identify new sounds. On a walk in the woods they can be encouraged to "listen to the quiet," as one child put it.

A study of sounds can include the sounds of toys; the sounds of household machines, such as a mixer, a sewing machine, or a clock; the sounds of people laughing, crying, or scolding; and the sounds of animals. Attention can be drawn to pitch, rhythm, and volume.

TABLE 8–2   *Number Concepts Understood*

Name	1	2	3	4	5	6	7 8 9 10	Rote to
John			$1 + 1 + 1$ $2 + 1$	$1 + 1 + 1 + 1$ $2 + 2$ $3 + 1$	$1 + 4$ $2 + 3$ $4 + 1$			20
Mary			$+1$ $2 + 1$	$+1$ $2 + 2$ $3 + 1$	$+1$ $2 + 3$ $4 + 1$	$+1$ $2 + 4$ $3 + 3$ $5 + 1$		15

Concepts of sound will be better learned if one has real-life experiences with the sounds. Though children learn to answer "Moo" when asked "What does the cow say?" they really understand after a visit to the dairy. "She *does* say moo!" confirmed a five-year-old.

Vibrations produce sounds. Children learn from making, feeling, and hearing vibrations. They discover they can stop vibrations with their hands. Musical instruments of various kinds offer numerous possibilities. Tapping various materials to hear the sound differences allows children to experiment with sound production. Further suggestions will be included in the music and rhythm chapter.

Listening to sound is, of course, the way the child develops his language in the first place. Promoting listening as well as talking is important in all communication. Suggestions to help foster language development will be included in the chapter on language arts.

Many children are concerned by night sounds. Some children have deep fears regarding sounds they hear when they awake at night. Experience identifying sounds can help them realize how the sound is being made so that it will not be frightening. Several stories can help initiate the discussion. They are *Noise in the Night*, by Anne Alexander; *Muffin in the City* and *Muffin in the Country*, both by Margaret Wise Brown; "Hiding in the Dark" and "Nighttime" from *Martin and Judy*, Volume I, by Verna Hills Bayley.

CHEMISTRY IN COOKING AND CLEANING.   The kitchen is one of the best chemistry laboratories. With the teacher's assistance children can stir up food mixtures of various types. The children can discover the effects of heating and cooling. For details related to cooking projects see the chapter on lunches and snacks.

Using solvents to clean up various substances also teaches children the nature of chemicals. For example, waxed crayon stuck to table tops is impossible to clean up with water, yet comes off readily when liquid wax is used. (Teachers should remember this and avoid using harsh cleansers on smooth finishes.) Children can learn that the use of detergent or soap makes the water more effective for removing the dirt from their hands.

COLORS. Concepts of color develop during the years before six. Color is closely related to the creative art materials discussed in Chapter 7. Discussion of color should be included in any experience in which it is relevant. The use of the prism to refract the light showing the colors of the rainbow gives children a pleasant way to discover color. Children learn the names for common colors.

TIME. Americans, more than peoples of many other cultures, are time oriented. Children become time conscious early partly due to their TV programs. A phrase like "after *Sesame Street*" is a common time-orienting phrase used by mothers. American children learn early that it is important to be on time for an appointment.

Teachers help children's time orientation by developing regular routines; for example, juice is served about 10 A.M. A cardboard clock placed under or beside a real clock can be set with the time for a looked-forward-to event. Children will keep their eye on the real clock to see when it moves to the set time. They are learning to tell time.

The calendar may interest some young children. Little by little they learn the days of the week—that Monday is the first day of school in the week and Friday the last. They will be able to remember some of the names of the months. A class calendar can be marked with special dates—holidays and birthdays. Some teachers like to permit one child to mark the day's weather on the calendar each day. Both calendars and clocks give children experience with numbers. Much of this is very abstract, with depth of understanding to be developed in the children's later years.

As children begin to gain an understanding of time, they are also learning the routine of seasonal changes, the sequence of the sun rising and setting, and their own routine during the day.

Historical time is a difficult concept for young children. When visiting a historical train exhibit, a four-year-old said, "It was an old-old train, and an old-old man showed it to us. He was fifteen or sixteen." The phrases "olden days" and "when you were a little girl" are often used by children to designate times long gone.

GEOLOGY. Mike, a five-year-old, showed a favorite rock at "show and tell," saying, "This is a quartz crystal. My brother's Scout leader gave it to me." With Mike's enthusiasm as a starter the entire class became immersed in a study of rocks that was carried on throughout the school year. The children brought rocks and fossils found along streets and alleys in their neighborhoods. The teacher brought her rocks. She had pumice that floats, obsidian used by the Indians for scrapers, and lava she had collected in lava beds in Central America.

The lava led naturally to a discussion of volcanoes. The teacher brought slides and set up a viewing area, where some children looked over and over at color photos taken of an erupting volcano. The children pored over the encyclopedia—"the important books," as they called them—looking for pictures of volcanoes. Some volcanoes were pictured with prehistoric animals. This fact led them into a study of dinosaurs. Combining the two interests led naturally to the museum to see minerals under ultraviolet light and to see dinosaur skeletons.

A few rocks and a magnifying glass can start the study of rocks. Purchasing a labeled collection can encourage a beginner, whether teacher or child, to identify, classify, and label. Nearly every locality has its rock hounds (collectors) who are usually eager to share their hobbies with children.

In mining communities and oil-producing areas special emphasis can be placed on the local minerals. Children can learn something of the formations, the method of extracting, and the economic importance of the mines or wells—especially the energy resources used by a family.

Understanding Mathematical Concepts

"How old are you, little girl?" asks a kindly old lady in the grocery store. Little Mary shyly puts up three fingers. She may say, "Three." Chances are that Mary couldn't do this old parlor trick at two, and after five she'll probably just give a verbal answer. Mathematical learning begins at a young age, especially when concepts are closely related to the child. Mary is beginning to learn mathematics.

Numbers surround us. In fact, with the advent of the computer many people feel that they are being dehumanized by being assigned numbers that can be fed into machines. The child often has a social security number at a young age; he has phone number, a house number, a number of brothers and sisters, one tricycle, many books, a few dolls, or so many pennies. He sees his mother using money, a cup of sugar and two eggs in a cake; she divides the candy bar in half; or she pours the glass half full of his favorite soft drink. The child hears about a TV program on channel 2 at eight o'clock. He sees his mother scurrying around to keep an appointment at a certain hour, or he goes for a visit on a given date, and hears of plans for next year.

Such incidental happenings as the above may be the child's mathematical experience as he enters school. The teacher's role is one of clarifying his present concepts and adding new concepts in a meaningful way. The fallacy of teaching children to parrot the "right" answer should be clear. There will undoubtedly be problems in the future that teachers today do not have the "right" answer for. It is hoped the tools of reason and the attitude of experimentation she leaves with her children will encourage some of them to become the future Einsteins. An adult might memorize a calculus formula and be able to recite it perfectly. However, without the undergirding understanding and experience, he would have limited use for the material he had memorized. So it is with children. They can learn to verbalize numbers, but if they do not understand the basic reasoning leading to them, so-called knowledge will be useless.

Children must become physically involved in learning mathematical concepts. The mathematical teaching must start with the child and remain relevant to him. He will be ready for abstract thinking at an older age. Teachers of young children should plan ways to incorporate mathematics into the children's total school experience. Words denoting mathematical ideas are used whenever possible. Rote counting is related to real objects.

For example, when making cupcakes the teacher says, "Let's count the children to see how many cupcakes we need." The teacher and the children point to each child and count. "We need fifteen cupcakes for our group. Let's count out fifteen cupcake papers." This project gives three opportunities to relate counting to a practical problem at hand. Such an opportunity will mean different things to each child participating. One may not know about counting, another may not know all the numbers, another may not understand how to determine quantity after counting by rote, and another may have full understanding of the process. Through careful observation the teacher determines the level of each child's ability and helps him to add to his concept. The teacher learns to select for each child a mathematical question that he can answer, because success with numbers, like success with other areas of learning, will keep the child willing to explore and try.

The teacher tests an individual child's concepts. She can keep ten cubes or pennies in her pocket. If the child is momentarily unoccupied or stops for a chat with the teacher, she can play a game of hiding the cubes or pennies, then bring out a given number, saying, "How many are there?" The teacher can continue the game, arranging cubes in various sets until she gets a clear idea of the child's ability. She can make a chart, such as the one in Table 8–2, to record the concepts each child understands. This study can guide her in planning further number experiences.

Mathematics for the young child includes counting, adding, subtracting, and dividing. He learns the fraction *one half*. Mathematical vocabulary should be taught as it relates to real experiences the child is having. The next chapter, on structured learning, will suggest

FIGURE 8–10. *What sinks? What floats? What's dry? What's wet? Does water run down hill? These concepts and many others are learned by experience when water play is provided. (Kansas State Child Development Laboratory School.)*

further how mathematical concepts are part of young children's experience and learning.

Conclusion

Stimulating the child's mental growth is of foremost importance during the years before six. The work of Landreth and Piaget suggests how this growth takes place. The child makes a serious attempt to make sense out of the world he lives in. Nursery schools and kindergartens can offer many projects and experiences through which children can discover concepts and build on the concepts they already have. A creative teacher, who herself has a well-developed sense of wonder and curiosity, will encourage her children to discover, think, and reason. She will help them make inferences and generalize.

The cumulative plan or building-block approach is suggested; each concept should be firmly based on what the child already knows. Experiences the teacher plans should remain highly relevant to the child's here-and-now experience throughout his early years. Many experiences can be repeated frequently, with children learning each time. The teacher's role is one of being certain that there is a wealth of things to learn throughout her program and that the children feel free to experiment, think, and discover new ideas. The science curriculum for the nursery school or kindergarten should be planned carefully and concretely. It is well to build on spontaneous experience of the children, but a program that relies wholly on such experiences will be cheating the children. Children want to learn and they can learn. Teachers must have faith in each child's ability. Learning science need not be a grim business but a really satisfying, invigorating experience that brings joy to lips and smiles to faces. Should a child turn away and show no interest, his behavior suggests that the teacher must search elsewhere for a meaningful experience for that particular child. It is a teacher's obligation to do this searching.

ADDITIONAL READINGS

ALMY, MILLIE. *Young Children's Thinking: Studies of Some Aspects of Piaget's Theory.* New York: Teachers College Press, Columbia University, 1967.

BIBER, BARBARA, et al. *Promoting Cognitive Growth.* Washington, D.C.: National Association for Education of Young Children, 1971.

BRUNER, JEROME S. *Toward a Theory of Instruction.* Cambridge, Mass.: Harvard University Press, 1966.

FREEMAN, IRA, and MAE FREEMAN. *Your Wonderful World of Science.* New York: Scholastic Book Services, 1967.

FROST, JOE L., and G. THOMAS ROWLAND. *Curricula for the Seventies, Early Childhood Through Early Adolescence.* Boston: Houghton Mifflin Company, 1969.

HOPMAN, ANNE B. (ed). *Helping Children Learn Science.* Washington, D.C.: National Science Teachers Association, 1966.

LANDRETH, CATHERINE. *Early Childhood: Behavior and Learning.* New York: Alfred A. Knopf, Inc., 1967.

LEEPER, SARAH H., et al. *Good Schools for Young Children.* New York: Macmillan Publishing Co., Inc., 1974.

NAULT, WM. H. (ed.). *About Me, Childcraft Annual.* Chicago: Field Enterprises Educational Corporation, 1969.

Ranger Rick's Nature Magazine. A children's magazine published by the National Wildlife Federation, 1412 16th St. N.W., Washington, D.C.

RASMUSSEN, MARGARET (ed.). *Young Children and Science.* Washington, D.C.: Association for Childhood Education International, 1964.

READ, KATHERINE. *The Nursery School.* Philadelphia: W. B. Saunders Company, 1971.

ROEPER, ANNEMARIE, and IRVING E. SIEGEL. "Finding the Clue to Children's Thought Processes," in *The Young Child* by Willard W. Hartrup and Nancy L. Smothergill (eds.). Washington, D.C.: National Association for Education of Young Children, 1967.

SCHMIDT, VICTOR E., and VERNE N. ROCKCASTLE. *Teaching Science with Everyday Things.* New York: McGraw-Hill Book Company, 1968.

TAYLOR, BARBARA J. *When I Do, I Learn.* Provo, Utah: Brigham Young University Press, 1974.

TODD, VIVIAN E., and HELEN HEFFERNAN. *The Years Before School: Guiding Preschool Children.* New York: Macmillan Publishing Co., Inc., 1970.

WANN, KENNETH D., MIRIAM S. DORI, and ELIZABETH LIDDLE. *Fostering Intellectual Development in Young Children.* New York: Teachers College Press, Columbia University, 1962.

9

Structured Learning Activities

MARIA, standing at a small table, firmly dumped the six-piece wooden puzzle out on the table. She immediately began replacing the pieces in the frame, one at a time. The largest piece went in first. It was the duck's body. Next, in went the head, followed by the bill and the feet. Maria was deeply absorbed in the task and did not notice what others were doing nearby. As the last piece dropped in place, Maria, looking up from her task, clapped her hands joyfully and smiled with self-satisfaction. Something about doing the puzzle must have given Maria some reward, for no one was near who acknowledged her success, yet she flipped the puzzle over and began to work it again.

Puzzles are just one of a number of early childhood learning materials we call *structured* because their form or composition does not change with use. Structured learning materials have size, shape, weight, color, and texture that remain constant.

Values of Structured Learning Activities

Structured learning materials contribute to all five of Landreth's intellectual operations, which were discussed in the previous chapter. When the child recognizes the problem or task suggested by the toy, he is using *cognition*. In the case of Maria, she knew the task required putting the pieces back in the frame. *Memory* was used when Maria recalled other puzzles, recalled the picture, or remembered from previous experience where each of the pieces belonged. It is clear from her speed that she was using little trial and error as she may have during her first use of the puzzle. *Convergent thinking* was being used, for in this type of material there tends to be one right answer or use of the material, as contrasted with art materials, previously discussed, which encourage wide variation in use. However, *divergent thinking* or novel use or response is possible with many

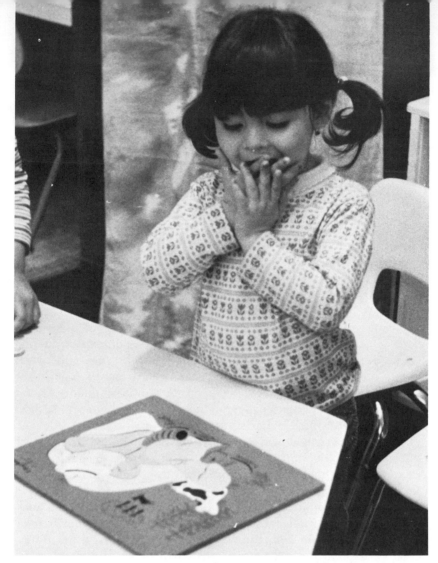

FIGURE 9–1. *Completing a puzzle gives the child an immediate sense of satisfaction. She knows when it is complete and that it is correct. (National Institute of Education Child Study Center, U.S. Office of Education.)*

structured materials, if the adults will permit novel uses. The puzzle Maria worked, for example, might have been put together on the table without the use of the frame, or upside down without the clues derived from the painted designs on the pieces. Or Maria might have traced around the pieces and made a drawing of a duck, a somewhat unusual use for puzzle pieces. *Evaluation* occurred when Maria put a piece in the wrong place and, realizing her error, retrieved the piece and placed it correctly. Many structured learning materials are self-correcting. That is, they won't work or be complete unless everything is in its correct place.

Sensorimotor experience is derived through structured learning materials. The child uses his senses and his small muscles to explore the materials. He learns most from having ample time to explore the materials—building, arranging, dismantling, and redoing. Having adults ply him with questions regarding the characteristics of the material or what he is doing with it is generally considered to be important but is secondary to exploration in the learning process for young children.

Eye-hand coordination is developed with many of the materials because they require seeing the pieces and manipulating them in specific ways. Puzzle pieces are arranged in the frame, beads are strung, pegs are placed perpendicularly in the holes of a pegboard. Many of the materials require small muscle coordination, but large muscles and eyes are also coordinated when planks and packing boxes are manipulated on the playground or in the block corner.

Concepts of many kinds develop through the use of structured learning materials. Size, shape, weight, color, and texture are experienced. Spatial concepts—large, small, thick, thin, up, over, around, under, beside, and so on—become clearer as the child uses these toys. The mathematical concepts of number, quantity, and equivalence are experienced as children count, exchange, measure, and balance with these materials.

Perception of whole-part relationships is gained with many of these materials. In Maria's puzzle, for example, she recognized the parts (feet, bill) and their relationship to the rest of the duck. You may observe children who do not recognize the pieces that are eyes or hands, for example, and see them try to fit them into what may appear to you to be illogical places. If so, they may need your help or verbal guidance. Attention can be directed to likenesses and differences. Perhaps in the duck puzzle the two feet are alike and interchangeable, but perhaps not, and the children then learn to note the difference between them. Color is also an important characteristic of many of these toys. Children learn to label and differentiate colors while enjoying puzzles.

Figure-ground perception is experienced through some of the toys. That is, one child may concentrate on the puzzle frame while another concentrates on the picture design of the pieces. Thus each child would be perceiving the task of the puzzle differently. The child's perception, then, influences how the adult offers help.

Vocabulary is continually growing as children talk about what they are doing, labeling the objects, the parts, and the process they are involved in. Some social conversation arises naturally as children share materials, cooperate on building or putting toys together, or have disputes over prior rights to a toy or a learning space.

Curiosity is developed and satisfied through the use of these structured materials. Motivation is high because children are generally attracted to things that come apart, things that move, and things that they can handle without admonishment. A sense of accomplishment is quickly achieved, and the child can select another toy or repeat his use of the original one. Certain of these materials reward persistence, as children easily note when the puzzle is worked or the lotto board is filled up.

Inventiveness and creativity are fostered by some of these structured learning materials. Structured materials may attract children who shy away from the messy, nonstructured art media. These children are finding an avenue of creative expression that is valid and comfortable for them.

Many prereading and prewriting skills are developed through these materials; for example, handedness, left-to-right progression, symbol correspondence, and observation. Ascertaining likenesses, differences, and whole-part relationships, which are inherent in many of these toys, contributes to these academic skills.

The self-pacing quality and generally individual use of the structured learning materials give the child a chance to explore, correct, test, and retest by himself, as he remains freer of competition than he may with some other materials or activities he finds in the early childhood center.

Types of Structured Learning Materials

A visitor to any high-quality child development center will discover many structured learning materials invitingly displayed where children can stop to use them for a moment or the whole morning. The materials may be called *manipulative toys* or *table games,* though either of these labels eliminates certain toys. For our purposes, structured learning materials may be classified into three groups: (1) perception, (2) construction, and (3) coordination. These groups are not mutually exclusive but may be helpful when one is thinking about the main purpose that a toy serves.

Perception

Perception materials help the child learn through the senses—touching, seeing, hearing, smelling, or tasting. The perceptual process includes judgment and subtle discrimination.

Sorting objects for likenesses and differences is called *classification* and is required by a number of toys, for example, the lotto games that are popular with late four-year-olds and with five-year-olds. Lotto games are generally developed so that the large card that the child holds has one general category of object, for example, things to eat. The small cards that the children turn up have matching cards. In a set of four cards each of the other children may have firemen's tools, or flowers, or motor vehicles. The perceptive child quickly notes that he has "things to eat" and passes over any card that does not fit that category. He quickly discriminates between his category and the others as each card in the pile is turned over. The less perceptive or less experienced child scans his card each time to discover if he has the card in question and usually reports to his friends each time.

When you are guiding the use of lotto games it is preferable to watch children play a time or two to discover at what level they are operating. Thus you avoid assuming the children are at a more immature level than they really are or vice versa. After a time you may profitably ask them to look at their cards and tell what is alike about the objects on each card. You might say, "What do you do with the things on your card, Jane?" or, "Who uses tools like the ones you see on your card, John?"

Uncle Wiggily, Candyland, and similar games require the ability to match, count, and take turns with peers. Delbert, Jamie, and the teacher, Miss Smith, were about to begin another game of Candyland. As happens from time to time with some structured learning activities, a dispute developed. Both boys were yelling, "I wanta be first! Let me go first." Miss Smith picked up a red token, placed her hands behind her back, and said, "Whoever picks the hand with the red token goes first." Both boys were satisfied. Miss Smith, like many good teachers, knows and utilizes various successful methods for settling disputes quickly—methods that avoid harsh discipline and that promote good relationships and facilitate a continuation of the desired learning activities.

Dominoes with either pictures or dots representing numbers also provide experience in visual discrimination. The children match from their "hand" in turn or simply work together or alone making a "train" of dominoes from the pile of dominoes as they match. The children discriminate primarily according to likenesses and differences without even counting the dots on the dominoes. The double-six set is sufficient for children through four years, but many fives can enjoy a double-nine set. Double nines even test the adults! For young children keeping score makes the game too complicated.

Card games such as "concentration" and "fish" can be enjoyed by some children in older groups. Some games require the collecting of cards that are alike. A simple way to use the cards with younger children is to let them sort the cards into their various categories.

FIGURE 9–2. *The game Candyland requires matching the card in hand with the spaces on the board and moving a token. Late four- and five-year-olds take turns as they play together. (Michigan State University Laboratory Preschool.)*

Small children can do this on a table in order to avoid the difficulty they have holding the cards in their hands.

Cubes, beads, pegs, buttons, bolts and nuts, bottle caps, and other objects can be used for sorting (classifying) experiences. In classifying you simply group things together that are alike in some way. Egg cartons or muffin tins are handy for separating small objects. Boxes can be divided into sections to accommodate larger objects. You might have little cars in several colors. You can work with a child, saying, "Give me one like mine." If he is learning colors, say, "Give me a red one." After the group has been sorted you can ask, "What color are these cars?" After they are mixed up again you might say, "Put your finger on the red block," helping the child learn the color labels.

In using pegboards and pegs or beads, the teacher might say, "You make a little design and I'll try to make one like it." Then after she matches the child's design she can suggest, "Now, John, you make one like mine." Children also enjoy making designs for others to match, unless the designs get too complicated or the game becomes too long. Give only one variable at a time; that is, if you ask the child to classify according to color, then save classifying according to shape for another day. According to research, once a young child has ordered objects in one way he has some difficulty at this young age seeing the same objects in another way.

Parquetry blocks require the child to organize basic geometric-shaped blocks according to designs in the bottom of the box. In helping a child new to parquetry, you can say, "Which block looks like this one?" as you point to a geometric shape. Children enjoy sorting the parquetry blocks into piles of "look-alikes" on the table and even like to arrange their own designs without the aid of the printed designs. This is a creative use of the toy that should be encouraged. Various other games encourage children to classify shapes. Teachers should go a step further and call the children's attention to shapes in their classroom and in the play yard. Even snacks come in interesting shapes, from triangle sandwiches to round cookies.

The imaginative teacher can make a classifying experience out of numerous common objects. Helping sort the plastic spoons and forks in the housekeeping corner is a classifying experience. The block corner, with its shelf of squares, triangles, cylinders, and so on, is a classification opportunity. With this perception, teachers realize that putting away the blocks is a valuable learning experience for children. This holds true in most areas of school; that is, the crayons all go together in one basket and the scissors in another, while the tricycles are all grouped in one storage closet.

Seriation is another perceptual activity described by Piaget. The child looks at at least three objects, determines whether they are the same, and then arranges them in a series, perhaps according to size. Maria Montessori, a pioneer early childhood educator, also felt that seriation was important. She presented children with numerous graduated cylinders with matching holes in a long bar. This matching game was self-correcting; that is, the child knew when he was correct by the way the cylinder fitted the space.

Nested boxes or cans are examples of seriation toys. Another is the Montessori "pink tower," built from graduated boxes stacked to make a tower. This toy has been replicated by numerous manufacturers since Montessori's day. Teachers can prepare tin cans of various sizes in the same way.

The stacking disc toy, consisting of a single spindle over which the child slips colored discs, is familiar to most. Graduated from the large base to a screw-on top, the toy is a challenge to perceptual, coordination, and seriation skills. When this toy is given to toddlers before the "age of accountability," they frequently use the spindle part for a hammer, much to the dismay of their educationally hopeful parents.

To learn discrimination of relative size, the child may line objects up in order. Many common objects found in the home and school— such as balls, pop bottles, and cold cream jars can be used for this purpose. In guiding the child's participation, be sure that you offer appropriate word pairs—tallest-shortest, biggest-smallest, longest-shortest and so on.

Children can also practice seriation in arranging chairs or tricycles in the room or yard. "Let's put all the large ones in the back," suggests the teacher. The children may need help with the labels describing these perceptual tasks.

Construction

Several types of construction materials allow children to build, thus helping them discover balance, weight, height, and depth. Some materials are quite small and can be used most comfortably on a table, whereas others are large and are used on the floor or in the play yard.

BLOCKS.   Blocks are probably one of the most important types of equipment supplied by a high-quality early childhood education center. They give children an opportunity to express their ideas, interpret what they observe, and express their feelings. The shelves of blocks may be the first equipment that impresses a visitor, as blocks are displayed in a prominent place and there are many of them. This arrangement encourages the children to incorporate them into many types of play. Children discover height, balance, and directionality as they use blocks. They learn to judge the amount of space required to enclose themselves or a toy animal or car. They experience distance as they select a block to make a bridge over their road. A child's ideas, information, and creativity are coordinated as the child uses blocks. He recalls a "house" and builds one for a doll family. He recalls a "bridge" or "overpass" and builds that over his road. Gravity is experienced as blocks topple down or the small toy car runs down the ramps the children build. Note the involvement of the children in the following incident.

Steve and Eddie were using the large hollow wooden blocks. Using the ramp, they found some excitement in running their cars down the ramp and seeing them shoot rapidly off to one side. They noted other ramps in the corner of the room and brought them to add to their ramp. It didn't work, they discovered, to lay the ramps together on the same level. Steve and Eddie surveyed their problem, then brought a large block to put under one ramp, creating excitement

FIGURE 9–3. *Shape matching and color matching are required by this perception game made by the teacher. (Michigan State University Laboratory Preschool.)*

for all when their cars swooshed down the two ramp run. Now they added two big blocks and a third ramp to make a three-ramp run. "Wow!" exclaimed Eddie, "Everybody stand back. This is really going to be a race now!" The downhill run proved interesting not only to Steve and Eddie but to other children who were attracted by the excitement, until numerous races developed out of the two boys' initial idea. Gravity had been discovered that afternoon, and it was a simple matter for the teacher to give the boys and the others a label for it as the activity came to a close that day.

Large blocks come in several varieties. The largest are usually about 22″ × 11″ × 5½″, with the smaller ones being half or one fourth the large size. Hollow wooden blocks have been available for many years and are extremely popular in both nursery schools and kindergartens. Though expensive, they are very durable, making them an almost permanent investment for the school. Large blocks are now being made of polyethylene and other man-made materials. These latter blocks have the advantage of being weatherproof and not splitting or peeling in moist climates. Auxiliary pieces, such as planks and ramps, greatly increase versatility. A set of sixty large

FIGURE 9–4. *Large, hollow wooden blocks are indispensable in the nursery school and kindergarten to aid children's exploration of space. Here two boys find creative use for the ramps. (Texas Tech University Kindergarten.)*

blocks for twenty nursery school children and a set of seventy-five for twenty kindergarten children are recommended.

Large packing boxes used in the play yard may contribute the same kind of learning as blocks, having the additional virtue of allowing the child to get inside them. When large wooden boxes are made specifically for school use, they should be made in several sizes. Children will learn that one size may be more useful for one activity than another. Hollow blocks and packing boxes can be combined in interesting and productive play. It is convenient to have a push truck in the play yard to encourage children to take the blocks where they see a use for them. Also, when the play is finished the blocks are easily loaded on the truck and returned to storage.

Cardboard blocks are an outstanding and less expensive substitute for wooden blocks. These approximately shoe-box-sized blocks are colorful, and they are made with an inside support that reinforces them, making them stronger than they appear at first glance. Surprisingly, even adults won't squash them if they stand on them. Parents who purchased a dozen cardboard blocks when their children were small say these blocks represent their best-spent toy dollar, because their children have used them extensively for many years. Five

FIGURE 9–5. *A steering wheel makes a useful addition to the block play, suggesting various types of dramatic play requiring transportation. (Texas Woman's University.)*

dozen will serve a classroom for a number of years for indoor block play. They are not appropriate for damp play yards.

Unit blocks are all multiples or divisions of the basic unit, which measures 1⅜″ × 2¾″ × 5½″. All are made of hard woods and are carefully sanded. Besides squares and rectangles there are columns, arches, triangles, quarter circles, and numerous other shapes. All fit together precisely. About five hundred pieces are needed in a typical nursery school and more in a kindergarten classroom. Storage for unit blocks should include enough shelf space to accommodate each shape and size of block without crowding. These shapes can be marked on the back of the shelves with a drawing to help children and adults find where the different blocks go at cleanup time. Obviously this sorting and classifying is an important opportunity for cognitive learning. Small trucks stored near the blocks encourage children to load and unload blocks as well as to build roads for the vehicles.

Small blocks are much smaller even than unit blocks and contribute especially to small muscle dexterity. These blocks are made of either wood or plastic. Many are very small, and though interlocking, they make somewhat fragile and unstable buildings; therefore, use at a table is usually preferred. The older four- and five-year-old children generally have the muscle coordination and patience to enjoy these small blocks, whereas younger children find them frustrating. Some sets are profitably kept in the "rainy-day closet" to be brought out only rarely, when a new activity is needed to replace "rained-out" activities.

Block substitutes are made by some inventive teachers and parents. They stuff one cardboard milk carton with newspaper; then as it stands upright, a second milk carton opened at the top is forced down

FIGURE 9–6. *Unit blocks may be combined with small airplanes, cars, or animals in a construction experience. Note the cardboard blocks stored on the top shelf. (University of Houston Parent-Child Development Center.)*

over the first carton. The edges can be taped with plastic or masking tape.

Guiding block play presents many opportunities for creative teaching. Children will use many blocks and build magnificent structures if the schedule is open enough to allow sufficient time and if adults encourage creativity. With all blocks, the teacher's role is to provide an adequate number for her group of children and to store them where the children have ample building space away from generally used traffic lanes. Auxiliary figures and toys stored nearby make outstanding contributions to block play. Carpeting on the block-playing area will absorb the noise made by falling blocks and the children's exuberant play.

Block structures are often knocked down. This is quite acceptable, but the teacher can also encourage children to use their creativity in taking down their block structures piece by piece. Sorting and categorizing skills can be learned while the blocks are being placed on the shelves. If the teacher works with the children as they put blocks away, saying, "You bring them to me, and I'll help put them on the shelves," she may be surprised at the resulting cooperation. With a cooperative air the children will help and others will join in the fun, even though they may not have used the blocks. If the teacher says, "Thank you," or "What a big load!" these rewards will usually be sufficient to get the children's happy cooperation. Singing a song, like "Pickin' up blocks and put 'em on the shelf," to the tune of "Pawpaw Patch," helps, too. By all means avoid having a curse placed on using the blocks by assistants too lazy to help with putting them away. All should avoid the admonition, "*You* got the blocks out, *you* put them away," which is sometimes heard. Such a technique discourages the children's use of this valuable educational resource.

Children should be warned that cleanup time is approaching, so that they can finish their building project and the imaginative play that accompanies it. The teacher may extend the play period to allow the children who have worked diligently to construct something a few minutes to use it. In this way the teacher avoids frustrating the children and shows her understanding of the children's need to use a building they have constructed.

Sometimes the teacher may permit the children to leave their block structures set up so that they can add to them from day to day. This practice is most feasible when a single group uses the room. With care it can be allowed when one teacher has two groups using a room or even when two teachers share a room—if good cooperation exists between the teachers.

OTHER CONSTRUCTION TOYS.   In addition to blocks there are many other interesting construction toys. Some are plastic and some are

FIGURE 9–7. *One-to-one correspondence is learned in this puzzle. This young child is ambidexterous, using the left hand for pieces on the left and the right hand for those on the right.*

wooden. Some pop together over a plastic bubble or knob; some fit together in precut grooves or join with snaps like the grippers on a child's pajamas. Like blocks these toys give the child an opportunity to build in three dimensions and to use his imagination. They also give practice in small muscle coordination. Some can be frustrating to young children who are not coordinated enough to handle them. Some come with patterns to copy, which are generally too difficult for young children and may inhibit creativity. Therefore extensive use of patterns should be avoided. Children should have ample opportunity to create their own designs and structures.

PUZZLES. Puzzles are popular construction toys, as indicated in the opening anecdote of this chapter. Puzzles differ from other construction toys, however, for the task calls for the child to assemble pieces in a specific and preconceived way to make a picture in its original form. This is a clear example of a convergent task—one calling for one right answer.

There are a number of different kinds of puzzles. The most popular for nursery schools and kindergartens are those made of wood. Recently some have been made in colorful rubber, which adds an interesting textural experience. Puzzles are very durable, withstanding years of use by classes of children if care is taken not to lose pieces. Choices of puzzles include such things as animals, vehicles, and familiar scenes from children's lives and from books they know. Usually each piece is an object, a part, or a body, enabling children to think about replacing a head, a foot, or a wheel. This arrangement helps the child grasp the concepts of whole and part. Another type of puzzle provides inlays of whole objects grouped with related objects—such as five fruits, five vegetables, or five objects to wear when it rains. Some puzzles have knobs for removing the pieces, but although knobs do give the child experience in grasping, they seem unessential to puzzles and are easily broken off. Puzzles can be stored in specially built racks, which aids their care and protection. Knob puzzles require special racks.

Puzzles must be selected according to the number of pieces with which the child is ready to cope. Development and experience are more important than chronological age; however, four to six pieces are usually appropriate for three-year-olds and up to thirty for advanced kindergarteners. Some kindergarteners may even be ready for the United States map puzzle.

Guiding a child's use of puzzles begins with selecting the level of puzzle the child is ready for—not too hard, not too easy. Sometimes a child gains confidence from putting together a simple, familiar puzzle before going on to harder ones. Sometimes suggesting removing one piece, then replacing it, helps a child who is having trouble proceeding. You can offer a little help and encouragement if a child seems ready to give up, though you should avoid compelling a child to complete a puzzle. However, a common situation is for the child to help the adult, for there is nothing so sobering as to be left to work a child's puzzle that you haven't seen whole! A graduate student had this happen to him the first day he worked with a four-year-old group. The man picked up the jumbled mass in honest embarrassment, asking himself out loud, "Now, how in the world do you do this?" Whereupon a child volunteered, "Here, I'll help you." And he did, with the eternal thanks of the young man.

Arranging the puzzle storage adjacent to tables encourages children to use puzzles and other structured learning materials on the tables, helps keep pieces from being mislaid, and helps keep the distractions of other tasks from interfering with the child's work. If a teacher checks the toys after each self-selected activity period, she can ask the children to help look for any missing pieces before the pieces are lost for good. Sometimes children absentmindedly place pieces in their pockets, so simply say, "Children, check your pockets to see if our missing puzzle piece is hiding there." Seek the coopera-

FIGURE 9–8. *Part-whole concepts are experienced by this four-year-old with the wooden-pieced puzzle that fits in a wooden frame. (Nazarene Child Care Center, Lansing, Michigan.)*

tion of the custodians too, so they won't sweep out your precious pieces. Once a puzzle piece is missing the puzzle should be retired for repair. One method of repairing a puzzle is to line the hole with plastic wrap and fill it with wood filler, letting it set. After it is set it can be painted, hopefully to match the rest of the puzzle.

Puzzles are a long-range investment. Some puzzles should be stored away to rotate as "new" from time to time. They are an activity that children can usually manage without much help or supervision, leaving teachers free to handle more complicated learning centers.

Children can occasionally make their own puzzles by selecting a magazine picture and gluing it to cardboard—men's shirt boards are good. Put the glued picture flat under books to dry, with a wax paper on top of the picture. Wax paper does not adhere to white glue. After the glue is dry, the pieces can be cut. A paper cutter is helpful in this task. Remember to make the pieces simple at first; then they can be cut further if the child is ready.

Coordination

One group of materials helps the child to learn small motor coordination and to practice these motor skills until they become unconscious and automatic. You, for example, once had to look at and think consciously about tying your shoelace; now you do it automatically.

Small motor coordination plays an important role in reading and writing, which are in their preliminary stages during the preschool years. Lugo and Hershey suggest four steps in the sequence of mastering a fine motor skill. First, the needed maturation of the visual and hand muscles must be present; second, the child notes the problem or task and is motivated to try to do it; third, he tries out the task; and fourth, he practices until mastery is achieved.[1] Children in our early childhood centers may be at any stage of this four-step sequence. A child may be more advanced in some skills than in others. Our task is to present the children with interesting materials and with support while they develop and practice these skills.

BEAD OR RING STRINGING.   Manipulative skills develop as the child strings beads or rings. Special laces with metal tips are available, making the task easier when the holes are small. In an emergency a piece of masking tape rolled securely around the end of a lace will make the tip firm and enable the child to get it through the bead. At a beginning level the child will mostly be concerned with transferring beads to string. Later he will become selective, perhaps choosing red beads, or square ones, or even alternating the beads to form a pattern.

Another lacing task is shoelacing. This is a practical task, and parents will be happy if their children learn to do it. There are several shoelacing toys available, but the inventive teacher can merely bring a discarded shoe for children to practice lacing and tying. However, both teachers and parents should remember that tying shoelaces is generally learned when the child is five or six years old. Also in the clothing line are items used to practice buttoning, zipping, and snapping. Though these, too, are available commercially, they can be made by anyone with some time, materials, and elementary sewing skills.

Lacing string or yarn in sewing cards and special lacing cards gives good practice. One drawback is that teachers generally must unlace the cards to prepare them for reuse, a task that becomes time-consuming and tedious. Sewing on burlap with yarn in large needles is a similar task, and the child is allowed to keep his creation.

[1] James O. Lugo and Gerald L. Hershey, *Human Development* (New York: Macmillan, 1974), pp. 365–366.

The teacher will want a needle threader to help with keeping the children's needles threaded. It is wise to start the day with a number of needles already threaded. Tacking burlap to wooden frames helps the children use it more successfully.

PEGBOARDS. Pegboards and a basket of colorful pegs especially intrigue the youngest preschoolers. First they select pegs at random and concentrate on fitting them in the holes. Later, children may create designs or follow a friend's pattern or the teacher's. Squares of ceiling celotex with holes can be used for pegboards, thus providing children another sensory experience.

Coordination practice is carried out in other situations in the school. The use of writing and drawing tools and scissors, the tearing of paper, and the squeezing of glue bottles are examples. Turning pages of books, placing the needle on the record player, and buttoning and zipping clothing all contribute to coordination practice.

Coordination skills are preliminary to many other motor skills, and teachers can encourage their practice by setting expectations that are individual. Age is not the best criterion, and some three-year-olds excel some fives. Competitive situations should be avoided, for when a child notes his failure, he may grow tense and begin to avoid the practice that would help him.

Guiding Structured Learning Activities

Purchasing a variety of structured learning materials and displaying them invitingly are the beginning steps in guiding children's use of them. Generally they are placed on shelves or in areas designated for their use, and the children move in and out of the areas as they become interested during self-selected activity periods. Because many of the materials are used by one child working alone, there are fewer quarrels over these materials, and less close adult supervision is usually needed than in some of the other areas of the school. This characteristic is a plus for overworked teachers, who can oversee these materials from a distance while they concentrate their energies in a more demanding area. Caution is advised, however, for children do need support, especially in their initial use of these materials. Teachers can encourage new uses of materials or encourage a child to think at a higher level if they keep close watch on how the children use the materials. Teachers should note which children use what materials and which children never use some of the materials. Teachers should then determine if these children are practicing perception, construction, and coordination skills sufficiently in other parts of the program. It is highly likely that they are, but if not, they may need some individual attention and encouragement.

FIGURE 9–9. *Imaginative play using parts from a structured game (left) and parts of an erector set (right). (Texas Tech University Kindergarten.)*

Teachers are cautioned against plying children with continuous questioning; many of these materials are used in an explorative fashion at first and the children cannot label what they are discovering. Their learning deepens as they gain experience.

In a rare case a child may learn to isolate himself from others by using these individual type activities. These materials may become a refuge for a withdrawn child. In such situations the teachers should plan ways to help the child learn to associate with others successfully and comfortably.

Many guidance problems can be eliminated if the space is arranged so that a child who is involved with one of these toys is not interfered with needlessly by children passing to and fro. With planned storage, children can learn to return these materials to their rightful place.

Conclusion

Structured learning materials are those toys in which size, shape, weight, color, and texture do not change. Their use helps children learn concepts about the physical world, stimulating many types of intellectual operations. Structured learning materials provide opportunities for three types of experience; perception, construction, and coordination. Many are manipulated individually and are self-

FIGURE 9–10. *Assembling a picture puzzle and joining parts cut in several pieces requires an advanced level of ability. (National Institute of Education Child Study Center, U.S. Office of Education.)*

paced and self-correcting. Inventiveness and creativity are fostered by many of the structured materials and may be an important avenue of expression for those children who do not enjoy nonstructured activities. Prereading and prewriting skills are being developed through the use of structured learning materials, for example, left-to-right progression, handedness, and symbol comparisons.

ADDITIONAL READINGS

ANKER, DOROTHY, et al. "Teaching Children as They Play." *Young Children,* Vol. 29, No. 4, May 1974, 203–213.
CARTWRIGHT, SALLY. "Blocks and Learning." *Young Children,* Vol. 29, No. 3, March 1974, 141–146.

EARHART, EILEEN. "Classification Training Curriculum." *Child Study Journal*, Vol. 2, No. 4, April 1972, 191–196.

EVANS, E. BELLE, et al. *Day Care*. Boston: Beacon Press, 1971.

HAMMERMAN, ANN, and SUSAN MORSE. "Open Teaching: Piaget in the Classroom." *Young Children*, Vol. 28, No. 1, October 1972, 41–54.

HESS, ROBERT D., and DOREEN J. CROFT. *Teachers of Young Children*. Boston: Houghton Mifflin Company, 1972.

HIRSCH, ELISABETH S. Ed. *The Block Book*. Washington, D.C.: The National Association for the Education of Young Children, 1974.

PARKER, RONALD K. *The Preschool in Action*. Boston: Allyn & Bacon, Inc., 1972.

SIGEL, IRVING E. "The Development of Classificatory Skills in Young Children: A Training Program." *Young Children*, Vol. 26, No. 3, January 1971, 170–184.

SPONSELLER, DORIS. Ed. *Play as a Learning Medium*. Washington, D.C.: The National Asociation for the Education of Young Children, 1974.

WEIKART, DAVID, et al. *The Cognitively Oriented Curriculum*. Washington, D.C.: The National Association for the Education of Young Children, 1971.

Language Arts

"HE TALKS all the time. He drives me crazy," a mother commented at the nursery school. "How unfair!" thought the visiting audiologist who earlier in the day had fitted a hearing aid for a small deaf child. The deaf child had never learned to talk. The audiologist had seen tears come to the mother's eyes as her child responded to her voice for the first time.

The years from infancy to six are crucial for language development. Speaking, listening, reading, and writing are all part of language development. Listening is called *aural* language, and speaking is called *oral*. Both precede reading and writing. The nursery school and kindergarten teacher's purpose is to give children extensive experience in listening and speaking. This is background for later writing and reading. The many concepts learned orally and aurally serve as a frame of reference for reading and writing. Reading and writing can be difficult for children if prereading and prewriting experiences are inadequate.

Biological factors may affect the child's speaking and hearing ability. Rubella (German measles) is one serious disease that can infect a woman in the early stages of pregnancy. Such infection may cause abnormalities in the speech and hearing organs of the fetus.[1] Birth injuries may impair the child's ability to speak and hear. Brain damage or injury to the speaking and hearing organs in childhood may be equally disabling.[2] Also, adenoids may grow into a child's ear and nose passages, interfering with hearing and breath control. A child who does not respond to verbal directions or who eats noisily may have a problem with adenoids. His parents should be alerted to the need for a medical checkup.

[1] Maurice H. Miller and Marcia Rabinowitz, "Audiological Problems Associated with Pre-Natal Rubella," *International Audiology*, **8:**1 (1969), 90–98.
[2] L. Fisch, "Causes of Congenital Deafness," *International Audiology*, **8:**1 (1969), 85–89.

FIGURE 10–1. *Telephones are a great asset for promoting language skills. Every school should have several telephones. (Michigan State University Laboratory Preschool.)*

Environmental factors play a major role in a child's language development.[3] Stimulation from parents, siblings, and playmates is extremely significant. Children want to communicate. Since birth they have been learning to interpret the words and actions of family and friends, and in turn, they learn the words and actions that these people will understand. Communication is a two-way street—individuals trying to let others know their thoughts and feelings while the recipients try to decode the messages. This is a marvelous human capacity, and we want the child to continue to grow in both his production and his comprehension of language.

According to Cazden, a researcher studying children's language,

[3] Joan C. Baratz, "Language in the Economically Disadvantaged Child," *Journal of American Speech and Hearing Research*, **10**:4 (1968), 142–145.

FIGURE 10–2. *When teachers associate closely with the children, the children are encouraged to speak and to listen. (Michigan State University Laboratory Preschool.)*

When we say that a child has learned his native language by the time he enters first grade, what do we mean he has learned? A set of sentences from which he chooses the right one when he wants to say something? The *meaning* of a set of sentences from which he chooses the right interpretation for the sentences he hears? Even if the sets of sentences and interpretations were enormous, the result would still be inadequate. Outside of a small and unimportant list of greetings like *Good morning* and clichés like *My, it's hot today,* few sentences are spoken or heard more than once. Any speaker, child or adult, is continuously saying and comprehending sentences he has never heard before and will never hear or comprehend again in the same way. Creativity in expressing and understanding particular meanings in particular settings to and from particular listeners is the heart of human language ability.

The only adequate explanation for what we call "knowing a language" is that the child learns a limited set of rules. On the basis of these rules he can produce and comprehend an infinite set of sentences. Such a set of rules is called a grammar, and the study of how a child learns the structure of his native language is called the study of the child's acquisition of grammar.

When we say that a child knows a set of rules, of course we don't mean that he knows them in any conscious way. The rules are known nonconsciously, out of awareness as a kind of tacit knowledge. This way of knowing is true for adults too.[4]

According to some research the necessity of coping with more than one language may, for some children, hamper the development of skill in a single language. It is necessary for them to learn two words for each concept. Other research suggests the opposite. For example, Smart and Smart report, "As international communication grows more and more important, it becomes more and more desirable for children to speak more than one language. In an earlier era, it was thought to be disadvantageous for a preschool child to learn a second language. Current research suggests the very opposite, that the best time to learn is early and the best way to learn is from a person who speaks that language as his mother tongue, that is, a native speaker. Advantages are in terms of ease of learning sounds, flexibility of brain function, and related cognitive development." [5]

Relationship of Language Development to Total Development

Language development influences and is influenced by all other areas of development. Social development, for example, is fostered when children have language skills. Language skill encourages a child to make social contacts. The solitary play of a two-year-old develops into cooperative play as the child matures in his ability to communicate. Then the child can approach another child verbally as well as physically. Children with the most advanced language skills make the most social contacts, lead others in activities, and organize the cooperative play.

Of course, the child's first social environment is the family. A child's language is influenced by his relationships with members of his family, especially his mother. If a good relationship exists, children have more advanced language skills than others in their age group.[6]

Emotional development is also fostered when the child has language skills. Both good and bad feelings can be expressed verbally.

---

[4] Courtney B. Cazden, "Suggestions from Studies of Early Language Acquisition," *Language in Early Childhood Education,* ed. Courtney B. Cazden (Washington, D.C.: The National Association for the Education of Young Children, 1972), pp. 3–4.

[5] Mollie S. Smart and Russell C. Smart. *Children: Development and Relationships* (New York: Macmillan, 1972), p. 267.

[6] Elizabeth Hurlock, *Child Development* (New York: McGraw-Hill, 1972), pp. 168–169.

FIGURE 10–3. *Pictures can be used effectively to prompt storytelling skills. Children can describe the action taking place, offer a description of the scene, and guess what the people might be saying. (Texas Tech University Kindergarten.)*

He is able to protest when things go against his wishes. The total emotional climate of the child's environment will affect the child's speech progress. Being very shy or insecure will negatively affect his ability to express himself.

Mental development and the child's conceptual framework are complexly interwoven with language development. The child's ability to express his ideas is related to his ability to understand verbal symbols. Words and names (symbols) given to objects and actions help the child learn, relate, remember, and compare.

Children sometimes learn words for concepts; then, through experience, they acquire understanding of the concepts. For fuller understanding, therefore, the child needs opportunities to relate experience to words.

A child's speech is creative. The "out-of-the-mouths-of-babes" stories told by proud mamas and doting grandmothers are usually the unique word combinations children invent. Children enjoy coining words, rhyming words, and experimenting with words. Unhampered by the "right" way to say something, children's expressions are colorful and original. On a hot day one child said, "I feel like I've had a bath in lollipop suds."

Physical and motor development affect the organs of hearing and speech. A malfunction in any organ can create language handicaps. Newborn infants are now tested for hearing in maternity wards. Hearing aids are fitted to the infant when a hearing loss is discovered. A hearing aid helps the infant hear all the prelanguage sounds commonly heard by normal infants.[7] A child whose speech and hearing therapy is left until later childhood may first require training in the infant languages of babbling, lolling, and gibberish. Finally, words are introduced.

The child who can speak and understand is a more lively companion in large motor activities at home and school. Language skill affects the child's self-concept. Positive feelings accompany successful communication. The years before six are very important years. A foundation is established for all future development.

How the Teacher Fosters Language Development

What does the nursery school and kindergarten teacher do to foster language development? A number of suggestions follow.

1. The teacher establishes a comfortably relaxed atmosphere that stimulates the children to talk freely with everyone. She encourages the children to exchange ideas, share information, and ask questions. Though she may make an effort to encourage "indoor voices" in the classroom, she appreciates children who are happy, lively, and talkative. Silence is not a sacred commodity. In fact, the young child's classroom or play yard is almost never quiet. The teacher may at times have to interpret the "noisy classroom" to other teachers, administrators, janitors, cooks, or parents. As Landreth says, "How can a child learn he has views if he is never permitted to express them?"[8]

2. The teacher values each child and finds time to let each talk to her. She serves as a model for the child's speech, speaking clearly and correctly, using words, gestures, and examples to help the child understand. She quietly seeks out children who are less assured and helps them feel at ease when talking with her and others. She visits children at home and talks with their parents to learn the personal interests of each child. When the teacher knows about family events, pets, siblings, or toys she can engage a child in conversation on

---

[7] Marion P. Downs and W. G. Hemenway, "Report of the Hearing Screening of 17,000 Neonates," *International Audiology,* **8:**1 (1969), 72–76.

[8] Catherine Landreth, *Early Childhood Behavior and Learning* (New York: Knopf, 1967), p. 199.

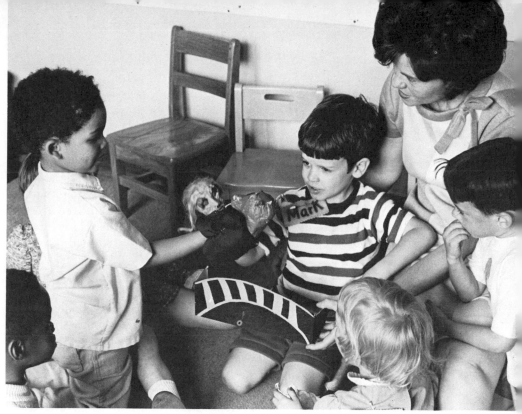

FIGURE 10–4. *Puppets encourage children to speak and listen. Puppets are especially useful for shy children who may be hesitant to speak for themselves but willing to speak for a puppet.*

subjects that interest him personally. The teacher may discover a subject that a child likes to discuss and reserve that topic for their private conversations. One child goes skiing; another goes fishing; another raises rabbits. One teacher learned a few words of Russian to be able to say "Good-bye" to a child who spoke Russian.

3. The teacher capitalizes on every opportunity to extend a child's vocabulary, to increase his ability to formulate sentences, and to describe an event in a sequence. Every learning experience is considered for its language arts possibilities. For example, following a cooking experience, the teacher asks questions to enable the children to practice the new words the experience has introduced. A few days later she may ask the children to recall the cooking experience and relate it to another project she has planned for them. She may ask the children to tell her what they plan to tell their mothers about the activities of their day in school. When children have been personally involved in activities, they can talk more easily. Verbalizing helps them remember. The teacher may send home materials that encourage the child to speak. His products give something to show and to explain to his parents.

4. The teacher gives clear directions. When giving directions, she demonstrates as well as talks in order to give the children clues to the meaning of what she says. She avoids putting too many ideas in a single sentence. She gets the children's attention and speaks clearly.

5. The teacher makes plans for the children's language development. She plans both talking and listening experiences. She assesses the needs of individual children to determine the activities that are most appropriate for each. She plans a variety of activities in order to interest the children and keep them eager to learn. She plans interesting displays of pictures and objects in the classroom to stimulate conversation.

6. The teacher who hears incorrect pronunciation and grammar allows the child to finish his statement. She believes that incorrect speech is preferable to no speech. Once she has responded to the thoughts in the child's communication, she may then, or later, use his words correctly to help him begin to hear the correct form. All teachers should be aware that though there is considerable uniformity in the country in language, there are regional accents and dialects that make it difficult even for educated people to communicate. Teachers must be most sensitive when helping children who are new in the community and children from various ethnic groups. The teacher's language is not "better" than such a child's, just as a New Yorker's language is not "better" than a Southerner's. With conscientious effort they can all communicate.

7. The teacher uses open-ended questions that encourage the children to elaborate on their ideas, information, and feelings—to use their skills in thinking and putting it all together. For example, the teacher says, "What do you think the boy will do now?" instead of, "Did the boy go swimming?" Or, "Tell me about your trip," instead of, "Did you take a trip?" The second question in these two examples can be answered with a yes or a no and does not call for further elaboration. The teacher might say, "Would you tell me about _____?" or, "I'm interested in where you found the _____."

8. The teacher strives to be the kind of person the children want to identify with. Identification is a powerful force in language acquisition. Children try to act and talk like people they identify with.

9. The teacher accepts the children as they are and avoids moralizing. To keep communication channels open, she avoids telling them how they "ought" to act, think, or feel.

10. The teacher pays attention to the children, and reflects their words and body language back to them to let them know she is listening and understanding their communication. For example, if

a child bites his nails and looks fearful, she recognizes his state—he's scared. She can say, "It's scary to get so close to the train, isn't it?" When she is competent at interpreting the meaning beyond the children's words she is really tuned in to children.

11. The teacher picks up on the children's verbal horseplay. If they chant, she chants. If they rhyme, she rhymes. She laughs with them and has fun with language—and all communication.

12. The teacher avoids being fussy about her own and others' names and titles; such fussiness can stifle the children's conversation. Surely a wise principal would not want to hear the teacher say, "Stop chattering and speak to our principal Mr. Smith correctly and with respect, Jonathan."

13. The teacher watches for the children who don't speak, for those who don't appear to hear, for those who don't respond to directions until after the others start, and for those who talk with a nasal twang or who eat unusually noisily. Such symptoms suggest to the teacher the need for medical referrals, hearing and speech assessment, and possible therapy. It is important to take care of problems before the child develops habits that are difficult to change.

14. The teacher writes down stories, songs, poems, and sayings a child expresses. She reads them back to him, showing that she values his words, and teaching him that there is a relationship between spoken language and the written words he finds in books.

Planning Language Arts Activities

Language is a two-way street—listening and speaking. Listening may be as important as speaking itself. Listening must be done with comprehension. Active thinking should accompany listening. Teachers can't be sure that a child sitting quietly is listening. The entire program, both indoors and out, affords numerous opportunities for involving children with language.

When the teacher starts a new project or a learning experience, she uses techniques to quiet the children and gain their attention. A song, a poem, finger play, a puppet, or a new picture can serve this purpose. She'll want them to follow the discussion, think critically about what she's saying, be stimulated to further interest, and react with new behavior or new understanding. All children will not respond to all projects. Therefore other activities are kept available for those with different interests. As each activity is planned, teachers should note new words and phrases that the children can learn. Plenty of time should be allowed for children's comments and questions as an activity progresses.

FIGURE 10–5. *Children's language skills are enhanced through reading stories and discussing them with an interested adult.*

Games

Games such as "Simon says" can be played with small groups to encourage listening and learning new vocabulary. The common "Simon says, 'Stand up'" can be altered to "Simon says, 'Put your hands *above* your heads'" or "'put your hands below your chair.'" Such a game can be played at the snack table while the children are waiting for the snack to come, or at the gate when they are waiting for their parents or a bus.

Guessing games can be created by the teacher as she describes the characteristics of familiar objects for children to guess. At first, the objects should be near at hand. Later, out-of-sight objects at home and at school can be described. After some experience the children can take turns describing objects.

The teacher can say, "I'm thinking of something that is—HOT. What could it be?" When the children catch on, a child can be invited to choose the object and the adjective, whisper the choice in the teacher's ear, and then tell the others whether they are correct as they guess.

A box or a bag with several objects for children to feel, describe, and name invites conversation. They can learn to use such words as *rough, smooth, large, small, hard, soft* as they try to identify the object. The teacher can select familiar items. *Large* and *small* can be learned more readily by using two sizes of the same object—buttons, Jell-O boxes, milk cartons, and so on.

Jokes

Five-year-olds who are beginning to appreciate jokes will enjoy correcting the teacher when she says absurd things like "Shall we wait until the street light turns purple?" Children like to play tricks on others, too, once their concepts are well enough formed so that they can recognize the absurdities.

Records and Tapes

Records and tapes are outstanding aids that encourage listening. A record player that is simple enough for the children to operate will encourage voluntary listening. The collection of records should be changed frequently. A quiet nook that is free of distractions is a good location for the record player.

Tape recordings of the children's conversations, stories, and songs encourage the children to listen for their own voices. Stories the children record can be typed and placed in a book, or they can be sent home. Thus their value is enhanced, and the children begin to see a relationship between spoken and written words.

Headsets for a record player or a tape recorder are valuable additions to equipment. Occasionally a child wants to hear a record that interferes with another child's activity, or a child may want to hear the same record over and over. Using the headset avoids disturbing others.

Music

Teachers can hum or play a tune or a rhythm for the children to guess. Children can learn to lead this listening game too. Children need opportunities both to listen to music and to participate. Songs help children add new words to their vocabularies. Further discussion of music and rhythm follows, in Chapter 13.

Literature

The use of good literature contributes to language. Poetry challenges children's listening. Children can help the teacher rhyme words. With only a little experience children will know that the word in a poem to rhyme with *ice* is *slice* or *mice*. Many good poems are available for children, which, when presented enthusiastically, will interest them. Suggestions for books, poems, and finger plays are given in Chapter 11.

Dramatic Play

Imaginative role-playing, so popular with young children, contributes to their language development. Children need to talk in making their wants known, they have concrete objects to discuss as they play, and they enact roles they have observed. All these conditions contribute to learning. Dramatic play is discussed further in Chapter 12.

Puppets and flannel board figures are useful aids for encouraging children to speak. Shy children find that speaking through a puppet or a figure is easier. Torrance, who has done notable work in children's creative language expression, gives children a "magic net," under which they imaginatively become whatever they wish. They wear the magic net and stand, walk, talk, or dance like the person, animal, or object they wish to become. Torrance used colored netting 36″ × 72″ and gave about ten children "magic nets" at one time.[9]

Telephones

Telephones are extremely useful in encouraging conversation, and every school should have several. The children will often talk to each other, and the teacher can talk to a child in casual conversation or ask for information she has been helping him learn, such as his telephone number or his home address.

Field Trips

Field trips and other special events will help extend the child's language. From firsthand experiences the child builds a frame of reference to which he compares new information, whether it comes through reading, listening, or experimenting. Details for planning field trips are given in Chapter 14.

Sharing Time

Sharing time, or "show and tell," is a popular activity in the kindergarten. This is an organized time when an individual child shows the group something he has brought from home or tells about some event. The activity gives the child an opportunity to speak before the group. He is encouraged to develop his discussion in logical sequence.

[9] E. Paul Torrance, *Encouraging Creativity in the Classroom* (Dubuque, Ia.: Wm. C. Brown, 1970), pp. 3–5.

FIGURE 10–6. *A rope ladder promotes language skills as children advise each other how to succeed at the climbing task. (Texas Woman's University Child Development Associate Program.)*

Children learn to listen and then ask the speaker questions. They all learn to take turns.

Parents should be enlisted to help the child select worthwhile things or ideas to share during "show and tell." They can help the child plan what he will tell. Parents can help their child keep track of which day of the week is his sharing day, for once the "show and tell" idea becomes popular in a class it is seldom feasible to let everyone speak each day. In a class of fifteen or more children the sharing time could take an hour—much too long to expect active listening. Overlong periods rob other meaningful activities of their rightful time in the schedule. A calendar can be arranged designating a certain day for each child to bring or tell something. Exceptions are made, of course, when a child has something very special for "show and tell": a new baby sister or the first flower of spring qualifies.

In some groups sharing time is held during snack time. When only a portion of the group is slated to speak, daily sharing time requires only a few minutes. Table conversation, a valued language experience, is also encouraged.

The key to success is the teacher, who must develop skill in directing sharing time in order to make it a pleasant learning experience for both the speaker and the group. She'll need skill in drawing out the shy speaker and limiting the verbose one. She will preserve the child's dignity and allow for individual differences in ability to participate. Learning can be increased if the teacher judiciously raises questions and directs the children's attention. Occasionally a teacher may designate certain things as being good for "sharing time," such as fall seeds or leaves.

A "sharing table" can be set up for children to display their specimens and treasures. The self-selected activity time can be used for individual discussion of these objects. As many three- and four-year-old children are not ready for an organized "sharing time," a "sharing table" may be substituted.

Dealing with Language Problems

Articulation

How does a teacher help children with obvious language deficiencies? The teacher cannot be a speech therapist. Children with severe problems should be under the care of a trained therapist. The therapist can help the teacher choose activities that will be helpful for a child with problems. Help at this young age includes games that might be played with children with normal speech so that attention need not be focused on the handicapped child.

All workers in a nursery school or a kindergarten should not attack a child's speech problems. Excessive pressure may add complications and lead to feelings that he pleases no one. The teacher who has the best rapport with the child should be the one to intervene actively. Other helpers may correctly restate words he misuses so that he can hear them, but they should leave the actual intervention to that one teacher. The total staff, including bus drivers and cooks, should be advised of the procedure because they, too, have an opportunity to help.

One helpful procedure is for adults simply to restate a child's mispronounced words or ungrammatical phrases in a corrected form so that he may begin to hear the correct pattern. Asking the child to repeat specific words or phrases often produces tension that causes further problems. Van Riper says that it is frequently ear training that is needed rather than mouth training. He suggests that only one sound be worked on at a time.[10] If a child says "wed" for "red," he may not be hearing the *r*. Speech therapists would not practice with him on the word *red* but on a word completely unfamiliar to him, such as *rebel* or *referee*. Therapists use nonsense words to advantage when helping a child relearn a sound.[11] The sounds can be practiced in isolation in games or singing or in mimicking animals or machines.

To expect children in nursery school and kindergarten to make all sounds correctly is expecting too much. For example, in a study of

[10] Charles Van Riper, *Speech Correction Principles and Methods* (Englewood Cliffs, N.J.: Prentice-Hall, 1963), pp. 248–249.
[11] Ibid., p. 279.

308 first-grade children, Roe and Milisen found that 88 per cent had trouble with *z*, 69 per cent with *g*, 45.7 per cent with *t*, and 17.6 per cent with *r*. Blends such as *st* and *dr* were easier than either *s* or *d* followed by a vowel for most of the children.[12] Many articulation errors are common and are eliminated without therapy as the child matures.[13] Templin's studies indicate that on the basis of cross-sectional data fewer children than anticipated had achieved adequate articulation at the beginning of the second grade. She found that boys were about one year slower than girls.[14]

Hearing

A child with hearing difficulties should also be under the care of a specialist. He can be integrated into a group of normal children if he wears a hearing aid and has had enough speech experience to make his wants known.[15] It is unfair to require a teacher to deal with a hard-of-hearing child in a group of normal children unless the child wears a hearing aid or unless the teacher has plenty of assistance. An extra assistant to work with the handicapped child would make it possible for him to be in a group of normal children. A child who cannot hear the story cannot be expected to listen while one is read. He naturally loses interest and distracts the others. He should do something he enjoys in another room or outdoors. The group should not miss their literature experience because one child cannot participate.

Foreign Language

A child who speaks a foreign language may fit comfortably into a group if the mother tongue is well developed. Skillful in his own language, he will begin learning the new language if the staff makes adequate efforts to help him feel secure and happy. He can be encouraged by a few moments of private language help from time to time and by words, smiles, and gestures indicating that he is liked and is doing well. There may be many learning experiences for the whole group that can incorporate a foreign child's language and

[12] Vivian Roe and R. Milisen, "The Effects of Maturation upon Defective Articulation in Elementary Grades," *Journal of Speech Disorders,* 7:1 (March 1942), 42.

[13] Anne S. Morency, Joseph M. Wepman, and Paul S. Weiner, "Studies in Speech: Developmental Articulation Inaccuracy," *Elementary School Journal,* 67 (1967), pp. 329–337.

[14] Mildred C. Templin, "Research on Articulation Development," *The Young Child,* ed. Williard W. Hartrup and Nancy L. Smothergill (Washington, D.C.: The National Association for Education of Young Children, 1967), pp. 109–124.

[15] Vivian W. Stern, "Fingerpaint on the Hearing Aid," *The Volta Review,* 71:3 (1969), 149–154.

previous experiences. In one group the five-year-olds were especially interested in their new German classmate. They ·wanted to know where he had come from, how he had traveled, and if he had gone to school in Germany. The teacher introduced a world map to locate Germany and taught the group a few German words. The new child was delighted. He soon felt at ease and spoke to the children in German. The unfamiliar sounds awed the children and the teacher had to reassure them that it was all right to speak to him in English. She explained that he could tell by their gestures some of the things they wanted him to do. In a short time he learned some English phrases that helped his social relations.

In the case of the German boy the parents were strongly in favor of the child's learning English. Occasionally the families speaking a foreign language do not readily accept their child's learning English. In this case the school must build a bridge of friendship and respect to the other culture to help the family accept and encourage their child's learning the new language.

It is natural for people to hesitate to give up their mother tongue. Perhaps the child will be unable to communicate with grandparents if he knows only English. In some neighborhoods those who emphasize English and speak it at home are criticized by their friends. Teachers should appreciate the ambivalence that may be associated with learning a new language.

Disadvantaged Children's Language

During recent years disadvantaged children's language has received considerable attention. Unfortunately language is usually only one of the areas of development that is inadequate. Diligent use of all the suggestions given above, plus more deliberate attempts at enrichment, may be called for. An apparently meaningful program has been developed for Spanish-speaking Head Start children at Colorado State College (Greeley) by Nimnicht, Meier, and McAfee. McAfee suggests a much more conscious effort with respect to language than may be called for in English-speaking groups. She especially advises against rote learning and verbalization. She stresses involving the children physically in their learning by using activities that require the child to put his hand *in front of* his face, *behind* his head, and *between* his legs. Numerous words denoting sameness, differences, location, position, relative size, and contrasting conditions are suggested for practice.[16]

[16] Glen Nimnicht, Oralie McAfee, and John Meier, *The New Nursery School* (New York: General Learning Corporation, 1969), pp. 41–53.

Working with Children with Nonstandard English

Young black children and others who come with a nonstandard English dialect present certain critical problems for teachers. Researchers who have studied the linguistic components of the black dialect find it simply different and not deficient. The dialect is usually well developed and expressive and serves useful purposes in the exchange of ideas, information, and feelings. There are numerous debates as to whether or not children should be taught standard English. A casual survey of black public figures—educators, politicians, artists, writers, and television commentators—generally reveals a high proficiency in standard English.

Researchers Cullinan, Jagger, and Strickland have concluded that it is a defensible objective to expand the language of black children with dialects to include standard English without reducing their proficiency in their native black English.[17] Children who speak black English must be fully accepted as equals, be encouraged to talk using their own language traditions, and be helped to develop new language forms through such opportunities for speaking and comprehending as have been suggested in this chapter and throughout the text.

Working with Spanish-Speaking Children

Teachers who work with young children from ethnic or language groups different from their own sometimes erroneously judge or downgrade the children's language abilities or may fail to have positive expectations for such children. Such judgments are unfair to these children and their parents. Children from such groups are often unusually quiet as new students in a strange school situation, just as vivacious adults often become tongue-tied when they venture into a new country, where the language and the customs are different from their own.

We must remember that the young children entering kindergarten and nursery school generally have very few experiences outside their home and neighborhood, regardless of their socioeconomic background. When they are confronted with a school situation in which the setting, adults, language, and ethnic mix are new, different, and perhaps uncomprehensible, it is not surprising that these children appear scared, shy, and quiet.

[17] Bernice E. Cullinan, Angela M. Jaggar, and Dorothy Strickland, "Language for Black Children in the Primary Grades: A Research Report," *Young Children,* **29:**2 (January 1974), 98–112.

Mrs. Rebecca Peña Hines, a recent vice-president of the National Association for the Education of Young Children, is a noted early childhood educator who grew up speaking Spanish at home and learning English at school. Now, as director of the Parent-Child Development Center in Houston, Texas, she expresses many concerns about the situation facing the Spanish-speaking child.[18]

Mrs. Hines indicated that Mexican-American parents, and especially grandparents, are usually deeply interested in their children's maintaining their Spanish language. Their attitude is, of course, defensible, because it is their language and the language of their ancestors—a beautiful language with a body of great literature. A large portion of the Western Hemisphere speaks Spanish. Some Mexican-American parents who want their child to function in the English-speaking world sometimes go to the extreme of speaking only English at home, creating some raised eyebrows among friends and neighbors who may look upon that family as "putting on airs." However, with the recent Chicano movement, the younger generation of parents and soon-to-be parents has revived an interest and a pride in maintaining the Spanish language, along with the other rich and positive aspects of the Mexican-American culture.

Chicano children (and any non-English-speaking children) may have an uphill language struggle in typical schools. Most schools do not teach Spanish in the kindergarten or elementary school, and English is not taught in a manner that builds on a Spanish-speaking child's already-developed language foundation. This makes it difficult for the child to learn either language well. Chicano children are often erroneously considered by observers to be "nonverbal" or "slow" when, in fact, these outsiders are merely observing the child's reaction to strangers and to a largely different environment.

Mrs. Hines finds that young Chicano children are generally friendly, open, and verbal if they have a teacher or an aide who speaks Spanish and who can build warm communication with the children and their parents through appreciation of their unique background and culture. Bilingual-bicultural aides and teachers are needed for young Chicano children. Bilingual adults will teach Spanish to these children, adding to their vocabulary for expressing their needs and concepts. Gradually English is introduced to the children on an individual and small-group basis—thus building a bilingual base for the children. They eventually learn two words for

---

[18] In making the following suggestions for working with children from Mexican-American homes I have drawn upon discussions with Rebecca Peña Hines and upon materials she presented at the annual meeting workshop of the National Association for the Education of Young Children in 1973.

each concept and expression, and at times they integrate the two languages in interesting and unique ways. Reinforcement of the cultural strengths in the children's background, such as Spanish music, literature, and festivals, serves to enhance further the children's feeling of who they are.

Mrs. Hines, whose work has been concentrated in Texas, California, and Washington, believes that English-speaking nursery school and kindergarten teachers can learn to communicate with Spanish-speaking children. The teachers can learn some key words and phrases in Spanish in order to understand and to respond, just as a teacher of a deaf child can learn to communicate with a few hand symbols. Spanish songs like those included in this book (Chapter 13) can be learned rather easily and sung with the children. The child's parents might be enlisted to help with pronunciation. Pictures including Chicano children and their families can be displayed and used for learning activities within the classroom. Curriculum plans can introduce cultural objects—piñatas, books, and foods—that are familiar to Mexican-American children, helping them with adjustment and with enhancing their self-concepts.

Even when the class includes only one or two Spanish-speaking children, these steps are important to those individuals and also to the other children, who will learn much from an introduction to different cultures such as the Mexican-American culture.

Teachers are advised to continue talking to the child in English even though they believe that he does not understand. Children frequently can understand much more than they can speak. Eventually the words will take on meaning. The tone of voice and the body language accompanying the words give clues to the child concerning meaning and also communicate warmth and interest in him. Likewise, English-speaking children in the class should be encouraged to talk with non-English-speaking children in order to develop peer relationships and provide models. Both groups will benefit as the children learn language expressions from each other. Important learning flows in both directions.

Any child has a right to expect teachers to respect his culture. If they have an attitude of respect and positive expectation, the children and the parents will be responsive to the teachers and the school. The children will then have a firm foundation for climbing up the educational ladder.

Teaching Foreign Language

"Why doesn't the school teach a foreign language?" "Are there advantages to teaching a second language to young children living in an English-speaking environment?" These questions are often raised by parents. There is a difference of opinion with regard to the optimum time to introduce a foreign language. Some authorities believe that the training should begin early. Others do not believe that all research supports early foreign language instruction.

In some situations the child must learn a second language. Many disadvantaged children are, in effect, learning a second language.[19] The school starts with whatever language skill children have and teaches them English much as a foreign language is taught.[20,21]

A five-year study of the effects of teaching Spanish to kindergarten children was carried on at Texas Tech University. The classes were made up of middle-class five-year-olds in the laboratory kindergarten. During the five years from 1962 to 1967 five groups received Spanish lessons. Lessons lasted from 10 to 15 minutes per day and varied from one to two semesters' duration. The study was designed to find:

1. Whether five-year-olds could be motivated to learn Spanish.
2. What could be taught to them.
3. What methods could be used effectively.

Lessons were carefully outlined with the Spanish staff of the Department of Foreign Languages. Spanish professors and students in language "methods" classes taught three years. The kindergarten teacher and Spanish-speaking child development majors taught the last two. The kindergarten teacher and college students had considerable enthusiasm for the language. Incidental events often became language lessons. For example, during snack time, the teacher would ask, «Quien quiere mas leche?» The children learned to hold up their hands and respond, «Mas leche, por favor.» ("Who wants more milk?" "More milk, please.")

The cooperation of the kindergarten teacher and the language instructors was important to the success of the project. The new language was never an isolated experience. Using trained language teachers gave the children good models to imitate. The kindergarten teacher's active participation protected the children from teaching that did not consider their individual needs and development. Be-

---

[19] Joan C. Baratz, op. cit.

[20] Marion Meyerson, "The Bilingual Child," *Childhood Education,* **45**:9 (1969), 525–527.

[21] George I. Sanchez, "Significance of Language Handicap," *Learning a New Language,* ed. Margaret Rasmussen (Washington, D.C.: Association for Childhood Education International, 1958), pp. 25–32.

cause of her participation the language and related experiences permeated the entire program.

Lessons were planned to focus on familiar objects, expressions, and situations at home and school. A single concept was presented in various interesting ways to keep the interest high. For example, when the children were learning to count, they counted the number of children, the number of girls, and the number of chairs. They also sang "Ten Little Indians" in Spanish and took turns counting individually. Counting was interwoven with other concepts that were being learned. Teaching aids of all kinds were used to present real things and models for the children to talk about. The lessons were short and they were fun.

The outcome seemed positive in most respects. The children leaped the language barrier with grace. Spanish was a natural choice for that community, which had a 20 per cent Latin-American population and a natural relationship to Mexico. The children learned about some of the festivals that are part of Mexican tradition. They were interested in learning the new language. Often they reported having heard Spanish on the radio (not uncommon in that part of Texas), or someone speaking it while they were shopping downtown, or at home where older brothers and sisters were studying Spanish for school.

The games and songs particularly appealed to the children. They liked being called on to participate individually, although they were never forced to respond until they indicated their readiness. Children who had trouble articulating English sounds were actually helped by saying the sound in Spanish. The child who spoke German, mentioned earlier, was given private help in English during the Spanish lessons. However, he had so much facility with languages that he learned a number of Spanish expressions from the children who were using them in their play.

The staff, the students, and the parents gleaned valuable information during these sessions. It was interesting to all to observe the children learning a subject about which one could assume no prior knowledge or home practice. Many early childhood education students expected to teach Spanish-speaking children in Head Start and felt they had learned teaching methods that would help them.

The importance of planning was clear. Deciding the concepts to teach, planning the sequence for teaching, and preparing the teaching aids took considerable time and thought. Concepts related closely to children were the best choices.

Better pronunciation resulted from individual participation than from group recitation. The teacher's verbal approval was of greatest importance. Approval was given both to the group and to individuals.

Whereas teachers with much teaching experience could keep a large group interested, beginning teachers were more successful with small groups. All planned activities that were fun. Involving children in a variety of songs, games, pictures, toys, stories, and role playing contributed to the success of the lessons. Teachers frequently shifted from one teaching method to another to maintain high interest.

Conclusion

Language development includes speaking, listening, reading, and writing. Language arts activities can accompany every learning experience in the nursery school and kindergarten. Suggestions to help teachers enhance the child's listening and speaking skills have been made. The teacher sets the stage for the children to exchange ideas, share information, and ask questions. She values a room with a busy hum of meaningful conversations more than she does one in which sterile silence reigns. The teacher encourages the children to speak. Teachers value the children's creative use of language.

ADDITIONAL READINGS

ANDERSON, VERNA D. *Reading and Young Children.* New York: Macmillan Publishing Co., Inc., 1968.

BEREITER, CARL, and SIEGFRIED ENGLEMANN. *Teaching Disadvantaged Children in the Preschool.* Englewood Cliffs, N.J.: Prentice-Hall, Inc., 1966.

CAZDON, COURTNEY B. *Language in Early Childhood Education.* Washington, D.C.: The National Association for Education of Young Children, 1972.

FROST, JOE L. (ed.). *Early Childhood Education Rediscovered.* New York: Holt, Rinehart and Winston, Inc., 1968.

LANDRETH, CATHERINE. *Early Childhood: Behavior and Learning.* New York: Alfred A. Knopf, Inc., 1967.

MANUEL, HERSCHEL T. *Spanish-Speaking Children of the Southwest, Their Education and the Public Welfare.* Austin, Texas: University of Texas Press, 1965.

MARTIN, BILL, JR. *Language and Literature: The Human Connection.* Washington, D.C.: Department of Elementary-Kindergarten-Nursery Educators, NEA, 1967.

MURPHY, LOIS B., and ETHEL M. LEEPER. *Language Is for Communication.* Washington, D.C.: U.S. Government Printing Office, 1973.

NIMNICHT, GLEN, ORALIE MCAFEE, and JOHN MEIER. *The New Nursery School.* New York: General Learning Corporation, 1969.

ROBINSON, HELEN F., and BERNARD SPODEK. *New Directions in the Kindergarten.* New York: Teachers College Press, Columbia University, 1965.

SCHULMAN, ANNE SHAAKER. *Absorbed in Living Children Learn.* Washington, D.C.: National Association for Education of Young Children, 1967.

SMITH, GRACE. "On Listening to the Language of Children." *Young Children,* Vol. 29, No. 3, March 1974, 133–140.

STRICKLAND, RUTH G. *The Language Arts in the Eelementary School.* Lexington, Mass.: D. C. Heath & Company, 1969.

VAN RIPER, CHARLES. *Speech Correction Principles and Methods.* Englewood Cliffs, N.J.: Prentice-Hall, Inc., 1972.

Children's Literature

"MY MOMMY got *this* book from the library and I love, love, love it!" exclaimed five-year-old Peter as he turned the pages of a picture book he had selected from the fresh supply neatly arranged in his kindergarten room. The teacher thought, "Being part of the wonderful way children respond to good books is one of teaching's intangible rewards."

Through literature children find the history of the human race, the hopes of the future, and the record of happiness and pathos. Between the covers of a book children find the mechanical, the artistic, the beautiful, and the ugly.

The Teacher's Goal

The teacher who wants children to live full lives will help them learn to love books. Because she is concerned with children's prereading experiences, she will enrich their lives with books in a variety of ways in order to create in them a strong desire to learn to read. Thus the teacher's goal when she offers literature to young children in the nursery school and kindergarten is to inspire in them a romance with books that will continue throughout their lifetime.

Attitudes Toward Books

The years before six are important years for developing children's romance with books. This is a period for the adults in children's lives to help them "catch" the enthusiasm for books. The best word is "catch" rather than "teach" because contagion is far more effective than teaching. Attitudes at home and school affect children's attitudes toward books. Loving books makes using them for learning and enjoyment much easier. Many people have lost or never have had a really good feeling associated with books. They may be college students who dread the thought of a library assignment, adults who seldom read, and citizens who are lost when the television is broken.

FIGURE 11–1. *Encouraging the informal sharing of books among children indicates that the teacher values books. (Nazarene Child Care Center, Lansing, Michigan.)*

When children have a happy introduction to books, they discover there is fun, laughter, adventure, romance, information, and enlightenment in them. They want more. They feel that books are their friends. They may want to carry them around or take them to bed. They like the sharing with parent, teacher, friend, grandparent, or sibling that books invite. Children, like adults who love books, will turn to books for solace in lonely moments or for a laugh when in a gay mood. Once a child is "hooked on books," so to speak, he'll want to learn to read. In fact, he can't help himself. Given a rich menu of books during his earliest years, a child will develop ideas, vocabulary, and grammar. He will discriminate between sounds and begin to differentiate between the symbols he sees on the printed page. Reading will come easily for him.

Some parents and teachers push children into the mechanics of reading before the children have been convinced that books really offer them something. Children have to feel that the task of learning to read is worth the effort. Reading could perhaps be likened to driving. Would it make sense to be required to learn to drive a car before one cared to go anywhere? Would the driver-to-be think the risks and tensions were worth the effort? Not likely. The reader-to-be may also be unconvinced of his need to read.

Neither a teacher nor a parent who lacks enthusiasm can infect a child with enthusiasm for reading. But many parents and teachers have overcome this handicap by working hard to learn about children's books in order to help their own children. In the process they have been inspired to capture the romance with books they missed in their own growing up. Therefore it is never too late. Two books by Annis Duff, *Bequest of Wings* [1] and *Longer Flight*,[2] will help adults who want to get acquainted with children's books. Anne Eaton's *Reading with Children* [3] and Nancy Larrick's *Teacher's Guide to Children's Books* [4] will offer stimulation.

Children's librarians know books and children, and their primary goal is to bring the two together. Teachers and parents will find librarians very helpful. Also, they exemplify the love of books that could well become a model for others. As one observes a librarian, he sees how she helps children find books. "Let's see, Jim, you liked that dinosaur story; here's another one about *Danny and the Dinosaur*," [5] said one librarian. She seemed to have an uncanny memory for Jim and his reading interests. After watching awhile the observer noted that Jim was not an exceptional case. The librarian helped children find an appropriate section of the library, noticed when they seemed lost or undecided, and encouraged them by offering assistance and calling them by name.

The weekly story hour was also revealing—well planned, well timed, and well integrated with mood-setting techniques. The librarian held over fifty children spellbound with a topnotch story. Teachers could learn from her.

The reading attitudes of the adults in children's lives—whether parents, teachers, grandparents, baby-sitters, or librarians—will influence children's literature experience and the pleasure they derive from it.

Books in the Nursery School and Kindergarten

The Library

The school's book collection should be given continuous attention. A sizable budget for new books should be available yearly to add new

---

[1] Annis Duff, *Bequest of Wings* (New York: Viking, 1944).
[2] Annis Duff, *Longer Flight* (New York: Viking, 1955).
[3] Anne Eaton, *Reading with Children* (New York: Viking, 1957).
[4] Nancy Larrick, *A Teacher's Guide to Children's Books* (Columbus, Ohio: Merrill, 1960).
[5] Syd Hoff, *Danny and the Dinosaur* (New York: Harper & Row, 1968).

issues and replace worn-out books. Teachers should keep abreast of the new books coming out by reading reviews in *The Horn Book Magazine*,[6] *Childhood Education*,[7] *Young Children*,[8] and *Parents' Magazine*.[9] Booklets such as *Recommended Children's Books,* published by the *School Library Journal*,[10] and *Bibliography of Books for Children,* published by the Association for Childhood Education International,[11] provide information on both new and old recommended books.

Filing

A system of filing books in the school library should be developed. Some teachers like to color-code the binding of each book with colored plastic tape to designate the subject matter of the book. Books might be grouped according to interests, such as children, animals, transportation, and plants. Books also can be filed according to author. This method encourages the staff to become aware of the names of authors. In either case a cross-listing in an up-to-date card file will help new users find the books they seek.

Books should be removed when they become unrepairable. Out-of-date books should be filed in a separate section to be referred to when they are needed for studies of "the olden days." Many picture books related to farming, housing, and transportation fall into this category now.

Repair

Books should be kept in good repair. If pages are torn, they encourage children's misuse. If pages are missing, the book should be replaced or discarded. Pictures from old books can be salvaged to make illustrations for flannel-board stories or homemade books.

When repair is feasible, a plastic book-mending liquid is available in school supply houses that is ideal for mending young children's books. The liquid dries clear and leaves no edge for small fingers to peel off. Parts of a page can be reattached if held together with paper clips or clothespins while the liquid dries. To mend several pages at

[6] *The Horn Book Magazine* (The Horn Book, Inc., 585 Boylston St., Boston, Mass.).

[7] *Childhood Education* (journal of The Association for Childhood Education International, 3615 Wisconsin Ave. N.W., Washington, D.C. 20016).

[8] *Young Children* (journal of the National Association for Education of Young Children, 1834 Connecticut Ave. N.W., Washington, D.C. 20009).

[9] *Parents' Magazine* (Parents' Magazine Enterprises, 52 Vanderbilt, New York, N.Y. 10017).

[10] *School Library Journal* (R. R. Bowker Co., 1180 Avenue of Americas, New York, N.Y. 10036).

[11] Association for Childhood Education International, 3615 Wisconsin Ave. N.W., Washington, D.C. 20016.

a time, place wax paper between the book pages. The plastic does not adhere to wax paper.

If liquid plastic is unavailable, a second choice is a plastic tape made especially for mending books. It is not glossy and does not discolor with age as does the more common mending tape. Clear plastic adhesive is available that is ideal for covering the entire book cover to increase its wearing qualities and help keep it clean.

The Book Corner

The book corner should be separated from the other play areas by dividers to provide a quiet, undisturbed atmosphere that encourages concentration. Carpeting will improve the atmosphere. A table will help the children handle books more carefully. Books should be invitingly displayed on a rack that allows the cover of the book to show. Because the book corner is available during the self-selected activity period, the children will browse on their own. Teachers will usually find several eager listeners if they will take time to read a story. A child who wants a story should be able to find someone to read to him. This area is often popular with new aides or college students who are getting acquainted with the children.

A fresh supply of books should be selected regularly. Certain favorites can remain available for a few weeks. Books can be selected to give information related to concepts being developed or to stimulate questions and observations regarding concepts the teacher anticipates emphasizing in the future. Books "just for fun" should always be available.

To ensure a wider selection of books in the book corner and to give children experience in the public library, a kindergarten teacher developed the custom of allowing a committee of three children to accompany an assistant to the library once every two weeks. They chose one book for each child in the class. Often the class made suggestions to the committee about books they'd like. The children became comfortable in the library, chatting with the librarians and looking over the exhibits. The names of the books were recorded and date-due cards removed as precautions against their loss before the books were displayed in the classroom.

Reference books such as *The Golden Book Encyclopedia*,[12] *Illustrated Golden Dictionary for Young Readers*,[13] and others will help answer some of the children's questions. They should have a perma-

---

[12] *The Golden Book Encyclopedia*, 16 vols. (New York: Golden Press, 1959).
[13] Stuart Courtis and Gainette Walters, *Illustrated Golden Dictionary for Young Readers* (New York: Golden Press, 1965).

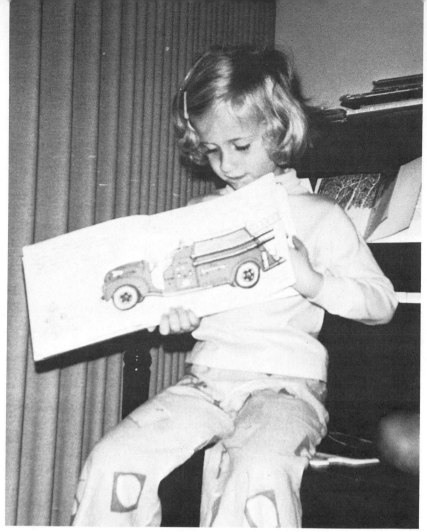

FIGURE 11–2. *Children frequently play "teacher," holding the book for their audience just as the teacher does. (Louisiana State University Nursery School.)*

nent place in the room. One group called such a collection "the important books."

If children are given opportunity and encouragement to use them, books can be taken outdoors during nice weather for a pleasant small-group story or individual reading. In climates where a major part of the school day is spent outdoors, a book rack can become standard outdoor equipment.

Puppets, flannel board, and flannel-board figures, if stored in the book corner, can readily contribute to literature and language experiences. A place to plug in the record player or tape recorder is also an asset, because these devices are used to advantage here.

Storytime

Storytime is one of the times in the nursery school and kinder-garten when the children come together in a group. The children will sense that storytime is an important time of day if the teacher (1) plans a smooth transition so that they know what to expect; (2) sets the stage for quiet listening-responding behavior; (3) plans some soothing activities; and (4) carefully prepares the story and illustra-tive materials. If, on the other hand, the teacher haphazardly plucks a book from the shelf and sandwiches storytime between snack time and going outdoors, or if the assistants are running around cleaning up the room while the story is in progress, the children can be ex-pected to feel that storytime is rather unimportant.

Size of Story Groups

Small groups of four or five children make more effective story groups, particularly for younger children. The youngest children like to feel close to the teacher and to be able to respond to the book individually—verbally and physically—which is sometimes difficult to permit in a large group. Gradually, as children mature, the groups can be combined. When there are a number of assistants in a group —aides, cooperating mothers, or students—it is especially sensible to use their help in order to divide the group for storytime. Even when the group remains together, the assistants should join the story-time. Their interest will encourage children's interest, and the as-sistants will become familiar with a situation they may be called on to take over in the future.

When the teacher really believes that there are books for every child, she will seek to interest every child in books. For one or two in the group it may mean an almost private story session.

Patty and Martha were examples of three-year-olds who could not tolerate a group storytime even in groups of four or five children. Patty was easily distracted. Martha wanted to sit directly in front of the book, which blocked others' view. These two found joy in books, however, when read to together. Sometimes they asked to hear sev-eral books that they had selected. Finally, at age four, they decided they would like to hear the story with the other children.

Patty and Martha could easily have become storytime distractors in the playhouse or at the puzzle shelf. But the teacher felt storytime too important to give up. She sought a combination that would in-terest them. The tiny group was the solution. In thinking of Patty and Martha, one must note that they were three-year-olds. Their ex-perience with storytime before coming to nursery school had been a

FIGURE 11–3. A *"little bumble-bee" finger play catches children's atten-tion and helps them get settled down for listening to a story. (Michigan State University Laboratory Preschool.)*

warm sitting-on-the-lap variety with their parents. Teachers may have to carry some of this practice into the school. Even in under-staffed schools, a cook might have been enlisted to read to Patty and Martha or to supervise as they listened to a story record. Com-munity or student volunteers could provide valuable assistance with such children. When children cannot be enticed to storytime, their activity should not be distracting to the children who do want to take part. Time during the self-selected activity period can be used to en-courage children like Patty and Martha to become interested in books.

FIGURE 11–4. *Careful planning is needed so that adults will have time to read a story to one or two children when they indicate an interest. (Iowa State University Nursery School.)*

Chairs or Floor for Storytime?

The choice between chairs or floor will be a personal one of the teacher's. Some like chairs because each child has a place and one does not block the view of another so easily. Others say chairs can become a distracting element—rocking back and forth—or that children on the ends of the circle may be slighted because they can't see the book and therefore lose interest.

Some teachers like to group the children on the floor, especially if it is carpeted. They feel this arrangement promotes a cosier, restful atmosphere. Rug sample "sit-upons" can provide individual places. The children can sit close together.

Whatever the choice, the children should be able to see. They should be able to relax and not be unduly cramped together. Teachers should arrange the group so that the children don't face the glare of the windows. The teacher can sit on the floor or on a low chair, whichever makes it easier for all the children to see.

The book or flannel board should be in good light so that the children can see the pictures. Pictures must be large enough to be seen by those in the back of the group. Some books are inappropriate for groups because the illustrations aren't clear from a distance. Children will readily become disinterested if they cannot see the pictures.

Transition to Storytime

Transitions or changes in activity can be made smoothly and with a minimum of fuss. When the children are expected to make such shifts in their routine, the teacher must first decide what she wants to take place and plan accordingly. Where do the children go first? Which path do they use? Is the path clear of obstructions? Will the children have room or will they run into each other? Are there distracting elements on the way? Having studied her plan through, the teacher explains it to the children and helps them learn to follow it. A regular routine should be worked out so that the children can predict what will take place and what their role is. Given a general routine with room for individual differences, children will behave in appropriate ways with only a little practice. Other transition suggestions are presented in Chapter 4.

Each teacher will work out the transition to fit her group and her room. To shift from snack to storytime, for example, it is common in some groups to have the children deposit snack dishes on a tray, then walk past a book rack and select books. They take the books to the corner of the room reserved for storytime. They relax and "read" their books to themselves, share them with a child sitting nearby, exchange them with others, or visit quietly until most of the group has arrived.

The teacher, too, relaxes. She talks with children informally, comments on pictures they are enjoying in their books, encourages a child to find a picture she knows will interest him, or just listens attentively.

When it appears that most children are through looking at their books, she sings a song, which is the cue to pass the books to her or to an assistant. She immediately begins a series of finger plays, poems, and songs. These activities are valuable for their literary and musical qualities and because they encourage children's attention and participation and help develop cohesiveness within the group. A discussion related to experiences that took place earlier in the day or about tomorrow's projects may be worked in around a wide selection of songs, poems, and finger plays. When everyone has arrived from snack and the listening mood has been established the teacher begins her story.

Choosing a Story

Choosing an appropriate story and deciding on a technique for its presentation are two of the most important aspects of the teacher's planning. Teachers should choose stories that they themselves like. It is not likely they will put their best effort into a story they don't enjoy. The story must be right for the children. They should be able to understand it. The story should be chosen with the children's ages and previous experience in mind. Teachers must look hard and long to find suitable stories for the youngest nursery school children. It is far better to present two short stories that will hold the children's attention than to select a longer story and lose their interest before it ends. However, when the teacher misjudges the children's interest and selects a story that fails to appeal, it is wise to skip hastily through the pages, telling salient parts, and conclude the storytime with something that does appeal to the group.

The following are general guides for selecting stories and books. Stories and books should

1. Be about young children and familiar people, animals, and activities.
2. Contain about one sentence per page for three-year-olds or up to three sentences for five-year-olds.
3. Have a vocabulary the child can be expected to understand or to learn.
4. Be illustrated with clear, whole pictures that depict the action taking place.
5. Be selected both "for fun" and for information.
6. If "for fun," be fantasies that do not harm children.
7. If for information, be accurate information about the real world.

Children's books may become obsolete, depicting technical or social concepts that are outdated. For examples, unless specifically designed to depict the historical, books about transportation and farming should be relatively new. Also, books indicating roles of boys and girls, and men and women, need careful scrutiny for sex role stereotyping. Recent research indicates that many picture books and other books used in early elementary schools depict girls as weak characters in observer, nonaggressive roles, and boys are pictured as leaders and as characters having the most fun and curiosity. Similarly, books showing children of ethnic groups other than white have been quite rare until recently.

Teachers must put extra effort into selecting books with new information. In the interim they can develop some homemade books for their groups. For example, with the aid of magazine pictures and photographs books can be made from heavy tagboard and notebook rings. Books with children from various ethnic groups can be made. There are several magazines devoted to black culture, and magazines from Mexico might be a source of pictures of persons of Latin heritage. Ethnic stereotypes should be avoided, such as the depicting of Indians only in headdresses. It is important for a child of an ethnic group to have some literature depicting his group, and it is also important that the children of each group learn about children who have different cultural and ethnic backgrounds.

Late in the kindergarten year, when the teacher is sure of the sophistication of her group, more fanciful stories and those with some distance in time and place might be selected.

Teachers should become familiar with their school library and with a selected group of outstanding books in order to be able to find a story that will appeal to their children even on a moment's notice. It often happens that emergencies arise—schedules don't work out, special performers are late, or rain pours just when an outdoor activity is planned. If the teacher can reach for a book that she knows has special appeal, she can hold her group together and avoid the disruptive behavior that emergencies often trigger in children.

Listed below are books that are predictable winners for each age listed. These books incorporate the characteristics of content, illustrations, length of sentences, and number of pages typically enjoyed by children of each age. Of course many other books could have been listed. However, it is each teacher's responsibility to learn to choose the right books for the children in a particular group. New students should study these suggested books, compare other books to them, and try out various books with children in order to learn to select books wisely.

For three-year-olds:
Flack, Marjorie, *Ask Mr. Bear.*
Gipson, Morrell, *Hello Peter.*
Jackson, Kathryn, *Busy Timmy.*
Keats, Ezra Jack, *The Snowy Day.*
Lenski, Lois, *Big Little Davy.*

For four-year-olds:
Brown, Margaret W., *The Noisy Book.*
Flack, Marjorie, *Tim Tadpole and the Great Bullfrog.*
McCloskey, Robert, *Blueberries for Sal.*
McCloskey, Robert, *Make Way for Ducklings.*
Rey, H. A., *Curious George.*

For five-year-olds:
Burton, Virginia Lee, *Mike Mulligan and His Steam Shovel.*
Daugherty, James, *Andy and the Lion.*
Gag, Wanda, *Millions of Cats.*
McCloskey, Robert, *One Morning in Maine.*
Petersham, Maud and Miska, *The Circus Baby.*
Zion, Gene, *Harry the Dirty Dog.*

Illustrations in Books

Teachers should learn to appreciate the art in children's picture books. There is much beauty, strength, and feeling in some picture books. Once she is acquainted with an artist's work the teacher's enjoyment of picture books will be enhanced. Pictures contribute a great deal to children's enjoyment of books.

The Caldecott Medal is given yearly to honor one of the earliest picture book artists, Randolph Caldecott. Caldecott, an Englishman, lived from 1846 to 1886. His children's books were illustrated after 1878.[14] It is interesting to study the evolution of children's books over the years. One method of study is to seek out the Caldecott Medal winners.

As one studies picture books, it is easy to become impressed with the wide variation in technique and medium that is used by artists. An hour-long film highlights a number of outstanding picture book artists, such as Barbara Cooney, Robert McCloskey, Maurice Sendak, and Ezra Keats. The film "The Lively Art of Picture Books"[15] selects artists' representations of lions, trees, and the Notre Dame Cathedral to show the wide variety of ways these objects are seen by artists and represented in children's books. The examples support the concept of creativity discussed in Chapter 7. Both teachers and parents appreciate this film.

Illustrations in books help the child understand what is happening in the story even if he doesn't hear or understand the words. Pictures should leave accurate concepts. Children are less confused if objects appear whole. Some books have small or abstract pictures that are difficult to see from a distance. The teacher should place the books she expects to use for group storytime across the room and judge whether the children will be able to see the pictures. When the children can't see the picture, they can be expected to lose interest and perhaps to misbehave. Books with pictures that are difficult to see can be used for individual reading. If the story is especially strong, the

[14] "Randolph Caldecott," Vol. 4, *Encyclopaedia Britannica* (London: Wm. Benton, Publisher, 1960), p. 565.
[15] *The Lively Art of Picture Books,* 16mm, sound, color, 57 min. (Weston, Conn.: Weston Woods Studio, 1964).

teacher can tell it, using other visual aids such as puppets or flannel-board figures.

One of the teacher's difficulties in choosing books will come when she tries to find books that tell stories of peoples of various races, colors, and creeds in this country and the world. For example, the total list of books with black children that are suitable in content and illustration to read to three-year-olds is quite limited. For four- and five-year-olds the list doesn't grow by many items.[16] The list is just as meager for the Spanish-American, Indian-American, or Oriental-American child.[17]

Not only do black children need books with black faces for identification purposes, but all children at some point will benefit from books with faces, homes, families, and customs different from their own; such books expand their knowledge of the world's peoples. What, then, can teachers do to remedy the problem of pure white picture books? First, they should keep asking bookstores, librarians, publishers, and writers for such books. Second, they may have to make their own.

Teachers have always been self-reliant. If they need something they can't buy, they make a substitute. By taking photographs; finding paper dolls, magazine, newspaper, or catalog pictures; or using some of the interracial teaching aids on the market, teachers can illustrate homemade books or provide visual aids for storytime. Homemade books will be discussed in a later section. Of course, it is worthwhile for children to watch puppets and flannel-board figures that represent minority children even when no children from that group are in the class.

Choosing a Storytime Technique

Storytime should never become the same old thing. The teacher can develop a number of techniques that will make it an event that is looked forward to. What are some of these techniques?

READING DIRECTLY FROM A BOOK. This technique is best when you have outstanding poetry or prose with outstanding illustrations. Certainly when the author and the artist provide a well-integrated piece of literature, it is well to let it carry the children along.

USING THE ILLUSTRATIONS OF A BOOK WHILE PARAPHRASING THE STORY. This technique works well with informational material that is too long and detailed for the children, yet has illustrations related to their interests.

---

[16] Marilyn Jasik, "A Look at Black Faces in Children's Picture Books," *Young Children*, **24** (October 1968), 43–54.

[17] Louise Griffin, *Multi-ethnic Books for Young Children* (Washington, D.C.: The National Association for Education of Young Children, 1970).

TELLING THE STORY.   Storytelling is one of the oldest arts. It certainly should not become a lost art in the nursery school and kindergarten just because publishers have given us many good books. Listening to a story without the aid of pictures requires more attention from children than listening to stories from picture books. A good storyteller needs preparation and practice.

The storyteller can use various props to invite attention and set the mood for the story. She can wear an apron when reading *Apron On, Apron Off* by Helen Kay,[18] or an old straw hat during *Who Took the Farmer's Hat?* by Joan Nodset,[19] or a pretty rose for *No Roses for Harry* by Gene Zion.[20] A collection of hats can illustrate *Caps for Sale* by Esphyr Slobodkina.[21] A plush bunny or doggy can sit beside the teacher during a pet story and tell the teacher "when everyone is ready to listen."

The teacher chooses a good story and learns to tell it. For a new story she might make notes on index cards to prompt her until she becomes familiar with the story. It is important to do the story well. The teacher should use vocal inflections to create the various characters and help the children differentiate between them. Eye contact with each listener will help hold his attention and help the teacher feel the impact her story is making: The teacher may move her head, body, or arms to help dramatize the story. However, teachers are cautioned not to select frightening stories or to build up unnecessary suspense or fear through their dramatizations.

The teacher can help children realize that they too are storytellers. She can type, write, or tape-record a child as he tells an exciting event. She can read this back to the child to help him realize he really did tell a story.

TELLING A STORY WITH FLANNEL BOARD.   You can make a flannel board by covering a large piece of cardboard with a piece of outing flannel. A neutral gray is a satisfactory color. An easel or some other stand for holding the board will be convenient. You can make another type of flannel board by covering the bottom of a large cardboard box; then cut the sides diagonally to support the flannel board at a 45-degree angle.

Figures that represent the characters in the story are cut out of felt, pelon, flannel, or paper. A small piece of sandpaper or masking tape attached to the back of the figure makes it adhere to the flannel.

---

[18] Helen Kay, *Apron On, Apron Off* (Englewood Cliffs, N.J.: Scholastic Book Services, 1968).

[19] Joan Nodset, *Who Took the Farmer's Hat?* (New York: Harper & Row, 1963).

[20] Gene Zion, *No Roses for Harry* (New York: Harper & Row, 1958).

[21] Esphyr Slobodkina, *Caps for Sale* (New York: Scott, 1947).

Figures are available commercially that represent community helpers, family members, and some traditional stories. Such items can be used in many stories. All the characters in a story need not be made. Sometimes a single figure or picture will provide the children a focus for their attention as they listen.

Children will enjoy and learn from using the flannel board figures. They will not only tell the story the teacher tells but will create their own stories. Such use can take place during the self-selected activity period. However, during the storytime the teacher may or may not let the children handle the figures. The decision will depend on goals. If she wants the children to hear a meaningful story in sequence, she may handle the figures herself, keeping them out of sight until time for them to appear. However, if encouraging individual participation is more important than story sequence, she may give each child a figure to place on the board when it is called for. This technique does detract from the story and may be hard on the figures. It is true that teachers may spend a great deal of time making these figures and often prefer that they remain "special" to add spice at storytime.

The true-to-life stories of Martin and Judy in *Martin and Judy*, Volumes I, II, and III, by Verna Hills Bayley [22] lend themselves to adaptation for the flannel board. The series has the advantage of featuring the same little boy and girl, with whom children readily identify. *Ask Mr. Bear* by Marjorie Flack,[23] *The City Noisy Book*, by Margaret Wise Brown,[24] and *I Can Count* by Carl Memling [25] are examples of stories that are readily illustrated on the flannel board.

TELLING A STORY WITH PUPPETS.   Puppets often inspire quiet children to talk. Children may appear tense during a story until they have an opportunity to be one of the characters through a puppet. Depending on her objective, the teacher will vary her decision as to whether she or the children will speak for the puppets. The choice of stories and the use of puppets will depend on the age and experience of the children.

Homemade hand puppets can be made of paper sacks, socks, vegetables, or cutouts on a stick. Finger puppets can be made of decorated styrofoam balls or of construction paper attached to the finger by a paper ring. Many commercial puppets are available. A worthwhile addition to the school is a set of family puppets made of molded plastic. The puppets come in both black and white families.

[22] Verna Hills Bayley, *Martin and Judy*, Vols. I, II, and III (Boston: Beacon Press, 1959).

[23] Marjorie Flack, *Ask Mr. Bear* (New York: Macmillan, 1932).

[24] Margaret Wise Brown, *The City Noisy Book* (New York: Harper & Row, 1939).

[25] Carl Memling, *I Can Count* (New York: Western Publishing, 1963).

By purchasing several sets, the teacher can enlarge the family. Extra adults can be grandparents or other relatives. Delightful for animal stories are plush bunny, dog, and lion puppets.

To encourage puppetry during the self-selected activity period a cardboard box can be cut to resemble a television set, or a table can be turned on its side to make a stage. The children will conceal themselves behind the "TV" or "stage," holding up the puppets for manipulation or speaking. If a few chairs are arranged for the "audience," the listeners will come and go as interested.

ROLE-PLAYING A STORY.   Children can become involved in a story through creative dramatics. The teacher may tell or read a story, then let the children present their version. Care should be taken to avoid indicating that there are certain words that must be said. The children may be encouraged to play various roles without attaching them to a story. The teacher might say, "Who would like to be the mother calling the children to come to breakfast?" Who will be the father? Or the children? A drama suitable for Broadway may result.

MAGAZINE PICTURE STORY.   The teacher selects a number of pictures she has saved from magazines and stacks the pictures in an order that might suggest a story sequence. For example, picture number one is a girl, number two is a dog, number three is a girl and a dog running, and number four is a dog doing tricks or eating. The teacher may start with the phrase, "Once upon a time there was a . . ."—then let the children take it from there. The first few sessions may produce very short stories, so teachers should prepare several sets. However, once the idea catches on, the children will enjoy elaborating on the details in the pictures and the action they can imagine.

This same storytelling technique is used to tell the stories with the pictures in *My Weekly Surprise,* a newspaper published for kindergarteners but usable with many fours.[26] The cover picture invariably is a good story starter. The children's imaginations do the rest.

FILMSTRIP STORIES.   Some filmstrip stories have been made from outstanding picture books. To see the enlargement of the drawings from such books as Robert McCloskey's *Make Way for Ducklings* [27] is to appreciate anew the great care he took in illustrating the book. One drawback of filmstrip stories is that they are used frequently on television and may not be new to the children. This, of course, may not lessen the enjoyment of them, but teachers should realize this fact and not be too disappointed if the children say, "We've seen that."

[26] *My Weekly Surprise* (American Education Publications, Education Center, Columbus, Ohio 43216).

[27] Robert McCloskey, *Make Way for Ducklings* (New York: Viking, 1941).

STORY RECORDS. Story records are popular with children. Stories usually include some music and sound effects that would be difficult for the teacher to add. Therefore the record offers the child a variation. Outstanding stories should be used for group time. The record jacket or a picture related to the story can be attached to the flannel board for a focus of attention. Children seem to enjoy having the turntable at eye level so that they can watch it. Records of published books are now available, so the book can be held for viewing while the record plays. Some records have both book and filmstrip available. Recorded stories will provide important listening opportunities for individual children during the self-selected activity period.

The following recorded stories are particularly popular with children. The asterisk (*) indicates that a picture book is available for that story. These records are available on 78 rpm records and in various combinations on 33⅓ rpm records.

"Sleepy Family"	* "Andy and the Lion"
* "Muffin in the City"	* "Blueberries for Sal"
* "Muffin in the Country"	* "Madeline's Rescue"
* "The Little Firemen"	* "Make Way for Ducklings"
"Little Indian Drum"	* "Georgie the Friendly Ghost"
* "The Carrot Seed"	* "Story About Ping"

A STORY SONG. A number of children's songs are complete with plot, suspense, and climax. The teacher will find eager listeners if she occasionally sings a story to her group. She may accompany herself on an instrument—guitar, autoharp, or piano. Also, she may illustrate the song at the flannel board as she sings. "Mary Had a Little Lamb," "John Henry," "Eency Weency Spider," or "Hush, Little Baby"—all familiar songs for young children—can be thought of as stories the first time they are introduced. "I Know an Old Lady," a humorous, fanciful story by Rose Bonne and Allan Mills, is delightful to sing in kindergarten.[28] Younger children, however, take the song too literally. Of course, the children will want to sing along, so let them!

CHILDREN'S OWN STORIES. Children can learn that their own words make stories and even books. A trip or an interesting discovery can prompt a story. The children dictate, the teacher writes. Dictation can be done individually during the self-selected activity period or with the group during storytime. Sometimes the class can be divided into groups to write several stories.

[28] Rose Bonne and Allan Mills, *I Know an Old Lady* (Englewood Cliffs, N.J.: Scholastic Book Services, 1961).

Young children won't have patience enough for the teacher to print carefully as they dictate their story, so the teacher takes the dictation on a lined tablet. She transcribes it later. She has to use her own version of shorthand to keep up with the flow of ideas. If two adults can work together, one can write while the other keeps the ideas coming and helps a child hold on to a thought until the writer gets it down. A tape recorder is very useful in these instances. When a lull comes in the contributions, the transcriber can read "the story so far." Then the children can be asked if they had other thoughts as they listened to their story. The story can be typed, posted on the bulletin board, and read at storytime the next day. A copy can be sent home to parents in a special booklet. The children will relive the event each time they hear the story.

Four-year-olds dictated the following story after a trip to see the train engine that is on exhibit on the Michigan State campus.

The Train

Monday we went to explore the M.S.U. train.

It was as high as the ceiling. No! It was high like a house. There were big, big wheels. Everything was black.

We climbed tall stairs to get to the top.

We got to pull the train whistle rope. It was an old, old train and there was an old, old man. He helped us ring the bell. He was sixteen or seventeen.

It had a dark scary coal car behind it. It was a coal engine. I think it was a steam engine.

We sat in the driver's chair. We found where the brakes were.

We pulled the track switch thing. It was broke. The train was on tracks—that's how it goes.

It was fun to visit that train!

A picture book can be made of the story. Pages can be cut of cardboard and fastened with notebook rings. A few lines from the story can be lettered on each page. It can be illustrated with drawings, with magazine pictures, with pictures copied from books on a Xerox copier, or with photographs if available. Because the children are the authors, the book will be one of the most popular in the school.

The following story was dictated by the four-year-olds, then made into a picture book.

Our Fall Trip

Once upon a time nineteen children went to the woods. It is called the Arboretum Park. We took the Sugar Bush Trail, or path, or road. We saw a squirrel. He was eating bread.

We saw cows with long horns. We saw prairie dogs and deer—reindeer.

We fed the racoon. They eat with their claws. They have a face that looks like a mask.

We found two caterpillars.

We jumped in a big pile of leaves under a tree. We made the pile. That was fun.

We saw the ducks. We fed them bread. Did you see three swans? Except one of them was a white duck.

We saw buflalo—two buffaloes.

We ate some bread, peanut butter, and Koolaid.

We came back to our school. We had fun.

Sometimes in place of a story the group dictates a thank-you letter to someone who has made a special event possible. An example follows. Mr. Caldwell was a police officer, and Prince was his trained police dog.

Dear Mr. Caldwell,

We liked your dog, Prince. Thank you for bringing him. We liked to see him climb up the slide and slide down it and climb over the boxes. We liked the commands you gave the dog. We liked to see him jump through the swing. His name sounds like "Prince Charming." We liked him to do everything. We liked to see you slide down the big slide. We liked to see him go up and down on the seesaw. We didn't know policemen and dogs went around at night playing on our seesaw!

Love,
The Kindergarten Children

Dictating a letter or a story is a creative literature and language experience. Each child derives satisfaction from his contribution.

He'll remember that contribution too as the story is read and reread to him! By recording children's expressions, one is readily impressed with the effects children achieve with language. When dictation is taken from children, care should be used to preserve their original and often charming phrases.

POETRY AND FINGER PLAYS.   Poetry tells a story. Poems can be used at storytime or spontaneously anywhere in the room or yard. The more the teacher uses poetry the more children will appreciate it. Children who hear poetry frequently will soon be rhyming words even in new poems. Poems contribute a great deal to the child's learning to hear sounds. They make an important contribution to his reading readiness.

In selecting poems for children, the teacher should take care to choose short poems on subjects of interest to children. As with books, the message should be clear and be presented in a vocabulary on the children's level. For the more symbolic poems, wait until the children are older.

In addition, teachers should choose poems that they also enjoy, and learn to read them with meaning. Various collections will help teachers choose poems. *Poems Children Will Sit Still For,* edited by de Regniers, Moore, and White,[29] and *All Together* by Dorothy Aldis [30] are examples of collections that can aid teachers when selecting poems. Of course, every child should get to know poems from A. A. Milne's collections: *When We Were Very Young* and *Now We Are Six.*[31] *The Human Connection* by Bill Martin, Jr., will inspire teachers to integrate poetry with their other teaching.[32]

The teacher can mark the table of contents of her books or type the poems on index cards. This latter method enables her to carry cards in her pocket and use poems spontaneously. Eventually she will know many from memory.

Finger plays are short poems with actions for the child to do as he says the words. The actions seem to help hold the child's attention and offer a good introduction to poetry. Teachers can encourage children to use finger plays creatively by adding new verses and motions. Hundreds of finger plays have been published in a variety of books, so the teacher has only to select those she likes and make them her own through memorizing them and using them frequently. *Let's Do*

[29] Beatrice S. de Regniers, Eva Moore, and Mary M. White, *Poems Children Will Sit Still For* (Englewood Cliffs, N.J.: Scholastic Book Services, 1969).

[30] Dorothy Aldis, *All Together* (New York: Putnam, 1952).

[31] A. A. Milne, *When We Were Very Young* (New York: Dutton, 1924); *Now We Are Six* (New York: Dutton, 1927).

[32] Bill Martin, Jr., *The Human Connection* (Washington, D.C.: Department of Elementary-Kindergarten-Nursery Education, NEA, 1967).

Fingerplays by Marion F. Grayson [33] and *Finger Playtime* by Mary J. Ellis [34] are examples of books of finger plays available. A few finger plays with suggested actions are given at the end of this chapter.

A finger play will quiet a group of fidgeting children quicker than nearly any technique, especially if the verse is begun in a quiet voice that makes children wonder what is taking place. The teacher then can use finger plays in place of saying "Shh!" It is helpful to type new finger plays on index cards and carry them in a pocket in order to have them handy for these moments. Finger plays are simple enough so that children can be encouraged to "Remember to say this to your mommy tonight." Parents enjoy such samples of their child's learning.

Finger plays can be soothing or they can be rollicking. The teacher learns to sense which type she needs to set the mood. For example, if she is getting the children ready to listen to a story, she would choose a quiet finger play—not one that would cause the children to get up and clap. Such behavior would dispel the mood she is trying to establish for the story. On the other hand, if the children have been listening quietly to a story, the teacher might choose a lively finger play to give them the cue that she is ready for them to get up and become active again.

Additional Tips for Storytime

The teacher who chooses a good story, perfects her technique, and plans a smooth transition between other activities and storytime still has some steps to take before she will complete a satisfactory group literature experience.

Once the group is ready, the teacher should proceed directly to the first sentence of her story. To tell young children about an author or discuss why the story is appropriate that day invites disruption of the listening mood the teacher has worked to establish. After a few pages it is sometimes possible to ask children why they think this story was chosen today. As for the author, after the book becomes a favorite— after many readings—the group might be interested in some interesting fact about the author.

Children will not automatically know the behavior that is expected at storytime unless the teacher teaches them. She can teach children gently but firmly, and a good story experience will be sufficient reward. Eye contact with each child throughout the story helps him

---

[33] Marion F. Grayson, *Let's Do Fingerplays* (Washington, D.C.: Robert B. Luce, 1962).

[34] Mary J. Ellis, *Finger Playtime* (Minneapolis: T. S. Denison and Co., 1960).

feel that the teacher is talking directly to him. The teacher therefore keeps her eyes moving from child to child. If a child appears to become distracted, the teacher may let her eyes rest on the child for a moment. In most instances that is enough to draw his attention back to the story. If a child seems about to become disruptive she can say, for example, "John, do you know what the old man said?" The child who is easily distracted can be invited to "Sit up here close to me, and I'll help you remember to be a good listener." She can then touch his knee or shoulder as a gentle reminder. Care should be taken to be sure the children understand that the place by the teacher is not a punishing seat—her offer is to "help" not punish. Also, a second adult who sits with the children is a great help in handling special problems that may arise. The teacher who is reading may then concentrate on holding the attention of the group.

Teachers develop skill in acknowledging a child's verbal contribution during storytime. One of the teacher's reasons for her choice of story is that it will have special meaning for the children. When she is successful, the children will be bubbling over with personal references stimulated by the story. This is good—just what the teacher wants. Yet she can only listen to a limited number of children before the group becomes impatient. They are egocentric. If they can't talk, too, and can't have the story, then they take things into their own hands. They may talk or even poke their neighbors. Sometimes the teacher's nod or smile will be sufficient recognition of a child's comment. Sometimes the teacher may pause to listen, then grasp the lead when the child pauses. She can teach a "secret sign," such as a nod, a wink, or a wave of her index finger, that means "Let's wait until we finish the story." Of course, when the story is complete, she must then hold a discussion, permitting the children to talk about the ideas in the story. Discussions, besides being excellent for language development, help the teacher correct misconceptions. Discussions help the teacher gain more understanding of individual children.

The Martin and Judy stories [35] are examples of stories that encourage personal identification. In such stories the teacher may read or tell awhile, then let the children talk about their experiences, and finally say, "Let's see how Martin and Judy worked it out." This statement helps regain their attention and the storytime can go on.

An old farmer said of the movies, "You gotta go to know if you shoulda gone." And so it is with storytime. The teacher's role is to lead children into an avenue of enjoyment. Then they will be happy to go to storytime each day.

[35] Verna Hills Bayley, op. cit. (see n. 22, above).

Reading

No one skill that children learn receives as much attention as reading. A number of writers have instilled fear and guilt feelings in parents and teachers whose children aren't reading by nursery school age.[36] Of course, all adults want children to learn to read. Reading skills are basic in modern society. However, no one has yet proved that early readers read with more comprehension or, as adults, are more devoted to literature than children who learn later.[37]

What Is Reading?

Reading can be defined as making sense out of letters or symbols. Note the requirement is "making sense . . ."—not merely pronouncing the symbols. To make sense means to comprehend or understand. In reading one must understand the concepts symbolized by the letters.

An example may help clarify this definition. Any adult with reasonable reading skills could probably read a book on nuclear physics —to choose one of the highly technical sciences. He could "read" in the sense of pronouncing the words. Yet would he be able to comprehend the content just because he could read it? Would his motivation be high for reading such a book if he did not understand it? The answer is "No" to both questions. Without experiences and background information that provide a frame of reference, the words would be meaningless. His motivation for reading them would be low. Therefore it seems logical that the young child needs experiences to support the words he reads.

Reading in the Nursery School and Kindergarten

Teachers should squarely confront the question of reading in the nursery school and kindergarten. They should formulate their answers to this issue. They should take the initiative to avoid a defensive stance. Parents want to know, the community wants to know, and even children want to know. Are you going to teach reading?

An honest answer is, "No, not in the sense that you expect the first grade teacher to teach reading." However, every experience the school offers will be a prereading and prewriting experience. Day after day a rich curriculum in science, language, art, music, and literature will

---

[36] Maya Pines, *Revolution in Learning: From Birth to Six* (New York: Harper & Row, 1967).

[37] Nila Banton Smith, "Early Reading Viewpoints," *Early Childhood Crucial Years of Learning,* ed. Margaret Rasmussen (Washington, D.C.: Association Childhood Education International, 1966), 60–64.

be providing the frame of reference so basic to recognizing symbols and understanding what is read.

Further than this, a policy can be stated that on an individual basis children will be encouraged to learn to read. If a child wants to read to the teacher or an assistant, he will find a ready helper. When a child points to a word and wants to know what the word is, someone will tell him. If a child volunteers to read to the children, he will be encouraged—yet the staff will avoid making others feel left out because they haven't learned yet. If a child memorizes a favorite story and wants to "read" it to some friends, he can. When the child corrects a teacher when she omits or changes a phrase in a favorite story, the teacher can take this in stride, knowing the child's memory for detail is a plus on his reading ledger.

The emphasis on reading will be entirely individually focused. For the group as a whole the teaching of reading will be left to the first-grade teacher, who has special visual aids and special techniques that the child will find fresh and exciting if they aren't usurped by the nursery school and kindergarten and labored over prematurely.

Prereading Experiences

What are the experiences that prepare the child to read? Is the school entirely responsible for prereading experiences?

Prereading experiences are those events that occur before the child begins to read. These experiences give him a background for understanding what he reads. Such experiences begin at birth and continue throughout the individual's life. For a child they are the home, the family, the school, the neighborhood, the television, and the events in which he participates, wherever they occur.

One of the first things a child must learn is that little black squiggles (symbols) have meaning. "This label says John. That is your name. Here it is on your locker," says the teacher. She helps him begin to learn that the symbols *J-o-h-n* stand for him. Over and over he sees *John*—on his name tag, on his paintings, on his coat, on his treasures from home. His friend Bill has a different symbol.

Teachers label many objects and write letters and stories, which support the idea that little black marks tell something and convey a message. The child must even learn to concentrate on the black marks—not on the white surrounding them on the page.

Many parents supplement the labeling that teachers are doing. "The red sign says *STOP*," says John's dad. Later, John reminds dad, "But you were supposed to S-T-O-P and you didn't." Thus he indicates he now understands both the symbol and the meaning.

The rich curriculum offered by the good nursery school and kindergarten is full of prereading experiences. These experiences help children develop a frame of reference for relating what is being read and what they will later read.

Vocabulary-building experiences are prereading experiences. In several chapters of this text the opportunity for vocabulary enrichment has been pointed out. The opportunity to practice letter sounds, blend sounds, words, and rhymes are all prereading experiences.

The child who learns to differentiate between largest and smallest, tallest and shortest, and longest and shortest is helped with his reading. These concepts help him to understand when his teacher points out differences in capital letters and small letters. Making lines and forms in art projects, seeing names written from left to right, and learning to write from left to right are all prereading experiences.

Differentiating puzzle pieces; fitting together the parquetry blocks, with their squares, diamonds, and triangles; choosing pegs and beads; arranging the block-city; aligning toys; and choosing blocks of a correct size and shape are all prereading experiences with structured media.

Games such as Candyland, Merry Milkman, Uncle Wiggily, dominoes, playing cards, and the various lotto games all require prereading skills. Such games contribute to number concepts. These games are especially useful in the kindergarten, where cooperative verbal skills and longer attention spans make sustained interest in games possible.

The child's experience of assuming various roles in spontaneous dramatic play gives him a feeling for the characters in the books he reads. The outdoor program, with its opportunities to extend the child's perceptions of nature and with its outlets for his energy and imagination, also makes contributions to a child's reading background.

Parents' Role in Children's Literature Experiences

It is important for teachers to encourage parents to make contributions to children's literature experiences. The school cannot assume the total responsibility if maximum learning is desired. Even highly educated parents often need guidance in helping their children.

Teachers can help parents become enthusiastic about children's books. Parental attitudes will influence children's reading. Whenever an opportunity arises, teachers can promptly suggest titles and authors of books on subjects of interest to parents. Suggestions on how books can be secured at the library or borrowed from the school's collection will be welcomed. Some parents need to know where the library is and how to get there, how many books they can check out, and how much they cost.

FIGURE 11–5. *Big sister reads to little brother when the library habit is developed in families. Some schools have lending libraries, letting children choose their favorite book to take home. (Southern University.)*

Get Books into the Home

Without books at home the child cannot look at books on his own and, of course, parents cannot read to a child. The school can operate a lending library if it has the resources. For example, in one school paperbacked picture books were secured, covered with clear plastic adhesive to increase durability, and loaned to the children. A large mailing envelope was labeled with each child's name to provide a safe place for carrying and storing the book. A 5″ × 7″ card was made for each child and carried the name of the books he had checked out. At a glance the teacher had an indication of a child's interest in books. Each time the child returned a book, he could choose another. The staff felt that because paperbacked books were relatively inexpensive, the cost of lost books would not be formidable. In practice, no books were lost.

The teacher should encourage parents to use the public library with their children. The library habit should be a family habit even for families who buy books. Of course, no family can buy the wealth of books available there. The library should become an enjoyable place to go. Then research assignments in later years won't hold so much dread for children. If the school can introduce children to the library, they in turn can encourage reluctant parents to take them. Many public libraries have a story hour to which young children are invited. The teacher can give this information to parents, along with her personal endorsement. Parents can be encouraged to use the story hour as an opportunity to check out books for home use.

Buying Books

Buying books is another way for children to have them at home. Parents can be reassured that picture books purchased during the child's nursery school days can be enjoyed over and over and will eventually serve as practice reading material. Therefore the money used for books is well spent. Some schools purchase paperbacked books in quantity and maintain a bookstore where children can spend their allowance. Buying books is, of course, a good way for the child to spend his money.

Teachers can help parents buy books by ordering them through the school. Of course, handling money is not one of the teachers' favorite tasks, but the responsibility is sometimes assumed when it means getting books into the homes of children.

There are a number of book clubs that parents may ask about. Parents also seek advice when buying an encyclopedia. Teachers can help children by helping parents make the best decision regarding books to purchase.

Reading to Children

It is enjoyable for the child if several family members take an interest in his books. Grandparents and siblings as well as parents can read to the child. Choices of books should include old favorites as well as new books that extend the child's knowledge.

Whoever reads should encourage the child to talk about the book. They can ask: "What was the dog's name? Who took the farmer's hat? How was Martin feeling? Why did the father say that?" Such conversation helps the child think about what he is hearing and gives him language practice. It strengthens his understanding and helps him remember too. However, questions should not be carried on to the point that pure enjoyment of the story is lost.

During the latter months of kindergarten, parents may express the feeling that picture books are "old hat." This may be their impatience over wanting the child to begin reading. The teacher can suggest series books such as *"B" Is for Betsy* by Carolyn Haywood [38] or *Henry*

---

[38] Carolyn Haywood, *"B" is for Betsy* (New York: Harcourt, Brace & World, 1939).

Huggins by Beverly Cleary,[39] to be read on a chapter-a-night basis. Such books carry children into the school age and extend their experience with books.

Parents can be advised to continue to read to their child even after he starts reading. The mechanics of learning to read are laborious and often discouraging even to children who have enjoyed a rich background of literature and are highly motivated to learn to read. Of course, the beginning reader needs time to practice reading at home, but the parents can continue a diet of stimulating, exciting books until he passes beyond the laborious read-aloud stage. Hearing books that are advanced beyond those the child can read will spur him on as he labors over his first primers. The parent can let the child gradually assume the reading role—perhaps at first on pages containing pictures. Or the parent may read the narrative parts while the child reads the conversation. Such reading is also good practice for vocal inflections. Any method that gives the child reading practice, yet keeps the story moving, will help keep reading motivation high.

Conclusion

The goal when offering literature to young children is to begin a romance with books that will last throughout their lifetime. A teacher values children's literature when she (1) reads to children often; (2) changes the supply of books available to them; (3) chooses reading material with regard to individual and group interests; (4) prepares adequately for group storytime; (5) encourages parents to enrich their children's lives with books; and (6) "loves, loves, loves" books.

FINGER PLAYS AND BODY ACTION POEMS

QUIET FINGER PLAYS

LITTLE BOY	FINGER ACTIONS
Here's a little boy	(Fist with thumb extended.)
That's going to bed.	(Cover fist with other hand.)
Down on the pillow	
He lays his head.	

---

[39] Beverly Cleary, *Henry Huggins* (New York: Morrow, 1953).

He wraps the covers
Around him tight.
And that's the way
He sleeps all night.

(Close hand around fist with extended thumb.)

BUNNY

There's nothing as soft as a
  bunny,
A wee little, soft little bunny.
He can hop on his toes,
And wiggle his nose,
And his powder puff tail
Is quite funny.

(One hand is an imaginary bunny being petted by the other hand.)
(Fingers hop).
(Hand on nose, wiggle it.)
(Move hand to rear to indicate tail.)

GRANDMA'S GLASSES

Here are grandma's glasses.
Here is grandma's hat.

(Fingers make glasses over eyes.)
(Two index fingers make pointed hat.)

Here's the way she folds her
  hands
And lays them in her lap.

(Fold hands and lay in lap.)

GRANDPA'S GLASSES

Grandpa lost his glasses,
Before he went to bed.
Guess where grandma found
  them?

(Fingers make glasses over eyes.)

Right on top of grandpa's head!

(Move glasses on top of head.)

THREE BALLS

Here's a ball

(Make round shape with thumb and index finger.)

Here's a ball

(Make round shape with two thumbs and two index fingers.)

Here's a great big ball.

(Make third ball with both arms.)

Let's count them.
One, two, three.

(Repeat for the count.)

TEN FINGERS

I have ten little fingers,
And they all belong to me.
I can make them do things.
Would you like to see?

(Extend fingers of both hands.)
(Point to self.)

I can shut them up tight (Make fists.)
And open them wide. (Spread fingers open.)
I can put them together (Clasp hands together.)
Or make them hide. (Put hands behind back.)

I can make them jump high. (Raise hands high.)
I can make them jump low. (Reach low.)
I can fold them quietly. (Fold and lay hands in lap.)
And hold them just so.

MY TURTLE

This is my turtle. (Make fist and extend thumb.)
He lives in a shell. (Indicate fist as shell.)
He likes his home very well.
He pokes his head out. (Extend thumb and wiggle.)
    when he wants to eat.
And pulls it back in (Hide thumb in fist.)
    when he wants to sleep.

MY EYE AND EAR

This is my eye. (Cover one eye.)
This is my ear. (Cover one ear.)
This is to see. (Look around.)
And this is to hear. (Cup hand around ear.)

BOISTEROUS FINGER PLAYS

MR. BULLFROG

Mr. Bullfrog sat on a big old (First with thumb up.)
    rock.
Along came a little boy. (Left hand walk.)
Mr. Bullfrog KERPLOP! (Both hands slap knee.)

PIG

I had a little pig (Fist with thumb up.)
And I fed it in a trough. (Make cup of left hand.)
He got so big and fat, (Make circle of arms.)
That his tail popped off! (Clap both hands and knees.)
So, I got me a hammer (One hand is hammer.)
And I got me a nail (Hammer on thumb of other
    hand.)

And I made that pig (Continue to hammer.)
A wooden tail!

FIVE LITTLE ASTRONAUTS

Five little astronauts	(Hold up fingers of one hand.)
Ready for outer-space.	
The first one said,	(Hold up one finger.)
"Let's have a race."	
The second one said,	(Hold up two fingers.)
"The weather's too rough."	
The third one said,	(Hold up three fingers.)
"Oh don't be gruff."	
The fourth one said,	(Hold up four fingers.)
"I'm ready enough."	
The fifth one said,	(Hold up five fingers.)
"Let's Blast Off!"	
10, 9, 8, 7, 6, 5, 4, 3, 2, 1.	(Start with ten fingers and put one down with each number.)
BLAST OFF!!!	(Clap loudly with "Blast Off!")

FIREMEN

Ten little firemen	(Lay all fingers out straight on knees or floor.)
Sleeping in a row.	
Ding-dong goes the bell	(Pretend to ring bell.)
Down the pole they go.	(Pretend to be sliding down pole.)
Jumping on the engine	
EE—RR—OOO	(Make siren noise.)
Putting out the fire.	(Pretend to use fire hoses.)
Then home so slow	
And back to bed again	(Lay all fingers in a row again.)
All in a row.	

LITTLE BUNNY

There was a little bunny	(Make ears over head with fingers.)
Who lived in the wood.	
He wiggled his ears	(Wiggle fingers.)
As a good bunny should.	
He hopped by a squirrel,	(Fingers hop along arm or on floor.)
He hopped by a tree,	
He stared at the squirrel,	(Cock head and look.)
He stared at the tree,	
But he made faces at me!	(Wiggle nose.)

COUNTING

One, two, three, four,	(Extend fingers one at a time.)
Mary at the cottage door.	
Five, six, seven, eight,	(Change to say "cookies," "celery," or whatever the child is eating.)
Eating (cherries) off her plate.	

FIVE LITTLE BIRDS

Five little birds, high in a tree,	(Extend five fingers.)
The first one says, "What do I see?"	(Extend one finger.)
The second one says, "I see a street."	(Extend two fingers.)
The third one says, "I see seeds to eat."	(Extend three fingers.)
The fourth one says, "The seeds are wheat."	(Extend four fingers.)
The fifth one says, "Tweet, tweet, tweet."	(Extend five fingers.)

FIVE LITTLE HOT DOGS

Five little hot dogs frying in a pan.	(Extend five fingers.)
The grease got hot and one went BAM.	(Clap.)
Four little hot dogs frying in a pan.	(Extend four fingers.)
The grease got hot and another went Bam.	(Clap.)
Three little hot dogs frying in a pan.	(Extend three fingers.)
The grease got hot and another went Bam.	(Clap.)
Two little hot dogs frying in a pan.	(Extend two fingers.)
The grease got hot and another went Bam!	(Clap.)
One little hot dog frying in a pan.	(Extend one finger.)
The grease got hot and another went Bam!	(Clap.)
No little hot dogs frying in the pan.	(Make fist.)
The grease got hot and the pan went BAM!	(Clap loudly.)

I'M THE LITTLE HOT DOG
My father owns the butcher
  shop.
My mother cuts the meat,
And I'm the little Hot Dog   (Clap on "Hot Dog.")
That runs around the street.

BABY BUMBLE BEE
I'm bringing home a baby   (Cup hand pretending to hold
  bumblebee.   bee.)
Oh, won't my mommy be so
  proud of me?
I'm bringing home a baby
  bumblebee.
Oops! He stung me!   (Toss hand excitedly.)

Moderately Active Finger Plays

FIVE LITTLE RABBITS
Five little rabbits   (Show five fingers.)
Under a log,   (Cover with other hand.)
One says, "Hark, I hear a dog!" (Show one finger. Hand behind
      ear.)
One says, "Look, I see a man!" (Point indicating eye.)
One says, "Run, as fast as you (Make fingers run.)
  can."
One says, "Pooh, I'm not afraid." (Thumbs in armpits.)
One says, "Shh, keep in the (Finger to lips.)
  shade."
So they all lay still   (Five fingers under hand.)
Under a log,
And the man passed by
And so did the dog.

FIVE LITTLE PUMPKINS
Five little pumpkins,   (Show five fingers.)
Sitting on a gate.
The first one said,   (Show one finger.)
"It's getting late."
The second one said,   (Show two fingers.)
"There are witches in the air."
The third one said, "We don't (Show three fingers.)
  care."
The fourth one said,   (Show four fingers.)

"Let's run, run, run."
The fifth one said,   (Show five fingers.)
"Isn't Halloween fun?"
"OOOOOOW" went the wind,
And OUT went the light.   (Clap on "OUT.")
Those five little pumpkins   (Five fingers roll behind child.)
Rolled fast out of sight.

HERE IS A BUNNY

Here is a bunny   (Fist with two fingers ex-
                                        tended.)

With ears so funny,
And here is his hole in the   (Thumb and index finger.)
   ground.
When a noise he hears,   (Extend fingers quickly.)
He pricks up his ears
And jumps in his hole in the   (Pretend to put bunny in hole.)
   ground.

TOUCH GAME

Touch your nose.   (Finger on nose.)
Touch your chin.   (Finger on chin.)
That's the way this game begins.
Touch your eyes.   (Fingers on eyes.)
Touch your knees.   (Fingers on knees.)
Now pretend you're going to   (Cover mouth with hand.)
   sneeze.
Touch one ear.   (Finger on ear.)
Touch two lips right here.   (Finger on lips.)
Touch your elbows where they   (Fingers on elbows—cross
   bend.   hands.)
That's the way this touch game
   ends.

ROBIN REDBREAST

Little Robin Redbreast   (Thumb and little finger
                                        extended.)

Sat upon a rail.
Niddle, noddle went his head   (Move thumb.)
And wiggle, waggle went his   (Move little finger.)
   tail.

Body Action Poems

DRESSING WARMLY

Let's put on our mittens   (Pretend to pull on mittens.)
And button up our coat.   (Pretend to button coat.)
Wrap a scarf snugly   (Pretend to tie scarf around
Around our throat.   neck.)

Pull on our boots,   (Pretend to pull up boots.)
Fasten the straps,   (Pretend to tighten straps on
And tie on tightly   boots.)
Our warm winter caps.   (Pretend to tie bow under chin.)

Then open the door   (Pretend to turn knob on door.)
And out we go   (Make fingers walk on floor if
Into the soft and feathery snow.   sitting or walk out door if
       standing.)

KEEPING DRY

Put up your umbrella   (Pretend to extend umbrella.)
To keep yourself dry;
Put up your umbrella,
There's rain in the sky.

Pitter, patter, pitter, patter,   (Make fingers tap on floor.)
Softly it falls.
Hurry home quickly
Before Mother calls.

WHIRLING TOP

I am a top, all wound up tight.   (Loop arms around knees while
       sitting.)

I whirl and whirl with all my   (Whirl around fast.)
   might.
And now the whirls are out of   (Whirl slowly.)
   me,
So I will rest as still can be.   (Come to rest.)

BOUNCE LIKE BALL

I'm bouncing, bouncing every-   (Children standing.)
   where.
I bounce and bounce into the   (Jump up and down with
   air.   rhythm.)
I'm bouncing like a great big
   ball.
I bounce and bounce, then   (Fall down in place.)
   down I fall.

THE ELEPHANT

The elephant is so big and fat.　(Circle arms.)
He walks like this, he walks like　(Walk.)
　that.
He has no finger, he has no toes,　(Point.)
But, oh my Goodness, What a　(Swing arm low for trunk.)
　nose!

GARDENING

This is the way I plant my gar-　(Bend down and dig.)
　den—
Digging, digging in the ground.
The sun shines warm and bright　(Make circle with arms over-
　above it;　head.)
Gently the rain comes falling　(Tap like rain on hard surface.)
　down.

This is the way the small seeds　(Open hands slowly.)
　open.
Slowly the shoots begin to grow.　(Bending down, put up arm.)
These are my pretty garden　(Stand proudly and smiling.)
　flowers,
Standing, standing in a row.

MY GARDEN

I dig, dig, dig,　(Pretend to dig in standing po-
　sition.)
And I plant some seeds.　(Pretend to drop seeds in row.)
I rake, rake, rake.　(Pretend to rake.)
I pull some weeds.　(Pretend to pull weeds.)
I wait and watch,　(Look at ground.)
And soon I know
I'll be here to watch
My garden grow.

MY RABBIT

My rabbit has two big ears　(Extend two fingers for bunny
　ears.)
And a funny little nose.　(Pat nose.)
He likes to nibble carrots　(Pretend to nibble.)
And he hops where'er he goes.　(Move hand, making fingers
　"hop," or if standing, hop on
　tiptoes.)

HAMMERING

Johnny pounds with one hammer,	(Pound palm with fist of other hand.)
One hammer, one hammer,	(Have one finger extended.)
Johnny pounds with one hammer,	
But Jimmy pounds with two.	(Have two fingers extended.)
Jimmy pounds with two hammers,	(Continue pounding palm.)
Two hammers, two hammers,	
Jimmy pounds with two hammers,	
But Betty pounds with three.	(Have three fingers extended.)

(Use children's names and continue up to five hammers.)

NOTE: All these finger plays and poems are by unknown authors.

ADDITIONAL READINGS

ANDERSON, VERNA D. *Reading and Young Children.* New York: Macmillan Publishing Co., Inc., 1968.

ARBUTHNOT, MARY HILL, and others (eds.). *Children's Books Too Good to Miss.* Cleveland, Ohio: Case Western Reserve, 1971.

CIANCIOLO, PATRICIA JEAN (ed.). *Picture Books for Children.* Chicago: American Library Association, 1973.

DE REGNIERS, BEATRICE, and others (eds.). *Poems Children Will Sit Still For.* New York: Scholastic Book Services, 1969.

ELLIS, MARY JACKSON. *Finger Playtime.* Minneapolis: T. S. Denison and Co., Inc., 1960.

GRAYSON, MARION F. *Let's Do Fingerplays.* Washington, D.C.: Robert B. Luce, Inc., 1962.

GRIFFIN, LOUISE (ed.). *Multi-Ethnic Books for Young Children.* Washington, D.C.: The National Association for the Education of Young Children, 1970.

LARRICK, NANCY. *A Parent's Guide to Children's Reading.* New York: Simon and Schuster, 1969.

LARRICK, NANCY. *A Teacher's Guide to Children's Books.* Columbus, Ohio: Charles E. Merrill Publishing Co., 1960.

MARTIN, BILL, JR. *Language and Literature: The Human Connection.* Washington, D.C.: Department of Elementary-Kindergarten-Nursery Educators, NEA, 1967.

STRICKLAND, RUTH G. *The Language Arts in the Elementary School.* Lexington, Mass.: D. C. Heath & Company, 1969.

TRESSELT, ALVIN, "Books and Beyond," *Childhood Education,* Vol. 51, No. 5, March 1975, pp. 261–266.

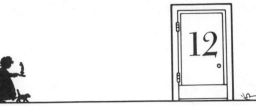

Dramatic Play

JIM BUSILY arranged the empty food boxes and egg trays on the shelves in the four-year-old nursery school's "store." He turned all the cash registers away except one. He stood behind it expectantly.

Nancy walked into the "store." "How much are the eggs?" she asked.

"Two dollars," replied Jim. Nancy started away with the egg container. "No, you didn't pay me." Jim said. He altered his voice slightly and continued, "Pretend to pay me." Nancy complied.

"You know why I have to use this big register all alone? Because my helpers aren't here today," explained Jim.

He tried to talk Nancy into buying more items. He said, "These are my secret sauce. These are my secret peaches." Nancy chose an assortment and paid him. "Thank you," said Jim giving her the change. He wanted to do some more business, but Nancy left the store.

"Let's pretend it's ten more days from now," Jim called over the divider that separated "store" from "house." It worked. Nancy returned and took some more groceries.

"Hey, you didn't give me any money and I didn't give you any money." Nancy was leaving and made no move to come back. Jim put his hand out in front of him and pretended to get the money. Then he closed up shop and went to the housekeeping area to join Nancy.

Nancy started out for the "store." Hating to see her go, Jim said, "No, the store closes at four o'clock and it's four o'clock now."

Nancy said, "But, I'm going to the other store," and left.

"Oh," said Jim, "I wonder where wife has gone now."

Scenes like this are common among young children. From their front-row seats teachers and parents are privileged to attend children's first performances as they step out on life's stage. No written lines are needed. Few props are called for. The child can be alone or with others when his feelings and ideas—real and imagined—spill out in spontaneous role-playing called *dramatic play.*

Dramatic play is the champagne of the under-six set. It gives the sparkle to home, school, or wherever children gather. Children are actors without stage fright. They perform as expertly to an empty barn as to a full house. They say what they feel and feel what they say. They unashamedly use erroneous conceptions and unintentional puns. Creativity abounds. Children ride a plank "horse," eat sand "cakes," and drink water "beer" without apology for their realism. If adults have sensitive ears, eyes, and hearts, they may be moved from deepest anguish to poetic ecstasy or be entertained by rollicking slapstick.

Values of Dramatic Play

Contributing to Total Development

All areas of a child's growth can be stimulated by dramatic play. Briefly, dramatic play contributes to development of the mental, physical, creative, social, and emotional components of the child's being.

MENTAL DEVELOPMENT. The child's dramatic roles expand as his world broadens. The child integrates concepts from every area into the imaginative play he develops. He wonders. He questions. He experiments. This active role helps him develop the depth needed to make concepts his own. While selecting roles and props he learns to make choices. He makes decisions beginning with whether or not to join an activity. Language skills, so crucial to concept formation, are called for and practiced in dramatic play. The example in the introduction to this chapter illustrates this fact.

PHYSICAL DEVELOPMENT. It is a rare child who needs encouragement to exercise. Given space, equipment, and a friend or two, activity involving exercise naturally occurs. Many dramatic roles require fast, rugged action. Good health and physical stamina are fostered.

CREATIVE DEVELOPMENT. Original thoughts, words, and deeds spill out effortlessly in dramatic play. "Pretend to pay me," said Jim. "Pretend I'm a gorilla," says a petite blond, and for a while she is a gorilla. Children on these untrod paths find new (to them) ways to do things, new things to do, and new uses for old objects—all creative discoveries.

SOCIAL DEVELOPMENT. In dramatic play the child develops his concept of his own sex role. He tries out numerous social roles and increases his depth of understanding of many other roles. He begins

FIGURE 12–1. *A tent encourages spontaneous role playing called* dramatic play. (*University of Houston Parent-Child Development Center.*)

integrating the rules of society. Often one hears him admonish friends who forget the rules. His conscience is developing.

EMOTIONAL DEVELOPMENT. The full range of feelings is expressed and experienced as the child plays with others in dramatic play. He knows joy and sorrow, affection and rejection, anger and pleasure, satisfaction and dissatisfaction. He learns to know himself as a person with feelings.

Providing Insight into Inner Thoughts and Feelings

"If we want to get closer to the truth we must look deeper into the reasons for our behavior," said Virginia Axline, a child psychologist.[1] Therapists such as Axline use the technique of play therapy, which includes spontaneous dramatic play, for discovering the source of a child's emotional disturbance. Axline explains, "We are seeking understanding, believing that understanding will lead us to the threshold

[1] Virginia M. Axline, *Dibs: In Search of Self* (Boston: Houghton Mifflin, 1964), p. 8.

of more effective ways of helping the person to develop and utilize his capacities more constructively." [2]

Teachers and parents too seek ways to understand children and thus to promote their development more effectively. Dramatic play, whether it occurs at home or at school, can give insights into the behavior of children. While the "normal" children usually enrolled in nursery schools and kindergartens do not have such deep-seated problems as those requiring play therapy, they may, nevertheless, have problems that could make them candidates for therapy should those problems continue unresolved. Teachers may have occasion to recommend therapy for a child after observing him for some time at school. [3]

Teachers should observe children's dramatic play carefully. Through a system of periodic observing and note taking, teachers develop evidence for decisions.

What can the teacher learn from such observation? She will note the recurring themes and the roles the child plays. She will know if certain children seldom participate in dramatic play. Her notes will show what he does instead. If a child is thought of as typically happy, or cross, or hostile, she notes whether one type of incident or a particular group situation invites his typical behavior.

In a typical classroom certain children will require more adult guidance than others. Observing helps the teacher determine at what point guidance is called for with such children. For example, a child may strike out each time the teacher asks him to wait for her attention. By observing this pattern in operation, the adults can make a concerted effort to satisfy his attention needs in some satisfactory way before he acts out. Observation will show certain children who never cause trouble. What are they doing? Notes often point out children who seem hungry or ill or who lack physical stamina.

The teacher seeking answers will observe and listen. What questions do the children ask? What concepts are they using? What misconceptions do they have? Who are the leaders? What characteristics do the leaders have in common? Do some children enter groups easily? What techniques do they use? The answer to these questions may give the teacher a clue as to how to help a child who has difficulty entering groups.

The teacher looks at all behavior, not just negative or troublesome

---

[2] Ibid., p. 9.

[3] Ibid., Chapter 1. Dibs was first observed by nursery school teachers who after a period of concern called in the psychologist for consultation. This is a report of her work with Dibs in play therapy. It is such a moving account that teachers everywhere should read it.

behavior. The positive relationships she observes will build confidence that all children can learn to relate to their friends and use their blossoming intellects creatively.

Helping a Child Solve Personal Problems

Teachers should be frank to admit when problems are beyond their training and experience or when they lack time for coping with children with special problems. When such instances occur, the teacher makes referrals to the guidance clinics of the community.

The teacher's focus will be on recurring themes in a child's relationships instead of on isolated incidents. A few examples of teachers' action follow.

The teacher helps build up the child's feelings of self-confidence—his positive self-concept. If children reveal that they feel little and helpless, she seeks ways to help them feel bigger and stronger. If they reveal that they feel left out, she finds ways to help them feel included and wanted. If one reveals his big brothers are bossing him around, she can accept his bossing in school, protecting only those children who can't protect themselves. If a child teases, she notes whom and when he teases and searches to understand why he finds teasing satisfying.

A child may reveal through his dramatic play that he is bothered by fears or that family relationships are difficult for him. The teacher helps him get his feelings out in the open. He can talk to her and play out his feelings with puppets or small figures. The teacher may read a story that initiates a discussion of his problem. She may endeavor to help him through his parents.

It is not uncommon to observe a young child playing the role of the opposite sex during dramatic play. That is, a boy selects women's clothing or a girl selects male's clothing for dramatic roles. Much of this play is natural curiosity about the roles of the opposite sex. The teacher, through close observation, can attempt to determine the significance of the behavior. Is the child merely trying out a role? How frequently does the play occur? Why does he seem to prefer the role? What is the child's place in the total group? Does the role reversal give him unusual attention from adults and children? What is his home situation? Do his parents accept his real sex role?

The term applied to persons who dress up in clothing of the opposite sex is *transvestism*. Bakwin and Bakwin have found that transvestism among boys greatly exceeds that of girls and that "the fact that transvestism is more common in children than in adults suggests that the deviant behavior corrects itself." They further state, "In a certain number of cases, when resistance on the part of the parents is encountered, or when the behavior seems deeply intrenched and fails to respond to general suggestions, psychiatric help should be enlisted." [4]

The teacher's role when dealing with children who play the role of the opposite sex is first to be certain that the dress-up closet contains many interesting men's as well as women's clothing. She can advise helpers to avoid giving undue attention to a child who dresses in this manner and to seek to show him attention at other times. She can talk to individual children and the group about their various "pretend" roles to help them differentiate real from pretend. She can observe and record incidents for staff consultation. She can refer the family to a pediatrician when she has enough recorded incidents to substantiate her observation. She may refer the child to a guidance clinic for observation. Ideas for dress-up are presented later in this chapter.

If a child has difficulty relating to others, the teacher may encourage his parents to provide a companion for him. Children who ride together in car pools often have their plans made when they get to school, so teachers often suggest a car pool to parents whose child is on the outside of the social groups. She may suggest that they regularly invite one of the classmates home for a visit. The teacher may carefully pair him with a child whose similar interests make him a prospective friend.

The teacher may observe that a child seems consistently tired or listless. She confers with his parents and may suggest a medical examination. If he appears hungry, she offers him his snack early and checks with his mother to learn about mealtimes at home.

Teachers can watch for physical complications. For example, if children breathe through the mouth and are unusually loud in their eating, they may have enlarged tonsils and adenoids. Need for corrective shoes may be revealed as children are observed running across a wide expanse. The teacher encourages the parents to consult a specialist when such problems are observed.

Satisfying the Child

What are satisfactions that the child derives from his dramatic play? In the first place, he has a good time. Having fun is a strong motivator for young children. If they can have fun, they will willingly go along with most other goals the adult has for them.

In the second place, he makes friends. He can choose his companions and be chosen. Friendships grow out of a mutuality of interests and needs. When the child is old enough for nursery school

[4] Harry Bakwin and Ruth Morris Bakwin, *Clinical Management of Behavior Disorders in Children* (Philadelphia: Saunders, 1960), p. 403.

and kindergarten, companions his own age become increasingly important to him. Even though he has a perfect home life, he is drawn to children of his own age.

Third, he has an opportunity to learn. Children are anxious to learn. They see their friends doing something and want to try it. They imitate their actions and their speech. Imitation is a great teacher. Children don't always tackle the easy. Dramatic play encourages them to do better, climb higher, and become smarter than before. Dramatic play offers children an informal opportunity to pit themselves against new ideas and against their peers.

Fourth, by trying out various roles, the child comes to understand himself better. A role repeated frequently can be considered to have special significance for the child.

Fifth, dramatic play offers the child the opportunity to release the abundance of energy with which he is blessed. Children thrive on action. While awake most are busily on the move. Freedom to keep moving and talking, which is allowed during dramatic play, permits the child to play as his energy level dictates.

Planning for Dramatic Play

In planning for dramatic play, the teacher takes into consideration the group of children and the developmental tasks confronting each one. She considers their age and their previous experiences at home, at school, and in the community. Her first plans are tentative. She firms these as she gets better acquainted with the group. She leaves room for spontaneous themes to develop. She willingly discards ideas that seem insignificant at a given time or for a given group. She plans to introduce numerous concepts and to reinforce learning through dramatic play. She frequently selects the specific ideas from the questions the children initiate, realizing that children will only be able to represent roles that they have observed. For example, children who have never been to a restaurant won't know how a waiter acts.

A rich, coordinated program is planned to open new vistas that children can incorporate into their dramatic play. Special visitors, trips, movies, pictures, books, and science discoveries are included in the curriculum plan. The plan, however, is more of a housecoat than a straitjacket.

Teacher's Role

The teacher must be a friendly, open, spontaneous, and creative person. She has many strengths that keep her personality on an even keel, even when emergencies arise. Deep personal regard for

FIGURE 12–2. *Small figures from home are shared in a moment of dramatic play. Though fragile for group use, these toys are suggestive of the type of play the child engages in at home. (Nazarene Child Care Center, Lansing, Michigan.)*

each child, which is conveyed openly and often, helps the children feel at ease in her presence.

Teachers must support dramatic play continuously if its values are to be realized. Just because the children are playing happily is no reason for the teacher to complete her office tasks or make a trip to the principal's office. Measures that prevent problems are more effective than mopping-up procedures. When the class is operating smoothly is the best time to record the positive examples that will sustain the teacher in moments of discouragement. Moreover, activities should be enriched and extended at every opportunity. The teacher who keeps close to the children, observing and listening to them, can more meaningfully plan the highly motivating, worthwhile nursery school or kindergarten program that each child deserves.

FIGURE 12–3. *Two telephones facilitate communication between house-holder and fireman. (Texas Tech University Kindergarten.)*

Atmosphere

The teacher establishes an atmosphere conducive to meaningful creative dramatic play. There is an air of freedom that the children sense. They seem to be like the old slave who got his freedom after the Civil War. Someone asked him if he wasn't as well off under slavery. They reminded him that he had the same master, the same food, and the same bed. He replied, "Yes, except there is a looseness about this freedom that I like."

There is a "looseness" in the nursery school and kindergarten that allows for spontaneous, impromptu, original, and different things to take place. There is a steady hum of talking, laughing, and learning as the children work individually and in small groups.

Time

Time is required for dramatic play to develop and for themes to be carried to satisfying conclusions. If the daily schedule is interspersed with many teacher-instigated activities, the children may find little opportunity to develop an idea before the teacher calls them to another circle. In such classrooms dramatic play soon withers.

In most schools dramatic play takes place during indoor and outdoor self-selected activity periods. If such play is to flourish, a minimum of 30 minutes, but preferably about 50 minutes, will be needed for the self-selected activity period. The teacher keeps the schedule flexible. For example, if the children have worked hard on getting a "train" ready for an imaginary trip, the teacher allows them to take at least one ride before announcing that it is cleanup time. On the other hand, if the train trip is over and the children seem at loose ends for a new activity, the teacher may decide that it is a good time to clean up even though the clock doesn't quite say so. The teacher warns the children when a transition is approaching; thus she encourages them to bring their activities to a close.

Space

Space is a requirement for dramatic play. Children need space to move around. Several areas of the room and yard can contain opportunities for dramatic play. Such areas are the work tables, the housekeeping area, the block area, the music area, the literature area, the woodworking area, and the outdoor area, which includes climbing areas, digging, wheel toys, and perhaps materials typically kept indoors. Having several areas provides alternative activities should congestion occur in one area.

Limits

Limits are defined, discussed, and maintained without punishment or harshness. Only those limits necessary to protect children, the learning environment, and property are set. Limits help children feel secure. Dramatic play should not become a free-for-all.

Suggested Props for Dramatic Play Themes

The following materials and equipment are suggested for enriching and extending the roles children play. Props are placed where they will be noticed by the children. They are stored so that the children can find them readily and are kept orderly to suggest constructive creative play and not disorganized destruction.

DRESS-UP. Both men's and women's clothing should be available. Castoff clothing makes good "dress-ups." Rummage sales are good sources of these materials. Children seem to be attracted to texture. Things of velveteen, satin, or fur are favorites. The crinoline petticoats of a bygone era are considered extremely elegant, especially when worn as "wedding dresses." Hats, purses, shoes, boots, and costume jewelry are popular items.

Big brother's shirts, sport coats, Scout uniforms, vests, boots, and shoes are a better size for young children than are dad's. Hats for

FIGURE 12–4. *Beauty shop play requires knowledge of the roles of patron and operator. (Louisiana State University Nursery School.)*

some community helpers—firemen, policemen, bus drivers—can be purchased from school supply catalogs. Farmers' and cowboys' hats are available in variety stores. The metal hat of the lineman is popular and can be purchased in hardware stores. Painters' hats are often free at paint stores.

Long circle skirts encourage role playing and creative dancing. A group would like a number of these, which can be made by a seamstress. She can use a simple waist pattern that fits the largest child, then cut an ankle-length circle skirt to fit the waist. A zipper should be placed in the front to make self-dressing easier. You can alter women's old skirts for self-dressing by putting elastic in the waistband or sewing velcro on the opening.

Other popular costumes that can be made by a seamstress are clown, drum major, bunny, doctor, and nurse outfits. Children like bright colors in their dress-up clothes. They should be made of lightweight material because children wear them over clothing.

"Dress-ups" should be stored so that they present a suggestive array from which children can choose and so that clothes stay in good condition. If clothes are stuffed into a trunk or a box, a chaotic disorder results that is not part of constructive learning. An open cupboard built at the children's level using regular coat hangers is one type of storage. Pegs may also be used. In most cases, some adult help will be necessary at cleanup time. Dress-up clothing should be laundered regularly.

A good-quality, full-length mirror is indispensable in the dress-up area.

HOUSEKEEPING. The housekeeping area or playhouse is perhaps the most common dramatic play area. This seems logical because the first roles the child assumes are family roles. Household routines and relationships affect young children very directly. They become alert to the people and the activities of the home. In the following example, roles are carefully assigned and played.

Five-year-olds are playing in the housekeeping area. They begin

FIGURE 12–5. *Shaving can be encouraged by the availability of shaving cream and a razor (minus its blade).*

FIGURE 12–6. *Glasses nearly always intrigue the young. Glasses can be made from the plastic rings that come around soft-drink or juice cans, with pipe cleaners to make ear pieces. (Michigan State University Laboratory Preschool.)*

building another room along the playroom wall outside the house-keeping area. They use chairs to enclose their room. They move a number of toys into the "new house." The three girls wear dress-up clothing. Susie is Mother, Ruth the baby, and Cindy a small child. Mark is the father. Baby says to Mother, "Pretend you came in and saw a baby." Mother pats Baby on the head and then says, "Now, Baby, you can get up. Your daddy is coming home." Father enters. Mother says, "Honey, will you put this toy in the box over there?" Father does as requested. The small child enters and starts to go out again. Mother commands, "Come back. Come back. Here, take this," giving the small child a toy. She then says, "Now you sit there and play until time to eat."

Furnishing the housekeeping area can be quite simple or very elegant depending on ideas and financing. Staff and parents who have ingenuity and skill with tools can furnish the area at little cost. Old tables can be cut down, cupboards can be made with wood and cardboard boxes. Stove grills can be painted on one end of a box. The cushion from a car's back seat can be purchased at a salvage yard and used as an upholstered sofa or a child-sized bed.

Durable dolls of various sizes and colors should be available. Dolls with molded hair are more durable and withstand the countless baths better than those with fabric hair. Doll clothes should be made so that children can manage the buttons and zippers. Slip-on pants and skirts can be made with elastic belts and are good for those children who are interested in undressing and dressing dolls.

Other furnishings are small dishes, pots and pans, silverware, several telephones, mop, broom, and carpet sweeper. A doll carriage, a bed, and a small rocker are popular. A small chest of drawers for the doll clothes is important. A few food tins, cereal boxes, and a milk carton or two can be added.

The children can be very helpful in putting the materials away each day. However, the teacher should check before their arrival to be sure the area is clean and tidy. Materials should be washed as needed and dangerous broken pieces disposed of or repaired. To make the area inviting or to stimulate its use, she may place a doll in the high chair and set out the baby food. Little mothers take over from there.

If children want to use water or play dough in the housekeeping area, the teacher must establish limits. These materials do add to the realism. However, if the teacher finds the mess excessive, she can ask the children to use water and play dough elsewhere and to "just pretend" in the playhouse.

The housekeeping area should be rearranged occasionally to stimulate the play. Changing the location in the room may bring it to the attention of a child who hasn't played there before. For example, when the housekeeping area is close to the large block area, the two areas may supplement each other, and the children will move back and forth between a block structure and the housekeeping area. Some of the housekeeping equipment may be moved to equip a block house or may be moved outdoors to help extend the role playing to the yard.

BEAUTY SHOP AND BARBERSHOP. The following materials invite beauty shop and barbershop play: A long mirror or several smaller ones, curlers, combs, a safety razor without the blade, whipped soap flakes for "shaving cream," and an old electric shaver. "Hairdryers" can be made of round commercial ice cream cartons obtained at an

FIGURE 12–7. *A family picnic was arranged in the block corner with a plank table especially built for the occasion.* (*Texas Tech University Kindergarten.*)

ice cream parlor or supermarket. The carton is taped to a yardstick, then taped to the back of a small chair and set against the wall for support. Don't forget a stack of magazines or books nearby!

After beauty–barber shop play, dip the tools in disinfectant. Avoid this play altogether if the children have infections on the scalp.

RESTAURANT. During various cooking projects—making pancakes, hamburgers, or pizzas—the housekeeping area can become a restaurant or a drive-in. Menus can be posted. Tablecloths can be made out of bright cloth. A cash register operator handles the money. Boys like Jim may like the play. He announced that he was the "cook" and this was his "restaurant." He methodically took orders. He indicated several times that a cook's role was acceptable for a boy in a restaurant but not in a house. The teacher took the opportunity during this role playing to discuss with Jim that some men cook at home. This was an effort to broaden his view of sex roles.

STORE. With a few shelves built of planks and blocks, a cash register, paper sacks, pencils, and note pads, children will enter into store play. A collection of grocery cartons and cans suggests a grocery store. The hats from the dress-up area change it to a hat store. Shoes make it a shoe store. Play is enriched by trips to a supermarket or a department store.

FIGURE 12–8. *Dressing up is a perennial favorite, especially with crinoline petticoats that make elegant dancing and wedding dresses. (Michigan State University Laboratory Preschool.)*

OFFICE. An old typewriter (provided free by some business machine companies), telephones, tables, and chairs will be sufficient furniture for the office. It is interesting to note children's concept of an office. In one group where even a number of the children's mothers had offices, the children first used such equipment for a "doctor's office." They altered the teacher's initial arrangement by bringing in a bed from the housekeeping area. They searched for the stethoscopes. After several days of playing "doctor," they thought of using the space as the parent's office. However, the roles they played were themselves. They indicated that the crayons and paper had to be available. Drawing seems to be the child's pastime when he visits a parent's office.

The typewriter is a very popular piece of equipment and probably should have a permanent place in the classroom because of its importance to modern living.

POST OFFICE.   Post-office play naturally follows the mailing of a letter to a friend or the posting of valentines. A schoolbag can be the mailman's satchel. A cardboard box can be painted to resemble the mailboxes the children see along the street. A collection of old holiday cards or inexpensive envelopes for the children to address provides mail.

A letter can be mailed to each child to prove that the postal system works. But if you give children stamps to put on their letters, many will lick off the glue, so be prepared with the glue bottle to help finish the job. A visit to the post office and a talk with the postman will add realism to the play.

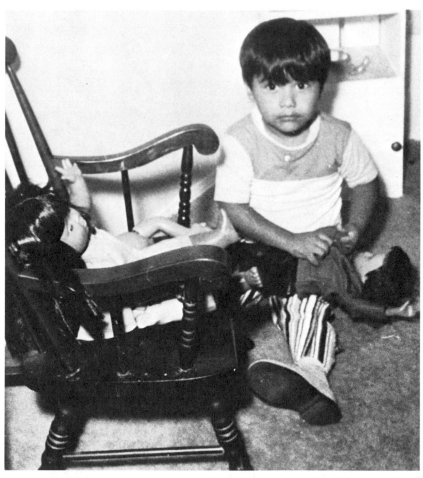

FIGURE 12–9.   *Dolls of many varieties contribute to imaginative play.* (*University of Houston Parent-Child Development Center.*)

FIGURE 12–10. *Culinary role-playing results from the use of play dough for cookies, pies, and cakes. (Texas Tech University Kindergarten.)*

MINIATURES. Small figures of people, animals, cars, and trucks also contribute to dramatic play. Children are the manipulators of the scene, moving the figures around and speaking for them. Small blocks and construction toys may supplement the play. A model house of a size suitable for the people figures prompts domestic dramas.

BLOCK AREA. Both boys and girls will develop a variety of dramatic play themes in the block area. Using the large hollow blocks, children design space in which they function as actors. After one group built a room using these blocks they all got inside and completely closed themselves in by placing a wheeled cart with a wire mesh side in front of the door. One boy said, "We are all in jail." His friends replied, "I knew we shouldn't have robbed."

During a period of reruns of "The Lone Ranger" on television, five-year-olds began building "horses" out of the large blocks. They stood three blocks upright, then stacked three lengthwise on top of the first three. They made a "neck" and a "head" with smaller blocks and finished their "Hi Ho Silver" with a tail of colored plastic scribble-sticks tucked into a crevice of the blocks in the appropriate place.

FIGURE 12–11. *"Just like painters," they say, using wide brushes and cans of water to re-create the home-decorating project they've observed. (Texas Woman's University Nursery School.)*

They mounted their horses and called, "I'll meet you at Ransom Canyon." (Ransom Canyon was a local picnic spot.)

The large hollow blocks and packing boxes are free of detail and therefore allow the imagination free reign. They are very strong and will hold numerous children at play.

Auxiliary toys add to block play. A mounted steering wheel suggests the building of a car, a bus, a train, or an airplane. Models of domestic animals suggest a farm and wild animals a zoo. Cars, trucks, and trains encourage road building. Housekeeping toys, especially telephones, are popular in the block area.

In the following example economic information is combined with building, the child with the broader experience leading the way. Later on during a discussion the teacher could let Bill explain more about his ideas.

Four boys finished building a tunnel through which they could drive their cars, trains, and trucks. Everyone was lined up to make the grand entrance into the tunnel. Bill said, "We forgot one thing." Jack said, "What's that?" Bill replied, "We forgot to put someone at the start to collect money from everyone." Jeff responded, "What?" Bill explained, "Yes, to help pay for building the tunnel." Jack hurried to the art table to get paper to make money.

FIREMEN.   A trip to the fire station, a fire in the neighborhood, or even a fire engine screaming past the school will often stimulate fireman play.

With a little help children can make their own fireman's hat. Using two sheets of a double-paged newspaper (30" × 23"), fold it in its original lengthwise fold. Bring the upper right and upper left corners together at the center line to make the usual three-cornered hat. (See Figure 12–14.) About 3 inches remain to turn up for the brim. Staple the brim to the hat body. Turn in one corner to the center peak and staple it in place. This leaves the other long corner to go down the young fireman's back. These hats may be painted.

The newspaper hats or commercial plastic firemen's hats team up with hoses, ladders, and red wagons when the children play out their helping roles, complete with sound effects.

GAS STATION.   Wheel toy "cars," of course, need gasoline. A large hollow block can become the gas pump if a piece of garden hose is attached to it. A plastic nozzle that comes with cleaning liquid can be attached to the hose. During warm weather the children can carry

FIGURE 12–12.   *Both boys and girls play the housekeeping roles.* (*Michigan State University Laboratory Preschool.*)

FIGURE 12–13. *Family roles are common among young children, for these are the roles they see more often portrayed. (Texas Tech University Kindergarten.)*

out the car-wash idea by washing the wheel toys. A few pairs of pliers and screwdrivers will foster mechanics play. Visits to a gas station, a garage, or a car wash will interest the young drivers.

TELEVISION. A window cut in a large cardboard box can serve as a TV screen. A few cereal boxes will encourage TV commercials. Puppets and musical instruments may invite performances. A few chairs or cushions can be arranged for the audience. A trip to a television studio will foster this play.

CAMPING. Camping has become a popular family experience. A small tent erected in the yard will provide the children many opportunities for camp-related play. A sheet can be draped over equipment when no tent is available. Suitcases and fishing poles might be added.

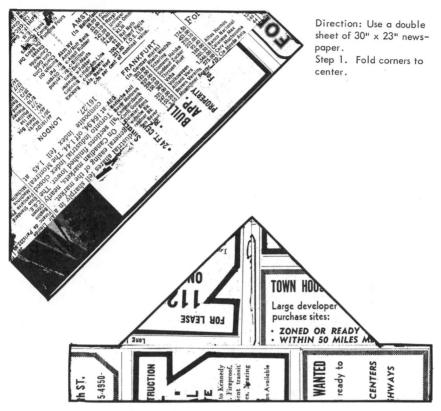

Direction: Use a double sheet of 30" x 23" newspaper.

Step 1. Fold corners to center.

Step 2. Fold up brim making a three-cornered hat. Staple brim and folds in place.

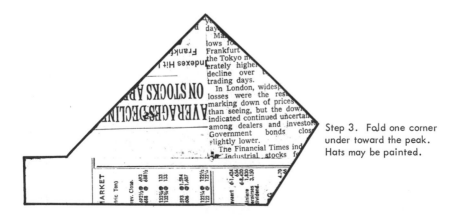

Step 3. Fold one corner under toward the peak. Hats may be painted.

FIGURE 12–14. *Making paper firemen's hats.*

FISHING.　The children can simulate fishing by tying string to a stick. Magnets can be added to the string. If paper clips are attached to paper or plastic fish or to the creepy crawlers made with liquid plastic kits, the children will enjoy their fishing. With this same setup, the children can "fish" numbers, colors, or the lotto cards out of a box. The paper clips should be securely attached to avoid a safety problem with very young children.

FARM.　Farm play is popular in rural neighborhoods. For city children, concepts learned on a trip to the farm can be reenforced through dramatic play. Models of domestic animals and farm machinery are available. Barns can be constructed out of boxes. Hay bales can be added to the yard to roll around, to walk on, and to hide behind.

For young cowboys an old saddle mounted on a wooden sawhorse makes exciting riding. Because guns do not contribute positively to the goals for the child's development, the school usually does not provide such accessories. In fact, teachers usually have rules against using any toy as a gun, and guns that are brought to school are kept in the teacher's office for safekeeping.

CONSTRUCTION.　Construction play is fostered when road graders, bulldozers, trucks, and shovels are provided. Digging can take place in the sandbox or other digging area. Construction and road building are particularly popular when children can see construction taking place in their neighborhood. Children like to get inside large cardboard boxes that have been opened at both ends. They roll around the yard and may be called "bulldozers" by young workers.

TRANSPORTATION.　Youngsters' imaginations can transform ordinary packing boxes into a train. One plank across another becomes an airplane. A boat or the skeleton of an old car can be placed in the yard for the little drivers. These should be kept well painted to avoid a junk-yard appearance in the yard. Traffic signs can be added to extend the play.

SPACE EXPLORATION.　Space exploration intrigues even the youngest. A large refrigerator carton can become the rocket that blasts off after the countdown. With the teacher's help opaque plastic milk jugs can be cut to resemble space helmets and large grocery bags can be made into temporary space suits by cutting out holes for the head and arms.

Conclusion

Dramatic play is the spontaneous, imaginative role-playing taking place in nursery schools and kindergartens during the self-selected activity period.

Dramatic play is a valuable activity because it contributes to the child's growth in all developmental areas; it affords adults an opportunity to gain insight into the child's inner thoughts and feelings; and it affords teachers the opportunity to help a child with some of the problems he might be having.

The child finds dramatic play satisfying because he can have fun with his friends in meaningful, energy-releasing activities. His creativity is encouraged, and he enjoys learning about himself by playing out numerous roles.

Planning is required to reap the benefits possible from dramatic play. An atmosphere of freedom is established by a teacher who is alert, warm, and responsive. Time and space are required and necessary limits must be set. An interesting array of materials and equipment will stimulate a variety of dramatic play themes.

ADDITIONAL READINGS

ANKER, DOROTHY, et al. "Teaching Children as They Play." *Young Children*, Vol. 29, No. 4, May 1974, 203–213.

AXLINE, VIRGINIA M. *Dibs: In Search of Self.* Boston: Houghton Mifflin Company, 1964.

BALDWIN, CLARA P., and HELEN T. M. BAYER. *Play Is Learning.* Bulletin No. 1155. Ithaca, N.Y.: New York State College of Home Economics, 1968.

BEYER, EVELYN. *Teaching Your Children.* New York: Western Publishing Company, Inc., 1968.

COHEN, DOROTHY H., and VIRGINIA STERN. *Observing and Recording the Behavior of Young Children.* New York: Teachers College Press, Columbia University, 1958.

D'EVELYN, KATHERINE. *Meeting Children's Emotional Needs.* Englewood Cliffs, N.J.: Prentice-Hall, Inc., 1957.

ENGSTROM, GEORGIANNA (ed.). *Play: The Child Strives Toward Self Realization.* Washington, D.C.: The National Association for the Education of Young Children, 1971.

LEEPER, SARAH H., et al. *Good Schools for Young Children.* New York: Macmillan Publishing Co., Inc., 1974.

SCARFE, N. V. "Play Is Education," in *Early Childhood: Crucial Years of Learning*, ed. Margaret Rasmussen. Washington, D.C.: Association for Childhood Education International, 1966.

SCHULMAN, ANN SHAAKER. *Absorbed in Living Children Learn.* Washington, D.C.: National Association for Education of Young Children, 1967.

SUNDERLINE, SYLVIA (ed.). *Bits and Pieces: Imaginative Uses for Children's Learning.* Washington, D.C.: Association for Childhood Education International, 1967.

Creative Music Activities

JENNIE JENKINS

Will you wear red,
O my dear, o my dear?
O will you wear red,
Jennie Jenkins?
I won't wear red,
It's the color of my head,
I'll buy me a fol-de-rol-dy
Til-dy-tol-dy seek-a-double roll
Jennie Jenkins roll. (1) [1]

THUS sang the kindergarten teacher introducing a new song. As the chorus ended, the children clapped and called, "Sing it again, teacher, sing it again." The teacher knew then that she had chosen well. She continued with other verses, using black, brown, blue, and green. The children picked up the rhythm and began clapping. They caught the repeat and chimed in on "roll Jennie Jenkins roll." The teacher sang a verse using "pink," they rhymed it with "stink" and laughed hilariously!

"Jennie Jenkins" became a favorite. The song would go on and on for as many verses as there were children present. They felt each must have a chance to choose a color before the teacher was permitted to terminate the song. Children liked to stump the teacher by choosing such variations as "skin color" and "striped" that were hard to rhyme.

Why was "Jennie Jenkins" a children's favorite? In the first place it has a catchy rhythm—a toe-tapping tempo that stays with you for a long time. It has a familiar element—colors—which each got a

---

[1] Each song is given a number the first time it is mentioned. By referring to the end of the chapter, the reader can locate a book containing the music for that song.

turn to name. "Jennie Jenkins" also has freshness—a surprise of nonsense words that especially tickle the funny bones of five-year-olds. But most of all, the children simply enjoyed the song—the most important reason for singing it in the kindergarten.

Of course, there were some secondary values offered by "Jennie Jenkins." By practicing the feel of words on the speech and hearing organs, children had a chance to say and hear words, rhymes, and sounds. They learned by rote, challenging their memory. Color concepts were introduced. Taking turns was required and practiced. Each of these values is important, but none is important enough for the teacher to sing the song if it did not bring joy to the children.

Music in the Nursery School and Kindergarten

Singing and dancing are creative arts. The emphasis in the school for young children is on the child's enjoyment of musical expression rather than on any particular outcome. Though the teacher may start with words or a tune that is well known, she encourages creativity by permitting the children to interpret the music in their own way, responding with new rhythms and words. This same emphasis on the process rather than on the product is suggested for all areas of learning.

The goal is to introduce music to children so that their lives will be richer. Music gives them another medium through which they can express their thoughts and feelings. Enjoyment is the first requirement. Any demand for perfection has no place at this young age. Care must be taken so music is not subverted, that is, used to upgrade deficiencies or learn concepts in a way that robs the child of his enjoyment of music.

The teacher considers children's developmental level when making plans for music activities in the nursery school and kindergarten. Music for these years is an action art—as opposed to a spectator art or a performing art. The young child should have an opportunity to become personally involved in his music, letting himself go, trying various expressions, using no patterns, and receiving neither coercion nor criticism.

Children are natural musicians. Their feeling for music begins early. Baby's first movements are rhythmic—two feet kicking, two hands waving. The infant experiments with different tones as he cries—long before he uses his vocal cords to speak.

Children can be musically creative, and teachers and parents should get as much fun out of their original tunes and dances as they do out of their original sayings. No one says a child lacks talent when his sentences aren't adultlike, so is it fair to say that when his

FIGURE 13–1. *A guitar is excellent both outdoors and in and can be played softly so as not to overshadow children's voices. (Michigan State University Spartan Cooperative Nursery School.)*

tunes aren't the same as adults'? Children do make many original compositions that are a result of experimenting with sounds, rhythm, and singing.

Music can occur at any time of day. It happens at work time, cleanup time, outdoor time, and at dressing and undressing time. Children compose songs, chants, and dances. In an atmosphere of freedom and trust the child will express his moods in spontaneous music.

Planning Music Experiences

Goals and Resources

Planning is required if children are to enjoy music, have a medium for expressing their thoughts and feelings, and lead richer lives because of their introduction to music. Just as is true of other areas of the curriculum, achieving the above goals requires meaningful music experiences that will not result from haphazard teaching.

Planning requires assessing children's developmental levels—physical, mental, emotional, social, and creative—then relating these findings to music. The teacher must discover what the children know and how they feel about music. She will survey the resources—in herself, her school, the families, and the community. She will be open to ideas that encourage creativity in the children. Planning requires sitting down regularly to evaluate what is being done and to decide on new experiences to provide in the future.

Search for Ideas

Teachers must search constantly for ideas for music experiences. Those teachers with a music background have many advantages, of course, because they can play or sing a new song or play an accompaniment for dancing without much effort. But a teacher without formal music training can also "have music wherever she goes." To these latter teachers much of the following will be most relevant, for there are ways for teachers to compensate for lack of formal music training. Some of the best musical experiences for children are provided in groups in which the teacher's formal training in music is almost nonexistent. The secret lies in opening up the teacher's creativity and overcoming a lack of self-confidence.

Most adults know many songs that can be used in the nursery school or kindergarten. The way to find out whether this statement is true of you is to make a list of songs you know. Start humming to yourself right now. Remember those old nursery songs your mother or grandmother sang? Or the camp songs for Scouts? How about hymns? Folk tunes? School songs? Popular songs? There you have six categories for your list. Add to it daily. Turn through songbooks, listen to records. You'll find a tape recorder useful for learning new song material from parents or other teachers. Before you know it, you'll have a much longer repertoire than you might believe was possible.

Get used to singing out on those songs on your list. Work at remembering tunes. Try picking up the tune in the middle of a song. Share a song that you know but have never seen in print with members of your class. Or maybe you remember a tune to which classmates can supply words.

You have songs on your list that you think aren't appropriate for young children. But wait. If you've remembered the tune for many years, it must have special holding power. Could you use the tune and adapt words to it?

An example of an adapted song is the old hymn, "Jacob's Ladder" (2). Using that tune and part of the words you can sing:

> John is climbing up the ladder,
> John is climbing up the ladder,
> John is climbing up the ladder,
> Reaching up so high.

Of course, once you start this, several children may want you to sing them up the jungle gym. You can also give John advice—musically, such as:

> John is holding very tight,
> John is holding very tight,
> John is holding very tight,
> As he climbs a way up high.

Have you heard the song, "Goodnight, Irene" (3) that the Weavers sang years ago? You could sing it at rest time merely by inserting each child's name where "Irene" appears in the song. Or you could use it outdoors when you want to help a child.

> Come here, Millicent,
> Come here, Millicent,
> Come here, Millicent,
> Come here, Millicent,
> I want to tie your bow.

Teachers should feel at complete liberty to adapt any song to their needs. Creativity is the word. It's fun for the teacher. The children will love it too. For example, here's the way "Old Roger Is Dead" (4) was adapted:

WE CAME TO OUR SCHOOL

> We came to our school and we painted with paints,
> Painted with paints, painted with paints,
> We came to our school and we painted with paints,
> It was so much fun!

As the teacher sings the last phrase, she points to a child who comes up with the next activity phrase, i.e., we climbed on the jungle gym, we played in the dollhouse, we built with the blocks, etc.

Children's records can be used to help teachers learn new material to teach. By listening to the record and writing down the words, you can learn quickly. You might like to take the record home and sing as you get supper ready or do your homework. Of course, you could simply use the record, having the children sing along with it. However a record often interferes with adapting songs to individual children or with adapting a song to the special needs of a group—such as giving them time to stand up, or to laugh about the words. You might not like the pitch or the tempo of the record. Having to operate the record player may also interfere with spontaneity. But the biggest drawback yet may be that the record is a crutch that teachers rely on when they could very well go it alone. Records can interfere with creativity—both yours and the children's.

Of course, records have an important place. After you've learned a song from one, put it out on the listening shelf; you'll get a response like this one from Johnny, who heard "Do-Re-Mi" (5) from

The Sound of Music. He was overjoyed. He ran to the teacher and pulled her to the music corner, "That's the song you taught us! We know that song. Teacher, I found our song. Listen!"

Children like to hear their favorites over and over. A familiar song is like an old friend that it's nice to run into. Therefore, teachers need not worry about using song material that some other teacher might use later on. Children will enjoy the song later if they like it now.

Also teachers should apply the principle of enjoyment to themselves as well as to the children. They should never try to teach a song or use a record they don't enjoy. In the first place, there is such an abundance of good material, why do it? Second, the children will sense a teacher's lukewarm attitude, so they won't enjoy it either.

Many adults lack faith in their musical ability. Perhaps this is because the modern world is flooded with music via recordings, concerts, and television. It's probably because they have never been encouraged to think of themselves as musical. But even when you think you can't carry a tune you can still help children find joy in music. Children are uncritical and readily respond to a teacher's effort. Their response will be rewarding and encouraging. With repeated successes the teacher's confidence grows.

A common concern for students is, "But I have to sing in front of my demonstration teacher." What they may not know is that the teacher went through the same conflicts herself when she was beginning and is likely to be the least critical of all. The demonstration teacher knows that children will respond with joy to music if adequate opportunities are being planned for them—even when the leader has stage fright.

Some nonmusician teachers feel embarrassed because they don't play an instrument. However, most songs that are suitable for young children can be sung without the piano. Rhythms too are possible without the piano.

When the piano is used for children's singing, it often overshadows the children's voices, so that neither they nor the teacher can hear them. Children may get lazy or become distracted by watching the pianist. Unskilled pianists are often slaves to the printed music and become flustered over deviations. Often they cannot watch the children and play; therefore a barrier exists between the teacher and the children. However, a mirror attached to the piano enables the teacher partially to overcome this barrier. Also, unless the pianist can transpose, the song may be played in a key that is suitable to neither the teacher nor the children.

On the other hand, an accompanist who can play by ear or one who follows the children rather than leads can be a great help at

FIGURE 13–2. *The autoharp, with its preset chords, can be played effectively by beginners. (Michigan State University Spartan Cooperative Nursery School.)*

music time. Unfortunately, this talent is rare. Therefore teachers can plan to sing unaccompanied or try the chording instruments discussed below.

The guitar makes a delightful accompaniment for children's songs. Its simple chords need not overshadow the children's voices. Even though it is large, the children will want to have a chance to strum and test the tones resulting from changing the finger position on the strings. Many books of children's songs have chords marked that are suitable for piano, guitar, or autoharp. The teacher needs only play a few chords, because it is best to keep the harmonies simple. In some songs only one chord is required for the entire song. See Figure 13–3 for the chords commonly used in children's songs.

A baritone ukulele is a melodious instrument that teachers find relatively easy to learn to play. Children call it a "guitar" because its size is about the same proportion to them that a guitar is to an adult. In areas where western and folk music are popular this instrument will contribute to role playing as well as to music. Because the baritone uke strings are tuned the same as the highest four strings of the guitar, any music showing guitar chords can be played. See Figure 13–3 for chord diagrams.

An autoharp is a popular instrument for schoolrooms. It is held on the lap or in the arms; therefore it easily goes to singing time either indoors or out. The autoharp has preset chords, so the player has only to push the lever to play the chord he seeks. A fifteen-chord autoharp offers the teacher the most variations. When the teacher wishes to use the autoharp during singing time, it is well to have it out during self-selected activity periods. Children will get their turn for experimenting. If they feel satisfied, the teacher can say at singing time, "It is my turn now to use the autoharp." The autoharp, like any instrument, should be kept tuned. If necessary the teacher may ask a music store or a musician to tune the autoharp for her. Guitar and piano chords can be played on the autoharp. See Figure 13–3.

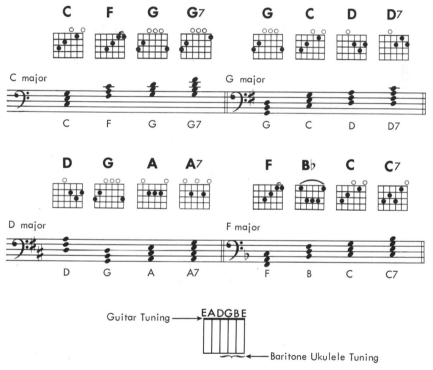

FIGURE 13–3. *Common chords for the scales most used. Four major keys with their common chords are shown. Four chords are sufficient for most children's songs. The diagrams represent the top end of the guitar— vertical lines represent the strings, horizontal lines the frets. The solid dots (·) indicate the placement of the fingers of the left hand on the strings. Circles (°) indicate open strings, and the absence of marks indicates that the strings are not strummed. The right hand strums the rhythm. For baritone ukulele chords, read the right-hand four strings on the guitar diagram. The four strings of the baritone ukulele are tuned like the right four strings of the guitar, as shown in the lower diagram.*

Singing

Singing can occur spontaneously in both children and teachers. Singing also occurs through the systematic introduction of songs at a regular group time.

New Songs

Though repetition is necessary for learning, variety is the spice of life in the nursery school and kindergarten, as elsewhere. Because every song the teacher presents will not appeal equally to all children, the teacher provides variety in hopes of touching every child. She will bring new material to them every week, and no one song gets overworked until someone cries, "Not that again!" Because it takes several hearings before children will be able to sing a song, they should have a number of songs in various stages of learning.

The teacher keeps up a constant search for new songs. She wants some songs to relate to concepts she is developing with the children. For example, as each season is studied, a number of songs are found that reinforce those concepts, let children practice the new vocabulary, and encourage them to express their feelings about the season. At the same time, songs related to their other interests are included, as well as nonsense songs and old favorite nursery songs.

One place to discover song material is to listen to the children. They often sing a song from home, television, or records that would be fun for the group. Children's records and songbooks will offer many suggestions. The nonmusician who needs help learning new songs can find songs in books and then locate them on records. Students and teachers often teach each other songs. Teachers make notes of songs they hear. Simply writing the words down helps them remember songs. The words help locate the song in a book or on a record.

New songs may be introduced as a story, or they may first be sung at the art or science table in the presence of only a few children. Because songs can accurately describe concepts, they may be used in this way. Having sung the song in a small group, children may want to hear it again during singing time.

If you are a student teacher, you will want to learn to manage the singing time without your demonstration teacher's help. Managing the children and handling discipline will be up to you. If the demonstration teacher feels required to step in to help you, it will be difficult for you to regain the children's attention. Therefore you must go to singing time with the confidence that your planning has been sufficient to carry you through.

Planning is very significant. It may look so easy and natural when the demonstration teacher leads singing—but she plans too. Your control of the group begins as you plan, long before you sit before the group. Make a list of songs that the children might request—those the demonstration teacher has taught them. Do you know all the words? Make a list of the songs you expect to teach. On index cards type the words to new songs and note the tune if the words are adapted from something familiar. Notes will help you keep from forgetting. They will offer suggestions when you feel "blank." Forgetting is easy when you have had many things to consider, watch for, and remember, as teachers do at singing time.

Sit with the children on the floor or on a small chair. The piano stool is too far away for an intimate singing time to develop.

Look at each child as you sing. Smile so he knows you enjoy singing with him. Shift quickly from a familiar song, to a finger play, to a new song. Pick up cues from the children so that you move with the group instead of pushing against what they want to do. More than anything, have fun singing with the group and you'll find the children listening, singing, and responding. Discipline will be no problem.

Teaching a New Song

Sing a new song straight through at normal speed—just as you hope the children will learn to sing it. Let them catch the song's flavor. Don't exaggerate any part. If the song is short, sing it several times so the children get familiar with the ideas and the repeats. Don't ask them if they want to hear it again, for someone will surely say "No." Just sing. By the time it has been sung this way several times, the children will be chiming in. Don't wear it out though, and don't dissect it—singing it a line at a time. This destroys the whole effect of the song. The next day repeat the same procedure. This time you can specifically invite the children to help you sing. By the third day many of your group will be beginning to sing. You will be able to tell whether they are going to like the song. If they fail to respond after three or four days, this indicates that the song apparently isn't for them at this time. Save that song until later. A song worth singing doesn't need to be pushed onto children.

Choice of Songs

Children are attracted by action songs. Such songs give them a way to participate with their hands and sometimes their whole bodies. The actions will attract some children who may do the actions long before they sing many of the words. Clapping can accompany some songs that don't suggest other actions.

ACTION SONGS

EENCY WEENCY SPIDER (6)

Eency weency spider went up the water spout,
Down came the rain and washed the spider out,
Out came the sun and dried up all the rain,
And the eency weency spider went up the spout again.

(Actions: Use fingers to imitate spider going up. Wiggle fingers to give rain effect, encircle face with hands for the sun, and make the spider climb again.)

WHERE IS THUMBKIN?

(TUNE "Frère Jacques," or "Are You Sleeping?") (7)

	ACTIONS
Where is Thumbkin?	(Hands behind back.)
Where is Thumbkin?	
Here I am.	(Bring hands out, thumbs
Here I am.	extended.)
Howdy-do dy day sir?	(One thumb bows to other.)
Very well I thank you,	(Other thumb bows in return.)
Run away, run away.	(Return behind child.)

Other verses: Pointer, middle, ring finger, and little finger. (The last two are difficult for small children to extend but they like to try.)

THE WHEELS OF THE BUS

(TUNE: "Mulberry Bush") (8)

	ACTIONS
The wheels on the bus (car)	(Children roll hands around
Go round and round,	each other.)
Round and round,	
Round and round.	
The wheels on the bus	
Go round and round	
All over town.	

Other verses: Money goes clink	(Short claps.)
Wipers go swish	(Fingers go back and forth.)

Horn goes beep	(Pretend to honk.)
Babies go waa	(Pretend to cry.)

IF YOU'RE HAPPY AND YOU KNOW IT (9)

If you're happy and you know it
Clap your hands (clap clap)
If you're happy and you know it
Clap your hands (clap clap)
If you're happy and you know it
Then your smile will surely show it
If you're happy and you know it
Clap your hands (clap clap)

Other verses: Pat your head (pat pat); Toot your horn (toot toot);
Touch your nose (tap tap).

Content of Songs

Elements of familiarity are important in songs. The teacher searches for songs about things the children know, i.e., children, animals, bugs, snow, wind, space flight, etc. However, she does not explain a song word for word but lets most of the song's meaning come to the children as they sing and as they experience their world. If a song has a catchy melody in a suitable range, children will sing it with gusto even if they do not understand it entirely. Their renditions of hymns and patriotic songs offer humorous examples of this fact. The range from middle C to D, a ninth above, is appropriate for kindergarten, with middle C to A being better for nursery school children who are learning to sing.

Concepts the children are learning can be the subjects of songs, but teachers should keep in mind that children must also enjoy these songs. By singing a new word, children receive a kinesthetic or sensory experience in the speech and hearing organs from which other understandings can grow. Of course, a counting song combined with pointing to objects—fingers or children—will help a child learn his numbers. The teacher sings "Mary Wore a Red Dress" (10); Mary stands up, and John sees her red dress and his color concepts are improved. If the children enjoy singing the ABC's to the tune of "Twinkle Twinkle Little Star" (11), there's no harm done and they get the kinesthetic experience necessary for beginning to know the alphabet. Teachers dealing with children of all languages can use songs to help build vocabulary and provide ear training.

SONGS ADAPTED TO TEACH CONCEPTS

COLOR SONG

(TUNE: "Pawpaw Patch") (12)

Children wearing red, please stand up.
Children wearing red, please stand up.
Children wearing red, please stand up.
So we can see your colors.

NOTE: The song continues designating the colors the children know, introducing new colors, and at the same time letting each child stand at least once.

DO YOU KNOW?

(TUNE: "Muffin Man") (13)

Do you know the firemen, the firemen, the firemen?
Do you know the firemen who drive a big red truck?
Oh, yes we know the firemen, the firemen, the firemen,
Oh, yes we know the firemen who drive the big red truck.

Other verses: Policemen—police car
                 Milkman—white truck
                 Garbage man—gray truck

COUNTING

TEN LITTLE INDIANS

(TUNE: Traditional)

One little, two little, three little Indians
Four little, five little, six little Indians
Seven little, eight little, nine little Indians
Ten little Indian boys.

Actions: Point to fingers as each number is sung. Verse can be changed to cowboys, spacemen, firemen.

OLD MACDONALD'S FARM

(TUNE: Traditional)

Old MacDonald had a farm,
E-I-E-I-O
And on this farm he had a duck,
E-I-E-I-O
With a quack quack here,
And a quack quack there,
Here a quack, there a quack,
Everywhere a quack quack,
Old MacDonald had a farm
E-I-E-I-O

Other verses: Let the children select the other farm animals to sing about.

UP IN A SPACE CAPSULE

(TUNE: "Up in a Balloon") (16)

Up in a capsule, boys,
Up in a capsule,
Flying 'round the little stars
And way out to the moon.
Up in a capsule, boys,
Up in a capsule,
Won't we have a jolly time,
Up in a capsule!

PARTS OF MY FACE

(TUNE: "Ten Little Indians") (14)

Eyes, ears, nose, and mouth;
Eyes, ears, nose, and mouth;
Eyes, ears, nose, and mouth;
Belong to my face.

NOTE: The children touch each part as they sing.

Spanish versions of songs are given below. You can use them when teaching Spanish or working with Spanish-speaking children.[2]

OJOS, OREJAS, NARIZ, BOCA

(TUNE: "Ten Little Indians") (14)

Ojos, orejas, nariz, boca;
Ojos, orejas, nariz, boca;
Ojos, orejas, nariz, boca;
Son parte de mi cara.

DIEZ INDITOS

(TUNE: "Ten Little Indians") (14)

Uno, dos, tres inditos,
Cuatro, cinco, seis inditos,
Siete, ocho, nueve inditos,
Diez inditos son.

NOTE: The Spanish "Ten Little Indians" can be adapted to say *ninitos*—children, *pollitos*—chicks, *perritos*—puppies, etc.

¿DÓNDE ESTÁ JUANITO?

(TUNE: "Pawpaw Patch") (12)

¿Dónde, dónde está Juanito?
¿Dónde, dónde está Juanito?
¿Dónde, dónde está Juanito?
¿El está alli?

¿Dónde, dónde está Maria?
¿Dónde, dónde está Maria?
¿Dónde, dónde está Maria?
¿Ella está alli?

Note: Insert each child's name, Use *el* for boys and *ella* for girls.

---

[2] Other songs in Spanish are suggested in *Fun Learning Elementary Spanish* by Margaret Anne Carlson and others (Albuquerque: University of New Mexico, 1961).

VAMOS A LA ESCUELA

(TUNE: "Pawpaw Patch") (12)

Vamos, vamos a la escuela,
Vamos, vamos a la escuela,
Vamos, vamos a la escuela,
A la escuela hoy.

Note: Ad verses with activities such as
a pintar—to paint
a jugar—to play
a leer—to read
a cortar—to cut
a dormir—to sleep

Songs that call for children's individual participation have strong appeal. Teachers will need as many of this type of song as they can find. They should feel perfectly comfortable adapting songs to the needs of their groups. Sometimes the child's name is used, sometimes he gets to select the animal or activity that goes into the verse. In the following song, the child's name is used and his colored shirt is designated:

WHERE OH WHERE?

(TUNE: "Pawpaw Patch") (12)

Where oh where is dear little *Jimmy*?
Where oh where is dear little Jimmy?
Where oh where is dear little Jimmy?
Way over there with the *blue shirt* on.

NOTE: When the teacher must sing everybody's name, she can put several together—Where oh where are Peter, James, and John?"

"What Shall We Do When We All Go Out?" (17) can be sung with each child suggesting a different outdoor activity. After a few days this song can become a cue song—like a closing hymn in church— that tells the children that outdoor time has come.

When "The Farmer in the Dell" (18) is altered to say "The Farmer Has a _____," each child can select a different animal or machine for the farmer. The children may eventually become quite imaginative, selecting such animals as deer, dolphins, or "dodo" birds. Their suggestions are usually indications of their imaginations, not their lack of concepts. Such jokes are signs of their increasing maturity.

Other songs calling for individual contributions are "When I Was a Young Maid" (19), which calls for occupations and tools, and "Monkey See Monkey Do" (20), in which the child suggests a motion for others to make.

Teachers should know lullabies as well as rousing songs. A quiet song is worth a thousand "Shhh's," just as are the quiet finger plays suggested in Chapter 11. A quiet song can help restore order out of chaos. The teacher can start a song like "My Pigeon's House" (35) in a I'm-telling-a-secret voice. She sings to two or three children sitting near her. She scans the group with her eyes, encouraging others to listen and join the singing. She nods and smiles to children who begin listening. The songs work their miracle as one child after another relaxes and begins to listen and sing.

SOOTHING SONGS

Kumbaya (21)

Mary's listening, Kumbaya,
Mary's listening, Kumbaya,
Mary's listening, Kumbaya,
Oh, Oh, Kumbaya.

Hush, Little Baby (22)

(TUNE: Traditional)

Hush, little baby, don't say a word,
Mommy's going to buy you a mocking bird.
If that mocking bird won't sing,
Mommy's going to buy you a diamond ring.

If that diamond ring turns to brass,
Mommy's going to buy you a looking glass.
If that looking glass gets broke,
Mommy's going to buy you a billy goat.

If that billy goat won't pull,
Mommy's going to buy you a cart and bull.
If that cart and bull turn over,
Mommy's going to buy you a dog named Rover.

If that dog named Rover won't bark,
Mommy's going to buy you a mule and cart.
If that mule and cart fall down,
You're still the sweetest little boy in town.

Guidance can be sung instead of spoken and is often more effective as a result. The teacher will have her own favorite tunes that pop into her head when needed. She can sing "Barry, walk around the puddle," or "Time to go indoors." Cleanup time can be lots more fun if everyone bursts into song as materials are put away. They can sing "Pickin' up blocks, put them on the shelf," instead of "Pickin' up pawpaws" (12). "Here We Go Round the Mulberry Bush" (8) readily becomes the following at cleanup time:

CLEANUP TIME

(TUNE: "Here We Go Round the Mulberry Bush") (8)

> This is the way we stack the blocks,
> Stack the blocks, stack the blocks,
> This is the way we stack the blocks,
> When it's time for cleanup time.

Other verses: Wash the easel, wash the paint brushes, or wipe the tables.

The late four-year-olds and five-year-olds will enjoy songs with cumulative verses. "The Twelve Days of Christmas" (23) is a familiar example. For such long songs the teacher can prepare drawings to illustrate each verse so the children can "read" as they sing. Drawings help them learn more quickly and help the teacher too. The following are songs of this type: "Had a Little Rooster" (24), "I Bought Me a Cat" (25), and "I Know an Old Lady" (26).

The use of sad songs is often discussed by teachers. Some believe that sadness should never be a part of a song for young children. Others believe that a sad song may help the child learn about feelings. They feel that a child may use a sad song to express his own inner sadness. The song may help bring his concerns out where he can deal with them. "Old Roger Is Dead" (4) and "Go Tell Aunt Rhodie" (27) are considered sad by some teachers.

Of course, a child's reaction to a song will depend on the way it is sung. Songs that seem sad to adults may not seem sad to children. Whether a teacher uses sad songs should be left up to her, because one of the requirements in choosing songs is that the teacher enjoy the music she presents to children. If a sad song has special meaning for a teacher, she should be free to try it with the children. They may sense her feeling and appreciate the song too.

Allowing children to select songs during singing time is important because it makes the period more their own. No harm can come from singing "Jingle Bells" (28) in June, so a seasonal choice should be honored as would any other. A teacher must, however, decide from moment to moment how much to lead and how much to follow the children. If the entire music period is regularly left in the children's hands, stagnation will set in very soon. The teacher's skill and tact are required to balance the offering of a new song with the familiar songs the children enjoy. Good balance results from planning and from being sensitive to children's moods. The teacher can train herself to sense the children's moods and follow the leads they give her. The length of the music period will vary from day to day depending on the children's response.

The following are examples of leads that a teacher might follow: If a child kicks his heels, perhaps the teacher can think of a song in which kicking might be an appropriate sound effect. If the children lie down as though sleeping, can she think of a sleeping song? If a child should pretend to play the guitar, can she think of a song that could work this in? If the children have been sitting for quite a while, can she think of a song that would get them up for a stretch, then get them to sit back down so that a story could follow? By following the children's leads, the teacher can make the singing experience fun, relaxing, and creative, yet organized enough so that it is pleasant for everyone.

When teachers establish an atmosphere of freedom and use music creatively throughout their teaching, it won't be long before the children will be bursting out in song wherever they play. Both their tunes and their words will be original. If the teacher can capture some of these compositions in her notes and sing them back to the child, they will show that she appreciates his accomplishments.

A little boy was heard responding to the question, "Do you need a push?" He sang:

> I can push myself so high
> I can just fly
> Into the sky.

Another sang:

> Hooray for today!
> I can play all day!

His exuberance for life showed when he sang:

> I love these snowy days!
> It's fun today!

This young child's spontaneity and zest for living were pleasurable to behold.

Creative Movement

Children are naturally rhythmical in their movements. Swinging, jumping, swaying, whirling, tapping, and running are rhythmic movements familiar to any teacher of young children. Movement is important to children. From the smallest wiggling finger to the largest leaps, the child loves to be in motion. The teacher's role is to establish the atmosphere of freedom that lets the children express their feelings, and there will be rhythm.

Many interesting rhythms are noted during activities that may not be thought of as rhythmical, e.g., cutting, painting, or rocking in the rocking chair or the rocking boat. Teachers may help children recognize these rhythms. They might develop a chant to go with one of them, like:

> Pound, pound, pound, pound, pound on the clay,
> Pound, pound, pound, pound, pound it down.

Spontaneous dancing often results when classical music is played on the record player. The children will enjoy wearing long skirts for whirling and twirling to the music. Long streamers of colored material or paper, or colored scarves will prompt a gentle flowing rhythmic expression.

Movement can also be accompanied by a piano, a tom-tom, a tambourine, or clapping.

Children need space so their movement doesn't interfere with that of others. However, once children are spread out in the room or the yard, they have difficulty hearing the teacher's suggestions and comments. Teachers know that shouted guidance is ineffective. The teacher can solve the problem by developing a signal so children will know when she wants them to come together. The signal could be one loud "bang" on the tom-tom or three taps. The teacher can call them to a "secret huddle" to talk over the plans for the next activity. The huddle will help her keep the children's attention.

Children can be encouraged to use their imaginations to suggest movements to make. They can name birds or animals to imitate. They can imitate machines—large like a bulldozer and small like mother's mixer. Sound effects go with rhythms, of course. This is rarely a quiet time of day.

Children can be encouraged to use their space by jumping their highest or crawling their lowest. They can experiment with different ways to move through space—walk, run, hop, jog, leap, twirl, skate, slide, creep, glide, gallop, skip, and BLAST OFF! The teacher can pick up the rhythm of a particular child and tap it out on the tom-tom. "John, your rhythm pattern is—tap, tap—tap tap tap." She may say, "That was a HIGH leap, Jennifer." "What a smooth glide you have, Dennis!" A child who wouldn't participate in dancing may happily jump on a jumping board or a mattress. The teacher can recognize his movement by tapping out his rhythm or singing a song to its beat.

A teacher may crumple a plastic film bag in the children's presence. They watch it unfold, then they pretend to be a crumpled-up plastic bag. Many get lovely, unusual movement. With older children, who won't mind if balloons break, setting several balloons loose in the room may stimulate skipping, leaping, and running to keep the balloons floating through the air.

If the children seem hyperactive during planned rhythm experiences, they may need to be more active or they may already be overtired. Children can be rested by doing small movements with eye, tongue, finger, head, and nose as they relax on the floor.

There should be no desire to get every child doing the same thing. Care should be taken to recognize each child's unique contribution. Children will be freer without their shoes.

Teachers can use children's creative imitations to help at transition time. "Hop like bunnies to get your coats" or "Now on quiet feet like a mouse, let's go to the film room."

Listening

The opportunity to listen is important for growth in music appreciation. Listening is also important for language development. Many of the opportunities offered through music make important contribu-

FIGURE 13–4. *Free dance to the beat of the tom-tom is enjoyable movement experience indoors or out.* (*Michigan State University Laboratory Preschool.*)

tions to language. Acuity is tested. Memory is developed through listening activities.

Records

An area of the room can be furnished with records and a record player that the children are allowed to operate. A simple player without an automatic changer is best. If there is room near the record player, the children will respond to their records physically—through dancing, marching, and the playing of instruments. They should also be able to listen uninterruptedly to a musical selection or a story record. Attention spans are often quite long when children are listening to music voluntarily during the self-selected activity period.

Records of good quality should be provided. The 78 and 45 rpm records that have only one selection are easier for the children to manage alone. Long-playing records make the selection of a particu-

FIGURE 13–5. *A Vietnamese student leads the children in a Vietnamese children's dance. The children make their own Vietnamese hats, which are essential in the dance. (Texas Tech University Kindergarten.)*

lar piece difficult for a small child. Also, teachers are understandably reluctant to give children the more expensive long-playing records. Children can be taught rules for caring for the records and the record player. A rack should be available for holding records so that the children can learn to place records in the rack rather than on chairs and tables. A small selection should be available and changed frequently. Other records may be available on request.

Sound

Many experiments with sound are related to music. Apple juice bottles can be tuned. Colored water in different amounts is added to eight bottles until the scale can be played, with a wooden mallet used for tapping. The advantage of tuning bottles instead of glasses is that lids can be placed on the bottles to prevent evaporation. Experiments also result from putting on and taking off the lids.

Vibrations cause sound. Children can feel instruments vibrate simply by placing a hand on the instrument. A shoe box can be strung with rubberbands of different widths and tautness, creating various effects. Children can relate the experiment to the guitar, the autoharp, and the piano. During such a study children will enjoy a trip to hear a harpist. Other stringed instruments may be brought into the school for listening and experimenting. Piano tuning is interesting for children to watch. Also, many listening experiences will be carried on by children as they play the piano. Rules should be established so that the piano is treated with the respect due a musical instrument.

Vibrations can be felt in one's own throat, and some children discover this themselves.

Special Events

A trip to a school music room can help children learn about the sounds made by various instruments. They will like a close-up view. They like to go to band practices and watch the players up close.

FIGURE 13–6. Body movement, such as rolling, creeping, or wiggling, is a creative activity for young children. (*Michigan State University Laboratory Preschool.*)

Frequently delightful music experiences can be provided by the parents and siblings of the children in a class. For example, a father who was an evangelist singer came to sing. He made up songs, using each child's name. Another father brought his banjo. After a number or two he had each child use a hollow block for a drum—what rhythm resulted!

One child's brother played the trombone, another a steel guitar. A sister twirled. Another sister came with her friend. Wearing a striking Spanish dress, the sister danced the exotic Spanish flamenco. The friend made a striking contrast with a slow, graceful dance in a pastel ballet dress and slippers.

A mother who played the lead in the community production of *The Sound of Music* taught children to sing "Do-Re-Mi" (5).

By singing songs from their countries, foreign students can help children learn about peoples of other lands. At the same time foreign students learn about American children.

Many opportunities such as those suggested will develop children's listening skills. Children also practice appropriate behavior as a mem-

FIGURE 13–7. *Body control is practiced through an obstacle course such as this. The child is using a gym scooter. (Michigan State University Motor Skill Project.)*

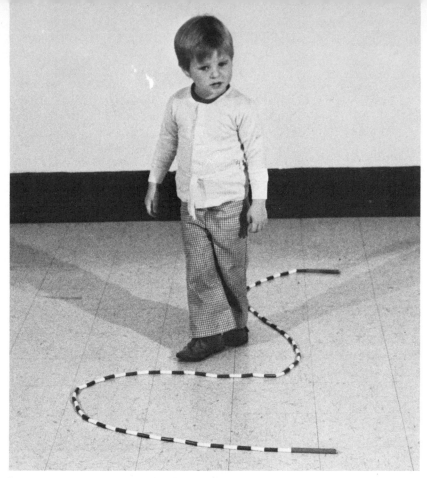

FIGURE 13–8. *Walking the crooked rope is a simple body-control exercise. (Michigan State University Motor Skill Project.)*

ber of an audience. However, each guest was advised ahead of time about ways to include the children in the presentation. The children thus became part of each experience. The involvement of family members is especially important to a child.

Rhythm Instruments

Rhythm instruments can be used creatively. They are placed in the music center so that the children will use them alone, accompany themselves in singing, or tap out a rhythm as a record plays. The children may organize their own band. When they do, the teacher will notice that they keep excellent time to the marching rhythm. A few records of good marches such as those of college marching bands will be sufficient stimulation.

Gone are the days of sitting everyone in a row to hold an instrument until time comes to tap just so. Rigid adult structure curtails creativity. When children organize a marching band, the teacher's role need only be to place a table or a collection of chairs in the center of the room to guide the direction of the march. Children think of a march tempo as "parade" music, so marching is important. If there is an insufficient number of the favorite instruments, the teacher may get agreement on a signal that tells the children when to exchange instruments. If the teacher plays the piano for the marchers, she is careful to emphasize the rhythm. Then the children can keep time.

Children have a number of opportunities to see marching bands on television. Attending a parade or visiting a marching band practice will create interest. If a child's sibling plays a band instrument, he can be invited to play. A twirler will interest children too.

Several good-quality tom-toms, bongo drums, and maracas invite individual and small-group experimentation with primitive rhythms.

Musical Guessing Games

The teacher asks, "What tune is this?" as she hums or plays a tune on the piano. The children guess. The children too can have turns humming tunes for others to guess.

Using the tom-tom, the teacher can tap out the children's names. She can start by choosing two children to stand up, then say, "Whose name am I tapping?" The teacher can plan ahead, selecting children whose names have contrasting beats.

By recording each child as he sings or talks, then bringing the tape for the children to hear, the teacher gives the children another guessing game requiring listening.

Singing Games

Some of the group games used with older children must be adapted if they are to be used with kindergarten children. Many are totally unsuited to nursery-age children. Too many rules, too many specific directions, and competition make them too complicated. Even the traditional manner of playing "The Farmer in the Dell" (18) is too complicated. Young children don't understand not being chosen. Some teachers improvise verses until each child is in the circle. Another alternative is to divide the group into several circles with an adult in each, then the game can be played in more or less traditional manner. If all the groups are in the same room, they can still sing together.

The game of musical chairs is popular with elementary school children but is not recommended for younger children because a child cannot understand being left out. In this game sufficient chairs are available minus one. The group marches around until the music

FIGURE 13–9. *Hula hoops have various uses for encouraging rhythmical movement. Here the child jumps from one hoop to the other. (Michigan State University Motor Skill Project.)*

stops, then everyone runs for a chair. However, if at this point the child who is left out gets to choose a rhythm instrument and becomes part of the band, his concern about not having a chair is somewhat removed.

Games requiring children to hold hands and move in a circle are also too structured. Often, however, it is just as well to let children stand where they will and move in their own circle. Late four- and five-year-olds will enjoy "Did You Ever See a Lassie?" (29), "Monkey See Monkey Do" (20), "Mulberry Bush" (8), "Round and Round the Village" (30), and "Punchinello" (31). Younger children may like "Ring Around the Rosy" (32), "Sally Go Round the Moon" (33), and "London Bridge" (34) if the teacher lets them move where they want to.

Singing games may be used to substitute in part for outdoor exercise when a sudden storm prevents going out. Children much prefer going outdoors; therefore singing games should be used for this purpose only occasionally. Tumbling and rhythms offer energy release in a similar manner.

Role of Parents in a Child's Musical Education

Numerous times in the previous sections suggestions have been made for involving families directly in the music program of the nursery school and kindergarten. Not only does a richer program result when families are involved, but each child whose parent participates gets a special boost. Parents make a significant contribution and feel more comfortable at school when they are invited to demonstrate some special skill to the children. By coming they gain a better understanding of their child and the school.

Teachers can keep parents informed about what their children are doing in music at school. As experiences are planned with the children's developmental level in mind, the teacher should be able to provide helpful suggestions for parents. Parents may seek guidance as to the appropriateness of piano, dancing, or voice lessons. The teacher should become familiar with the music programs offered in the community in order to guide parents.

Teachers may also encourage parents' enjoyment of music with their own children. Words to children's songs can be sent home. Then when the child is singing, the parents can refer to the song sheet and grasp more clearly just what the child is singing about. Perhaps they can even sing along. In some parents' meeting they may wish to sing some of the songs. Teachers can explain their purposes and demonstrate techniques for working with children.

Parents may seek guidance as to the type of record player and records to buy. Teachers can be more helpful if they visit record shops and have an idea of what is available locally. Sometimes a teacher can guide the choice that is offered by conferring with the owner of the record shop. Public libraries have recordings to lend, just as they have books. Parents may need this information, as many will not be aware that records are available for children's listening.

It is important for children to have their own songbooks. This is true even though no one in the family plays an instrument. Because children's songbooks are often beautifully illustrated, the child can "read" his favorite songs because he recognizes the pictures. Children will turn through the book and sing to themselves. Teachers can provide parents with names of appropriate songbooks. Some are available in libraries. Many families report having songfests with their children. Others say that bedtime singing sometimes takes the place of bedtime stories.

Teachers can watch for musical events in the community that families can attend to add to their enjoyment of music. Examples are a children's theater musical or a symphony concert planned especially for children. The teacher can see that parents have this information, including information on admission charges.

In some schools one traditional way of communicating with the home is to have the children present a program for the parents. However, caution is advised! If a teacher feels the tradition is harmful, she should ask to alter the format. The preparation for and the performance of the program should not be harmful in any way to even one child. No child should feel that he is being exhibited, left out, or embarrassed.

The children and the teacher can plan a simple program. They can decide together what things they would like to share with the parents. The program should be short, only 10 to 15 minutes. It should never be rehearsed until no fun remains in the numbers. (Sadly enough, overrehearsed programs are common at Christmas time.) No child should be allowed to star. This keeps competition from developing among children and parents. Memorized lines should be avoided.

An acceptable program would be "a day in school," for example, the singing and rhythm time as customarily carried on in the classroom. By seeing such a program, parents learn about the school's goals and techniques. There is room for the children's natural spontaneity to occur. The children will be at ease because the format is familiar.

Conclusion

Music in the nursery school and kindergarten takes specific planning, just as is required by other parts of the curriculum. Planning is required if the children are to enjoy music, have another medium for expressing their thoughts and feelings, and lead richer lives because of their introduction to music.

The children's developmental levels and their previous experience are taken into consideration in the planning of music activities.

Teachers without formal music training can provide a good music program if they make a special effort to overcome feelings of inadequacy. They will seek variety in the materials they present. They will watch the children for cues and leads in order to appreciate their creativity and adapt the program to their needs. Teachers will freely adapt material to suit the children. They will plan music for quiet and active moods. They will plan music to support the concepts that the children are developing, but the enjoyment of music will have priority. Teachers will involve the parents in the children's music experiences whenever possible.

SOURCES OF SONGS MENTIONED

NOTE: Each song was given a number in the text. It is listed below according to that number.

1. Jennie Jenkins, in *Exploring Music: Kindergarten*. E. Boardman and B. Landis, pp. 66–67.

2. Jacob's Ladder, in *Sing and Strum,* Alice M. Snyder, p. 20.
3. Goodnight, Irene, in *The Weaver's Song Book,* ed. Ronnie Gilbert, p. 34.
4. Old Roger Is Dead, in *Songs to Grow On,* Beatrice Landeck, p. 112.
5. Do-Re-Mi, in *The Sound of Music Vocal Selections,* Richard Rodgers and Oscar Hammerstein, pp. 16–21.
6. Eency Weency Spider, in *American Folk Songs for Children,* Ruth Crawford Seeger, p. 126.
7. Frère Jacques, in *The New Golden Song Book,* Norman Lloyd, p. 83.
8. Mulberry Bush, in *The New Golden Song Book,* Norman Lloyd, p. 44.
9. If You're Happy and You Know It, in *This Is Music, Book I,* William Sur, Adeline McCall, William R. Fischer, Mary R. Tolbert, p. 16.
10. Mary Wore a Red Dress, in *Songs to Grow On,* Beatrice Landeck, p. 12.
11. Twinkle Twinkle Little Star, in *The New Golden Song Book,* Norman Lloyd, p. 16.
12. Paw Paw Patch, in *Songs to Grow on,* Beatrice Landeck, p. 116.
13. Muffin Man, in *The New Golden Song Book,* Norman Lloyd, p. 35.
14. Ten Little Indians, in *American Singer: No. 1,* John W. Beattie, p. 94.
15. Old MacDonald's Farm, in *The New Golden Song Book,* Norman Lloyd, p. 20.
16. Up in a Balloon, in *More Songs to Grow On,* Beatrice Landeck, p. 12.
17. What Shall We Do When We All Go Out? in *American Folk Songs for Children,* Ruth Crawford Seeger, p. 59.
18. The Farmer in the Dell, in *The New Golden Song Book,* Norman Lloyd, p. 36.
19. When I Was a Young Maid, in *American Folk Songs for Children,* Ruth Crawford Seeger, p. 168.
20. Monkey See Monkey Do, in *Train to the Zoo,* Children's Record Guild Recording No. 1001.
21. Kumbaya, in *The Weaver's Song Book,* ed. Ronnie Gilbert, p. 156.
22. Hush, Little Baby, in *The Weaver's Song Book,* ed. Ronnie Gilbert, p. 24.
23. Twelve Days of Christmas, in *This Is Music, Book 4,* William R. Sur, et al., pp. 174–175.
24. Had a Little Rooster, in *More Songs to Grow On,* Beatrice Landeck, p. 34.
25. I Bought Me a Cat, in *Songs to Grow On, Beatrice* Landeck, p. 76.
26. I Know an Old Lady, in *I Know an Old Lady,* Rose Bonne and Allan Mills, p. 1.
27. Go Tell Aunt Rhodie, in *The Weaver's Song Book,* ed. Ronnie Gilbert, p. 99.

28. Jingle Bells, in *The New Golden Song Book*, Norman Lloyd, p. 56.
29. Did You Ever See a Lassie? in *The New Golden Song Book*, Norman Lloyd, p. 38.
30. Round and Round the Village, in *The New Golden Song Book*, Norman Lloyd, p. 37.
31. Punchinello, in *More Songs to Grow On*, Beatrice Landeck, p. 96.
32. Ring Around the Rosy, in *The New Golden Song Book*, Norman Lloyd, p. 39.
33. Sally Go Round the Moon, in *American Singer: No. 1*, John W. Beattie, p. 184.
34. London Bridge, in *Fifty Songs for Children*, Mary Nancy Graham, p. 2.
35. My Pigeon's House, in *Sleepy Family.* People's Record (611) 78 rpm, The Franson Corp., New York.

BOOKS CONTAINING SUGGESTIONS FOR CREATIVE MUSIC ACTIVITIES

* Indicates books that have coordinated records available

ANDREWS, GLADYS. *Creative Rhythmic Movement for Children.* Englewood Cliffs, N.J.: Prentice-Hall, Inc., 1954.

BEATTIE, JOHN W. (ed.). *The American Singer: No. 1.* New York: American Book Company, 1954.

*BOARDMAN, E., and B. LANDIS. *Exploring Music: Kindergarten.* New York: Holt, Rinehart and Winston, Inc., 1969.

CHERRY, CLARE. *Creative Movement for the Developing Child.* Palo Alto, Calif.: Fearon Publishers, Inc., 1968.

GERHARDT, LYDIA A. *Moving and Knowing: The Young Child Orients Himself in Space.* Englewood Cliffs, N.J.: Prentice-Hall, Inc. 1973.

GILBERT, RONNIE (ed.). *The Weaver's Song Book.* New York: Harper & Brothers, 1960.

GRAHAM, MARY NANCY. *Fifty Songs for Children.* Racine, Wis.: Whitman Publishing Company, 1964.

GUTTOLPH, EDNA G. *Music Without the Piano.* New York: Early Childhood Education Council of New York, 1966.

JAYE, MARY TINNIN. *Making Music Your Own.* Parkridge, Ill.: Silver Burdette Co., 1971.

JENKINS, ELLA. *This Is Rhythm.* Elkhart, Ind.: Lyons Band, Division of Magnavox, 1974.

*LANDECK, BEATRICE. *Songs to Grow On.* New York: William Sloane Associates, 1950.

*LANDECK, BEATRICE. *More Songs to Grow On.* New York: William Sloane Associates, 1954.

*LANDECK, BEATRICE, HAROLD C. YOUNGBERG, and ELIZABETH CROOK. *Making Music Your Own: No. 1.* Morristown, N.J.: Silver Burdett Company, 1967.

LLOYD, NORMAN. *The New Golden Song Book*. New York: Golden Press, 1966.

*SEEGER, RUTH CRAWFORD. *American Folk Songs for Children*. New York: Doubleday, Inc., 1948.

*SMITH, ROBERT. *Discovering Music Together: Early Childhood*. Chicago: Follett Educational Corporation, 1969.

SNYDER, ALICE M. *Sing and Strum*. New York: Mills Music, Inc., 1957.

*SUR, WILLIAM, et al. *This is Music: No. 1*. Boston: Allyn & Bacon, Inc., 1963.

WOLFE, IRVING, BEATRICE P. KRONE, AND MARGARET FULLERTON. *Music Round the Clock*. Chicago: Follett Publishing Company, 1963.

RECORD SUGGESTIONS

The following are examples of records suitable for young children. Children should be allowed a range of responses. They may listen quietly or respond actively to the suggestions on the record. Individuality can be encouraged and children challenged to think of new movements. The following titles can be located in a number of catalogs. They are available in single records and also appear in varying combinations on long-playing records. Single presentations (45 or 78 rpm) are considered more satisfactory when children use records at the record player. Long-playing records (33⅓ rpm) require more adult help.

Music participation records:

Circus Comes to Town
Jingle Bells and Other Songs for Winter Fun
Little Gray Ponies
My Playful Scarf
My Playmate the Wind
Rainy Day
Sunday in the Park
Train to the Zoo
What the Lighthouse Sees

Music interpretation records:

Hungarian Dance No. 1 by Brahms
March of Toreadors by Bizet
Sousa Marches
Waltz of the Flowers and Dance of the Sugar Plum Fairy by Tchaikovsky

Field Trips and Special Visitors[1]

THE TURKEY FARM

At the turkey farm there were 5,000 turkeys. They were white turkeys and black turkeys. The girl turkeys were white and the boy turkeys were black. All the sick turkeys were in the back pens. Mary found a feather that was both black and white.

They fed the turkeys grain—it was maize.

The turkeys make loud noises—it was gobble gobble.

One was following me. Some got out. One of them flied! The teachers caught a turkey and let us pet him. It didn't scare me.

It smelled awful. It smelled like bacon. It smelled like chicken do-do-do—ugh!

It was fun to go to the turkey farm.

THE KINDERGARTEN children dictated this story to the teacher following a Thanksgiving-time trip to a turkey farm. Such field trips take the child to an observation that cannot readily be brought into the classroom.

Field trips and special visitors are educational methods used to provide children firsthand information, observation, and study. As children discuss and dictate stories about their new experience, opportunities are presented for clarifying misconceptions and expanding knowledge.

"Because a young child is a laboratory rather than a lecture stu-

[1] Acknowledgments is due *Childhood Education* for permission to reprint portions of my article "Trips for Preschoolers," *Childhood Education* (May 1967), 524–527.

dent, teaching him is largely a matter of providing him with materials and activities in such a way that he can learn from his own experience and generalize in his own words," writes Catherine Landreth, a noted specialist in child development and in early childhood education.[2] She means that children learn most by having opportunities to see for themselves, to touch, to taste, to smell, to hear, and then to talk about their experiences. Their concepts are broadened through firsthand experience. Field trips and the special visitors invited to the nursery school or kindergarten offer the child experience that helps him understand more fully the life going on around him, the books that are read to him, and books he will later learn to read. Pictures, films, recordings, poems, and songs will also have more meaning following firsthand experiences.

Planning Field Trips

Considerations

Five considerations are weighed by the teacher in her decision to use the field trip method for a group of young children. These considerations are: (1) the educational goals for the group; (2) the suitability of the available field trips; (3) the time required; (4) the costs involved; and (5) the dangers involved.

Educational Goals

Before the field trip educational goals should be well established. A field trip can be used to stimulate interest in a subject as well as to extend information. It can also be fun and add variety to the school program. Although the latter purposes are valued, most teachers would agree that the first two are the more important purposes of field trips.

The teacher will have some tentative goals based upon her knowledge of and experience with children of the age she teaches. However, the teacher's decision on specific field trips must be made after a period of assessing the needs of a particular group of children. She will want to know: What experiences have they had previously at home and school? What questions are they asking? What interests them? What do they talk about? What books do they select? From such study she can decide what information needs extending and what interests should be stimulated.

2 Catherine Landreth, *Preschool Learning and Teaching* (New York: Harper & Row, 1972), p. 161.

FIGURE 14–1. *Field trips are useful for enlarging children's horizons—if trips are planned with care. (Texas Tech University Kindergarten.)*

Suitability of Available Field Trips

Teachers will continuously survey their community for ideas for worthwhile field trips and special events. The interest and cooperation of the parents of the children should be enlisted in order to provide a rich curriculum. For example, one group visits the television studio because a child's father works there and helps arrange the visit. Another group goes to the police station because a child's father works there. Parents can assist on buses, drive cars, and act as guides.

There will be differences among groups, so there is a fallacy in saying, "Kindergarteners always go to the fire station." In some schools every child goes on every trip no matter what his age or previous experience. Can this practice be justified?

Attending nursery school may be a sufficiently new, strange, and stimulating adventure for a three-year-old. Teachers must determine whether it is best to take him on field trips before he is at ease in the school setting. A trip may undermine his security just when he is beginning to feel comfortable away from home. Tammy is an example. Usually a confident, happy three-year-old, she wondered, "Will my Daddy find me here?" during a walk less than a block from the nursery school. She verbalized a concern that many of the others may have felt.

Field trips for first-year nursery school children should be simple and close to school. Teachers may explore the possibility of taking only a few of the children, leaving behind those who aren't ready for outside experiences. Such a plan, of course, requires activities, helpers, and perhaps some explanations for those who remain.

Field trips usually serve their purposes best for those late four-year-olds and kindergarten children who are confident with the teacher and in the school situation and are fully ready for broadening adventures. This age is ready for more things to look at, to talk about, to think about, and to use creatively in their schoolwork.

Communities offer many more resources for field trips than teachers sometimes recognize. The following are listed because they are known to have been successful for some groups. The list is not exhaustive, and teachers should use it to help them find resources in their communities. There is no set list of experiences every child should have. Therefore the teacher should develop the curriculum that makes sense for her age group.

Field Trip Suggestions

ANIMALS

Farm—sheep, cattle, horses, pigs, turkeys, chickens
County fair—animal exhibits
Dairy at milking time
Rodeo horses
Ducks in pond
Zoo
Hatchery
Wildlife exhibit
Bird sanctuary
Aquarium
Pets—in pet shop or in child's home
Museum—animal and bird exhibits

PEOPLE AND PLACES

Artist's studio
Bakery
Barbershop
Beauty shop
Bowling alley
Car wash
Children's houses
County-fair-style show
Dairy bottling
Department store windows

PEOPLE AND PLACES (*Continued*)

Musicians—band, orchestra, individual instrumentalists, singers
Health clinic
Lunchroom kitchen
Museum—old fashioned house, doll collection, Indian houses, historical exhibits
Science classroom
School—kindergarten for nursery children, first grade for kindergarten children
Office
Post office
Potter's studio
Puppet show
Print shop
Restaurant
Dormitory room
Fire station
Foreign student or family
Garage mechanic
Home economics classroom
Ice skating rink
Library
Police station
Swimming pool
Teacher's house
Television studio
Grocery
Mother and baby
Ice cream parlor

GROWING THINGS

Botanical garden
Christmas tree farm
Flower garden
Nature walks—four seasons
Orchard
Park
Woods
Farm

TRANSPORTATION AND MACHINES

Airport
Train ride
Train station
Exhibited train
Model train
Construction site
Street repair
Farm machinery show
Elevator
Escalator
Streetcar ride
Car dealer's showroom
Bus ride
Museum—machine exhibit
Museum—space exhibit
Boat ride

OTHER

Museum—geology exhibit, Christmas trees, children's art
Science classroom—skeleton, insect collections, botanical collections
Planetarium
Seashore
Ecology walk—litter pickup

Time Required

The time required to plan and carry through the field trip should be considered from the standpoint of the children, the teachers, and other adults who may be requested to assist. Time is a valuable resource and should be used wisely. The teacher must ask, "Is the time required for this field trip the best use of everybody's time?"

Costs Involved

Many field trips are free. Some may require admission fees. Transportation is a cost even though it may be borne by a school district or by a number of parents who drive their private cars. A total cost should be calculated if there are numerous fees. Careful determination should be made as to whether the trip is the best use of the resources. For example, if a train trip is calculated to cost $100 for fifteen children, would this be the best use of $100?

Dangers Involved

There are added dangers associated with taking children away from school, whether by bus, by car, or on foot. No concerned teacher assumes the responsibility for a group of children without giving some thought to possible accidents. The school's legal liability in case of accident is one consideration. Liability insurance for private automobiles is another. However, insurance is a hollow consolation to a teacher if an accident does occur. Parents should feel that utmost care for children's safety is planned. Trips that are planned haphazardly often do not give safety sufficient attention.

Preparation

Five further steps are outlined below, which if considered carefully should assure the enrichment of the children's experience that the teacher seeks. These steps are

1. The teacher's preparation.
2. The children's preparation.
3. The field trip.
4. Follow-up activities.
5. Posttrip activities.

These steps can be applied with modifications to special events brought into the school by a visitor or the teacher.

TEACHER'S PREPARATION. The teacher becomes fully informed about the subject of the trip she has chosen. She makes a trip there ahead of time to see specifically what there is for the children to learn. She decides what things she may have to point out to the children because, as inexperienced observers, they may miss important points unless helped in their observation. She will plan for parking, note any hazards that might endanger the children's safety, and recruit additional adult helpers if needed.

She talks with the guide. She will want him to appreciate the level of learning of the children. Many adults have little idea what will interest children. For example, at a bus station, when children were anxious to get aboard a bus, the guide tried to inform them how to get a refund on a ticket. Needless to say, the children's attention wandered! A teacher can decide how she might help the guide if he fails to show the things she feels are important or if he talks above the children's level. Having developed rapport prior to the actual event, it is easy for her to say, "Mr. Arthur, could we see those baby calves? I know the children would enjoy those." Or after a complicated explanation, she might say, "What Mr. Arthur means is that those calves get some special food to see how they will grow."

Choosing the right day of the week for the trip is an important decision. Several things must be considered. First, what immediate preparation will the teacher give the children and how many days will that take? What kinds of follow-up activities does she hope will result, e.g., dramatic play, art activities, rhythm responses, and science experiments? She knows that through reliving the experience, the children work out some of their concepts, roles, and feelings. If she hopes for a great deal of this type of follow-up, she will schedule the trip early in the week so that there will be maximum carry-over into the school activity. The amount of carry-over will be greatly reduced if a weekend intervenes and will be almost nonexistent if a vacation follows the trip. For example, children play firemen for days after a trip to the fire station. They wear their self-made firemen's hats, carry ladders on little red wagons, and put out fires in their "houses" made of packing boxes and wooden planks.

Where in the daily schedule is the best place for the trip? This is an important consideration. The date and time must be convenient for the host or owner of the place to be visited. The teacher considers the energy demands of the trip on the children. An active trip such as a walk on the seashore or on a farm would logically follow a quiet interlude at school rather than a period of outdoor play. A trip to hear a harpist play and accompany the children's singing logically follows a period of active play. Children's bodies will then be ready for the behavior that the situation demands. Active and quiet play have good balance in a program that meets children's needs. Some readjustment in the routine activities will be necessary to fit the trip into the schedule.

The teacher plans for sufficient time for the total trip, including leeway for any emergency. In addition, a bonus experience may occur on any trip. For example, on a walk to the museum a cement mixer was observed dumping its load of cement. What a tragedy if the schedule would not permit even a little peek!

An important part of the teacher's preparation is to think through her rules for walking and riding during field trips. Walking trips will come first, while the teacher is still learning about her group. She can appoint a pair of leaders—she might call them "engines" and "cabooses." They should all practice certain signals so that the leaders will know when to stop and when to go. Learning that "red light" means stop is more fun than just having the teacher call "stop." "Green light" permits them to proceed. Practice sessions can be held in the classroom before the trip. The meaning of traffic lights should be understood and practice sessions held in the classroom to help the children learn their meaning.

When crossing streets, the teacher may ask the child who has been designated the "engine" to stop the "train" at some landmark they see on the other side. She then remains in the middle of the street until all chidren have crossed.

Transportation is often essential for field trips. In public schools teachers can usually depend on buses with qualified drivers. This is a real advantage. In other schools parents may be asked to drive several children. Care must be taken not to overload a car, thereby interfering with safe driving. Only insured cars should be taken on trips.

Thought should be given to deciding which children ride together. Two children who are noted for being hard to handle should be separated. When a parent is driving, his child should be allowed to ride with him. It is essential to have an extra adult accompany each driver. The drivers should be given a list of the children who ride in their car and their phone numbers to use in any emergency. Also, the address and phone number of the destination, and detailed instructions for getting there should be written out for each driver. To depend on one car following another in city traffic with a car full of children is hazardous. Drivers can lose each other and may end up not knowing where to go.

Some schools require a signed permission slip from parents for each trip. These slips are often difficult for teachers to get returned because they are easily misplaced or forgotten. Other schools have parents sign a permission slip that covers all trips throughout the year. Such slips can be taken care of during the child's enrollment. Teachers should also clarify with the school's legal adviser, the problem of liability in case of accident.

Teachers should inform parents of planned trips. Not only will parents then be able to dress the child appropriately, but they can more intelligently supplement the teacher's goals if they don't have to guess what is taking place. That is, parents can ask questions to draw out the child's information and reactions to the trip, answer questions he asks, and arrange family trips that further supplement the school's efforts.

CHILDREN'S PREPARATION. Preparing the children for the field trip is essential for maximum learning. Preparation for a field trip may cover several months, with the trip serving as a capstone, or in some cases the trip may appropriately be initiated after a few days' discussion, with most of the learning to come after the event.

Through pictures, stories, records, role playing, and discussions, the children can become aware of the details they can expect to find on field trips. A fireman expressed amazement at the vocabulary of a group of kindergarteners. If they didn't readily find a tool they asked the fireman where it was. They used the correct name. These children had learned about the fireman's tools during the week prior to the trip. Sometimes there are exceptions or differences in what the child sees in his picture book and what he will find on the trip. The teacher can warn the children of these exceptions ahead of time and help avoid disappointment. For example, new fire stations may not have the traditional fireman's pole. This is a source of disappointment to children who are expecting it.

Stories, songs, and poems may be used to help children learn about a subject they will be seeing on a field trip. The books by Ramona Emmons and Billy N. Pope in the *Your World* series make excellent resource material for both preparation and follow-up activities.[3]

Role playing helps children learn more about the trip. It will help them feel self-assured in a strange place. Prior to a train trip one group arranged chairs as they expected their train seats to be arranged. Young artists designed tickets and took turns being the conductor who punched their tickets. They talked about the difference between their trip of 15 miles and one they might take with their parents—luggage, sleeping on the train, costing more, and not returning for several days. Reassurance was necessary for a child or two who wondered when they were going to return. The children

---

[3] Ramona W. Emmons and Billy N. Pope, *Your World*, Series I through VII (Dallas: Taylor Publishing Co., 1966–1969).

pretended to see the parents' cars waiting at the station as the train pulled in. Their make-believe ride included what they were seeing from their train window. It made them better watchers as the real train rolled along a few days later.

The Field Trip

The day of the field trip finally arrives. All should be in readiness, including the enthusiasm of the children. Keep talk in a low key to avoid overstimulation. The teacher gathers the group around her for a brief review of what they are going to see. Next her talk turns to how they are expected to behave—"quiet in the museum" or "quiet in the egg-laying barn." Perhaps they have to think about how quiet quiet is and why it is necessary.

Toileting cannot be forgotten when one is dealing with young children. After specifically reminding the children to go to the bathroom before leaving the building, the teacher will check on children who are known to have difficulties. Also, it is helpful if adults carry small packages of tissues. Drinks, too, are another consideration. On warm days a picnic jug of water and some paper cups are essential. A sack of cookies will add a festive air to the excursion.

On walking trips the teacher makes assignments for "engines and cabooses" according to the practiced routine. When the children clamor for this responsibility, the teacher may keep a list to be sure she passes the favor around.

For trips by car the teacher makes car assignments by giving each driver a list of the children who will ride in his car. She must make it clear that the same children should always ride in the same car throughout the trip. The teacher discusses with the children the need to sit down in the car. She tells the children in the presence of the drivers that if they stand up, the driver will stop the car beside the road until all are sitting down again. The children's safety has high priority.

The teacher checks last minute details. She advises drivers where to park and what to do until she arrives. She asks the drivers to act as guides for the children in their car. She asks them to ask questions that will help the children notice details, to listen to the children's comments, and to answer their questions. The guide should also be alert to the group's safety. Unless the teacher specifically requests it, outsiders may be hesitant to assume this helpful role. Occasionally the teacher may hold a briefing for the guides in order to better coordinate the trip.

When the group arrives, they wait for the guide who will show them the things they came to see. The children are given lots of time to look, find details, and relate what they are seeing to what they have studied. After a while the adults can point out things they feel the children have missed. A relaxed, nonrushing atmosphere is important. If unexpected learning opportunities arise, the teacher should be happy to take time to observe these too.

The children should wear their name tags. Name tags aid assistants who do not know all of the children's names. They could help police should a child get lost. The children may be curious about this requirement, as was Billy, the oldest four-year-old in the class, who was sitting with three younger friends en route to a wooded park. "I wonder why we have to wear our name tags at the arboretum," he said, fingering his name tag. An adult said with a twinkle in her eye, "That's so the ducks will know your name." There was a moment of silence, then Billy laughed hilariously. "I think that's the funniest thing I ever heard, that we're wearing our name tags so the ducks will know our names." He continued to chuckle. The other children did not crack a smile. Billy, being more mature, recognized the humor that his younger friends missed. Of course, after the joke the adult stated the legitimate reasons.

The Follow-up

The follow-up occurs during the ensuing days and helps the children develop further in their learning. The children may use new concepts in the self-selected activity period. Science materials, blocks, books, pictures, dress-up clothes, records, and art materials may all be used. Sometimes the teacher brings out a new or stored piece of equipment to stimulate dramatic play. A steering wheel, for example, contributes to transportation themes.

Creative art activities may result from the trip. After visiting the prairie dog town, Cindy drew her version of what she had seen. The mounds were as big as mountains, each topped with a family of the animals, just as they were seen. Between the mounds were trees—of the same height as the mounds, giving the observer an idea that Cindy found the mounds more important than the trees as she viewed the scene. Making a fireman's hat, stringing an Indian necklace, or modeling a caveman's house from clay may result, depending on the stimulus from the trip. Freedom to use crayons, chalk, clay, and paints for interpreting the trip in the children's own way is important.

The stimulation of language expression is a prime value of a field trip. Generalizing in his own words from his own experience promotes the child's learning. Every opportunity should be taken to encourage the children to talk about what they saw. Discussing what they saw, how they felt, and how it sounded and smelled is thoroughly enjoyed by the children and helps them remember. Frequently teachers are afraid of open discussion because they fear it will get too loud and out of hand. Having a few pet finger plays, songs, or poems in mind to use as attention getters helps draw young talkers back to the fold. Verbal self-expression is very important for all children, but especially for those children who haven't had much to talk about before. Thus teachers should hesitate before squelching children's language expressions.

Written expression can result too. A dictated letter to the individual who so kindly permitted the visit is one type of expression. Making a poem and dictating a story are others. The opening story in this chapter is an example of a story dictated by the children. Other examples are offered in Chapter 11.

Posttrip Activities

Posttrip activities provide for the children's continued learning after the original emphasis passes and the class goes on to other subjects. This step can continue from the time of the trip to the end of the year. The teacher can place a book on the library shelf or read a story that will cause the children to recall their trip. She can play a record which reminds them. She can reread their own story or letter of thanks. When these stories are sent home, the parents too can carry on posttrip activities. Communication with parents enables them to add family experiences that build on the foundation the school initiates.

Special Visitors Invited to the School

Because of the complications surrounding field trips, it is often more desirable to bring special visitors to the children. The visitor should be one who can help extend the children's information and stimulate their interest. The children should be carefully prepared for these events. Many of the steps suggested for field trips are applicable here.

Following is a list of some suggested special visitors who might be invited to the school:

Mail carrier	Clown	Rock collector
Police officer	Artist	Insect collector
Highway patrol	Santa Claus	Mother and baby
Musicians	Storyteller	Custodian
Twirlers	Magician	Rope twirler
Dancer	Nurse	

The daily schedule may have to be adjusted so that the children will be ready for the type of behavior the event requires. Some visitors

FIGURE 14–2. *A father who is a highway patrolman can help children think about safety rules in a car. (Texas Tech University Kindergarten.)*

can function well during the self-selected activity period. They can talk to small groups of children, letting them come and go from their exhibit. This works for visitors with musical instruments and for those with various collections. The children who are most interested will stay a longtime; those with less interest will spend their time elsewhere.

If the visitor will be working with the group as a whole, then special plans should be made so that the children are ready for the listening behavior usually required. The teacher might want a period of vigorous outdoor play to precede the event, for example. Transition times should be given special thought. A visitor may cause overstimulation of the children. At the same time the teacher will be distracted by playing hostess to the guest. The situation is just right for chaos to develop.

An assistant might be designated to meet the guest, special songs can be prepared to use in case of delay, and activities can be planned that relax the children rather than add to their excitement.

When the visitor is a child's parent, his child too should get to be in the limelight. He should get to introduce his parent, sit by him, and help in any way. The parent should know that giving his child this bit of recognition is part of the plan. Otherwise he may be embarrassed at what seems to be quite possessive behavior on the child's part. Children definitely enjoy having their parent to show off and to show around.

Visitors should be helped to understand the interests of the children. For example, musicians welcome suggestions of songs the children know. Visitors like to know how much the teacher expects the children to become involved. For example, a ballet dancer can simply perform her dance, or she can lead the children in their own ballet, which, of course, makes the event much more meaningful for

FIGURE 14–3. *A father can help as children learn about a dog "attending" school for "show-and-tell."*

FIGURE 14–4. *Parents and siblings can contribute to the program by sharing their talents and hobbies. This mother, who was playing the lead in* Sound of Music *for the civic theater group, brought her two other children to share the singing fun with her kindergartner's class. (Texas Tech University Kindergarten.)*

the children, The teacher should be alert to help, where needed, to be sure that the visitor has a pleasant experience too.

Special visitors also deserve children's thank-you's. The following is how one group said thanks to a young mother who brought her baby for them to see.

Dear Mrs. Smith,

Thank you for letting us see the baby. Thank you for telling us how he eats the cereal. Thank you for letting us see him eat his apple juice. Thank you for putting on the bib.

Thank you for letting us see his toes. Thank you for letting us see his hair—his little black fur. Thank you for letting us see his shoes or his slippers—his bootsies! Thank you for coming.

Please come again. Thank you. Thank you. Thank you.

Love,
The Kindergarten Kids

Conclusion

Field trips and special visitors are appropriate methods to use with young children. In some instances children are better off remaining at school than being taken on field trips prematurely.

For these methods to give maximum educational benefit, these considerations should be weighed: the educational goals for the group, the suitability of available field trips, the time required, the costs, and the dangers involved. Teachers should make adequate preparation, prepare the children, and consider details of the special event, the follow-up and the posttrip activities.

The parent can make significant contributions to this aspect of the school program, through participating directly as a visitor with a special talent or exhibit or through helping as a guide during a field trip.

ADDITIONAL READINGS

EMMONS, RAMONA W., and BILLY N. POPE. *Your World*, Series I through VII. Dallas: Taylor Publishing Co., 1966–1969.

LEEPER, SARAH H., et al. *Good Schools for Young Children*. New York: Macmillan Publishing Co., Inc., 1974.

RUDOLPH, MARGUERITA, and DOROTHY H. COHEN. *Kindergarten: A Year of Learning*. New York: Appleton-Century-Crofts, 1964.

WANN, KENNETH D., MIRIAM S. DORI, and ELIZABETH LIDDLE. *Fostering Intellectual Development in Young Children*. New York: Teachers College Press, Columbia University, 1962.

Snack, Lunch, and Cooking Experiences

"WE'RE having jelly today," sang the teacher as she helped pass out the food for snack. Robert, a sturdily built five-year-old, matched her song with his, "Oh, good, I'm having jelly in my belly."

Robert was sitting next to Betty, his regular snacktime friend. The menu didn't please Betty so much. "I don't want any bread," she said. The teacher said perhaps someone else would like it then. Betty repeated, "I don't want any bread."

Robert's hearing acuity is good, and his reaction time was evident in the haste and skill he displayed in slipping a napkin over both of her pieces of bread and jelly and pulling them toward his place.

His snacktime friend asked him if he wanted her glass of milk as well. He replied as he pointed to his own and rhymed his answer, "Never fear. I've got some right here." He drank three glasses of milk and ate his own sandwich and the sandwich of his snacktime friend. He left one scraggly crust after inspecting it carefully to be sure there was no hint of jelly still adhering to it.

Children don't learn well when they are hungry.[1] However, meals and other food experiences in the nursery school and kindergarten do more than satisfy hunger. Through helping with food preparation, eating foods, and talking about them, children's curiosity and interest may be stimulated. They may even become interested in a program that otherwise appears not to be reaching them. Important also is the rest children receive while eating.

Goals for Children's Experiences with Food

By providing experiences with food the teacher helps young children learn:

---

[1] Richard H. Barnes, "Effects of Malnutrition on Mental Development," *Journal of Home Economics*, **61**:9 (November 1969), 671–676.

1. That plants and animals grown on farms are primary sources of food.
2. That the grocery store supplies some food products that are ready to eat and others that are ready to prepare.
3. That children need certain foods for growth and energy.
4. That they may like new foods if they try them.
5. That foods have names, physical characteristics, and flavors.
6. That the preparation of food includes such processes as heating, cooling, freezing, beating, and grinding.
7. That cooking tools, equipment, and processes have names.
8. That the scientific method of observing, relating, interpreting, and generalizing can be related to food.
9. That safety and cleanliness are important in the kitchen.
10. That both men and women like to cook and eat.

Planning Experiences with Food

The kitchen might be considered the chemical laboratory of the school for young children. It may be the regular school kitchen, with a small table in one corner where an adult and a few children prepare their foods. Some schools have elaborately furnished child-sized kitchens. Or a table or two in the classroom can become the cooking center. A hot plate and utensils can be brought in on a tray and removed when the cooking project is completed. The latter arrangement is probably the most common. Teachers often bring equipment from home. In public schools having lunchrooms or home economics classrooms, teachers often can use school equipment. Lacking cooking facilities, children's mothers can be enlisted to take food home to bake after it is mixed by the children. Numerous possibilities exist. Each teacher explores the options and makes the arrangements when she wishes to provide opportunities for the children to explore the world of food.

When planning a food experience for the children, the teacher should first think through the goals mentioned above. What does she expect the children to learn? She decides on a project that will contribute most to her goals. She avoids food with high sugar and fat content because rich foods would replace foods containing essential nutrients.[2] She carefully checks supplies and equipment to be sure she has everything she needs. She may prepare the food herself in her apartment or in the school kitchen to refresh her memory of the exact steps and to note possible problems that may occur as the children do it.

[2] Ruth Leverton, *Food Becomes You* (Ames, Ia.: Iowa State University Press, 1960), pp. 139–140.

The teacher and the assistants discuss their roles during the cooking project. For example, will the assistants help with the food? Or will they carry on other activities? If so, which ones? If it is necessary to take food or children outside the room, who is to go? Will each child's product be labeled, or will it be placed in a common pan? What if a child wants to put his product in his locker or take it home? Who cleans up after the project?

The children's ongoing experience with food is the place to start selecting projects. The foods that are commonly found in the children's homes and those served in the school will be of primary interest. Learning will be most effective when it is related to the particular children.

As the children eat their food products, the teacher should remember to discuss the food. Naming, labeling, and restating the procedures used will help children remember. Helping them think of adjectives to describe the appearance and the taste of the foods adds to their vocabulary. Reminding them to tell their parents about the project further strengthens their learning and helps tie the home and the school together. Every opportunity should be used to help children learn about foods that are required for good health. Learning is more thorough when a few concepts, rather than many concepts, are introduced in a given lesson or project. Most food projects are worth repeating, and concepts can be expanded next time. For example, rather than overloading children with learning five foods, use only two or three, and let them do more things with those examples.

Sources of Food

As far as most children know, the grocery store is the source of food. The children may help the teacher buy food there occasionally. Money concepts develop as they discuss the cost and the number of coins required to pay for a purchase.

Teachers can use visual aids, a field trip, or a garden to help the children further their understanding of the primary sources of most foods.

Interest is guaranteed if the children have picked the apples for apple sauce or the pumpkin for pumpkin custard, or if they have watched the cows being milked for the milk in ice cream. Garden products, too, will be pronounced "delicious" after they have been cared for by the children. The teacher can discuss the subject of primary sources by asking, "Where is this food grown?" or "What happens to it before the grocer gets it?"

It is not easy for a child to understand how a cute little squealy pig relates to the breakfast bacon. Some children like animals so

FIGURE 15–1. *Making cookies is a favorite food project. Careful planning and guided participation is required. (Texas Tech University Kindergarten.)*

much that they really don't want to think about killing them to eat. Even a college student said, "How could you kill a chicken that you had known personally?" The children can be told the sources of meat, but the teacher need not speak of the butchering process unless the children ask. If asked, give a factual answer.

Because families today buy so many foods already prepared, even adults almost forget how a food is grown or how it appears in its primary state. The chance to plant, care for, pick, clean, cook, and then eat a food crop is experienced by fewer and fewer people as the society becomes more and more urban. A garden helps children understand that some food is first a growing plant. Occasionally a window box can be used for growing plants.

If it is not feasible to grow the plants (and teachers could never grow all of them), it may be possible to visit gardens and farms to see plants growing. Teachers can ask local citizens or at a farmer's market for suggestions of local primary sources. The children might go to see such crops as wheat, corn, potatoes, fruit, pumpkins, or beans. Sometimes they may be allowed to pick a sample to take back to school.

A trip to the milking parlor of a dairy will help the children learn the source of their most common food—milk. A trip to the bottling and ice cream plant will add further to their information.

Because commercial egg producers generally won't admit visitors to egg-laying pens (because they excite the hens, so that they may stop laying), children may never see a hen lay an egg. A student teacher was telling the children that hens lay eggs, when one inquisitive child wanted to know, "How does the egg get out?" The student hadn't anticipated this question and was searching for a way to explain it when a knowledgeable five-year-old saved her. He squatted henlike, then jumped around and squawked! It was real enough for everybody, and the discussion continued.

Pictures may be the only resource for teaching the primary source of many foods. Care should be taken to secure accurate information. One teacher was heard talking about pineapples growing on trees— certainly an incorrect thing for children to learn.

Tasting Food in Its Fresh State

Many foods children eat are canned, bottled, or frozen. Teachers can look for ways to show children food in its fresh state.

Trays of fresh food can be arranged so that the children will taste various foods. Vegetables or fruits can be diced and the children can serve themselves with toothpicks. An example of the whole food should be reserved so that the children can relate physical qualities— color, shape, size, and weight—to flavor and internal characteristics as they eat.

Orange juice is a familiar food. However, many families buy it frozen or canned. Squeezing their own oranges and drinking the juice will delight children. Lemons can be squeezed for lemonade. Fruits such as apple, grape, and cherry must be heated to extract the juice. The children can help with this process too if reasonable precautions are taken with the hot liquids.

Children will enjoy cutting apples, bananas, celery, carrots, tomatoes, peppers, and cucumbers for their snack. To prevent discoloration, the teacher should remember to dip apples, bananas, pears, and peaches in citrus juices or in a solution made of ascorbic acid (available in the freezer supply section of the grocery store) mixed in a little water or syrup. Fruits can be served alone or in a fruit cup. Celery stuffed with cream cheese or peanut butter is popular.

Changing the Consistency of Foods

The children learn that through various processes in the kitchen —heating, cooling, freezing, grinding, beating—the food is made ready to eat. Children can observe some of the changes that take place.

Peanut butter, a longtime favorite, can be made from peanuts ground in a blender. The children can shell the peanuts and place them in the blender. After the peanuts are ground, add jelly or honey to give a consistency that will spread. Serve a spoonful to each child and pass the crackers. Watch them spread the peanut butter and eat!

When making gelatin dessert, the children can see the effect of the hot water on the granules. Then they note the change to a solid after chilling. If gelatin is started at the beginning of the day, cooled with ice water or ice cubes, and poured into individual paper cups, it is possible to have it ready to serve for snack the same day. For variation, set the gelatin outdoors on a cold day. The children will conclude that "it's cold as a refrigerator outdoors."

Making homemade ice cream teaches children that ice cream really does contain all the good foods that their mothers say it does. They can actually see the milk, eggs, sugar and flavoring go into the ice cream as it is being made. Either an electric or a hand-turned freezer can be used—and the children will help! The proof is in the eating. M-m-m! Good! For a variation, one group brought in snow to use in place of the ice.

Making butter gives the children yet another chance to see a change take place before their eyes. Use a pint of whipping cream for fifteen to eighteen children. Pour one cup of whipping cream into each of two quart jars and tighten the lids. The children pass the jars around the table, shaking and counting off five shakes per child. The cream first whips, then begins to separate, giving buttermilk and globules of butter. When sufficiently churned, the butter collects ("gathers") together. The buttermilk can be poured into small paper cups so that everyone can have a taste. The butter can be served on individual serving plates. Give the child a small plastic knife and watch him spread his crackers. Even children who say they hate butter will like both butter and buttermilk if it is presented to them with "Let's see how it tastes," instead of "Who wants some buttermilk?" or "Would you like some buttermilk?" Because whipping cream is sweet, the buttermilk tastes only slightly different from other milk.

Apples can be cooked into apple sauce. The children will observe the changing of the hard apples into the mushy sauce and the effect of sugar on the tart apple. Leaving the skin on the apple makes it easier for the children to do more of the project. Allow one apple per child. It is convenient to use the special apple cutter that cuts the apple in six sections and cores it all in one operation. The children can accomplish this operation with a minimum of help. If cooking takes place in the room, the tantalizing aroma will attract other cooks.

FIGURE 15–2. *The cutting and coring of apples for apple sauce is a popular project. The safe use of knives must be taught.* (*University of Idaho Nursery School.*)

Stir the cooked apples, and add sugar and a bit of cinnamon. Serve for snack. The children will surely go home and ask their mothers to let them repeat this project!

Popcorn is a child's favorite. The addition of heat to corn makes such an aromatic odor that people in the building will drop in to the classroom. An electric popper or skillet is handy for this project. Follow the usual safety precautions.

Eggs change consistency with heat. They can be boiled or scrambled. If shells are needed for dyeing, the inside of the egg can be blown out and scrambled. To blow: first use a paring knife to tap a hole about one-quarter inch in diameter in each end, then BLOW. Let each child blow his egg into a single cup. If bits of shell break off, the shell can more easily be retrieved. The children can help beat the eggs, adding seasoning and one tablespoon of milk per egg. The children can take turns stirring the egg in the electric skillet and watching the coagulation occur as the cooking process progresses. Serve for snack or lunch. Arrange timing to serve warm.

Breads of many varieties can be made in the classroom. The children learn more if they are made from "scratch" than when they are made from mixes. Actually breads have few ingredients. Recipes can be posted near the cooking table. What could be more fun than mixing, cooking, then eating your very own pancake? Pancakes can be served with jelly or powdered sugar. Biscuits, muffins, tortillas, and banana bread are other suggestions. Yeast bread can be made, but the project may require two days.

Cakes, cookies, and gingerbread can be made with various mixes. However, mixes simplify the process so much that understanding of the total ingredients required is reduced. Cookies and cakes may be made for a special day. Sometimes at the close of school a group makes a birthday cake for all the children who have summer birthdays. The group sings "Happy Birthday" to each child!

Directions follow for making special sugar cookies in the classroom. By noting the concern for detail in this outline, the teacher may be helped with planning other projects.

MAKING SUGAR COOKIES WITH YOUNG CHILDREN [3]

1. Use a sugar cookie recipe suitable for rolled cookies. Add a little more flour than is needed if an adult is going to roll them. A recipe will make fewer cookies than the recipe states because the children will not roll them very thin.

2. The children can help put the ingredients together. Mixing may be done the day before the cookies are baked, or the teacher can have the cookie dough ready when the children arrive. The time element will be the deciding factor. The rolling, cutting, and baking is usually enough for a half-day group to do.

3. Divide the dough into balls—enough for each child to make three or four cookies. Make a few extras in case of an accident.

4. Have the supplies on a tray—several rolling pins, flour, sifter, spatulas, cookie cutters, colored sugars, raisins, and plenty of cookie sheets.

5. Use a low table so that the children can stand to work. Cover

---

[3] Acknowledgment is due *The Progressive Farmer* for permission to reprint parts of an article by the author, "A Cookie Making Party" (February 1964), 106.

the table with clean tea towels. Pull them tight and tack the edges or secure them with masking tape. Sift flour on the area where each child will roll the dough.

6. Be sure the child washes his hands just before he comes to help. Supervise the hand washing, or hands may not be clean enough for food handling.

7. The children will be inclined to push down hard on the rolling pin, so tell them, "Let the rolling pin do the work." You may have to stand behind each child, helping him barely press the rolling pin down.

8. When the dough is rolled enough to cut, be ready with this statement, "Let me tell you a cook's secret." Then show him how to fit several cookie cutters on the dough before he cuts any. Children are inclined to cut one cookie out of the middle and then have to re-roll the dough. Help the child place the cookies on a greased cookie sheet.

9. The cookie decorator's table is set up nearby. It is another low table and should be covered with paper or a cloth for catching the sugar. The children can sit to decorate cookies. Colored sugar is provided in shakers. Raisins and red hots are also popular. The children spend a long time here getting just the right effect. When a child gets so much sugar that it might burn and stick to the pan, the cookies may need to be transferred to a fresh baking sheet.

10. One adult is required to supervise the oven as soon as a pan of cookies is ready. Set a timer because cookies bake quickly. Children enjoy peeking in the oven, so let them take turns as cookie watchers.

11. It is generally best to avoid keeping track of which cookie is whose. Some get broken, or burned, so if they are mixed up no one is disappointed with the finished product.

12. Of course, the proof of a cookie is in the eating. As soon as the children are through rolling their cookies and sufficient cookies are out of the oven, it is time to bring out the milk for the pleasurable moment of eating their own cookies.

Additional Suggestions

Main dishes for the lunch menu or a more substantial snack can also be made by children.

No child will pass up a vegetable soup if he helps cook the soup bone one day, chops the vegetables the next, and watches "our soup" simmer to completion the next. By that time everyone will literally have had a finger in the soup and surely will pronounce it "good."

Hamburgers, broiled hot dog bits, or pizza can be made. An electric skillet with temperature control is safest for hamburgers. The children can cut the hot dogs and watch with the teacher as they broil. The children can make pizzas by patting out canned biscuits and covering them with mildly seasoned pizza sauce and cheese. Then they are baked.

Canned soups, cheese sandwiches, cinnamon toast, or cereal-marshmallow treats can be made.

Children can help make jellies using the noncooked method. The recipe for "freezer jelly" is found on the pectin box. Sugar is stirred into fresh, canned, or reconstituted frozen juice. The pectin is boiled for one minute with three-fourths cup of water and then added to the juice and sugar. The jelly sets in a day or so. Children delight in using their "own" jelly and in spreading their own sandwiches with plastic picnic knives. It is a messy job, so teachers should prepare the table with a clean sheet of wrapping paper. Children will get jelly from ear to ear too, so a wash-up must follow the snack period. The recipe makes enough jelly for several sandwiches for a class of fifteen.

Teachers will choose the food experiences for their groups on the basis of the children's interests and questions. They should consult a recipe book for complete recipes of the foods suggested here. Foods can be prepared to serve either at snacktime or at mealtime. In serving foods to children, one should remember that children like mild-flavored and mild-temperatured foods best. They typically let their soup get cold and their ice cream gets mushy.

Children learn safety concepts along with other concepts during cooking projects. It is best to choose cooking projects that offer a minimum of danger to the children. Nearly any project requiring heat or the use of knives requires adult supervision at all times. Locate electric cords out of traffic lanes so that the children won't trip over them. Foods just out of the oven or just off the stove are extremely hot. Care must be taken that the children are not burned. Provide a cutting board for each child and reasonably sharp knives. Take time to show the children safety measures in cutting and handing tools to each other.

Mealtime in the School for Young Children

A visit to a school lunchroom is often a revelation to parents, especially if they can observe out of sight of their child. Parents make comments like the following: "He eats so well!" "I didn't know he could pour his milk!" "Doesn't he ask you to feed him?" The child may eat quite differently in a group of his peers and when guided by a skilled teacher.

When children are old enough for nursery school, they may have recently entered an eating stage that frustrates their parents. The infant grows rapidly, so food consumption is high. At age three the growth curve has leveled out and food needs are reduced.[4] About this same time children reach a stage where they want to assert their independence. They say "No" frequently and may refuse to eat foods they have been eating all along. Parents with a child of this age may get into the habit of bribing, cajoling, threatening, then finally feeding the child, just to get some food into him. When he enters nursery school, day care, or kindergarten, he brings his home experience with food with him.

Goals for Mealtime

During mealtime the teacher wants the child:

1. To eat a well-balanced diet.
2. To enjoy mealtime.
3. To taste and ultimately enjoy eating a wide variety of food.
4. To learn to feed himself.
5. To sit at the table and develop acceptable table manners.

A balanced diet will be planned by the nutritionist. Each food, including the dessert, is calculated to make a contribution to the child's essential nutrients. For this reason, dessert is not used as a reward for a clean plate. When school meals differ from home meals in both type of food and type of service, there is considerable adjustment for the child to make. The teacher understands that the children will need time to become accustomed to the school food.

Food can be pretty as well as tasty. Plan a variety in the color, texture, and shape of food. Tables and service should be orderly and attractive. Family style is the usual method of serving, with each table of five or six children having the dishes of food served by an adult at the table.

Children enjoy assuming some responsibility for meal service. Even three-year-olds can help set the table. Four- and five-year-olds will vie for the honor, and the teacher may need to keep a list of the helpers to be sure she passes around the favor. The children can also assist in cleaning up the tables following the meal. This training is good for all children but may be especially beneficial to children whose home routines appear inadequate.

Every effort should be made to arrange the setting so that it is pleasant, satisfying, and relaxing for both children and adults. The

---

[4] Thelma Waylor and Rose S. Klein, *Applied Nutrition* (New York: Macmillan, 1965), p. 257.

FIGURE 15–3. *Scrambled eggs are pronounced "good" after some children break, beat, stir, and cook the eggs during the self-selected activity period. Place cards help children know where their space is and provide a pre-reading experience. (Michigan State University Laboratory Preschool.)*

children should be seated on comfortable-height chairs that enable their feet to touch the floor. The youngest may need bibs. You can make self-help bibs by attaching a piece of elastic to a washcloth for the child to slip over his head.

Each child should have a special seat. Sometimes a teacher fosters a friendship by pairing a child who needs a friend with a potential friend during lunch. Although socializing is permitted at mealtime, the primary goal is to eat. The teacher may also wisely plan to seat the children who need special help near an adult, to disperse children who tend to be behavior problems, and to place independent eaters where they can be imitated by more dependent children. A seating arrangement that allows teachers to relax and get some nourishment too is important, because they may be required to spend several more hours that day tending to the children's needs.

Breakfast is served in some groups that arrive early, such as in a day-care center, in Head Start groups, or in other groups where it is known that home breakfasts are not meeting the children's nutritional

FIGURE 15–4. *Tasting new things is a goal of many preschool food projects. (Michigan State University Laboratory Preschool.)*

needs. Some children may want to eat immediately on arrival, whereas others may prefer to play awhile and then have their breakfast. Breakfast is usually more informal than lunch. One teacher takes care of the eaters, and another supervises those who are playing.

Most teachers feel that when children have a quiet time just prior to lunch, they eat better. Children can do their toileting and washing and then gather around the teacher for quiet stories and songs. The period should not be rushed. It is not the best time to demand the most responsible behavior, because children who are tired and hungry are more prone to anger.[5] When conflicts are common, teachers may wish to schedule lunch somewhat earlier, provide a more substantial midmorning snack, or plan a less taxing morning program.

An orderly transition to the lunch tables from the story circle helps retain the quiet atmosphere. The teacher can say, "Children who sit with Miss D, creep like little hungry mice to your lunch table."

The teacher serves the food, adjusting the amount to her estimation of each child's appetite for a certain food. Many foods will be served in teaspoon-sized servings, especially foods that are new or less popular. The teacher assumes that each child will taste the food. When she knows the child well, she will more accurately gauge the portions, and the "clean plate" will occur more often. Enjoyment of food is more important than a clean plate. "There are three peak periods for the development of obesity in children: late infancy; early childhood, around six; and adolescence," according to nutrition researchers. "Obesity interferes with both health and psychological functioning." [6] Teachers and parents are cautioned by nutritionists about requiring a clean plate when that means urging the child to overeat.

The teacher's small servings permit the child to ask for seconds and to serve himself. Children enjoy this measure of independence. When they want more milk, the teacher will pour the amount appropriate for the glass in a small pitcher and permit the child to pour his own milk. If she pours more than a glassful, the child may run it over. Children will drink numerous servings when they get to do the replenishing.

A typical serving arrangement allows children to take their dirty plates and silverware to a serving cart and return with their desserts when they have finished the main course. This gives them a chance to move a bit when they have been sitting for a time. They like this measure of confidence that they can walk without spilling their dessert.

Guidance During the Meal [7]

Guidance during the meal will be related to the goals stated earlier. A positive expectation that the goals will eventually be accomplished is necessary.

[5] Catherine Landreth, *Early Childhood: Behavior and Learning* (New York: Knopf, 1967), p. 142.

[6] Myron Winick, "Childhood Obesity," *Nutrition Today,* **9**:3 (May/June 1974), 9–10.

[7] For more detail see Chapter 11, "Guiding Children's Eating Behavior," in *Guiding Young Children* by Verna Hildebrand (New York: Macmillan, 1975).

FIGURE 15–5. *Experience pouring one's own juice and having to decide how much is provided at snack and lunch periods. (Michigan State University Laboratory Preschool.)*

In the first place, the teacher realizes that the growth rate for children of this age has slowed down, so she won't expect the child to be a big eater. She will further believe that he is the best judge. If the child is actively participating in the school program and is in good health physically and emotionally, he will eat what he needs to grow and to restore his energy. Teachers do not fall into a pattern of bribing, cajoling, or feeding children individually.

Children are great imitators and want to be independent. As one child watches other children happily going about the business of eating, he too becomes more independent. Even a three-year-old senses that his teacher can't spoon-feed five or six children (the number she probably has at her table). He begins to help himself.

The teacher recognizes growth in independence and rewards the child with praise and smiles. He'll pour his milk, cut his beans in two, and go to the serving cart for his dessert because he feels big doing these things for himself.

Children's meals at home may be come-and-go affairs, so they may think they can eat a little now and a little later even at school. The teacher can simply say, "If you are finished eating, put your plate on the cart. If you are hungry, sit at the table and eat." The teacher will give the child the choice, and after he has made the decision, both teacher and pupil will live by it. A few days of finding food served at a regular time will help the child realize the necessity of eating at the designated time and place.

The teacher guides the child quietly in brief, positive statements, letting the child know what he should do. She uses statements like: "Use your toast stick," to the child using his finger to get food on his fork; "A spoon will work better," to a child eating apple sauce with a fork; "Hold your glass up straight," to a child whose milk is about to spill; "Swallow before you talk," to the child who is talking with food in his mouth; or "Keep your food on your plate," to the child who litters the tablecloth.

The teacher uses demonstrations. She shows the child how to grip his fork for eating or cutting. She may guide his hand to help him put her advice into practice. For example, when she says, "Point the spoon toward you," she may guide his hand to make the tip turn toward his mouth.

Children generally feel bad about spills. Children are sometimes scolded harshly at home and may expect the same treatment at school. When the teacher occasionally spills something, the children may feel a new sense of comradeship. Spills do occur. They should be taken in stride. Extra silverware and napkins are kept close by to replace dropped items. A sponge, dust pan, and broom should be available in the serving area. When accidents are frequent, a slight change in arrangement might help avoid them. For example, if the table is cluttered, it may help to place serving dishes on a side table within reach. Teachers will prevent some spills if they are alert to remind a child to place his glass back away from the edge of the table.

When the child has finished eating, he takes his plate and glass to the serving cart and leaves the dining area. An adult, designated to guide him, takes over for the next steps. It is important that children who remain at the lunch tables not be neglected because of all the adults becoming involved with the children who have finished eating. A routine should be established so that children know what to do next. Generally they go to the bathroom to wash and urinate, then either prepare for going home or for taking a nap, depending on the type of school.

In day-care centers the nap room should be prepared while the children eat; then, as children finish lunch, they should be prepared immediately for naps, to take advantage of the quieting effect of eating.

Snack Time

Midmorning and midafternoon snacks serve several purposes for young children. A snack provides time to rest and food to restore energy. It provides an informal, social conversation time good for summing up the day's activities. Snack may be a fairly organized time of day or it may be informal. In groups that remain at school for lunch, the teacher may plan an early snack to avoid interfering with lunch appetites. Some children are slow starters. They eat very light breakfasts but then are famished by snack time. They eat so much snack that they aren't hungry for an early lunch. If snack is served in an informal come-when-you're-hungry arrangement during the first hour of school, it meets the need of such children. In groups that take a midday nap at school, it may be customary to let a few children at a time eat their midafternoon snack as soon as they wake up. This plan offers the teacher time to talk with small groups while others are still napping.

In other groups teachers may like to hold a quiet time immediately following the self-selected activity period, then follow this with a group snacktime when everyone eats together. In this way the half-day group accomplishes some of the goals that are achieved with a lunch program. No one plan is "best." The important rule is to make a good plan for a particular group of children.

The numerous suggestions for cooking projects and experiences with food offered in the first part of this chapter will contribute most if the children work together preparing the food, eat it together, and talk about it, thereby reinforcing the learning.

Of course, the children do not prepare every snack. The fare offered should be varied. There surely is no need for children to say, "Not that again!" in disparaging voices when they see the snack tray. Interesting food, attractively arranged and enthusiastically presented, will encourage the children to enjoy eating. They will be not only feeding themselves but learning about food as well.

Children can be designated "helpers" with snack. Perhaps one can serve the beverage, another place the napkins, another take the responsibility for helping serve the food. A poster showing a paper

FIGURE 15–6.   *Finger foods are good snack choices for young children.*

cup, a plate, and a napkin can be used to designate helpers—the names being removable and rotated during the weeks.

It is helpful to arrange in advance individual servings of food and drink at each child's place to eliminate prolonged waiting for the refreshments. For example, a glass of juice, a napkin holding three cookies, a dish of fruit, or a cupcake liner holding a serving of raisins can be set out on a tray from which the helpers can distribute the servings around the table before the children arrive at their places.

Imagine the impatience felt by the children who waited for one frustrated little girl to count out three cookies to each child in a class of twenty-five youngsters. Not only did they want three cookies, but they didn't want any broken ones. Several children could have been designated to help. The broken cookies should have been made into crumbs and used for some special dessert, as they were undesirable in the broken form.

Guidance suggestions made for serving lunch apply to snack. The Children remove their glasses and napkins when they are finished, placing them on a tray for removal to the kitchen.

Communicating with Parents

Close coordination of the school and the home feeding programs may avoid unnecessary confusion for the child.[8] Parents can be invited to observe snack or lunchtime occasionally so that they will better understand the experience their child is having. They should understand the goals the teacher has for a child of this age and the techniques she uses to foster those goals. Lunch menus can be sent home regularly.

Informing the parent when there have been special projects that the children may ask them to duplicate helps the parents carry through the learning begun in the school. Metheny et al. found that 34 per cent of the children in their study requested their mothers to prepare food they had eaten at school.[9] Recipes can be exchanged. Occasionally the teacher may visit the home to demonstrate how to prepare a food that the child has liked at school. When the teacher and the mother develop rapport on such domestic interests as recipes, it may strengthen the communication between the family and the school.

Parents may enjoy contributing an item for snack or lunch. Some sanitary codes forbid it. However, the school policy will be stated by the teacher. Parents are asked to inform the teacher ahead of time so that school food projects won't overshadow the parents' contribution. Duplications can then be avoided and parents' choice of a contribution can be guided so that it is appropriate in kind and amount. A typical occasion is a birthday or a holiday. A simple celebration at school is far easier on child and parent than giving a party at home.

In one kindergarten the teacher left the snack completely up to the parents. If they wanted their child to have a snack, they had to send it to school. What happened in practice was that a group of disadvantaged children regularly sat through the snack period and watched their more well-to-do classmates sip from cans of juice and eat cookies. It is hard to understand how a thinking, feeling teacher could permit such a cruel situation in her class.

If the advantaged parents had realized what was happening, they surely would have been willing to pool their funds to purchase a

---

[8] Reva T. Frankle, Miriam F. Senhouse, and Catherine Cowell, "Project Head Start: A Challenge in Creativity in Community Nutrition," *Journal of Home Economics*, **59**:1 (January 1967), 24–27. The authors give numerous practical suggestions for helping children learn to eat nutritious foods and make suggestions for working with parents to improve nutrition in the home.

[9] Norma Y. Metheny, Fern E. Hunt, Mary B. Patton, and Helene Heye, "The Diets of Preschool Children," *Journal of Home Economics*, **54**:4 (April 1962), 306.

snack for all the children. It seems that, in fairness, what is available for one should be available to all.

Conclusion

The serving of food is complete with ritual in nearly every culture. It is an important time of day in the nursery school and kindergarten. Not only are goals accomplished that relate scientific concepts to real-life experiences of the child, but the child also learns to eat a well-balanced diet. He learns to enjoy mealtime, to taste and enjoy a variety of foods, and to sit at the table and acquire appropriate table manners. The teacher keeps parents informed and invites their participation in experiences that will further their child's knowledge of foods.

ADDITIONAL READINGS

DEUTSCH, RONALD M. *The Family Guide to Better Food and Better Health.* Des Moines, Ia.: Meredith Corporation, 1974.

FERREIRA, NANCY J. *The Mother-Child Cook Book: An Introduction to Educational Cooking.* Menlo Park, Calif.: Pacific Coast Publishers, 1969.

HATFIELD, ANTOINETTE KUZMANECH, and PEGGY SMEETON STANTON. *Help! My Child Won't Eat Right.* Washington, D.C.: Acropolis Books, Ltd., 1973.

LAMB, MINA W., and MARGARETTE L. HARDEN. *The Meaning of Nutrition.* New York: Pergamon Press, Inc., 1973.

LEVERTON, RUTH M. *Food Becomes You.* Ames, Iowa: Iowa State University Press, 1965.

MARTIN, ETHEL AUSTIN. *Nutrition in Action.* New York: Holt, Rinehart and Winston, Inc., 1965.

MORRIS, PORTIA. *Food for Your Preschool Child.* East Lansing, Mich.: Michigan State University Cooperative Extension, 1967.

Nutrition and Feeding of Infants and Children Under Three in Group Day Care. Rockville, Md.: U.S. Department of Health, Education, and Welfare, Maternal and Child Health Service, 1971.

Project Head Start Bulletin No. 3, *Nutrition;* No. 3a, *Food Buying Guide and Recipes;* 3b, *Nutrition Instructors Guide;* 3c, *Leader's Handbook for a Nutrition and Food Course;* and 3d *Nutrition—Staff Training Programs.* Washington, D.C.: Office of Economic Opportunity, 1967.

Quantity Recipes for Child Care Centers. Philadelphia: Public Documents, 5801 Jabor Ave.

Recommended Dietary Allowances, Eighth Revised Edition. Washington, D.C.: Food and Nutrition Board, National Academy of Sciences—National Research Council, 1975.

SUNDERLINE, SYLVIA (ed.). *Nutrition and Intellectual Growth in Children.* Washington, D.C.: Association for Childhood Education International, 1969.

WAGNER, DOROTHY. *Nine Week Menu Cook Book.* Portageville, Mo.: Extension Division of University of Missouri, 1973.

WAYLER, THELMA F., and ROSE S. KLEIN. *Applied Nutrition.* New York: Macmillan Publishing Co., Inc., 1965.

WOHL, MICHAEL G., and ROBERT S. GOODHART (eds.). *Modern Nutrition in Health.* Philadelphia: Lea & Febiger, 1968.

Program Planning and Evaluating

THE TEACHER or the student teacher who confronts the puzzling task of developing the total program for children must weigh many factors relevant to decision making. There are unique factors in each classroom. Ultimately the program that reaches the child must be transmitted by a teacher who is in that classroom with that child.

Planning may seem contrary to the type of freedom and spontaneity that has been advocated in this volume. Quite the opposite is true. Adequate planning leaves a teacher free to respond to more of the human factors in teaching. Planning is a flexible structure that combines meaningful goals, the needs of the children, and the available resources.

The teacher's planning may be analogous to a mother's skill in home management. When the mother plans wisely and well, she has more of all resources to channel toward better human relationships in the family. The teacher who plans can also relate to children in a deeper, more relaxed manner, knowing that certain aspects of the program are taken care of in advance.

Planning Programs for Young Children

If a teacher were asked, "What is your major consideration when planning the program for your group of children?" she probably would answer, "The children." This is, of course, as it should be. However, there are a number of other factors that teachers must also take into consideration. Some forces are national in scope, some are statewide, and others originate in the community, the school, and the particular families of the children.

Various Factors That Influence the School

IMPACT OF THE FEDERAL GOVERNMENT. The democratic form of government of the United States influences teachers as they educate children to live in a democracy. In an authoritarian country the child

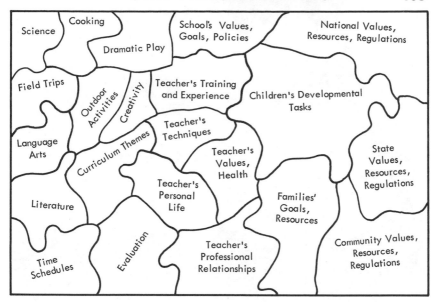

FIGURE 16–1. *The teacher's puzzle.*

is educated to function in that system. An example of national influence is the Supreme Court decision forbidding racial segregation in public schools. Also, the 1964 program of federal aid to education has stimulated communities to initiate Head Start and Title IV programs and to plan them according to federal guidelines. Many research projects and day-care centers were assisted through federal funds.

Private schools are indirectly affected by federal action. For example, the standards established in Project Head Start regarding the 2–15 teacher-pupil ratio will give parents, teachers, and administrators in private and philanthropic schools a standard they did not have prior to 1965.

IMPACT OF STATE GOVERNMENTS. State governments too have an impact on the teacher as she plans for her group of children. States generally hold the power to set and enforce standards, grant licenses to schools, and grant certificates to teachers. Over forty of the states provide state aid to public schools providing kindergartens. To receive this aid the schools are required to meet certain standards for curriculum, qualifications of teachers, and minimum number of days in a school year. State legislation may set some standards concerning facilities, children's medical examinations, or the number and ages of children admitted to classes.

INFLUENCE OF THE COMMUNITY. The community influences the program planning. In a public school, authority is vested in an

FIGURE 16–2. *When planning is well done, the teacher will have time for reading to a few children in the literature corner and for discussing the books with them. (University of Houston Parent-Child Development Center.)*

elected board of community citizens that acts through a school administrator. Also, a city commission may hire the director of a community day-care center or the director of the community action program. Philanthropic agencies, churches, or universities have special objectives that affect the teacher's planning. Local government agencies may also be responsible for enforcing certain fire and health regulations. Teachers must be aware of regulations as they plan.

INFLUENCE OF THE SCHOOL ADMINISTRATION. The school itself establishes policies for all the classrooms in a system. School administrations control the funds that are spent for supplies, new equipment, janitorial help, and paid assistants. School traditions, such as admission policies or parent participation, will influence planning. Some coordination of programs is required when several classes use the same equipment and play yard. Ideally, the teacher will be called upon to take part in decisions affecting her area of specialization.

INFLUENCE OF THE PARENTS.   Parents of children in a group can influence a teacher's planning. They know something of the impact the teaching is having on their child. When open communication exists between the teacher and the parents, the school gets valuable feedback regarding the positive and negative aspects of a program. The teacher's attitude toward parents can make the difference in parents' vital concern for or apathy toward school matters. If teachers listen to parents and actively involve them in school, parents can have a positive influence. Parents can also be a source of relentless pressure if their interests are consistently ignored.

In a study completed by the author on "Value Orientations for Nursery School Programs," [1] parents rated "individuality" and "socialization" as their two most preferred value orientations for nursery school pograms, when given a choice of nine orientations depicted through nine short stories. The nine value orientations were socialization, intellect, morality, aesthetics, authority, health, freedom, individuality, and economics. The economic value story was generally rated last. A teacher must be aware of and attempt to open discussion with parents regarding their value orientations. If parents expect a type of program that is completely unacceptable to the teacher, then the two parties will have to work out some accommodation, or the teacher may decide to teach in another environment. No one value is "right," nor is it entirely unrelated to the other values, but there must be some meeting of minds between teachers and parents or the children's early education experience may suffer.

THE TEACHER'S INFLUENCE.   Classrooms have unique characteristics because teachers are different. Teachers have different professional training and experience. Each teacher associates with her fellow teachers to a different extent. Programs will reflect how the teacher feels about young children. Her personality, creativity, health, and values will make a difference.

In the study referred to in the previous paragraph, teachers, paraprofessional teachers, and students in teacher preparation programs also rated "individuality" and "socialization" stories as their first and second choices of value orientations for nursery school programs.

The teacher's personal life away from the school will have an im-

---

[1] For a summary of the study see Chapter 2 of *Guiding Young Children* by Verna Hildebrand (New York: Macmillan, 1975).

pact on the class, just as the satisfactions she gains from teaching will affect her personal life.

The qualities of a good teacher for young children and the techniques she uses were discussed in Chapter 5. As important as professional know-how are the goals, procedures, and ideas necessary to develop a stimulating curriculum. Many ideas were discussed in detail in Chapters 6 through 15.

The teacher will plan to use the available resources to buy new equipment, supplies, and teaching materials. She will, as needs arise, submit requests for painting and cleaning her classroom through appropriate channels in order to have a physical environment of high quality.

THE CHILDREN'S INFLUENCE.   Last, but not least, the children influence the program. The school is there for them. The teacher seeks ways to incorporate everything she knows about child growth and development into a day-to-day program that strives to help each child reach his fullest potential. Goals for children and characteristics of various age groups are discussed in Chapter 2, along with methods teachers have for learning about the individual child's needs.

Program Guides

A fifteen-point guide for planning an effective program for children is outlined below. Teachers may also use the guides as a checklist for evaluating their programs.

1. A good program is planned from the point of view of the whole child in his immediate environment. Whether the child is from a small or a large family, from the city or the country, from an advantaged or a disadvantaged home, his ongoing experiences are the basis for all planning. The child is taken from where he is in his learning experience and guided through sequential steps to new heights of accomplishment.

2. A good program values the child's healthy, happy, responding, secure approach to living. The teacher expects the children to respond fully and learn appropriately for their age. An important goal is for them to learn to love school and learning, teachers, and other children. She wants them to develop a self-confidence that says, "Whatever there is to do, I can do it."

3. A good program provides for the emotional growth of the child. It accepts the child as he moves from the protected, individualized home experience to a group experience. Every effort is made to help him feel secure in the new setting—this goal being paramount for some time, depending on the child's need. Parents are helped and guided during this transition period.

4. A good program balances active and quiet activities. Within large time blocks the child has freedom to select the type of activity he feels he needs. The teacher's schedule balances routines and learning experiences in logical sequences of events. Both extremes of prolonged sitting and prolonged physical exertion are avoided. Tensions build up during enforced sitting, and fatigue contributes to lack of inner control that interferes with maximum learning.

5. A good program provides appropriate opportunities for children to grow in self-direction and independence. It provides an opportunity for them to learn to make choices through experience.

6. A good program establishes and maintains limits on behavior for the protection of individuals, the group, and the learning environment. By helping a child learn the reasons for various rules, the teacher encourages him to develop selfdiscipline.

7. A good program is challenging to children's intellectual powers. They are encouraged to think, reason, remember, experiment, and generalize. The laboratory rather than the lecture is used almost exclusively.

8. A good program provides media of self-expression. Creativity is valued, fostered, and recognized in every learning center. Art, literature, and music are part of every day's activity.

9. A good program encourages children's verbal expressions. To learn words and sentence structure, children must have an opportunity to talk. Being quiet is not necessarily valued.

10. A good program provides opportunities for social development. Each child gains increased understanding of himself. He learns through experience to share, take turns, and interact with individuals and groups. He learns to choose friends and to be chosen. Yet the program also allows time for him to be alone if he desires it.

11. A good program encourages children to learn about and care for their bodies. A routine of washing, eating, resting, and eliminating is established. Safety training has priority, both to protect children and to teach them to protect themselves.

12. A good program provides opportunities for each child to use his whole body in a daily period of outdoor activity. When bad weather prevents going outdoors, adequate provision is made for gross-motor activities in semisheltered or indoor areas.

13. A good program is action packed. It is frequently noisy compared to traditional upper-age classes. The reasons action, noise, and talking are permitted may have to be explained to administrators and others so that programs for children are not curtailed unnecessarily. Carpeting, draping, or other soundproofing should be provided in classrooms to cut down the noise level.

14. A good program is fun for children. Learning themes and ma-

terials are selected that especially attract young children. Their interests determine the choice of learning experiences in most cases. When a theme or a concept lacks appeal, others replace it.

15. A good program considers the interests and needs of the parents as well as the children. The parents are helped to feel and be important to their child's growth and development. They are counseled directly and indirectly so that they will make significant contributions to the child's growth and development. Positive help is provided to individuals and groups to foster this principle. Referrals are made to appropriate agencies when the teacher recognizes a need for help she cannot provide.

Time Needed

Time is required for planning. There is a common fallacy abroad that to teach young children, one has only to drop into the classroom and set out a few toys. However, nothing could be further from the truth if the teacher expects to provide the good program set forth in the fifteen-point guide. Not only must the teacher and her staff take the time to read, to study, to generate ideas, and to make plans, but they must also prepare materials before the children arrive at school. When the children arrive before the teachers are ready, they find activities to amuse themselves—which may mean they disorganize something the teacher has partially organized for their learning. Or it more often means that the children get into some kind of trouble that starts the day off on a negative note.

A program that meets the fifteen-point guidelines does not happen by chance. It develops as the staff confers on a regular basis when no children are around to interfere with thinking. Goals must be outlined, curriculum ideas suggested, and procedures agreed upon. Long-term goals and plans, as well as short-term goals and plans, are continuously before the teachers. Obviously the day-care teacher who plans for fifty-two five-day weeks each year has a more extensive planning task than the teacher of a parent-cooperative school that meets only three days per week during the winter months. However, both teachers should have long-range plans.

Many schools make no provision in the teacher's schedule for planning or evaluating. Not infrequently, teachers are paid for the hours they spend in actual contact with children. They are not paid for time in planning and evaluation conferences. Teachers are even scheduled for as many as ten contact hours daily, with no time away from children that could be used for planning. This is a short-sighted view on the part of administrations. If teachers are to do the creative job that should be expected, they should be compensated for the

FIGURE 16–3. *Adequate planning allows assistants to relax and interact with children in their assigned area, knowing other areas are properly attended. (Texas Tech University Kindergarten.)*

planning that is basic to that job. If one cause could be singled out as the root of current criticism regarding the lack of significant learning in schools for young children, the absence of planning would surely be that cause.

Student teachers too may unrealistically assume that their "required hours" are merely the children's class hours. However, for students to make the most of their opportunity to learn with an experienced teacher at their side, they must be willing to attend the necessary planning conferences as well as to search for and prepare resource materials outside the children's class hours. Because the dual role of teaching and studying is heavy, students are well advised to lighten their other obligations during student-teaching assignments.

Tasks for the Planning Session

Teachers meeting in planning sessions should set long-range and short-range goals. Schedules and assistants' assignments require attention. Themes for activities must be suggested and agreed upon. The resources necessary for developing the themes must be pinpointed. The room's arrangement, cleanliness, and attractiveness also require work and discussion.

In planning sessions, assignments should be discussed to insure that all members of the teaching team, male and female, share equally all tasks such as affection-giving, disciplining, housekeeping, toileting, and playground teaching. Remember, all members of a team are serving as models for the children they teach.

An outgrowth of conferring is the *esprit de corps* that can develop when the teachers, aides, students, volunteers, and parent-helpers meet to plan for the children. The group has a common interest—young children. They have a particular interest—a particular group of children. Their commitment to their teaching roles will be strengthened if they can participate and share their thinking with colleagues. Part of each person's job satisfaction is derived from friendships and from appreciation for each other. Such appreciation can grow through conferring.

SETTING GOALS.   Goals have been discussed in detail in Chapter 2. Each curriculum chapter has pointed up the goals and values derived from using that medium with children. The planning sessions must change general goals into specific goals for individual children. Goals are refined further as teachers increase their knowledge of a particular group of children. Goals must be both long-term and short-term. Program planning is done yearly, periodically, weekly, and daily. Goals can be set in terms of basic concepts that can be achieved through any number of different kinds of experiences.[2]

CURRICULUM THEMES FOR ACTIVITIES.   Six themes are suggested to serve as the basis for planning throughout the year. The themes are

1. The child—his name, sex, health, safety, and relationship to his family, the school, the community, and the world.
2. The community—its people, its workers, its institutions, and its traditions, including festivals.
3. The world of plants—especially those the child sees every day and those that provide his food.
4. The world of animals—especially those the child sees every day and those that provide his food.
5. The world of machines—including vehicles and other large and small machines.
6. The physical forces in the world.

[2] Kenneth D. Wann, Miriam Selchen Dori, and Elizabeth Ann Liddle, *Fostering Intellectual Development in Young Children* (New York: Columbia University, Teachers College Press, 1962), p. 131.

FIGURE 16–4. *Planning often includes preparing a game, such as this shape-matching game, for teaching concepts to children. (Michigan State University Laboratory Preschool.)*

One approach to planning would be to use these six broad curriculum themes concurrently throughout the school year. The phrase *cumulative plan* is descriptive of this approach and was discussed in Chapter 8. The teacher envisions a calendar of the school year before her. At the beginning of the school year she starts with the simplest concept in each theme and builds on it continually throughout the year. New concepts are related to previous concepts in each theme. Themes are interrelated and coordinated. Because the themes are running concurrently, the cumulative plan enables the teacher to adapt her teaching to the children's interests and leaves flexibility to cover fascinating current events. Human relationships and the building of the child's positive self-concept are easily kept in the forefront under a cumulative plan.

Another planning approach is the *resource unit plan*, wherein one concept may be presented for a number of days or weeks, then dropped, and another concept selected. Such plans create programs that often seem choppy and unrelated. Also, the spontaneous interests of the children are often ignored. Frost and Rowland indicate that unit plans have a reputation "of being broad and shallow." [3]

[3] Joe L. Frost and G. Thomas Rowland, *Curricula for the Seventies* (Boston: Houghton Mifflin, 1969), p. 383.

Also, a unit is apt to become too long for small children, as illustrated in the following example. A four-year-old asked her mother, "Why does Miss T talk about food every day?" A study of the basic four food groups had been carried on in great detail. Although the children probably had some interest in food, the unit had become too much lecture and not enough laboratory to hold the four-year-olds' interest.

With a resource unit plan, a unit on "community helpers" might be taught in a single week. Thus children of varied interests aren't given enough opportunity to explore their interests before some topics are terminated for the year and new topics started.

In a cumulative plan, "community helpers" is a concept that is discussed from time to time. For example, throughout the year many people, including the parents of the children, are recognized for their contribution to the community.

Holidays too are one aspect of the child's community. However, with a cumulative plan, the temptation to hop from one holiday to another for major themes is avoided. It must be quite boring for children to hop from Halloween to Thanksgiving to Christmas and so on for all the years of their elementary school. Surely more child-oriented themes, with incidental activities related to holidays where they are appropriate, would be more interesting and educational over the years. Nursery school and kindergarten teachers should build their curriculum around a broad concept of what the children want and need to know—which goes far beyond the few holidays of the school year.

Prepackaged kits of teaching materials that encourage each child in every class to join in lock-step education should be avoided. Both the children's and the teacher's creativity are seriously jeopardized when the plan becomes more important than the children. Packaged materials can help teachers, but teachers should feel a definite responsibility for screening materials and adapting them to each group of children.

RESOURCE MATERIALS. Resource materials are necessary for teaching each theme. The teacher will develop files of materials and ideas for teaching numerous concepts. By developing many materials, a teacher will have sufficient ideas to use in developing teaching plans to fit a particular group of children. She will be selective—choosing, for example, just the right poem or song for her group. She need never panic because of a shortage of material.

A resource file is assembled over time. If the teacher has a good filing system, she'll have a place to file newly discovered material. When needed, the material will be easily located.

One filing system uses manila folders with a different color tab for

RESOURCE FILE COVER PAGE

Subject _____

1. Statement of concepts to be learned:

2. Vocabulary to develop:

3. Science activities:

4. Art activities:

5. Dramatic play themes:

6. Stories, poems, finger plays:

7. Songs, rhythms, records:

8. Outdoor activities:

9. Field trips and special visitors:

10. Pictures:

FIGURE 16–5. *Cover page for each resource material file.*

each of the six themes. The colored tabs are bought where office supplies are sold. For example, all animal folders are labeled with a pink label. The file may have only two folders at first: (1) domestic birds and animals, and (2) wild birds and animals. However, as the file grows, the teacher will divide the material until she has a file for each animal she has occasion to discuss with children. Figure 16–5 is the suggested cover page for each folder; it can serve as the teacher's summary of the materials the file contains. Each folder can contain:

1. A statement of the concepts to be developed.
2. Vocabulary to develop.
3. Science experiments that teach concepts.
4. Art ideas.
5. Dramatic play ideas.
6. Stories, poems, and finger plays.
7. Songs, rhythms, and records.
8. Outdoor activities.
9. Field trips or special visitors.
10. Pictures.

SCHEDULING.   Scheduling means designating events for a fixed future time. Both long-term and short-term scheduling are needed in nursery schools and kindergartens. In scheduling, the teacher looks ahead to the whole year, to a convenient period of weeks, to the week, and to the day. In addition she plans a daily routine or sequence of events that is more or less the same each day.

To schedule long-range plans it is helpful to arrange a calendar of the entire school year in such a way that the total year can be seen. Some suitable commercial calendars are available, but a teacher can make her own with a large sheet of wrapping paper. A space for notes with each date provides a ready reference for checking progress toward goals.

With the calendar before her, the teacher blocks out the number of school days. From the administration calendar she can mark holidays and other days that have significance for her planning. She might want to write in children's birthdays. Many entries can be indicated in pencil so that they can be shifted as events dictate. Events that are regular occurrences can be placed on the calendar. For example, an end-of-school picnic or the kindergarten visit to the first grade can be noted tentatively at the beginning of school. Community events, such as a Lion's Club parade that typically occurs when the children can watch, are set months in advance and can be placed on the planning calendar. The teacher's diary can

DAILY PLAN OF ACTIVITIES

Date_____

ACTIVITY   WHO IS RESPONSIBLE?

Things to remember:

Art projects:

Science projects:

Dramatic play:

Literature-language area:

Music area:

Group time:

Outdoor activity:

Transition:

Snack menu:

Diary:

FIGURE 16–6.   *Sample of form for daily plan of activities.*

provide other tentative dates, such as when to plan a spring nature walk.

Periodic planning may mean a month, six weeks, a quarter, or a semester—whatever is a convenient administrative time unit in a particular school. For example, in a university laboratory school where plans involve the schedule of university students, the students' schedule also becomes the period for planning for the children. If student teachers typically assume certain levels of responsibility at different points during the term, these dates are marked on the planning calendar.

The teacher and the assistants meet on a weekly basis to plan the following five days' activities. Each day is planned in considerable detail at that time. See Figure 16–6. It is understood that plans can be changed to meet day-to-day situations. When interesting learning opportunities arise unexpectedly, the plans are flexible enough to

WEEKLY ACTIVITY PLAN					
Week of_____					
	MON.	TUES.	WED.	THURS.	FRI.
Art:					
Science:					
Dramatic play:					
Lit.-lang:					
Music area:					
Group time:					
Outdoor act.:					
Transition:					
Snack:					
Trips:					
Planning notes:					

THEMES   The child learns about: 1. Himself   3. Animals   5. Machines
2. Other people   4. Plants   6. Physical forces

FIGURE 16–7.   *Sample of form for weekly activity plan.*

incorporate them. However, advanced planning helps assure a program with educational goals for children. Some teachers prefer to be able to assess the week at a glance and would like to use a form similar to the one in Figure 16–7.

An *activity plan* could be made for every learning experience offered in the school. It is a challenging exercise to look at each piece of equipment or learning episode in the school and attempt to make an activity plan. Each of the ideas offered in Part Two of this book will help with this thinking. Figure 16–8 is an example of a completed plan for using one type of equipment. The items entered under each heading on this sample activity plan will vary depending on the activity you select. For many activities, you can refer to the curriculum chapters to help you formulate relevant and rather complete entries fitting the requirements of each heading. It is critical that you think through each step in the activity plan. Unless you are highly experienced with children and with the activity, you will readily cope with the variety of children's responses and behaviors only if you are super prepared.

In planning a finger painting project, for example, you will find in Chapter 7 all the information for your activity plan. You will find that this medium gives children an opportunity to practice small motor skills and to create their own designs. These could be your *Developmental Goals* for a particular day. Your *Objective* for children on a particular day could be to manipulate the fingerpaints with fingers, hands, and arms and create a design of their own choosing. Likewise, *Materials Needed, Procedures*, and *Guidance Suggestions* can be found in each chapter where a particular activity is discussed.[4]

The beginning student may want to try developing several activity plans, especially if she expects to be responsible for certain learning projects. The experienced teacher may need only to note "spring nature walk" on her calendar to know the amount of preparation she'll want to make for herself and the children before that date arrives. Each teacher does planning. One may write more on paper, whereas another carries the ideas in her head. The amount of written planning will depend on the experience of the teacher.

Besides planning the activities for each day, the earliest planning sessions give attention to the daily schedule or sequence of events. Once established, this routine may remain in effect for a number of months, perhaps with only minor alterations. This type of scheduling

---

[4] If additional information and help with activity plans is desired, see the introductory section of the second edition of *A Laboratory Workbook for Introduction to Early Childhood Education* by Verna Hildebrand, Macmillan Publishing Co., Inc., 1976.

ACTIVITY PLAN

(with sample plan)

NAME OF ACTIVITY: *Parquetry blocks*
Developmental Goal:
    1. Vocabulary development.
    2. Perceptual development.
Objectives:
    1. To match colors.
    2. To match shapes.
    3. To name colors.
    4. To name shapes.

MATERIALS NEEDED: *3 parquetry sets*

PROCEDURE:
    Place parquetry sets in an inviting location in the room.
    Sit with children. Observe their use of the sets.
    Let them discover and teach each other.
    Answer any questions. Note their use of vocabulary.
    Encourage naming of shapes and colors.

GUIDANCE SUGGESTIONS INCLUDING LIMITS:
    Play a game: "Show me the (*red square*)."
    Encourage them to make their own designs after they accomplish matching.

SPECIAL OBJECTIVES:
    To see if Amanda is able to name colors.
    To see if John can count to four. Encourage his practice.

EVALUATION:
    Hide shape and/or color—ask child to name it when it is uncovered.
    Check chart to see which ones they know.

SUGGESTIONS FOR FUTURE USE:

FIGURE 16–8.　*Sample of a form for the activity plan.*

was discussed in Chapter 4 for the benefit of students who might be observing or participating on a daily basis. Figures 16–9 and 16–10 are repeated from that chapter to bring together a more complete picture of scheduling here.

DAILY SCHEDULE

A.M.	P.M.	
9:00– 10:00	1:00– 2:00	Self-selected activity indoors.
10:00	2:00	Cleanup time (can vary a few minutes either way). As the child finishes helping with cleanup, he goes to the toilet, if necessary, and washes his hands.
10:15– 10:25	2:15– 2:25	Snack. With older children, sharing time * goes on at the same time as snack.
10:25– 10:45	2:25– 2:45	The children move to a story group or groups. They sit on the floor. They select a book for "reading" as they pass the shelf. They look at the book or just talk quietly. The teacher finishes the period with some songs, a special story, planning, or discussion.
10:45– 11:30	2:45– 3:30	Outdoor self-selected activity.
11:30– 11:40	3:30– 3:40	Cleanup time. Preparation to go home.
11:45	3:45	Dismissal.

* Sharing time—A period when children are called on to share some article or news they have brought from home. Discussed in detail in the chapter on language arts.

FIGURE 16–9. *Sample of a daily schedule.*

Three to six large time blocks are suggested for the schedule or sequence of events. Chapter 4 discusses the number of time blocks and the amount of time contained in each. Briefly, decisions depend upon:

1. The goals for the group.
2. The special needs of the group.
3. The time of day the children arrive.
4. How long the children stay at school.

TIME BLOCK PLAN *

Time Block I   Self-selected Activity (Indoors)

      Art   Music
      Science   Dramatic play
      Table games   Small, wheeled objects
      Blocks   Language arts
      Books

Time Block II   Teacher-Instigated Activity

      Cleanup
      Toileting, washing hands
      Snack
      Quiet time:
        looking at books
        music
        storytime and discussions

Time Block III   Self-selected Activity (Outdoors)

      Climbing   Riding tricycles
      Swinging   Sand play
      Running   Science

Time Block IV   Lunch Period

      Washing hands, toileting
      Resting prior to lunch
      Eating
      Washing hands
      Going home or preparing for nap

Time Block V   Nap Time

      Dressing for bed   Toileting
      Sleeping   Dressing

Time Block VI   Self-selected Activity

      New activities
      Snack
      Outdoor play

* Blocks I, II, and III are typical of half-day programs in nursery schools and kindergartens where lunch is not served. The six blocks are more typical of day-care centers. Blocks I and III may be interchanged for variation and for meeting the needs of the children as discussed elsewhere.

FIGURE 16–10.   *Sample of a time block plan.*

5. What happens at home before the children come to school each day.
6. The season of the year.

PLANNING FOR ASSISTANTS.   A teaching team of a minimum of two adults per group has been the rule in nursery school classes for decades. Unfortunately kindergarten teachers have often been expected to manage alone. However, Head Start recommends two adults per fifteen children. Today most teachers are able to involve others in their programs. Many have paid aides; others have community volunteers, high school and university students who assist in various capacities, and parents who volunteer or serve as part of a cooperative plan. It is up to both the teacher and the assistants to make most meaningful use of all the available help.

The teacher will want the best learning situation for the children. Assistants extend in numerous ways the efforts the teacher can make for the children. She will want each assistant to make a contribution to the children's learning and to have a satisfying experience with the children.

If at all possible, the assistants should be involved in the weekly planning. They need to feel they know what is going on. It is a very uncomfortable feeling when a youngster says, or implies, "I've been here longer than you have, I know the rules," as one child was heard to say.

Conferences before each day of school are essential for those adults who work directly with the children. Such conferences are more important than ever when individuals have missed the weekly planning sessions. All will feel much more comfortable knowing the goals for the day—for the group and for individuals. Helpers must be advised of unusual circumstances that confront certain children, such as Jimmy's mother going to the hospital or John's father leaving for the army.

Adults can choose the learning center for which they will be responsible. Such assignments may be agreed upon in weekly planning conferences. Each individual may assume the responsibility for bringing in the materials needed to enhance the learning in a particular area of responsibility. Regular teachers can assume responsibility in areas offering new learning situations, whereas others take the areas that offer experiences more familiar to the children and for which guidance is more predictable.

It seems to be more effective from the children's point of view for each adult to be assigned responsibility for an area of the room or yard. For example, if the adult's assignment is in the language arts area, such a plan makes it acceptable for her to remain in the language arts area with a child even though she hears chaos reigning in the block room. She can assume that a competent adult is in charge in the block room and will send out an SOS if assistance is needed.

An alternative plan is to let everyone move where "needed." In such a plan, however, teachers may never sit down and take time to extend the learning of children. They feel obligated to other parts of the school—particularly to trouble spots. When they hear chaos in the block room, they are likely to flock there. As a result, less troublesome children who remain absorbed in some task may be slighted, or some area needing the watchful eye of an adult may be left unattended.

Of course, when no children are at work in a learning center, the adult should feel free to observe or assist in other areas until children again show interest in her assigned center. However, she may take advantage of the lull to reorganize her center, to bring out some fresh materials, or even to clean it up if a transition time is approaching.

Space is provided in the Daily Plan sheet (Figure 16–6) for noting the assignment of assistants. Some teachers write the daily plan on a blackboard so that all helpers can see at a glance who is taking responsibility for a given area. Such posting avoids duplication of effort or concern that no one has an area covered.

All assistants should make their preferences and talents known so that their capabilities can be utilized in the best possible way for the good of the children. If all assistants complete a card such as that in Figure 16–11, they can be contacted for special projects.

Of course, in all groups teachers and assistants should be learning along with the children. Each should be willing to volunteer for an activity in which she does not feel she is an expert. For example, a person with little confidence in music should be encouraged to volunteer to work in the music area. Other adults can support her until she gains the confidence she needs to carry on alone.

A daily summing-up session is required at the close of each day. Teachers and assistants alike need a chance to reflect on the day, ask questions, share observations, and apply theoretical knowledge to the practical situation. The daily summing up is even more important when assistants come and go on a day-to-day basis. Goals for future days can be suggested at this time. For example, the staff may conclude, "We must help shy little Sara find a friend."

ROOM ARRANGEMENT, CLEANLINESS, AND ATTRACTIVENESS.   The important tasks of planning conferences are effective room arrangement, ensuring cleanliness, and providing attractiveness. Details regarding room arrangement were discussed in Chapter 4 under "Set ting the Stage." As a teacher starts a new group of young children, she will find it important to keep the room arrangement the same for a while to give the children security in their new environment. However, after they are comfortable in school they will enjoy variety. Some weeks the housekeeping area and music areas can change places. A little shifting may create interest for a child who seems not to have noticed an area before. Changing the schedule or sequence of events will also add variety, although it also creates uncertainties among the children, which teachers should anticipate in advance.

New objects on shelves and on bulletin boards can give the children plenty to look for as they arrive each day. Children's art, neatly and colorfully arranged, should be changed regularly.

Beauty should be part of the environment. A tacky, unpainted look can change overnight if a civic group with a do-good bent lends a hand. Parents can be enlisted to help. Student groups may enjoy assisting the teacher to improve the attractiveness of a classroom.

INFORMATION CARD

Name _____

Address _____ Phone _____

Group _____

Day and hour of assignment _____

Yes_____ No_____ Do you have a car that could be used for field trips?

Yes_____ No_____ Do you have a talent that you could share with the children?

List talents and describe:

Your personal goals for this term:

FIGURE 16–11. *Sample of an information card.*

Teachers should seek such sources of assistance when maintenance funds are inadequate.

Cleanliness and order should be important to the teacher. The children can help with getting materials back in their proper places each day. However, a continuous effort is required of the housekeeping staff to be sure that finger marks are washed off furnishings and walls, that wilted flowers are tossed out, that broken equipment is sent out for repair, and that general order is maintained in room, yard, and storage areas.

Evaluating a Program

Rosenthal and Jacobson reported in *Pygmalion in the Classroom* that teachers' positive expectations influenced children's school performance positively.[5] If Rosenthal and Jacobson are correct, then teachers should have firm expectations that each child will make progress. Teachers will look for evidences of progress to guide their planning. To begin the evaluation process they will ask: What has each child learned? How is the group progressing? What things can be taught better? Where does the program need changing? Are goals being met?

The comment "The children enjoyed that a lot" is frequently heard in evaluation conferences. However, children also "enjoy" an amusement park; but, one might argue, that little of educational significance is learned there. Schools differ from amusement parks. They have educational goals. Goals for progress in every area of the child's development must be considered along with his enjoyment of the school situation.

Evaluation of a general and specific nature should be done by the teaching staff on a continuing basis, not left until the end of a term or a school year. Only through evaluation can the teacher determine if educational progress is taking place.

General evaluation can begin by a checking of the daily plans against the diary of actual events. This provides a picture of what there was available to learn. Even a short diary written at the bottom or on the back of a daily plan sheet will provide information for evaluation. To be realistic, a diary generally must be brief, otherwise teachers won't have time to keep it.

A regular check of daily and weekly plans and diaries against the fifteen-point guidelines discussed earlier in this chapter will provide information on where a program is adequate and inadequate. By summarizing the daily plans the teacher can see at a glance how

[5] Robert Rosenthal and Lenore Jacobson, *Pygmalion in the Classroom* (New York: Holt, Rinehart and Winston, 1968).

FIGURE 16–12. *Planning creative play equipment makes any playground more versatile, interesting, and educational. (Kansas State University Child Development Laboratory School. For further description of this playground see Ivalee H. McCord, "A Creative Playground," Young Children, Vol. 26, No. 6, August 1971, pp. 342–347.)*

much variety she has offered the group. For example, if she realizes that she has repeated the same art projects, she can make efforts to bring in some new ones or add something new to the old ones.

Knowing what has been offered does not tell the teacher what individual children have learned. Teachers also must make an effort to know how individual children are progressing.

Teacher's Observations

Chapter 12 gives numerous suggestions regarding the teacher's observation notes and their value. Through routinely observing each child and recording evidence of progress toward educational goals, teachers can begin to assess a child's progress. Notes will help teachers in conferences with staff and parents.

Staff Conferences

It is helpful for teachers to get together to discuss individual children to gain the benefit of the thinking of others regarding each child. An outsider may be asked to observe and take notes on certain children to add more objective insight into the handling of behavior and learning problems. University student observers can contribute to such conferences. Students gain from learning to relate theory to practice.

Testing

A serious problem with nearly any evaluation is its subjective nature. For that reason those desiring more objective measures turn to tests. Tests taken at the beginning of a term are compared to those taken at the end. This is called pre- and posttesting. It would be helpful if there were more reliable testing materials to measure the growth that takes place in young children during the years they are in nursery school and kindergarten. Regardless of numerous inadequacies, pre- and posttesting is being done increasingly in schools across the country. Perhaps eventually, with improvements, more confidence can be placed in the results of such measures.

There are some problems encountered in the testing of young children. In the first place, the children are too young for the more easily administered pencil and paper tests that are common in upper age groups. When paper and pencil tests are used with kindergarteners, the teacher cannot be sure that the children completely understand the directions. The children may copy from their neighbor, making their test an inaccurate measure.

Individual testing is time consuming and rarely done on any scale. Individual testing, too, has its drawbacks. A teacher rarely has time to test all the children. Outside testers must not only know tests, they must have considerable knowledge of children generally and be willing to take time to get acquainted with individuals before starting to test. Testers may play with some children several hours before the children are ready to be tested. Even removing a child from the classroom to a testing room may cause anxiety and reduce motivation because he'd rather be back in the room with his friends.

Tests generally tend to be oriented toward white middle-class society, and therefore may be seriously unfair to others. Even so, the IQ score obtained from tests given at a young age has very low predictive value, according to data from the longitudinal study by Bayley.[6] In fact, Frost and Rowland predict that "The I.Q. will be abandoned as false and unworthy—especially as educators realize that it is a sample of behavior taken at a specific time under limiting conditions. Educators will cease to attribute to the I.Q. the power to

---

[6] Nancy Bayley, "On the Growth of Intelligence," *American Psychologist,* **10:**12 (1955), 805–818.

predict or determine the progress of a child; actually, the I.Q. never had such power, but it was used in a perverted way." [7]

The IQ tests have been criticized because they were developed with a white middle-class bias that makes them grossly unfair to children from other cultural orientations. Adrian Dove, a black sociologist, attempted to point this up with what has become known as the "Chitling Test." [8] This is a test for whites that uses black English. In a humorous fashion, Dove has shown how the cultural bias influences one's score on a test. Therefore, until testing can eliminate such bias, one should not take its results too seriously.

If teachers expect to use test results, they should be aware of the shortcomings of the tests. They should know how to interpret the results. Psychologists generally agree that it is unwise to give parents number scores from tests because they use them incorrectly, remember them inaccurately, and may use them for their own aggrandizement.

Two examples illustrate even teachers' confusion with test scores. A parent was told, "Betty didn't do well on her math test." The mother thought of the "S" mark (satisfactory) the teacher had put on the report grade and asked, "What did she make on her test?" The teacher replied, "Only fifty per cent." On further investigation, the mother, who was more knowledgeable than most, found that the teacher meant that the child ranked at "the 50th percentile" on math as compared to ranking at the "76th percentile" on her reading. The meaning of the percentile score was that Betty, when compared to all other children taking that test, scored in the middle of the group on mathematical reasoning and in the top one-fourth in reading.

Another teacher interpreted a score of 56 on a reading-readiness test to mean that the child had an IQ of 56. The mother naturally reacted with considerable alarm to this report. She had worked as an aide in a school for retarded children and had heard IQ scores bandied about. She had a vague notion of how scores were applied. When, after many worry-filled days, she talked to someone more informed, she learned that the teacher had confused percentile rank with IQ score.

Certainly, if tests are to be used, they should be administered expertly, interpreted correctly, and used in conjunction with other information, especially when recommendations regarding a child's future are being made.

---

[7] Joe L. Frost and G. Thomas Rowland, *Curricula for the Seventies* (Boston: Houghton Mifflin, 1969), p. 435.

[8] "Taking the Chitling Test," *Annual Editions Readings in Human Development '73–'74* (Guilford, Conn.: Dushkin Publishing Group, Inc. 1973), p. 298.

Reporting to Parents

A face-to-face conference is much more satisfactory for reporting a child's progress to parents than is a written form. Schools are allowing released time for such conferences in many schools today. By meeting parents in a conference, the teacher can help them think through possible alternative solutions to problems. In a written report the parents' reaction to information could cause negative instead of the desired positive result for the child.

For example, one kindergarten teacher checked "lacks social skills" on the report card of a quiet, withdrawn child. Had she mentioned this problem to his parents, she might have noted their defensive reaction and been able to suggest remedies that would have helped the child improve his social skills. However, the report card merely went home to the parents, who reacted by punishing the child. They kept him in the house every night after school instead of allowing him to play in the courtyard with his friends of the neighborhood. Surely the parents reacted in the worst possible way to the teacher's good intention. For the child's best interests it would have been better to have discussed the problem with his parents along with suggestions for helping the child.

Parent conferences require planning. The teacher must conscientiously think through each child's progress. She must have examples to support her conclusions regarding his growth in each area. She may find the conference more helpful for learning from the parent about the child and the impact of the program than she finds it for reporting. Conferring with parents requires different skills than teaching children, and teachers should spend some time developing those skills.

Conclusion

Planning is of utmost importance if meaningful programs are to be developed for young children. Goals must be clearly defined. Children's developmental tasks must be understood. Procedures for accomplishing the goals must be incorporated into action on an hourly, daily, weekly, periodic, and yearly basis.

Planning includes determining themes for activities, collecting resource materials, designating persons to be responsible for learning in each center, and arranging the room appropriately.

Evaluating children's progress is a difficult but necessary part of the teacher's responsibility. Reservations are suggested regarding the use of tests with young children. Teachers' observation notes should be used in addition to tests.

Parents can be helped to react positively to a teacher's suggestion if reports are made in private conferences where various plans can be discussed for alleviating the child's difficulties.

ADDITIONAL READINGS

FULLER, ELIZABETH M. *What Research Says to the Teacher About the Kindergarten*. Washington, D.C.: National Education Association, 1961.

GRAY, SUSAN W., and others. *Before First Grade: The Early Training Project for Culturally Disadvantaged Children*. New York: Teachers College Press, Columbia University, 1966.

HARTRUP, WILLARD W., and NANCY L. SMOTHERGILL (eds.). *The Young Child*. Washington, D.C.: National Association for Education of the Young Child, 1967.

HYMES, JAMES L., JR. *Teaching the Child Under Six*. Columbus, Ohio: Charles E. Merrill Publishing Co., 1974.

LAW, NORMA, et al. *Basic Propositions for Early Childhood Education*. Washington, D.C.: Association for Childhood Education International, 1965.

LEEPER, SARAH H., RUTH J. DALES, DORA SKIPPER, and RALPH L. WITHERSPOON. *Good Schools for Young Children*. New York: Macmillan Publishing Co., Inc., 1974.

NIMNICHT, GLEN, ORALIE MCAFEE, and JOHN MEIER. *The New Nursery School*. New York: General Learning Corp., 1969.

RASSMUSSEN, MARGARET (ed.). *Play—Children's Business: Guide to Selection of Toys and Games—Infants to Twelve-Year-Olds*. Washington, D.C.: Association for Childhood Education International, 1963.

SUNDERLINE, SYLVIA (ed.). *Toward Better Kindergartens*. Washington, D.C.: Association for Childhood Education International, 1967.

TARNAY, ELIZABETH D. *What Does the Nursery School Teacher Teach?* Washington, D.C.: National Association for the Education of Young Children, 1965.

TAYLOR, BARBARA J. *A Child Goes Forth*. Provo, Utah: Brigham Young University Press, 1975.

PART THREE

Professional Considerations

Teacher-Parent Relations

THERE is a growing consensus that efforts of home and school must be united if each child is to benefit fully from his educational opportunity. Hymes says, "We have to end the separation of home and school. Too much is at stake to let the foolish lack of communication persist. The left hand must know what the right is doing; the two hands must work together."[1] Nowhere in the long educational continuum is the parent-teacher relationship more important than in the child's early years. Being the child's first teacher, the nursery school or kindergarten teacher is in a strategic position to set the stage for early and continuing parent-school interaction. Fathers as well as mothers are encouraged to participate.

When university students hear of the importance of teachers' relations with parents, they ask: "Should the teacher be the one who initiates the parent-teacher relationship?" "How do I learn to relate to parents?" "How can teachers encourage parents to help a child?" "What do I do if parents don't seem interested in their child's schooling?"

Parents too have their concerns about relating to teachers. They hope the teacher will like their child and that he will like her. They hope that she knows subject matter and how to get it across to children. Parents worry when problems come up. Will the teacher react to a discussion of a child's failure by taking offense? Will she blame them, his parents? Will they appear to be asking for special favors for their child if they seek help?

Teachers find that some parents have a very accepting leave-it-to-the-experts attitude. Such parents believe, and teach their children, that "the teacher knows best." They rarely criticize the school. Should the child have trouble, such parents usually feel he deserves it.

---

[1] James L. Hymes, Jr., *Teaching the Child Under Six* (Columbus, Ohio: Merrill, 1974), p. 80.

Parents who have had little formal education are more likely to be tolerant, or accepting, of the school. They hesitate to go to school even to enroll a child. They have experienced many rebuffs in their lives and may have failed in school. By avoiding school, they protect themselves from being hurt further. They have real and imagined reasons for not taking advantage of a teacher's overtures toward them.

On the other hand, some parents expect to be involved in educational matters. They are concerned lest their child be unprepared for the future he faces. If they disagree with the goals or the methods of the school, they say so. Highly educated parents will make more demands for their children. Yet they may be so busy in their business or professional lives that very little time is given to school matters. For instance, some parents say that their days are filled with meetings and that they would rather stay at home with their family in the evening than hire a baby-sitter in order to go out to a parents' meeting.

Plans for relating to children's parents, like plans for educating children, must be based on knowledge of the families concerned. This chapter will focus on relations between parents and teacher more than on parent education, because of the belief that the teacher's first task is to relate to parents. Education may follow. However, the teacher may derive more education than the parent. Ideally, a meaningful two-way dialogue will develop and be of substantial benefit to the teacher, the parents, and the child.

Values of Teacher-Parent Relationships

Each teacher wishes to build the most relevant program for each child. By getting to know each child's parents and his home situation, the teacher can more accurately assess the experiences the child has had before coming to school. She uses this background to build stepping-stones to new experiences.

Reporting to parents on a child's school experience initiates exchanges with parents from which teachers gain valuable feedback regarding programs.

By knowing parents, the teachers can better encourage parental efforts on behalf of a child's education. Through various techniques teachers can help parents use the many hours at home with the child to further education.

As teachers and parents get acquainted, they will learn of each other's educational goals and values. Ideally, less conflict will arise between the two to cause confusion in the child's mind.

FIGURE 17–1. *Short parent-teacher conferences may be held when the parent picks up the child at school. Appointments for longer conferences can be set at this time.* (*Michigan State University Laboratory Preschool.*)

Even some highly educated parents have little knowledge of or appreciation for little children. Teachers can help all parents develop the understanding necessary for enjoying their children more fully.

The parent-cooperative nursery schools and kindergartens have a long and positive influence on parents. In addition to the objectives for the growth and development of the children, the cooperatives have objectives for both parents' growth. Parents often mention the changes in themselves that have occurred as a result of having their child in the cooperative nursery school or kindergarten. For example, you hear parents commenting, "I didn't know anything about little kids, I had never been around any but my own, until I came to the coop." "I was scared. I was afraid I'd do something that would harm the children!" "I got a lot out of talking with the other parents." "My husband and I made friends in the coop that have been our best friends for years."

Parents in cooperatives learn about child development, about teaching children, about curriculum, about supplies and equipment, and about financing the operation. Such ideas usually elude parents who choose other types of schools for their children. For many the financial savings offered by the coop make the difference between school and no school for their children. Cooperatives encourage a heavy dose of self-education for parents by offering them books to browse in and discussion groups and workshops in which they can share their most recent thoughts concerning their child's development.

From its beginning, Project Head Start encouraged teachers to know and work with parents. Many community resources have been coordinated through the school to improve the living situation of the Head Start children and their families.[2] Many day-care centers are making creative efforts to communicate with the parents of the children they serve.

Teachers add to their own understanding of children, parents, and families by making the effort to develop good relationships. Even though each family is unique, like the individuals in them, each experience improves the teacher's ability to relate to other families in the future.

Parents' Presence During Beginning Days

Schools have differing procedures for introducing new children to a group. Most nursery schools introduce only a few children at a time. This procedure gives the teacher time to relate to each child and leaves plenty of space for a mother to stay with her child until both the teacher and the mother feel the child is confident enough to remain for a period of time without the mother's support. Mothers without jobs or without other children at home may prolong this introductory period longer than the child needs, unless the teacher is able to help the mother in the separation process. Some mothers feel guilty, thinking that "good" mothers take care of children at home

[2] *Project Head Start Points for Parents*, Booklet No. 10 (Washington, D.C.: Office of Economic Opportunity, 1967); *Project Head Start Parents Are Needed*, Booklet No. 6 (Washington, D.C.: Office of Economic Opportunity, 1967).

when they can. Or a mother may be reluctant to leave her child with a stranger. Therefore it is essential for the teacher to communicate her regard for the mother and the child and reassure them that she can handle the situation. She can, of course, assure a mother that she will telephone her if any need arises.

Debbie was an example of a three-year-old who was reluctant to enter nursery school. A number of weeks were needed before she felt secure in the school. Her previous social experience had always included her mother. In fact, the parents had taken her many places but had never left her alone, even to stay with her grandmother. Intellectually, Debbie's mother wanted Debbie to go to school, but psychologically she hesitated to leave her. The process was not rushed. Some days the mother stayed all morning. Sometimes she left for an hour, then returned to take Debbie home. Debbie could easily have become a nursery school dropout if the teacher had displayed less confidence in herself, in the child, or in the mother. Eventually they were rewarded for their patience when Debbie stood at the nursery school door shouting, "Let me in," with a smile of confidence lighting her face.

Teachers in day-care centers will seldom have the time to let a child adjust as Debbie was able to do. They must use every technique available to help the child feel secure. Part of the problem is an outgrowth of the hurry-scurry felt in households when mothers are getting ready to go to work. Mothers have mixed feelings as they rush their child off to the day-care center and themselves off to work. Mothers often leave behind many undone tasks that may lead to guilt feelings.

Sometimes the day-care teacher's role is to help the parents make parting easier for the child. If the mother has time to stay during the introductory phase, she should do so. If she is required to leave because of her job, she should go. If she says she is going to leave and then lingers if the child cries, she teaches him that crying will keep her longer. Parting may be difficult for both child and mother; but an off-again-on-again leave-taking only complicates the matter for all.

Some parents may want to sneak out and leave the child at school. However, it is far better for the long-run adjustment if the child waves a tearful good-bye as he is held in the teacher's arms than for the child to discover suddenly that the parent is gone.

Kindergarten children often need a gradual introduction to school. If this is their first school experience they may experience anxiety, but usually not of the duration felt by a younger child. Short days, staggered schedules, or many assistants may help the kindergarten teacher as she introduces a new group to the new environment.

Types of Contacts with Parents

Initial Meeting

Parents may base their first opinions concerning the teacher on little information. Perhaps they notice her at a PTA meeting. They may ask other parents about her personal qualities, her teaching ability, and whether their child liked her. They gain some idea of the teacher's patience as she answers their questions during a telephone call. Because teachers have a professional obligation to the public, they should be consistently patient, fair, and friendly with parents wherever they meet them.

Home Visit

The teacher may arrange to meet the family at home. She calls in advance and asks if she can come to "say hello" and get acquainted with her new pupil. A home visit has many lasting values for helping the child make an adjustment to the school situation with a minimum of difficulty. Both child and parents will feel more at ease in their home than elsewhere. The home is more congenial for a discussion focused on the child. Before the teacher has any information to give, she gives parents an opportunity to inform her.

The home visit can help the teacher assess the child's psychological position in the home. She may sense sibling competition or favoritism as she observes interaction between family members. If the child appears to be overprotected, this may become apparent. Parents may volunteer information on a problem area as the child wanders out of the room.

Parents and child also learn from the visit. The next time they see the teacher they will know her. They can tell that she likes children. They can ask questions they might hesitate to ask in a strange setting or when others seem to be waiting for their turn to speak to the teacher. If the teacher can put parents at ease during the initial home visit, they will look forward to other contacts with her. Additional home visits are planned as needed. For further details regarding home visits see Chapter 3.

School Visit

Some teachers arrange their first meeting with a child and parent in the school setting. This plan brings the focus more quickly to the school, its equipment, and its procedures. The meeting should be private, with an effort made to learn about the child and the family. Both parents and children will feel more at ease if they have had a chance to look over the school setting when no other children are there.

Parents should always feel welcome at school. They should be invited to attend for a moment or an entire period, at their convenience. They should be able to arrive unannounced. The school program can continue on a routine basis with no alteration because of the visitor. When parents are told that they should call before visiting, they may feel unwelcome or worry that children are mistreated when visitors aren't present.

The parent's presence during a visit, or on the day a parent-co-operator participates, may cause some difficulties in the handling of that parent's child. Children sometimes exhibit dependent behavior that is not characteristic of them. It is natural for a child to want to be near his parent. It may be difficult for him to share his parent, as is necessary in parent-cooperatives. If the parent reacts by admonishing him to "run and play," the child may feel rejected. It is best to work *with* his feeling of possessiveness rather than *against* it. During a parent's visit, for example, the teacher can encourage the child to give his parent a guided tour. She can encourage the parent to follow the child and sit near him until the excitement wears off.[3]

When a parent brings a special exhibit, or in other ways helps with the program, that parent's child should be involved in the plans for the day. The child can help his parent get materials ready or share the "secret" of a special event that will surprise the other children. Parents should be aware that one of the values of their participating in special events is the recognition their child receives. If they don't understand this, they may be embarrassed by what seems like the child's inability to share. Talking to a child about "sharing" does nothing to ease his jealous feelings. Once the child feels that having his parent help others is no threat to his position, he'll be able to go about his business as usual.

If other children do not seem to understand why the visitor's child gets special attention, a simple explanation such as the following may be all that is necessary: "You know how you like to be near your mother when she comes? That's how John feels today."

Casual Visits

Many casual visits between teacher and parents take place as children are delivered and picked up at school. Visits may occur in the supermarket or at social events. At such times the teacher can report pleasurable moments the child has had in school. Parents may report an unusual family event that aids the teacher as she works with the child during the day. Because the teacher must focus attention

---

[3] For a touching account of a mother whose child felt hurt when she had to share her mother with others, read, "But You're MY Mommy," *Early Years,* 4:6 (February 1974), 52, 62–63.

FIGURE 17–2. *Parent-cooperative nursery schools and kindergartens invite parents to learn as they work with children and visit with other parents. (Michigan State University Spartan Cooperative Nursery School.)*

on the children and the other parents who are coming and going, there is little time for discussing difficulties a child might be having. However, an appointment for a conference can be arranged, or the teacher may ask the parent to call when it is convenient to talk.

Telephone Conversations

It is a rare parent that would abuse the teacher's invitation to "Call me whenever there is any problem that concerns your child and school. If I can be of help I want to be." The "on-call" attitude of professional teachers separates them from nine-to-five workers. Teachers know that children sometimes go home confused or with real or imagined slights. They may leave a dearest treasure at school. A call to the teacher can straighten things out so that the family's evening goes smoother. Parents should feel that it is all right to call the teacher at home.

Some parents in our mobile society live far away from family or friends with whom they might discuss their children. A call to the teacher may help that parent think through some difficulty. Teachers can encourage friendships between mothers, which will help alleviate the loneliness of a mother in a strange city.

Conferences

When parent conferences are the rule rather than the exception, parents will approach teachers with less anxiety. According to D'Evelyn, "With this procedure all children—not just those with adjustment problems—receive the benefit of thinking and help from those two very important influences in their lives." [4] The following letter is an example of the invitation to a conference that parents receive:

Dear Parents,

Now that we have had two months of school, I'd like for us to get together so we can talk about how your child has been getting along since school started. Private conferences are being arranged with each child's parents. This conference and others will be used in place of formal report cards.

Your conference is scheduled for   Nov. 2 at 2:30 p.m.   in my office—106 Wilson School. If this hour is inconvenient, you may trade with another family or call me (345–9996) for a better time.

Volunteers will supervise all of the children in the classroom during our conference. As you recall, to enable teachers to hold conferences, there is no school during the afternoons next week.

Please do not alarm your child about this conference. You can say, "Your teacher and I are going to talk about what you like at school. What shall I tell her?"

Of course, both parents are invited to the conference when it is possible for you both to attend.

Sincerely,
Mrs. Verna Hildebrand
Teacher

Note the content of the letter. The date, hour, and place of conference are stated clearly. The letter suggests some flexibility by letting parents exchange times or call for a change in schedule. The purpose of the conference is stated, as is the fact that all parents are involved. Baby-sitting has been arranged that will help parents solve one problem they always have when the child is not in school and when they may have several younger children. Also of importance is the advice regarding interpreting the conference to the child. Having worked to develop rapport with a child, the teacher would hope that the parents would not say, "Your teacher is going to tell me how bad you've been."

---

[4] Katherine D'Evelyn, *Meeting Children's Emotional Needs* (Englewood Cliffs, N.J.: Prentice-Hall, 1957), p. 142.

The teacher's purpose for arranging the private conference is to learn the parent's impressions of the program, to gain a better understanding of the effect of the program on the child, to get more information about a child, and to encourage parents' understanding and support of the program.

Parents will feel some obligation to attend conferences. The conferences should not be threatening to the parent. Discussion should be kept to the stated purposes unless parents indicate other things they wish to discuss.

Parents will be anxious to know how the child does in school and how he relates to other children and the teachers. They may want some indication and reassurance that he is a good learner. They may be concerned with reading or writing.

Teachers should make thoughtful preparations for conferences. They should collect some samples of a child's work and make notes on his participation in school. When there are problems that must be discussed, the teacher should think about possible solutions ahead of time in order to be able to make suggestions for discussion. Without suggestions for alleviating a difficulty, some problems may better remain undisclosed.

Teachers should avoid making a premature diagnosis of the cause of a child's behavior. One mother was completely surprised when her child's teacher telephoned and asked whether she and her husband were having marital difficulty. The mother replied, "No. Why?" Then the teacher explained that their daughter was acting strangely, so she "just wondered." Months later the mother was still wondering what the child did or said that prompted the teacher to ask. Certainly, if the couple had been having problems, this was hardly an appropriate approach.

When the teacher has called the conference, she will start the discussion by saying something like, "Now that we've had a few weeks of school, I thought it would be helpful for us to talk together. How do you feel things are going for Jack?" This question is usually easy for parents. They talk about things the child likes. The teacher can then ask, "How about things that have bothered Jack—things he didn't like? Do you think he's getting too tired?" By inviting negative reactions she lets the parents know that she isn't just looking for praise for her program.

Nearly every parent enjoys talking about his child to someone who wants to listen. During the first conference the teacher would hope to convince parents that she is deeply interested in the child, knows what the child has been doing at school, and likes the child and his parents.

While talking with parents, it is of greatest importance to avoid arousing their defensive feelings. Such feelings are aroused if the child is criticized. There are ways of stating a concern regarding a child's behavior without fixing blame or being angry or annoyed. When too forcefully confronted with a child's problem behavior, the defensive parent may deny that the child behaves that way at home and suggest that the behavior must be the product of the school situation. Then comes the teacher's turn to be defensive. Sometimes the teacher may better say, after citing examples, "These are the things we see. Do you have any indication as to why John feels this way at school?" Not having to defend themselves, parents may volunteer the information that they are having similar problems at home.

Parents may say, "I know I'm to blame." To which the teacher can say, "Rather than fix a blame, let's think together about how we might remedy the situation. Now, here at school we've tried [enumerate a few examples]. Is there something like that that you might try at home?" Such a discussion suggests possible solutions for examination. Parents can realize that problems have various solutions and they can try one that fits their situation.

Most parents are grateful to teachers who bring their child's problems to their attention. Problems can develop without being noticed by parents. Parents often praise a teacher for helping them work through a problem. Common, too, is criticism of teachers who wait until difficulties are full-blown before mentioning them. The teacher's solution is usually not to ignore the child's problems but to think through possible meanings, causes, and solutions before calling parents in for a conference. If parents and teacher know each other through many pleasant instances, and mutual trust has developed, each can weather discussion of a child's problem without personal threat unless one of them has his own deep-seated problems.

Parents often have the feeling that teachers just couldn't know how it is to be in parental shoes. As teachers grow in experience and draw on the experience of others, they may help parents realize that other parents before them have solved similar problems. Of course, teachers avoid using names or current classes for examples.

Teachers should be humble. It is extremely difficult really to know the family situation. There is very little that is clear-cut. An outsider should recognize uncertainties when giving advice. Parents' self-confidence must be protected and bolstered. If the conference is to be of any help to the child, the parents must have hope for succeeding as parents.

When parents request a conference, they are often ready to deal with some problem they face with the child. Again the teacher's role is more that of a listener and a suggester of alternatives than a giver of answers. The teacher should be willing to refer parents to other professionals whose training, experience, and available time leave them better equipped to cope with people who have problems.

A file of referral agencies should be on every teacher's desk. When teachers decide to make a referral, they should make some preliminary contacts with the agency in order to be able to give precise information to parents. Parents need to know where to go, when to go, what it will cost, and something about the personnel and procedure used. If the teacher knows the professionals in the agency by name and can personally endorse their qualifications, she may encourage the parents to follow through with the referral. Parents are understandably reluctant to face new people with their personal problems.

The teacher has the professional obligation to protect the confidentiality of personal information the parent reveals. Any notes the teacher makes should be kept private. Therefore information that is available to students and parent volunteers necessarily omits certain personal facts.

Occasionally in conferences and casual visits one parent seeks information about or is critical of other parents. The teacher must use diplomacy while turning the discussion back to that parent's own situation. Parents occasionally ask university student helpers about other children; students, too, must learn to handle such comments and avoid discussions that might be construed as gossip. Any information about the children should be discussed in a professional manner and in a professional setting.

For a discussion regarding the interpretation of tests and the reporting of test results to parents, see Chapter 16.

Organized Meetings

Getting parents together at meetings is one method of communicating with them. Meetings early in the year may help parents get acquainted with each other. The teacher may use the meeting to discuss her goals for the children and outline the ways she expects the school to meet these goals.

The needs and interests of parents will determine how many organized meetings are planned. The teacher may leave this decision up to the group. She may encourage them to organize their own group, elect a chairperson, or appoint a committee to plan future programs. The more the parents are part of the planning process the more interest they will have in attending meetings. Involvement of both fathers and mothers is important. An effort must be made to adjust meeting hours so as *not* to exclude working fathers or working mothers.

Some schools plan workshop programs that involve the parents in learning about nursery school or kindergarten activities. For exam-

FIGURE 17–3. *Parents' night at school is an event looked forward to in many schools. (Iowa State University Nursery School.)*

ple, the parents may meet, mix finger paints and play dough, then use the materials to further their understanding of the creative experiences their child is having at school. Some groups plan programs using films or speakers to stimulate their exchange of ideas. They may prefer small-group discussions in which the focus is on their specific child-rearing problems. Occasionally the topics parents suggest for meetings seem far removed from the child in the school. For example, parents may suggest meetings on meal planning, sewing, fashion, hairdressing, or even jewelry making. In the long run, these meetings may be helpful in developing rapport between home and school. Even when the teacher feels she is not able to be a resource person for such topics, she can help the group locate someone who can. Through meeting the personal needs of parents, the child's needs are often served. If the parents are given a positive experience in the school, there will be a good chance that their interest will eventually focus more directly on the child.

Once a meeting has been planned, the teacher can help advertise it. She may send home several notices encouraging parents' attendance. Her first notices will encourage parents in advance to reserve that date on their calendars. On the day of the meeting another notice can remind them. Through personal contacts she can generate interest and enthusiasm for the meeting. A committee of parents can contact others to encourage participation and offer transportation. Through such personal contacts parents will feel that they are wanted in the group.

Name tags help parents get acquainted and can help to break down formality because people can more readily use each other's names. It may help to put "Mrs. Estelle Jones—John's mother" on the name tag so that other parents can associate the mother with a name they may have heard their child mention from day to day. It is a common joke among mothers that they lose their identity once their child goes to school. Because young children rarely know each other's last names, they refer to adults as John's mother or Bettie's daddy.

Better attendance results when baby-sitting is arranged. Transportation may also be a problem for some parents. Some schools hold meetings during the child's school hours. Extra volunteers supervise a children's program while the teacher and parents meet in another part of the building. A space may be arranged for infants and toddlers, or little ones may accompany the mother to her meeting. This practice may cause distractions because of the needs of the child.

Evening meetings may not be well attended because of baby-sitting problems. When children must be brought to meetings, their bedtimes are delayed. Some teachers hold early evening meetings so that parents can return home again for their children's usual bedtime.

Some groups use gimmicks to attract parents to meetings. Gimmicks may be door prizes, recognition for the child's classroom, or performances by the children. Although gimmicks might be used occasionally to attract parents who cannot seem to be interested in other ways, their long-range value is questionable. Likewise, the threat that the child will be deprived of his place in the school if the parents do not participate is also questionable. A better way of attracting parents to meetings is through the personal interest of the teacher and other parents. When personal contacts are adequately made, a friendly atmosphere prevails, and if parents feel the program meets their needs, they are likely to make an effort to participate. The teacher's first meetings and first contacts set the stage for parents' participation. Well-planned, relevant programs are essential for good attendance.

Parent Effectiveness Training (P.E.T.) is a course or set of experiences designed by Thomas Gordon [5] to help parents with their interactions with their children. Sometimes these courses are offered to parents by a parent-educator or a mental health consultant. Aside

[5] Thomas Gordon, *P.E.T.: Parent Effectiveness Training* (New York: Peter H. Wyden, Inc., 1970).

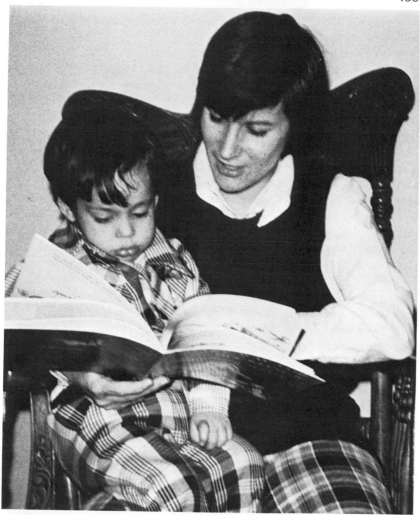

FIGURE 17–4. *Parents contribute to the "hidden curriculum" as they read stories to children at home. Children with this type of encouragement at home will seldom have reading difficulties. (Michigan State University Laboratory Preschool.)*

from learning some fruitful ways to deal with their youngsters of various ages, the participants gain from sharing their problems with parents having similar concerns. The techniques also have relevant applications to teaching children in the classroom.

Each chapter of Part Two of this book has suggested ways of involving parents in that particular area of the curriculum. Each curriculum area offers numerous possibilities for parents' meetings.

Printed Communication

Teachers usually rely on mimeographed letters to inform parents of school affairs. A brief letter written in an interesting, warm style will encourage parents to read it and to feel that it was written especially for them. Underline dates that are to be remembered.

Through letters the teacher can support other community agencies and their programs for families. The exact hours of a public health clinic might be important to some parents. Information on the hours the public library is open and when the children's story hour is held is helpful to parents and encourages library use. Parents can be reminded about musical events, art shows, exhibits, and lectures that are relevant to the many facets of the educational development of parents or children.

To emphasize to the child and to the parents that the teacher considers these letters important, she gives them special care. She seals them in envelopes containing each child's name. The name helps her keep account of undelivered letters. The letter can be attached to the child's coat with a safety pin. Children enjoy the responsibility of serving as "mail carriers" between their teacher and their homes.

Booklets and Newsletters

One form of written communication parents really appreciate is a newsletter or a booklet of class-related materials prepared by the teacher, duplicated, and sent home to parents. Some teachers prepare communications once a month, and others prepare them two or three times a year.

The content varies. The following materials have proved popular with parents:

1. The names and addresses of the children in the group.
2. Recipes for finger paint, play dough, and paste.
3. Recipes for food projects enjoyed by the children.
4. Words to songs and finger plays the children are learning.
5. Stories and letters the children have dictated at school.
6. Toy-buying guides, including suggestions for appropriate gift items.
7. Suggested activities for the children's winter or summer vacation.
8. Examples of correct ways to learn manuscript writing.
9. Suggested books for children.
10. Suggestions for parent reading on the various school activities, family life, or sex education.

Pretty covers can be made for booklets from construction paper. One teacher helps the children place their hand prints in white paint on the colored paper. Older children can make a drawing or cut out a magazine picture for their booklet. Collage designs can be made by the children to cover their parents' booklet.

A booklet like this makes a nice gift for the children to give to their parents. The children feel the materials are theirs. They like to take the booklets home to share with the whole family. Such an educational device stimulates additional learning and often involves the whole family.

Experiences for Students and Beginning Teachers

Students often wonder how they can go about gaining the experience that enables them to feel comfortable in situations with parents. There are, of course, numerous counseling, family relations, and parent education courses that will help the student. One practical suggestion is for students to use every opportunity just to talk to people who have children. Knowing families from many walks of life also contributes to understanding. A good opportunity for the student is to volunteer for baby-sitting to get acquainted with parents and to observe how they relate to their children. As students go home for vacations, they can listen to their relatives and encourage both the eldest and the youngest parent to talk about his concerns about and pleasures from child rearing. Every parent the student has the opportunity to know will provide experience that will help her develop better teacher-parent relations when she is the teacher.

Explaining the Need for Parent Work

Very often the steps that have been outlined here for parent-teacher relations are carried on by teachers in addition to a full day of working with children. If a teacher has fifty or sixty children in two kindergarten classes, it is easy to see why she would be unable to carry through all the suggestions made here. However, the situation will never improve unless the teacher discusses the problem with her administrator, who can lighten her class load, give her released time, or hire an assistant so that she can have some time for parent work. Teachers must take a nothing-ventured-nothing-gained attitude while continuing to do the best they can for the children in their groups.

A better plan is for the teacher to work half days with children, using the other half day for planning and for work with parents. This arrangement strengthens the program on two important fronts.

Special parent-educators are hired in some schools to coordinate programs for several teachers. They can readily organize parent meetings, meet with committees, and support leadership training that can be the outgrowth of a good program. However, even with a specialist in parent education the teacher will still need to maintain the relationships that have been discussed in this chapter. The work of any specialist should be incorporated into the planning for the class; therefore communication between the teacher and the parent-educator is essential.

Conclusion

Teacher-parent relationships are of utmost importance in the education of the young child. When the school and home are closely united, the child will more likely be able to reach his fullest potential.

Teachers will take the leadership in initiating contacts with parents. They will maintain an open, friendly approach to parents, yet remain professional at all times.

The teacher will value relationships with parents as a teaching

FIGURE 17–5. *Parents are encouraged to give each child some time when his learning can be recognized. (Project Head Start, Office of Child Development.)*

FIGURE 17–6. *Valuing the completion of a task by commenting to the child helps him know when he has pleased the parent. (Project Head Start, Office of Child Development.)*

experience and, perhaps even more important, as a learning experience with respect to the child and his parents.

Plans for the parents, like plans for the children, will be made after the needs and interest of the group have been determined. The teacher may initiate some meetings while leaving others up to the leaders of the group.

Teachers should be prepared to explain to the administrators of their schools the importance of developing relationships with parents. Teachers should seek recognition that their work with parents on a one-to-one basis as well as on a group basis makes an important contribution to each child's education.

ADDITIONAL READINGS

AUERBACH, ALINE B. *Parents Learn Through Discussion.* New York: John Wiley & Sons, Inc., 1968.

AUERBACH, ALINE B., and SANDRA ROCHE. *Creating a Preschool Center: Parent Development in an Integrated Neighborhood Project.* New York: John Wiley & Sons, Inc., 1971.

AXLINE, VIRGINIA M. *Dibs: In Search of Self.* Boston: Houghton Mifflin Company, 1964.

D'EVELYN, KATHERINE. *Meeting Children's Emotional Needs.* Englewood Cliffs, N.J.: Prentice-Hall, Inc., 1957.

D'EVELYN, KATHERINE. *Individual Parent-Teacher Conferences.* New York: Teachers College Press, Columbia University, 1963.

DREIKURS, R., and V. SOLTZ. *Children: The Challenge.* New York: Duell, Sloan and Pearce, 1964.

DUVALL, EVELYN. *Family Development.* Philadelphia: W. B. Saunders Company, 1971.

GINOTT, HAIM. *Between Parent and Child.* New York: Macmillan Publishing Co., Inc., 1973.

GORDON, THOMAS. *P.E.T.: Parent Effectiveness Training.* New York: Peter H. Wyden, Inc., 1970.

LEEPER, SARAH H., RUTH J. DALES, DORA SKIPPER, and RALPH L. WITHERSPOON. *Good Schools for Young Children.* New York: Macmillan Publishing Co., Inc., 1974.

MARKUN, PATRICIA MALONEY (ed.). *Parenting.* Washington, D.C.: Association for Childhood Education International, 1973.

MEDINNUS, GENE R. (ed.). *Readings in the Psychology of Parent-Child Relations.* New York: John Wiley & Sons, Inc., 1967.

MOORE, BERNICE MILBURN, and WAYNE H. HOLTZMAN. *Tomorrow's Parents: A Study of Youth and Their Families.* Austin, Texas: The Hogg Foundation for Mental Health by The University of Texas Press, 1965.

Parent Involvement: A Workbook of Training Tips for Head Start Staff. Washington, D.C.: Office of Economic Opportunity, 1969.

ROSENTHAL, ROBERT, and LENORE JACKSON. *Pygmalion in the Classroom.* New York: Holt, Rinehart and Winston, Inc., 1968.

RUEL, MYRTLE R. *Where Hannibal Led Us.* New York: Vantage Press, Inc., 1967.

SAYLER, MARY LOU. *Parents: Active Partners in Education.* Washington, D.C.: American Association of Elementary-Kindergarten and Nursery Educators, 1971.

SEARS, R. R., E. MACCOBY, and H. LEVIN. *Patterns of Child-rearing.* Evanston, Ill.: Row and Co., 1957.

TODD, VIVIAN E., and HELEN HEFFERNAN. *The Years Before School: Guiding Preschool Children.* New York: Macmillan Publishing Co., Inc., 1970.

The following journals will be helpful to teachers as they work with parents:

Adult Leadership. Published by the Adult Education Association of the U.S.A., 1225 19th St. N.W., Washington, D.C.

The Family Coordinator and the *Journal of Marriage and the Family.* Published by the National Council on Family Relations, 1219 University Avenue Southeast, Minneapolis, Minn.

Parent Cooperative Preschools International Journal. Published by Parent Cooperative Preschools International, 911 Alton Parkway, Silver Spring, Md.

The Profession—Past, Present, and Future

After one has an opportunity to become acquainted with current ideas, issues, and practices in a professional field, one's curiosity may be aroused about the history of that profession. In early childhood education a number of historical eras are significant and numerous individuals have made contributions. The reader is encouraged to pursue additional sources on topics of particular interest.

European Roots

For those who might be inclined to think that early childhood education has only recently been discovered, it is well to note that the early Greeks Socrates (469–399 B.C.), Plato (425–347 B.C.), and Aristotle (384–322 B.C.) spoke out regarding the education of the child.

During the Industrial Revolution of the eighteenth and nineteenth centuries, European philosophers wrote about educating the young child. In Rousseau's mind (1712–1778) the best education for the child in the later part of the eighteenth century was the education that least hampered the development of the pupil's natural ways.[1] Pestalozzi, a Swiss (1746–1827), was influenced by Rousseau. Especially concerned with education of the poor, he developed a home for paupers and a school for refugees. He felt that schooling should directly involve the child and suggested methods appealing to the senses.[2] Many ideas from the eighteenth-century philosophers are still in practice today.

---

[1] Jean Jacques Rousseau, *Emile,* trans. Barbara Foxley (London: J. M. Dent & Sons Ltd., 1911), p. 50.

[2] Johann Heinrich Pestalozzi, *How Gertrude Teaches Her Children,* trans. Lucy E. Holland and Francis C. Turner (London: George Allen and Unwin Ltd. 1894), pp. 200–201.

The era of nursery school–kindergarten education that heavily influenced the American movement occurred in early nineteenth-century Europe. Mothers and older siblings were going off to work, leaving small children uncared for. The first institution for the children of working mothers was founded in Germany in 1802.[3]

Friedrich Froebel (1782–1852), a German philosopher, believed that educating children was similar to cultivating plants, and so he coined the term *kindergarten* meaning "garden of children." He founded the first kindergarten in 1837.[4] Froebel's philosophy was naturalistic. He felt that children should be allowed to play, but that teachers could arrange play for them that developed their minds, bodies, and senses. Froebel had become convinced through work with older boys that their problems were really rooted in their earlier experience. In 1817 he admitted boys just three years old to his school. Froebel's writings later provided the philosophy for the kindergarten movement in America.[5]

Another historic early childhood education movement occurred in Scotland in 1816, when Robert Owen, a socialist, established an infant school. In France in 1833 Jean Frederic Oberlin founded a nursery school. *Crèches* were organized in Vienna, Austria, in 1847; in Spain in 1855; and in Russia in 1864.[6]

The McMillan sisters, Rachel and Margaret, organized the first English nursery school in London between 1908 and 1910. The McMillans' school and writings were inspirations for American schools.[7]

Dr. Maria Montessori, founder of schools bearing her name, was born in Italy in 1870 and died in 1952. She was trained before the turn of the century as a medical doctor and psychologist. Her major work centered around training feebleminded children in an Italian slum housing project. Her teaching stressed cleanliness and self-help. She designed numerous tasks and felt that children should learn these tasks in a designated sequence. She appears to have been quite successful in getting children to learn.

Montessori schools using Montessori methods and materials have continued to be formed throughout the world. Some of these schools seem to hold a semimystic faith in Montessori's ideas. Surely Dr. Montessori would make some changes if she were alive today. She

[3] "Nursery Schools," *The Encyclopedia Americana*, Vol. 20 (New York: American Corporation, 1967), pp. 554–557.

[4] Ilse Forest, *Preschool Education: A Historical and Critical Study* (New York: Macmillan, 1927), pp. 154–183; Friedrich Froebel, *Pedagogics of the Kindergarten* (New York: D. Appleton and Co., 1917), pp. 1–33. See also, Friedrich Froebel, *Mother Play and Nursery Songs*, trans. Elizabeth Peabody (Boston: Lothrop, Lee and Shepard, 1878).

[5] "Nursery Schools," op. cit.

[6] "Nursery Schools," op. cit.

[7] Margaret McMillan, *The Nursery School* (New York: Dutton, 1921), p. 22.

was a woman ahead of her times. Probably such a creative woman would use any scientific knowledge and experience available and update her methods accordingly.[8]

Nearly all nursery schools and kindergartens today emphasize the idea of self-help and the development of independence—both stressed in Montessori schools. Children generally help care for their room. "Self-correcting" materials similar to Montessori's have been adapted for general use. In most schools children are allowed to use learning materials in as many creative ways as the mind can suggest. However, in a strict Montessori school, there is only one correct way to use a learning material.[9]

Early American Roots

"Nursery for the Children of Poor Women in the City of New York" was the lengthy title given the first day-care program in the United States in 1854. There wage-earning women left their children (ages six weeks to six years) for as long as twelve hours.[10]

The first American kindergarten was founded in Wisconsin in 1856 by Mrs. Carl Schurz, who had been a student of Froebel. The kindergarten was taught in German. Mrs. Schurz's husband, an editor and later a senator, was a leader of the German element against slavery. The first kindergarten for English-speaking children was organized in Massachusetts by Elizabeth Peabody in 1860. These kindergartens were organized under private auspices. In 1873 the first public-supported kindergarten was established in Saint Louis. Patty Hill of Teachers College, Columbia University, and Alice Temple of the University of Chicago were early American leaders in nursery-kindergarten education.[11]

Lizzie Merrill-Palmer, in her will of 1916, provided funds for establishing a center in Detroit to train girls for motherhood.[12] Today the Merrill-Palmer Institute enrolls both men and women and contributes outstanding leadership to studies of children and families.

The Laura Spelman Rockefeller Memorial provided for increased emphasis in child-centered research when in the 1920s it was used to sponsor child study centers at a number of major universities. The University of California, the University of Minnesota, Columbia Uni-

[8] *Montessori in Perspective*, publication No. 406 (Washington, D.C.: National Association for Education of Young Children, 1966).

[9] Lois Barklay Murphy, "Multiple Factors in Learning in the Day Care Center," *Childhood Education*, **45**:6 (February 1969), 317.

[10] "Nursery Schools," op. cit.

[11] Ilse Forest, op. cit., pp. 170–182.

[12] Ilse Forest, op. cit., p. 297.

versity, and Yale University were four involved.[13] Early research supported the idea that nursery schools contribute to the child's physical progress as well as to his ability to respond to intelligence tests. Children who had behavior problems seemed to be helped when attending nursery school. Nursery schools were looked upon as a supplement to the home and not a replacement of it.

In the years between 1920 and 1930 the number of nursery schools in the United States grew from 3 to 262.[14]

The first White House Conference concerning children was called by President Theodore Roosevelt in 1909. Since then conferences have been called by each President at the beginning of each decade. Out of the first conference came the recommendation for and subsequent organization of the Children's Bureau, which was first housed in the Department of Commerce and Labor. It is now housed in the Department of Health, Education, and Welfare.

The final meeting of the 1930 White House Conference was reported in *The New York Times*, November 20, 1930: "Dr. F. J. Kelly of University of Chicago summarized the needs of the child in a machine age, expressed opposition to lock-step education and supported the statement that the cardinal principle in education should be the development of each child to his or her highest level of attainment because 'the danger of a dead level of mediocrity is more grave in a democracy than in any other form of government.'"[15]

Also reported in *The New York Times* was a classic document that came out of the 1930 Conference. It was *The Children's Charter*, reproduced here so that the reader can see that many of the 1930 problems are with us today—especially when one thinks of the world as the community and of our increasing concern for the world's children.

CHILDREN'S CHARTER [16]

1. Every child is entitled to be understood, and all dealings with him should be based on the fullest understanding of the child.

---

[13] Mary Dabney Davis, *Nursery Schools: Their Development and Current Practices in the United States*, U.S. Office of Education Bulletin No. 9, 1932 (Washington, D.C.: Government Printing Office, 1933), pp. 1–10.

[14] Gertrude E. Chittenden, Margaret Nesbitt, and Betsy Williams, "The Nursery School in American Education Today," *Education Digest* (January 1949), 46–51.

[15] "19 Point Program of Child Aid Carried," *The New York Times*, November 23, 1930, p. 20. (© 1930 by The New York Times Company. Reprinted by permission.)

[16] Ibid.

2. Every prospective mother should have suitable information, medical supervision during the prenatal period, competent care at confinement. Every mother should have post-natal medical supervision for herself and child.

3. Every child should receive periodical health examinations before and during the school period, including adolescence, by the family physician or the school or other public physicians and such examinations by specialists and such hospital care as its special needs may require.

4. Every child should have regular dental examination and care.

MEASURES FOR PROTECTION

5. Every child should have instruction in the schools in health and in safety from accidents, and every teacher should be trained in health programs.

6. Every child should be protected from communicable diseases to which it might be exposed at home or at play, and protected from impure milk and food.

7. Every child should have proper sleeping rooms, diet, hours of sleep and play, and parents should receive expert information as to the needs of children of various ages as to these questions.

8. Every child should attend a school which has proper seating, lighting, ventilation, and sanitation. For younger children, kindergartens and nursery schools should be provided to supplement home care.

9. The school should be so organized as to discover and develop the special abilities of each child, and should assist in vocational guidance, for children, like men, succeed by the use of their strongest qualities and special interests.

10. Every child should have some form of religious, moral, and character training.

11. Every child has a right to play with adequate facilities therefor.

12. With the expanding domain of the community's responsibilities for children, there should be proper provision for and supervision of recreation and entertainment.

PROVISION FOR THE HANDICAPPED

13. Every child should be protected against labor that stunts growth, either physical or mental, that limits education, that deprives children of the rights of comradeship, of joy and play.

14. Every child who is blind, deaf, crippled or otherwise physically handicapped should be given expert study and corrective treatment where there is the possibility of relief, and appropriate de-

velopment or training. Children with subnormal or abnormal mental conditions should receive adequate study, protection, training and care. Where the child does not have these services, due to inadequate income of the family, then such services must be provided to him by the community. Obviously, the primary necessity in protection and development of children where poverty is an element in the problem is an adequate standard of living and security for the family within such groups.

15. Every waif and orphan in need must be supported.

16. Every child is entitled to the feeling that he has a home. The extension of services in the community should supplement and not supplant parents.

17. Children who habitually fail to meet normal standards of human behavior should be provided special care under the guidance of the school, the community health, or welfare centre or other agency for continued supervision, or, if necessary, control.

18. The rural child should have satisfactory schooling, health, protection and welfare facilities.

COORDINATED ORGANIZATION

19. In order that these minimum protections of the health and welfare of children may be everywhere available, there should be a district, county or community organization for health education and welfare, with full-time officials, coordinating with a Statewide program which will be responsible to a nation-wide service of general information, statistics and scientific research. This should include:

    a. Trained full-time public health officials with public health nurses, sanitary inspection and laboratory workers.

    b. Available hospitals beds.

    c. Full-time public welfare services for the relief and aid of children in special need from poverty or misfortune, for the protection of children from abuse, neglect, exploitation or moral hazard.

    d. The development of voluntary organization of children for purposes of instruction, health, and recreation through private effort and benefaction. When possible, existing agencies should be coordinated.

The Great Depression Era

The Great Depression of the 1930s was felt by children, families, and teachers. The federal Emergency Relief Administration organized schools for young children. In 1934–1935 there were 75,000 children benefiting from a program designed more to put teachers to work than to educate children. The number decreased when conditions improved, but in 1942 there were still 944 nursery schools operating for 38,735 children. Kindergartens slowed their pace of growth soon after 1930, after sixty years of progress toward acceptance as a public school service. From an enrollment of 15,000 in 1888, to 725,000 in 1930, enrollment dropped to 600,000 in 1934.[17]

World War II Era

Child-care facilities received a major boost during World War II. They were essential to free women who were needed in production plants. The Lanham Act of 1942 provided funds for the day care of young children and for the extended day care of school-age children. These schools were held in quickly built "temporary" buildings. The facilities were in many cases a vast improvement in design and convenience over the renovated buildings that commonly housed nursery schools. The direct relationship with the public school system was also a step forward. The U.S. Office of Education and the U.S. Children's Bureau were designated to assume responsibility for the program. Children were the secondary concern of the planners of Lanham Act nursery schools—the war effort's need for women workers being their first concern.

In 1945, at the close of the era, there were over 50,000 children enrolled in almost 1,500 child-care centers, and there were 18,000 receiving extended day care. Kindergartens enrolled 700,877 in 1944.[18]

Sigmund Freud's (1856–1939) theory of human motivation[19] began having an impact on early childhood education. For example, play therapy and dramatic play in the nursery school and kindergarten contributed to the understanding of a child's inner feelings. The importance of the parent-child relationship and the significance of the early years, much emphasized by Freud and others, began to guide the early childhood programs.

The Early Post–World War II Era

The post–World War II era witnessed a return to normality as far as the nation's young children were concerned; that is, federal funds

[17] Bess Goodykoontz, Mary Dabney Davis, and Hazel F. Gabbard, "Recent History and Present Status of Education for Young Children," *Early Childhood Education* (46th Yearbook), Part II, National Society for the Study of Education (Chicago: University of Chicago Press, 1947), pp. 45–46.

[18] Ibid., p. 45.

[19] Sigmund Freud, *The Basic Writings of Sigmund Freud,* trans. and ed. A. S. Brill (New York: Random House, 1938).

for operating child-care centers were no longer available. States were allowed to continue operation of their Lanham Act child-care centers, but most permitted them to close. However, women did not all go back to the cookstove after World War II. They either needed or wanted to remain in the labor force. The need for day-care facilities continued and continues today.

It is of interest to note that the 1950 White House Conference dealt with the components of a healthy personality for children and youth. Mental health was finally receiving attention after being neglected so long. In the 1960 Conference there was a recommendation for public kindergartens and day-care facilities.[20]

In 1959 the Office of Education reported that 70 per cent of the public elementary schools maintained kindergartens and 5 per cent maintained nursery schools.[21] Private and cooperative schools increased during this time. The shift to the suburbs, improved standards of living, smaller families, smaller housing, increased mobility, and the increased level of parental education are frequently cited sociological factors contributing to the interest of parents in early education for their children.

Research at Yale by Dr. Arnold Gesell provided normative data to which parents and teachers could compare a child's growth.[22]

During the postwar decades Dr. Benjamin Spock's book *Baby and Child Care* sold millions of copies in a pocket edition.[23] Parents of young children needed the reassurance of a more experienced hand, and Spock substituted for the older generation's Grandma next door.

The United Nations, which was organized in 1945, contributed to better communication between the peoples of the world. Several specialized agencies dealt with the health and well-being of children and families. These were the World Health Organization (WHO), the Food and Agriculture Organization (FAO), the United Nations Educational Scientific and Cultural Organization (UNESCO), and the United Children's Emergency Fund (UNICEF).[24]

The War on Poverty Era

The "War on Poverty" was begun in the 1960s. The accelerated migration of rural America to the cities to work, the need for more

[20] Kathryn Close, "Impressions of the White House Conference," *Children* (May–June 1960).

[21] S. E. Dean, *Elementary School Administration and Organization*, U.S. Office of Education, Bulletin No. 11 (Washington, D.C.: U.S. Government Printing Office, 1960), p. 19.

[22] Arnold Gesell and F. L. Ilg, *Infant and the Child in the Culture of Today* (New York: Harper & Row, 1943).

[23] Benjamin Spock, *Baby and Child Care* (New York: Pocket Books, Simon & Schuster, 1953).

[24] United Nation's Visitor's Guide (New York: United Nations).

technically trained workers, the rising school dropout rate, and the growing unrest among minorities woke the nation to some festering ills in its midst. The war in Vietnam contributed to the inflation and required resources that might have been used domestically.

The Economic Opportunity Act was passed in March 1964 and, on April 11, 1965, the Elementary and Secondary School Act became law.[25] Finally, after long years of debate, federal aid to education was granted. Federal aid was expected to equalize the educational opportunities between the country's rich and poor states, just as state aid helped to equalize opportunities within a state. For decades district financing has helped to equalize educational opportunities among families of a district.

Head Start programs for disadvantaged children under six became one of the more popular programs in President Lyndon Johnson's War on Poverty. The program was heralded with great expectation in many quarters. Education for young children was given professional leadership and funds. Leaders were saying that Head Start is a program for educating children, not an employment program for the poor. If this attitude did, in fact, guide the leadership, it represents the first time that the needs of children were given top priority in any emergency program. However, the Head Start program maintains a strong commitment to involve local parents and school dropouts.

Margaret Rasmussen, editor of *Childhood Education*, reported in September 1965 that the first summer of Head Start had involved 536,108 children, 39,463 professionals, 44,589 paid neighborhood residents, 54,996 neighborhood volunteers, and 40,187 other volunteers throughout the nation.[26]

Early Head Start planners held out for a trained, qualified teacher and a low pupil-teacher ratio—two paid teachers for fifteen disadvantaged children, plus volunteer helpers. Short courses were estalished by universities across the country to train teachers, assistant teachers, and aides for the programs. In 1969, 3,600 paraprofessionals, as such assistants were called, were trained in 150 colleges.[27]

The Head Start program also includes the Parent and Child Center, which "represents the drawing together of all those resources—family, community, and professional—which can contribute to the

[25] J. William Rioux, "New Opportunities Economic Opportunity Act and Elementary and Secondary Education Act of 1965," *Childhood Education*, **42**:1 (September 1965), 9–11.

[26] Margaret Rasmussen, "Over the Editor's Desk," *Childhood Education*, **42**:1 (September 1965), 65.

[27] Harriette Merhill, "Highlighting the National Conference on the Paraprofessional, Career Advancement, and Pupil Learning," *Childhood Education*, **45**:7 (March 1969), 369k.

child's total development. It draws heavily on the professional skills of persons in nutrition, health, education, psychology, social work, and recreation. It recognizes that both paid and volunteer nonprofessionals can make important contributions. Finally the concept emphasizes that the family is fundamental to the child's development. Parents should play an important role in developing policies; they should work in the Centers and participate in the programs." [28]

Another development with federal support was Project Follow Through, which encourages utilizing Head Start concepts and practices in children's later school experience. According to Omwake, "Project Follow Through provides a second chance to effect some needed reforms in Early Childhood Education, another opportunity to try to break through the rigidities and stultifying practices which characterize so many of our public primary schools." [29]

The late 1960s were noted for the focus on disadvantaged children and their needs. Researchers and educators vied for grants from the federal government to try out various approaches to the problems. Listed below are thirty-four such programs and their locations. Each is written up in a small booklet that can be obtained for twenty cents from the Superintendent of Documents, Washington, D.C. 20402. These booklets were prepared for the 1970 White House Conference on Children held December 1970.

The Day Nursery Association of Cleveland, Ohio

Neighborhood House Child Care Services, Seattle, Wash.

Behavior Analysis Model of a Follow Through Program, Oraibi, Ariz.

Cross-Cultural Family Center, San Francisco, Calif.

NRO Migrant Child Development Center, Pasco, Wash.

Bilingual Early Childhood Program, San Antonio, Tex.

Santa Monica Children's Centers, Calif.

Philadelphia Teacher Center, Pa.

Cognitively Oriented Curriculum, Ypsilanti, Mich.

Mothers' Training Program, Urbana, Ill.

The Micro-Social Preschool Learning System, Vineland, N.J.

Project PLAN, Parkersburg, W. Va.

Interdependent Learner Model of a Follow Through Program, New York, N.Y.

San Jose Police Youth Protection Unit, Calif.

---

[28] *Project Head Start Points for Parents*, Booklet 10 (Washington, D.C.: Office of Economic Opportunity, 1967), p. 1.

[29] Eveline B. Omwake, "From the President," *Young Children*, 2:4 (March 1969), 194.

Exemplary Center for Reading Instruction, Salt Lake City, Utah

Dubnoff School for Educational Therapy, North Hollywood, Calif.

Demonstration Nursery Center for Infants and Toddlers, Greensboro, N.C.

Responsive Environment Model of a Follow Through Program, Goldsboro, N.C.

Center for Early Development and Education, Little Rock, Ark.

DOVACK, Monticello, Fla.

Perceptual Development Center Program, Natchez, Miss.

Appalachia Preschool Education Program, Charleston, W. Va.

Foster Grandparent Program, Nashville, Tenn.

Hartford Early Childhood Program, Conn.

Model Observation Kindergarten, Amherst, Mass.

Boston Public Schools Learning Laboratories, Mass.

Martin Luther King Family Center, Chicago, Ill.

Behavior Principles Structural Model of a Follow Through Program, Dayton, Ohio

University of Hawaii Preschool Language Curriculum, Honolulu, Hawaii

Springfield Avenue Community School, Newark, N.J.

Corrective Reading Program, Wichita, Kan.

New Schools Exchange, Santa Barbara, Calif.

Tacoma Public Schools Early Childhood Program, Wash.

Community Cooperative Nursery School, Menlo Park, Calif.

In addition to programs for children, for parents, and for teachers, Head Start established research programs to evaluate the results of Head Start programs. Additional research support encouraged many scholars to help discover more about children's learning generally and especially to shed light on those learning barriers facing disadvantaged children.

The Nixon Era

After President Richard M. Nixon was inaugurated in January 1969, Head Start parents and teachers waited anxiously to see what might happen to the Head Start program. Despite early presidential speeches generally supporting child care, the Nixon Presidency did not maintain the momentum for early childhood education that the previous period had established. However, the Head Start program largely survived, mostly because of strong grassroots support—demonstrating again that community organization is essential if the case for early childhood education is to be developed effectively.

On August 8, 1969, the President gave day-care advocates reason to hope for help from federal sources, when he said, "As I mentioned previously, greatly expanded day-care center facilities would be provided for the children of welfare mothers who choose to work. However, these would be day-care centers with a difference. There is no single ideal to which this administration is more firmly committed than to the enriching of a child's first 5 years of life, and thus helping the poor out of misery at a time when a lift can help the most. Therefore, these day-care centers would offer more than custodial care; they would also be devoted to the development of vigorous young minds and bodies. As a further dividend, the day-care centers would offer employment to many welfare mothers themselves." [30]

The Comprehensive Child Development Program

The writers of the Comprehensive Child Development Program, which was submitted to the President for signature after it had passed both houses of Congress, considered day care much more than a welfare program. The writers designed the bill to serve other children as well. The President vetoed the bill on December 9, 1971, indicating that it was fiscally irresponsible and administratively unworkable and had family-weakening implications.[31]

Many individuals and groups helped write and had worked for passage of the Comprehensive Child Development Program. In addition, many forums of the 1970 White House Conference on Children had addressed the needs for day care and the issues related to the family of today.[32] High-quality child care was a need felt in many quarters of the country. After the veto individuals and groups continued to work for day care and early childhood programs at local and state levels despite the lack of White House support.

The Women's Movement

The women's movement increased its momentum throughout the country during these years, and women pressed for increased and improved child-care services. No women's meeting was complete without at least one workshop on the need for child care, and the

---

[30] Richard M. Nixon, *Weekly Compilation of Presidential Documents* (August 8, 1969), 1108.

[31] Richard M. Nixon, *Weekly Compilation of Presidential Documents* (December 13, 1971), 1634–1636.

[32] See "The 1970 White House Conference on Children: Reports by NAEYC Official Delegates," *Young Children*, **26**:4 (March 1971), 194–201. See also *Report to the President—White House Conference on Children* (Washington, D.C.: Government Printing Office, 1971).

need was usually dramatized by provision of child care for the children of the women in attendance. Through such organizations as the National Organization for Women (NOW), the National Women's Political Caucus, and the Women's Equity Action League (WEAL), women were raising their voices for equal access to education, jobs, and the political arena. Child care would enable many women to pursue career goals and to provide their children more than custodial care.

Standards for Child Care

Custodial care is thought by some to be a relic of the past. However, at nearly every meeting of social service personnel and others who are in daily contact with child-care services, horror stories are heard concerning children who are being poorly and unsafely housed in centers, poorly fed, inadequately educated, and even mistreated. The minimal standards imposed by most states do not protect all children. In fact, the licensing regulations that control child-care centers are so minimal that children sometimes suffer. The recommended adult-child ratio for three- to five-year-olds is one adult to ten children. For an accurate calculation of this ratio custodial personnel and directors who do not help with the children in the classroom or yard are excluded.

Recognizing the need for improved standards for day-care licensing, the U.S. Office of Child Development held forums on licensing. With the help of representatives from licensing agencies of the fifty states and some cities, and from national and state organizations with interest in day care, a model for state licensing was prepared. The outcome was an excellent publication, *Guides for Day Care Licensing*,[33] which was designed for use by states and cities to improve their regulatory functions. Monitoring day care was considered by many to be as critical as monitoring restaurants—a practice that has been accepted for years. As services previously carried on in the home are moved out of the home into the commercial arena, governments must move to protect consumers. Day-care services are consumer services as surely as food, health, or dry cleaning services.

Child Development Associate

In 1971 the Child Development Associate (CDA) program was proposed by Dr. Edward Zigler,[34] then director of the U.S. Office of Child Development, to help in preparing teachers for child-care programs.

---

[33] *Guides for Day Care Licensing* (Washington, D.C.: Department of Health, Education, and Welfare, 1973).

[34] Edward Zigler, "Contemporary Concerns in Early Childhood Education," *Young Children*, **26**:3 (January 1971), 141–156.

The CDA program, it was hoped, would bring forth a career ladder that would encourage workers to get training for their jobs and would lead eventually to credentialing. The program was to be based on competencies exhibited by trainees rather than on courses per se. Initial pilot projects were funded by the U.S. Office of Child Development. The assessment measures are now being completed. When the Child Development Associate credential is finally awarded it "will be a professional award of competence and not a legal license—since issuing licenses is the business of the states,"[35] according to Williams.

Community Coordinated Child Care

The Community Coordinated Child Care (4-C) program was initiated by the Nixon administration. Jule Sugarman explained, "The underlying purpose of this program is to encourage agencies providing day-care and preschool services to work together to stretch their resources, cut out waste and duplication and improve and expand the quality and scope of their services. If they do so, more families will be reached; staff competence will be improved; parents will have a more effective voice in policy and program direction."[36] As an additional incentive, the states were encouraged to believe that with such coordination they would be able to receive joint funding from federal sources. Many states and communities did organize 4-C councils, composed of representatives from various areas of the state and from various agencies concerned in child care. A great number of high-cost professional hours went into the 4-C councils. The outcome in terms of children's programs is still to be evaluated. The promise for joint funding did not materialize to any major extent.

Research

Research related to children's programs ground to a snail's pace during the Nixon era. By the beginning of Nixon's Presidency in 1969, the "in" thing was the grantsmanship related to federal funding that centered on children's learning, disadvantaged children's needs, program models, and teaching styles for early childhood programs. As the period wore on, many grants were not renewed and the enthusiastic researchers were forced to move to other arenas. The development of educational "hardware," such as packaged learning materials, educational toys, and other educational kits, were the outgrowth of a new area of federally funded research. Commercial enterprises picked up these materials and manufactured and sold them

[35] C. Ray Williams, "CDA—'75," *Childhood Education*, 51:5 (March 1975), 267–272.
[36] Jule M. Sugarman, "The 4-C Program," *Children* (March 1969), 76–77.

to nursery schools, kindergartens, and day-care centers. These materials were expensive, and some programs were advertized and sold with hard-sell tactics designed to pressure teachers, parents, and school boards.

One of the important components of many of the research programs of the late 1960s and early 1970s was that of parent education. Earl Schaefer, summarizing such research wrote, "The accumulating evidence suggests that parents have great influence upon the behavior of their children, particularly their intellectual and academic achievement, and that programs which teach parents skills in educating their children are effective supplements or alternatives for preschool education. These data should influence future education policies and programs. A critical decision will be whether to devote manpower and money to child-centered extensions of academic education or to develop a comprehensive system of education that strengthens and supports parental education in the home, effective use of the mass media, and collaboration between the school, the home, and the mass media. This review suggests that an exclusive focus upon academic education will not solve the major educational problems. A major task for our child care and educational institutions and professions will be the development of a support system for family care and education. Major changes in professional roles and responsibilities, in training, and in educational policies and programs will be required to achieve a goal of equal education in the home as well as in the school." [37] Such findings are encouraging researchers and educators to make additional efforts to prepare professionals to work with parents.

State Action

During this era some states increased their tax support for certain groups of young children. For example, Texas and North Carolina have included kindergartens under state funding, thus providing kindergarten for all children. In some states new projects for three- and four-year-olds, using public school facilities, were developed. Some had federal support. Others had private funding for tuition or organized contributions from parent cooperatives.

The credentialing of teachers became an issue as states attached preschools to their public school systems. Children with special needs began receiving more attention in many states—even children as young as newborns became eligible for some state services when they had certain handicaps. These programs called for child develop-

[37] Earl S. Schaefer, "Parents as Educators," *The Young Child: Reviews of Research*, ed. Willard W. Hartrup (Washington: D.C.: National Association for the Education of Young Children, 1972), pp. 198–199.

ment professionals with skills and knowledge related to the handicaps of these young children, a difficult combination to find.

The Ford Era

President Gerald R. Ford's administration has mammoth problems with unemployment and with one of the country's worst inflations— facts that may endanger the new programs in child care that are badly needed, unless the education of young children receives some priority. With the high cost of living two salaries may be increasingly needed to keep familes solvent. With unemployment a real possibility a second job in the family is a sensible type of family economic insurance. Day care is a necessity for two-breadwinner families and also for single-parent families. Ford has not indicated the extent of his awareness of the needs of children and parents in our changing society.

The Future

The use of the term *preschool* may become outmoded in the years ahead. *Preprimary* may be the new descriptive term as the concept of school for three-, four-, and five-year-old children becomes generally accepted.

The "full day" kindergarten may be on the horizon. Instead of two groups of children, each sharing teacher and classroom for a half day, each group will have its own teacher and classroom. The number of hours children spend at school would be increased somewhat, though still leaving more time for teachers to do more planning, more individual pupil assessment, and more conferring with parents than the present double load permits. Twenty children per kindergarten will become the accepted standard, and teachers will expect to have one or two paid assistants.

Staffing schools for young children with adequately prepared teachers will become increasingly difficult as more and more programs are initiated. Community colleges are developing programs to help fill this gap. Inservice training is expanding in many schools, helping to keep teachers abreast of the times and challenging them to improve their teaching. If salaries for nursery school teachers were upgraded to equal those of public school teachers, some of the future teacher shortage would be alleviated. At the present time teachers who are highly qualified to work with young children are drawn toward upperage levels because salaries at those levels are more attractive. If young children are not to be slighted in the future, salaries for teaching young children must reflect the teacher's professional preparation and experience and the complexities of the assignment.

Assistants in programs (sometimes called *paraprofessionals*) will receive encouragement to become more professional through higher salaries and certification. The National Association for Education of Young Children passed a resolution at their 1969 annual meeting favoring "certification for all teaching roles in the field of early childhood education, including aides, assistant teachers, teachers, and supervisors." [38]

Colleges, universities, and state departments of social services and of education are now wrestling with the problems of determining the characteristics of good programs for teachers of young children and translating those values into teacher certification requirements.[39] Universities, despite other pressures on scarce resources, must devote increased emphasis and resources to training teachers of young children if the university is to provide an improved learning situation for the increasing number of students in early childhood education.

Television and computers will be more widely used in training teachers, in evaluating teachers, and in related child study and research. Closed-circuit television will enable teachers to see themselves as others see them. Through self-viewing, teachers will be able to direct their own self-improvement. Currently such possibilities tend to frighten teachers and student teachers. Some feel their spontaneity will suffer. However, as teachers become accustomed to the idea, and as safeguards are instituted to protect the individual's right to decide whether television tapes are to be made available to others, television will probably be accepted.

Research from many fields is expected to influence increasingly the teachers' classroom operation. More rapid and more effective methods of disseminating information will speed up changes. Teachers will be more interested in participating in research when prompt feedback enables them to use results with the children where data were collected.

With many aspects of the teaching and learning process becoming subject to research and quantification, teachers will need to participate in more studies and scrutinize more research results for useful guides for improving learning for young children.

[38] National Association for Education of Young Children, Annual Meeting Resolution Number 6 (November 14, 1969).

[39] Martin Haberman and Blanche Persky, eds., *Preliminary Report of the Ad Hoc Joint Committee on the Preparation of Nursery and Kindergarten Teachers* (Washington, D.C.: National Commission on Teacher Education and Professional Standards, NEA, 1969).

Finally, the future will depend to a great extent upon the activity of early childhood education associations at the local, state, national, and international levels. At the various levels these associations generally can be active not only in developing programs but in generating community and political support for the high-quality education needed for all young children. In many cases, an effective action is the passage of resolutions by associations and the transmittal of these resolutions to the communications media and to the appropriate political bodies.

For example, the National Association for the Education of Young Children regularly introduces, discusses, and approves resolutions at open sessions of the annual meeting. These resolutions are widely disseminated, generating a public discussion of issues and a thoughtful and considered impact on political decision-makers. The resolutions of this organization are usually printed in the January issue of *Young Children*, the association's journal.

Actions by organizations are often the most effective way to bring matters to the attention of elected officials and political bodies. Political bodies generally welcome and respect the views of organized constituents. The future quality and availability of early childhood education depends upon the maintenance of a continual community dialogue in which significant issues are presented, discussed, and evaluated. Don't hesitate to fulfill your responsibility to your profession and to children by making your thoughtful contributions to the dialogue concerning the future course of early childhood education. As many will testify, you and your organization can make a difference!

Conclusion

Between Socrates and Head Start are over two thousand years of ideas and experience contributing to the education of young children today. Yet, in a sense, early childhood education is still a young profession, with many ideas to be tested and evaluated.

Growth in early childhood education has resulted from recognized crises. The plight of women workers who needed a safe place to leave their children stimulated initial programs as the Industrial Revolution proceeded to gain momentum. The economic depression of the 1930s and World War II led to a major expansion of early childhood education in the United States. In the first instance, the need was for jobs for numerous unemployed people, in the second, the need was for child care for the children of women working in war industries. However, in the United States no period equals the 1960s for interest in the education of young children. Since 1965 large numbers of children have been enrolled in Head Start and many professionals, volunteers, and parents have become involved.

Head Start programs were initiated to help overcome our recognized national failure to support in word *and* action the American ideal of equality of opportunity for numerous disadvantaged children. In a real sense, whether people will survive and thrive on this planet depends upon the development of the full constructive potential of *all* children—children who will be capable of building a harmonious world community. Thus early childhood education becomes a relevant and vital movement with which to be associated if one wishes to help solve significant problems.

ADDITIONAL READINGS

Children and Youth in National Development in Latin America. New York: United Nations Children's Fund, 1965.

DAVIS, MARY DABNEY. *Nursery Schools: Their Development and Current Practices in the United States.* Washington, D.C.: U.S. Government Printing Office, 1933.

FEIN, GRETA G., and ALISON CLARKE-STEWART. *Day Care in Context.* New York: John Wiley & Sons, Inc., 1973

FISHER, DOROTHY C. *The Montessori Manual.* Cambridge, Mass.: Robert Bentley, Inc., 1964.

FOREST, ILSE. *Preschool Education: A Historical and Critical Study.* New York: Macmillan Publishing Co., Inc., 1927.

FROST, JOE L., and G. THOMAS ROWLAND. *Curricula for the Seventies, Early Childhood Through Early Adolescence.* Boston: Houghton Mifflin Company, 1969.

McFADDEN, DENNIS N. (ed.). *Early Childhood Development Programs and Services: Planning for Action.* Washington, D.C.: National Association for the Education of Young Children, 1972.

McMILLAN, MARGARET. *The Nursery School.* New York: E. P. Dutton and Co., Inc., 1921.

MONTESSORI, MARIA. *The Montessori Elementary Material.* Cambridge, Mass.: Robert Bentley, Inc., 1965.

MONTESSORI, MARIA. *The Montessori Method.* Cambridge, Mass.: Robert Bentley, Inc., 1965.

Montessori in Perspective. Washington, D.C.: The National Association for Education of Young Children, 1966.

NEHRT, ROY C., and GORDON E. HURD. *Preprimary Enrollment of Children Under Six: October 1968.* Washington, D.C.: U.S. Department of Health, Education, and Welfare, 1968.

STEIN, HERMAN D. (ed.). *Planning for the Needs of Children in Developing Countries.* New York: United Nations Children's Fund, 1964.

INDEX OF AUTHORS

SUBJECT INDEX